some like it *HOT*

ALSO BY CLIFFORD A. WRIGHT

ON COOKING

Little Foods of the Mediterranean

Real Stew

Mediterranean Vegetables

A Mediterranean Feast

Italian Pure & Simple

Grill Italian

Lasagne

Cucina Rapida

Cucina Paradiso

CONTRIBUTOR

"Harold l'Américain" in Saveur Cooks France

ON POLITICS AND HISTORY

Facts and Fables

After the Palestine-Israel War

some like it
HOT

Spicy Favorites from the World's HOT Zones

Clifford A. Wright

THE HARVARD COMMON PRESS

Boston, Massachusetts

For my oldest son

Ali Raphael Kattan-Wright

one hot kid

The Harvard Common Press
535 Albany Street
Boston, Massachusetts 02118
www.harvardcommonpress.com

Printed in the United States of America
Printed on acid-free paper

Library of Congress Cataloging-in-Publication Data
Wright, Clifford A.
  Some like it hot : spicy favorites from the world's hot zones / Clifford A.
Wright.
    p. cm.
  Includes bibliographical references and index.
  ISBN 1-55832-268-X (hc. : alk. paper) — ISBN 1-55832-269-8 (pbk. : alk.
paper)
  1. Cookery (Spices) 2. Cookery, International. 3. Spices. I. Title.
  TX819.A1W75 2005
  6341.6'383—dc22   2005004953

ISBN-13: 978-1-55832-268-4 (hardcover); 978-1-55832-269-1 (paperback)
ISBN-10: 1-55832-268-X (hardcover); 1-55832-269-8 (paperback)

10 9 8 7 6 5 4 3 2 1

Cover recipe: Shredded Shrimp and Serrano Chile Tacos, page 257
Cover photograph © 2005 Nina Gallant
Cover design by Night & Day Design
Interior design by Richard Oriolo
Illustrations by Paul Hoffman

contents

acknowledgments

I can't imagine having written this book without the Internet and people from around the world to help me. Although there is a cast of hundreds behind this book, besides individuals mentioned in the recipes themselves, I would also like to thank Taoufik Ben Azouz and Sofia Azouz, Neelam Batra, Rick Bayless, Gene Bourg, Unjoo Lee Byars, Cayobo, Bonnie Lee, Youssouf Mariko, Thomas Payne, Sarah Pillsbury, Nattera Roajphlastien, Martha Rose Shulman, Su-Mei Yu, and Dawn Zain for their help on culinary matters. Most of the recipes in this book were consumed by myself, Sarah Pillsbury, and my son Seri Kattan-Wright, who now understands the expression "chile burns twice."

I would also like to thank my agent, Doe Coover, and at The Harvard Common Press, my editors, Pam Hoenig and Valerie Cimino; managing editor Christine Corcoran Cox; production editor Abby Collier; copyeditor Ann Cahn; and, on the marketing side of things, Skye Stewart and publicist Liza Beth. Finally, I would like to thank my publisher, Bruce Shaw, for *Some Like It Hot*.

the world of spice

Our eyes nearly popped out of our heads when my daughter Dyala and I saw our Chongqing Spicy Chicken arrive. The platter was covered with hundreds of red chiles. I don't think I'm exaggerating, although we didn't actually count them. We were slightly alarmed, but game. The other diners in this San Francisco restaurant were gringos, and they whispered as they rubbernecked toward our table. It was clear to us that this dish was not on the menu and that we had successfully communicated to our Chinese waitress that we might look like Americans, but our culinary souls were Sichuan. The platter sat in front of us for a while because we weren't sure whether we were supposed to attack it or cleverly dodge the chiles like a soldier ducking withering fire. We decided to eat, slowly, and with chopsticks, picking around the chiles. It was amazing! The chicken knuckles—that's what I called them—were actually a section of the wing and so tender that you could eat the delicate bones as well. The flavor was intense, very intense, and delicious, very delicious, and hot, very hot. We started sweating and continued eating, quietly, without a word to each other. We ate all of it and looked up, sniffling, and Dyala said, "That was incredible, Dad. Do you really think you can re-create it?" I must, I responded, because I must have this again. Well, this book has Chongqing Spicy Chicken (page 156) and 300 other amazingly hot recipes from what I call the "Hot Zone," the spiciest, hottest cuisines in the world.

No, I'm not a masochist and I'm not a chile-head. I have simply become fascinated with the cuisines around the world that are so piquant. Why do some people love spicy food so much? And why do others abhor it? I brought to this book a lot of assumptions about very spicy food, and in the course of several years of research and recipe testing, almost all of them evaporated and a whole new world opened up. This is the world I hope to bring to you. It is a new world of taste, and, appropriately, the story begins in the New World.

How It All Began

WHEN I WAS A CHILD, I learned that Columbus discovered America after sailing the ocean blue. Over the course of a lifetime I've learned that there is a lot more to Columbus besides the man and his famous voyage. There is "the Columbian exchange," a reference to the exchange between the Old and New Worlds. Plants were exchanged in both directions and so were animals. But the "exchange" refers to much more than that because the Old World also brought pestilence, guns, and science to the New World.

The horticultural transference from the Old World to the New and the New to the Old really begins with the second voyage of Columbus, when he returned to Hispaniola with 17 ships, 1,200 men, and seeds and cuttings for the planting of wheat, chickpeas, melons, onions, radishes, salad greens, grapevines, sugarcane, and fruit stones for the founding of orchards.

From a culinary point of view, arguably the most important thing that came about from Columbus's discovery of America is the chile. That might seem nonsensical when we think of beans or tomatoes. Or what about the potato, you may

exotic ingredients

Do you want the real thing? Can you get the real thing? This book probably could not have been written 15 years ago. But today, with all our ethnic groceries and Internet Web sites, everything is available. So, yes, you can get the real thing, and some of the ingredients in this book are pretty exotic. But nearly every recipe suggests substitutes that you are likely to find in your supermarket. And when you see "Thai fish sauce" and no substitute listed, don't give up—it's in your local supermarket, believe it or not. Just remember how big your supermarket is and remember all those aisles you may have never been down. Well, you'll go down them now, especially the international/Asian/Latino aisle.

protest, which played a huge economic role in countries from Ireland to India? Ah, yes, the potato—but I said culinary, not economic. The chile changed the world as much as the potato did. In culinary terms, it provided gustatory heat, or spiciness, far beyond the hottest spice known until then, black pepper. In economic terms, it's possible the chile contributed to killing off the absurdly profitable spice trade that had existed between the Indo-Malaysian archipelago and Europe for two millennia. (In the reverse direction, of the most important foods brought to the New World from the Old there are many to choose from, but one would have to agree with Alfred W. Crosby, Jr. in his *The Columbian Exchange: Biological and Cultural Consequences of 1492* [Greenwood Press, 1972], that it all began with sugar.)

Some like it hot, and those who do live within a globe-encircling band between the Tropic of Cancer and the Tropic of Capricorn—more or less. Here in this area some call the Hot Zone, a temperate to tropical climate lends itself to a cuisine that is blisteringly hot, where people enjoy fiery hot foods spiked with chiles and spices that dance in your mouth. Whether it's the *moles* of Mexico or the kimchi of Korea or the curries of India or the *piri-piri* of Africa, this is a world cuisine of very exciting food that has captivated the American palate. One can dream up all kinds of adjectives to describe this cuisine from the Hot Zone: hot, zesty, jazzy, furious, blistering, electrifying, incendiary, piquant, pungent, lustful, sensual, sultry, torrid. It's all that and more, because these cuisines are delicious, too.

There is an interesting phenomenon about this spicy zone, this Hot Zone: it cannot be entirely described in geographic terms because, contrary to popular thought and contrary to the first sentence of the previous paragraph, it is not exclusively centered in the Tropics or around the equator. High in the cold Andes, or in the highlands of Mexico City, or on the frigid Korean peninsula, people are eating some very spicy-hot food. The chile, the hottest spice, may also be the oldest spice, as it seems to have been used by humans as early as 7000 B.C. It traveled well and was readily accepted elsewhere, probably because it had attractive and appetizing-looking fruits produced in a short period of time and because it yielded fruit year round in most climates where it thrived. There was another benefit, too: the fruits could be dried for storage or transport and used later. Because of its pungency, a little chile went a long way, and that must have been very attractive to poor people eating readily available bland, starchy foods.

Why People Like Very Spicy Food

I HAVE TO SAY IT AGAIN—I'm not a chile-head. What is a chile-head? It's someone who loves chiles in their own right and who loves to put a lot of them into everything. I am not a chile-head, or an artichoke-head, or a beef-head . . . you get the picture. As a cook I believe passionately in the blending of flavors to create taste. No one ingredient is a Holy Grail for me. But I am fascinated with spices. Chile is a most interesting spice because it is also a vegetable.

When people say "spicy" they mean piquant, that is, spicy-hot in the mouth, usually as a result of chiles or black pepper. But few spices are pungent, and before the discovery of the chile in the New World it's hard to think of any food being truly spicy. Throughout this book, you will read short boxes about other hot spices used in the world's cuisines. Some, such as garlic, one hardly thinks of as a "hot" spice, and others, such as grains of paradise, you may never have heard of. Today the hottest foods, and the most piquant cuisines, are that way because of chiles. We don't know exactly why humans like extremely piquant foods, but several theories have been offered to explain why they do, and why these extreme cuisines use gustatory heat to the max. I've identified 15 important hypotheses as to why this might be the case.

The Preserving/Masking Hypothesis

The preserving/masking hypothesis proposes that piquant spices were used in ancient times and through the Middle Ages to preserve meats and/or to mask the taste of spoiling or rotten foods.

We know this hypothesis is false for reasons I explained in my book *A Mediterranean Feast* (William Morrow, 1999). Basically, spices have never been used for their preservative effect because, first, they have traditionally been expensive and, second, there are better and cheaper ways to preserve food, namely salting, sun-drying, air-drying, smoking, and using vinegar. Another reason against the second part of this hypothesis, that spices were used to disguise rotten or rotting food, especially meats, is that in the Middle Ages, when the spice trade was at its height, freshly butchered meat was readily available to all classes. Meat wasn't rotten, and there was no need to preserve it. There is quite a bit of evidence for this, including municipal regulations prohibiting the sale of meat slaughtered more than one day previous in summertime and three days previous in winter, as well as statistics concerning the number of animals slaughtered daily in Europe. As the historian Jean-Louis Flandrin has said, "If medieval gastronomy is to be criticized, it has to be for consuming meat that was insufficiently aged rather than rotten."

The Status Symbol Hypothesis

The status symbol hypothesis states that the nascent bourgeoisie emerging in a Europe hungry for spices between the thirteenth and sixteenth centuries bought expensive spices in order to demonstrate their socioeconomic superiority over other segments of the population by flaunting expensive luxuries. Before the chile arrived in Europe, black pepper was the main spice for piquancy, and its high price made it also a symbol of wealth.

This hypothesis is weak because although it is true that black pepper was expensive, the chile was not. Second, it doesn't explain the abundant use of the chile in all the piquant culinary cultures, none of which are European.

The Physiological Hypothesis

This hypothesis has a corollary in the macho/thrill hypothesis (see page xiv). The explanation here is physiological, suggesting that the love of chiles comes from the high or rush derived from eating something that appears dangerous or poisonous, leading to a euphoria as the volatile ingredient, capsaicin, wears off. There is a modern explanation, in fact, based on biochemical reasons, which says that the body interprets piquancy in spices as pain and reacts by secreting "painkillers," that is, endorphins, which have not only an analgesic effect but also a stimulating and euphoric effect.

There may very well be some truth to the physiological explanation, but it seems unlikely that all the cultures in this book use piquancy for a "high." When asked, people who love chiles say they love the taste, not the rush they get.

The Health/Food Safety Hypothesis

This hypothesis argues that chiles provide a kind of food safety by killing or otherwise retarding bacteria. Chiles also seem as if they might inhibit intestinal disease. Pre-Columbian peoples recognized the chile's pharmacological uses. Healers prescribed them for a wide range of ailments, and lovers favored them as aphrodisiacs.

It is possible that primitive people thought food was made safe by using chiles; however, there was no theory of bacteria at the time, and there is no modern scientific evidence of any antibacterial effect.

The Medicinal Hypothesis

The medicinal hypothesis sees the ingesting of chiles as helping nasal congestion caused by the common cold by opening up the sinuses.

The medicinal hypothesis is indeed true: eating chiles makes one's nose run and opens up the sinuses to provide relief. But it's unlikely that this was the reason people initially adopted the use of chiles in cooking. Furthermore, people love eating chiles even when they don't have colds.

The Nutritional Hypothesis

The nutritional hypothesis states that chiles are good for you. We know now that chiles are remarkably nutritious, supplying vitamins A and C as well as various forms of vitamin B. There is more vitamin A and C in one jalapeño chile than in three oranges. In fact, chiles are estimated to provide one-third of the vitamin A in the rural Mexican diet.

One problem with this hypothesis is that the nutritional benefits would not be obvious to the populations adopting the chile. The purported health benefits of eating chiles seems not to be the reason for the acceptance of chiles into a cuisine, but, rather, a particular benefit after having been accepted. It seems unlikely that cultures would adopt the eating of chiles for health benefits alone.

The Tropical/Perspiration Hypothesis

This hypothesis posits that chile-loving cultures are found in the hot and steamy tropics, where the ingesting of chiles causes perspiration that helps cool the body.

This hypothesis is not convincing for three reasons. First, habitual chile-eaters in the areas of the Hot Zone report that they eat chiles because they like the taste and they are convenient. They never mention the benefits of perspiration.

Second, some of the Hot Zone countries are not hot, such as Korea, where people have no need to perspire due to the temperate climate with cold winters. Third, one hardly needs to ingest chiles to perspire in hot tropical climates; one will perspire on one's own simply because it's so climatically hot.

The Addiction Hypothesis

This argument states that people who like chiles are addicted to them. But there is no evidence that chiles are psychologically or physiologically addicting.

The Familiarity Hypothesis

The familiarity hypothesis states that people like chiles because they are familiar with the heat of the spice. Individual chile eaters eat chiles because they exist in a culture that eats chiles. People eat the foods they do because they are exposed to these foods through their culture. For example, it is well known that American children between the ages of 5 and 15 don't like to eat vegetables but Indian children of the same ages do. But it is not well known that this is because neither their American parents nor their American culture introduced them to real fresh vegetables when they were 18 months to 4 years old, the critical ages for food acceptance. The perception of food, the eating and enjoyment of food, is an event that is a critical social event.

The major problem with this hypothesis is that a reason based on familiarity may be true at some point, but it doesn't explain why the spice was adopted in the first place.

The Mastication Hypothesis

This hypothesis is based on physiological reasons: that the ingestion of chiles stimulates the flow of saliva and the gastric juices, helping to overcome loss of appetite and aid weak digestive systems as well as facilitating the chewing and digestion of bland, high-complex carbohydrate foods. This point was confirmed as long ago as the sixteenth century, when Francisco Hernández (1514–1578), who was physician and historian to King Philip II of Spain and who lived in Mexico from 1570 to 1577, wrote that chiles were used not only to season food but to stimulate the appetite. This explanation is the most valid of the ones presented so far, because it applies to all the cultures we're looking at, but it falls flat because it doesn't explain why *all* cultures don't eat chiles.

The Monotony of Diet Hypothesis

This hypothesis says that in all the cultures where the chile was adopted, the existing cooking was based on poor, often subsistence level cooking and was often based on a bland staple food, a complex carbohydrate. For example, in Peru and Bolivia the staple food was potatoes, while it was rice in India, Thailand, Korea, and Sichuan, maize and beans in Mexico, millet and yams in West Africa, cassava in the Amazon, and millet and barley in North Africa. Chiles were used to literally spice up these foods.

This seems a quite valid reason—to an extent. However, it does not explain those cuisines that have remained dull, and the cultures that have found no need to "spice" up the food.

The Beautiful Fruit Hypothesis

The idea behind the beautiful fruit hypothesis is that people began to eat chiles because they are brightly and invitingly colored red, green, orange, and yellow. This led early prehistoric Andean man to eat them wild and then to cultivate them and populations around the world to accept them once the chile started to diffuse. The fact that they were so hot and seemingly poisonous, yet benign, may have made them even more attractive.

Although this explanation may lead the way to understanding why a culture would adopt the chile, it doesn't explain why other cultures didn't.

The Macho/Thrill Hypothesis

There may be a macho purpose behind the eating of chile-hot foods. Eating chiles may be a "cheap thrill" experience, a benign masochism like riding a roller coaster, or it can prove one's manhood by self-torture.

The major problem with this argument is that it only explains the eating of chile in one culture, namely, in the United States, where eating chiles seems to be some kind of weird rite of passage for men. In every other piquant culinary culture, chiles are eaten for their taste, not their heat. In Mexico, for example, where sex roles are highly differentiated, there is little difference between men and women concerning the liking or disliking of chiles.

The Economic Hypothesis

The adoption of the chile in pre-Columbian American cultures and its rapid adoption by many Old World, especially tropical, cultures is a puzzle. It is even more of a puzzle when we consider that other New World foods such as tomatoes or maize had nowhere near the rapidity of acceptance in the Old World that the chile did. This leads one to consider the economic argument that the widespread adoption of the chile in the Old World was due to a preexisting culinary substratum of piquant foods based on relatively expensive spices, most importantly black pepper. Chiles, which were easy to grow almost anywhere and required little processing, were simply a cheaper spice. But, as Paul Rozin, a psychologist who has written extensively on the liking of chiles, has said, "This only postpones the problem because we will eventually have to supply an explanation for the original popularity of black pepper."

The Good Taste Hypothesis

The most obvious reason that people like chiles is that they taste good and that the sensation in the mouth is pleasing. They provide zest to bland foods. This seems more than likely in that the chile is most prevalently used in cultures where the staple food is a starch, bland, and a provider of most of the calories in the diet. This is true of all the Hot Zone cuisines except one, the modern American Southwest, where there is no staple food. As chiles do activate the digestive system, causing salivation and gastric secretion, it makes a lot of sense that they would be adopted. Along with good taste, chiles are also attractively colored and have pleasant aromas and flavors. This hypothesis explains a lot. But it doesn't explain, first, why all cuisines haven't accepted the chile and, second, why the hot cuisines are so spectacularly hot.

There are few studies on why people like chiles. One study was done in 1980 that attempted to find out more about why some people like chiles, working with people in the United States and Mexico. The researchers found that when chiles were eaten, the same pain receptors in the mouth were affected and the same message went to the brain in both chile-lovers and chile-haters. The chile burn was liked by the chile-lover and disliked by the chile-hater, which is a category that also includes infants and animals. The researchers Paul Rozin and Deborah Schiller called this behavior "benign masochistic activity." The eating of chiles for the chile-lover was a "contained risk" because he or she knew that there was no dangerous or life-threatening possibility resulting from eating chiles. In other words, eating chiles was a cheap thrill. There is a "rush" felt by the chile eater, which heightens the sensation in the mouth of the "pain" and of the food. On top of all this, the chile eater will also have some physiological effects, including sweating on the scalp and a runny nose. But, interestingly, gustatory sweating apparently does not occur in normal chile eaters in cool climates such as one finds in Mexico City or Cuzco,

Peru, or presumably Seoul, South Korea. More than 95 percent of both the Americans and the Mexicans in the study said that they like chiles because of the taste, but the discrepancies between the two populations showed up on the more folkloric side of things: 92 percent of the Mexicans and 3 percent of the Americans agreed with the statement that chiles "make me strong." On the culinary side of things, 41 percent of the Americans said food tastes bland without chiles, while 100 percent of the Mexicans agreed with the statement.

The Extremely Hot Cuisines

THIS BOOK IS NOT JUST about hot foods or spicy foods, but about those 14 or so cuisines around the world that are by any definition of piquancy simply off the charts. These are the most piquant cuisines in the world. They make veal paprika or lobster fra diavolo look like the blandest foods ever. They make steak au poivre look like child's play. Many of these foods prepared authentically will defeat the typical American palate, and when you encounter them in restaurants in the United States, rest assured you are not eating the real thing. In this book, you will meet the real thing. This doesn't mean that all of the preparations in these cuisines are piquant. Some dishes aren't. And it doesn't mean that everyone in these populations loves chiles. Some Mexicans don't care for them, you may be surprised to learn. But there is one thing for sure—the majority of these people do love very hot food.

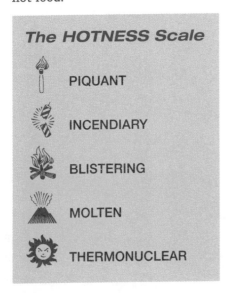

The HOTNESS Scale

PIQUANT

INCENDIARY

BLISTERING

MOLTEN

THERMONUCLEAR

Remember that tolerance and appreciation for piquant foods must be built up slowly and incrementally. Therefore, if you are unfamiliar with spicy foods or want to get a better sense of the range of how hot these cuisines are, you can do one of two things. First, you can start by choosing recipes marked with this symbol (see box), and then move up to those marked, and so on. Second, you can Americanize the recipe. Americanizing means reducing the amount of chiles called for by half or three-quarters for the hottest recipes— those marked with a, , or. You can desensitize yourself to the irritation of the capsaicin, and once you do the burning sensation slowly dissipates, leaving an agreeable flavor and heightened awareness of the other flavors of the dish as well as a pleasant warmth. A novice wine drinker believes all wine tastes the same, and a novice chile eater feels only the heat of the chile. As with the subtleties of wine, chiles are as varied in heat as they are in taste and smell. Chiles, too, have a floral bouquet and various aromas and tastes, depending on their species, their cultivars, their stages of ripeness, and their processing (whether they are cooked, smoked, dried, left whole, or ground). The recipes, though, are written as if you were eating in those 14 cultures—these are the real thing.

Tolerance for foods made hot by the use of chiles is an acquired trait, and you can gradually increase your tolerance to the point that others may consider you mad. The neophyte will claim that the heat dulls their senses—and that is true. That's why one increases tolerance slowly and gradually, for at the other end of the spectrum the foods that are very hot heighten the sense of taste and the ability to detect subtle flavors.

As a tenderfoot, or should I say "tendermouth," the first thing you encounter when you eat spicy-hot food is the flash of hotness. You will not taste anything but only feel the pain and burn on your tongue. Remember that you can no more plunge into chile-hot food than you can a swimming pool without knowing how to swim. You must start slowly and build up your tolerance for hot foods. After a while, that hot flash and discomfort recedes to the background, admittedly a hot background, and the subtle tastes of the other ingredients in the dish begin to emerge. Like an unraveling arabesque, there is a freshness, a richness, a saltiness, a savory aroma, a tang, a bitterness, a sweetness, and a heightened sensitivity to the complexity of flavors. It is all seemingly enhanced by that initial jolt of heat. Your taste buds seem more discriminating, but only if you relax and let that chile do its work. Fanning your open mouth is a useless gesture and distracts you from paying attention to the tastes and flavors of the dish. Relax and let your senses become acute, and you will enjoy the experience of eating like you never have before.

Many people believe the hottest cuisines are around the equator, as one culinary band circling the world, or that they are associated with very hot climates. But what makes these fiery cuisines so interesting is that many of them are culinary islands and there is no contiguous geographical belt of culinary spiciness.

The hottest cuisines in the world are Peru-Bolivian, including the Amazon Basin, Mexican, Southwestern United States, Louisiana Cajun, Jamaican and some other Caribbean islands, West African and a few Central and southern African countries, Algerian-Tunisian, Ethiopian, Yemeni, Indo-Pakistani, Thai, Indonesian-Malay, Sichuan, and Korean. Now it should be understood that these are general categories and they include subcuisines, "sub" meaning not of the cultural variety but of the piquancy variety. So, for example, in the general category of Peru-Bolivian, I will refer to a handful of dishes in northern Chile and a few in Ecuador that are very hot. But these categories are often piquant islands, since, for example, the foods of neighboring Venezuela or Argentina are not hot at all. Guatemala, which is next to Mexico, does have a hot dish or two, but in the main one would never call that country's cuisine hot.

The Southwestern United States is a special example because the cuisine is not universally hot and most of the culinary heritage is Mexican anyway. In the Southwest, the experimentation with piquant foods is happening mostly in restaurants and with certain individuals who call themselves chile-heads. This is also the only cooking of those mentioned that uses chiles self-consciously. What I mean by that is that chile-head cooks operate outside a culinary culture, creating dishes that use chiles simply because they are chiles and because they are so piquant. Southwestern cooking refers to a kind of cooking—and it is not the dominant cooking in this region—that one finds mostly in certain kinds of restaurants in Texas, Arizona, New Mexico, southern Colorado, and southern California. Cajun cooking is a style unique and particular to the Bayou country west of New Orleans in Louisiana.

In the Caribbean it is quite notable that Jamaican food is really hot and nearly no other Caribbean island cuisine is except for a dish here and there in Martinique or Trinidad—but Jamaican food is over-the-top, mon! Although there is a style of piquant cooking in Bahia in Brazil, and in Guyana and parts of the Amazon, that one might think of as a subcuisine of Peru-Bolivian, I place it as a subcuisine of the Caribbean because it is based on the habanero chile, the same species prevalent in the Caribbean and known as the Scotch bonnet chile or malagueta pepper, while the Peru-Bolivian chiles of choice are from other species.

Once we jump the Atlantic to West Africa we meet a world of hot. In unreflective moments I call this the hottest cuisine of the world. But, seriously, how do you compare? Anyway, by West Africa I mean the contemporary countries of Senegal, Gambia, Guinea-Bissau, Guinea, Sierra Leone, Liberia, Ivory Coast, Ghana, Togo, Benin, Nigeria, Mali, and Niger. A subcuisine of this area is still western, but considered, geographically, part of Central Africa, as represented by the contemporary countries of Cameroon, Equatorial Guinea, Gabon, Republic of the Congo, Democratic Republic of the Congo, and Angola. These countries have hot cuisines here and there, but remember that Africa's political boundaries are artificial and have nothing to do with culinary cultures. I throw Mozambique into this mix, even though it is southeastern Africa, and also the Cape Malay cooking of South Africa although it is more closely related to Indonesian-Malay and Indian cooking. The only other hot cuisines in Africa are the Algerian-Tunisian of North Africa and the Ethiopian (including the subcuisine of Somali) of East Africa. These are all culinary islands, although one could argue that Yemen belongs to the Ethiopian island. Uh-oh! This is getting complicated, but don't worry, it won't matter once you're in the kitchen.

Now we can make a big jump across the Indian Ocean to India, which has very hot cuisines, as do Bhutan and Sri Lanka to a lesser extent. Remember that Pakistanis and Indians have a lot in common except their religion, although there are a huge number of Muslim Indians in India. Culinarily, one can think of this region as one. And it is a piquant island. Persian cuisine to the west, Afghan cooking to the northwest, Tadzik and Xinjiang cooking to the north, Tibetan cuisine to the northeast and east (the Himalayas are a natural boundary), and Burmese to the east are all non-hot cuisines.

Thai cooking is not totally a piquant island because it merges into Indo-Malaysian cooking in the south, which itself swings through the archipelago to include the only hot cuisine in the Philippines, the cuisine of Bicol on the island of Luzon. But surrounding this area are the mild cuisines of Australia to the south and New Guinea and Polynesia to the east, as well as Indochina to the east of Thailand. The only hot foods in Indochina outside of Thailand are some dishes in the border regions of Laos and Cambodia. Vietnamese food is anything but hot. To the north, Thai cuisine is culinarily separated from China's Sichuan province by Burma, Laos, and the southern portion of Yunnan province. Sichuan has one of the hottest cuisines around, although the three regions to its south and southeast, Yunnan, Guizhou, and Hunan, should be considered subcuisines as their food is piquant.

In any case, one has to travel much farther north to find our last piquant cuisine, which is in the Korean peninsula surrounded by the blander cuisine of Manchuria to the north, Beijing to the west, and Japan to the east. That, in a nutshell, is the culinary hot world.

But this book is more than a catalog of piquant cuisines. As you cook this food from around the world, at some point you will wonder, why are there hot cuisines rather than not? Why are these cuisines so much hotter than the food from Minnesota, Canada, England, France, Holland, Norway, Sweden, Germany, Russia, and Japan?

The star of this show will be the chile, for it transcends the next hottest spice, black pepper, by a quantum leap. But to understand why these cuisines I've identified as being the hottest are that way, we will also need to look and see if there existed already an underlying culinary substratum of piquancy when the chile arrived from the New World after 1493. In other words, when the chile arrived in India, did cooks think, Oh, boy, this is even hotter than black pepper!? Or did a new sensory appreciation develop that led to the forming of a new and more piquant cuisine?

There's no doubt that the fruit of this shrubby perennial, from its earliest appearance in Tehuacan, Mexico, before 5000 B.C. through today, has been much appreciated by cooks.

The "Hot" Spices

A spice is defined as any of various aromatic vegetable products used to season or flavor foods. This is an interesting definition because one of the oldest and most important spices, salt, is a mineral, not a vegetable. Humans are the only animal that not only turn raw food into cooked food but also then season that food with spices. Spices are used to change the way food tastes. The expression "to spice it up" means to add spice to food to make it taste better or more interesting. Spices also seem to play a role in aiding digestion and in food conservation by inhibiting bacterial growth (in the case of salt), but their most important use is making food taste better.

The flavor of spices comes from volatile oils in their chemical composition. But several spices do more than that. They also create a hot or burning sensation in the mouth. For millennia a small number of spices provided a piquancy that enlivened the taste of food, although there was in traditional societies a powerful medicinal reason for the love of spices, too. In the Old World—Europe, Africa, and Asia—black pepper, mustard, ginger, and some other spices provided gastronomic heat. In the New World, a single plant was so powerfully spicy that it was the single piquant spice. The chile plant provided both the Incas in Peru and the Aztecs in Mexico with a powerful burning sensation, although the plant was being used thousands of years before the Incas and Aztecs. Once the New World was discovered by Europeans and the chile plant began its diffusion throughout the world, it replaced black pepper as the hottest spice, although it did not replace any spices wholesale; it simply joined them in the pantry of the cook.

No spice comes close to the piquancy of the New World chile, from where all chiles come, and so chiles provide the focus for this book. Before the discovery of the New World the spices used for piquancy in the Old World were limited to several spices that had varying degrees of "hotness." They varied not only from each other but could also vary depending on the cultivar, where they were grown, when they were harvested, how they had been aged or stored, and some other factors. These spices, which you will encounter in boxes and recipes throughout this book, are: garlic, ajwain, clove, galingal, grains of paradise, ginger, black pepper, long pepper, and mustard.

Several other spices are generally considered pungent, but not piquant or hot: Sichuan peppercorns (the only one of this category I use in these recipes), wasabi, cubeb pepper, Ashanti pepper, horseradish, horse-radish tree, Negro pepper, water pepper, jungle chile, jungle pepper, and Tasmanian pepper. Finally, there is one quite pungent plant, the radish, a member of the cabbage family, which is actually never used as a spice but as a vegetable and therefore is not included in this roundup.

The chile, however, is at the center of the story, a story illustrated with authentic recipes from these 14 cuisines. It will be difficult for you, a home cook, to stock your pantry with all the foods needed to cook from so many diverse cuisines, but it can be done, thanks to the ethnic markets that are increasingly found in all American cities, and thanks also to the Internet. Sometimes I don't believe it myself, but my pantry is now stocked with every food mentioned in this book. It's a pretty wacky pantry, but I can now identify the food when someone asks, "What's that smell?"

The Hot Zones

One of the most interesting phenomena about piquant or hot cuisines is that although America, outside of the two regions mentioned on page xviii, is out of the Hot Zone geographically and its food can hardly be called spicy, it has the most gastronomically open cooking in the world. We Americans also seem to be the people who most enjoy blowing our tops and burning our tongues. Americans crave spicy food with a kick. According to a recent poll conducted by *Food & Wine* magazine, 75 percent of Americans love spicy food, 53 percent like "food with a kick" (that is, just a little heat), and 22 percent "crave fire." This popularity continues, as

reflections on authenticity in cuisines

In writing this book I've thought a lot about authenticity and what that means. When I was testing the recipes I would begin first by stocking the pantry entirely with all the food I might possibly need, so that I could cook a particular cuisine on a whim. This approach made both the testing and eating less of a hassle and quite pleasant, as well as shortening the learning curve. I would also stick with a particular cuisine for weeks or months, immersing myself in the culture so that I could get to the point where I could legitimately invent recipes (although only two or three of these innovative recipes are in this book). With cuisines I was unfamiliar with, I would educate myself by reading, traveling, eating at the restaurants, and relying on natives of that culture. One of my friends is a Korean who is also a very good cook. She set up a schedule for my "Korean" education, which included shopping together in Korean markets in Koreatown in Los Angeles and cooking together. What I found so interesting, and which showed me how rigid my idea of authenticity had been, was that she took all kinds of shortcuts that makes cooking easier for her without the loss of "authenticity of taste." She said that I shouldn't worry about how her grandmother did it since how she does it is just as "authentic." So, she argued, I shouldn't confuse "antique" or "old style" with "authentic." The modern way of a young Korean cook living in America is just as "authentic." What all this means for the recipes in this book is that they are "modern authentic world cuisine," where each individual culture is respected. This is not fusion cuisine, but world cuisine for American cooks. It's okay for you to buy that jar of kimchi because Korean Americans no more make kimchi at home than German Americans make sauerkraut.

evidenced in new products such as the Red Fire Bar, a chocolate bar made of Mexican ancho and chipotle chiles and dark chocolate, and the hot sauces now sold with colorful and indicative names such as Acid Rain, Bubba's Butt Blaster, Dave's Ultimate Insanity Sauce, Nuckin' Futs Sauce, Rectal Rocket Fuel, Scorned Woman, and Vicious Viper (I didn't make these up). New Mexico State University has its Chile Pepper Institute, and for the real chile-head there is the Transcendental Capsaicinophilic Society at www.io.com/~m101/tcs/ for those who are dedicated to worshipping all chiles and making fun of people who "just can't take that spicy food."

Although the recipes in this book are organized according to traditional cookbook style—appetizers, salads, meat, side dishes, and so on—within each chapter the recipes appear geographically starting with Peru and Bolivia and moving north and east around the world. These are hot recipes. A Peruvian *chupe de camarones* (page 74) is a fiery hot (there's a phrase that will get overused in this book) shrimp soup with chile, corn, potatoes, rice, tomatoes, eggs, and garlic. Another Peruvian dish that will send heads spinning is *ají de gallina*, chicken and potatoes in a walnut and chile sauce (page 119). In Mexico, we will encounter the famous mole and red sauce (see pages 126 and 410). When we move on to Cajun country, we'll slurp up some shrimp bisque, all red and inviting (page 78). In Jamaica, a jerk pork will make eyes widen and mouths flare (page 233).

Now we travel across the Atlantic to Africa, just as the chile did 400 years ago. In West Africa, the ancestral home of nearly all African Americans, in countries such as Senegal, Guinea, Sierra Leone, Liberia, Ghana, and Nigeria, the locally impoverished people have created exciting cuisines based on local ingredients and the chile. The *Poulet Yassa* of Senegal (page 135) is a delightful dish of chicken marinated in chiles, onions, and lemon juice, which is then grilled before being simmered in the pungent marinade and is served with rice to absorb the flavors and the heat. In Mozambique, a real treat is Grilled Shrimp with *Piri-Piri* Sauce (page 274), fat shrimp skewered and grilled with an extremely hot and inviting orange-colored chile sauce and then dipped in melted lemon butter.

The North African countries of Algeria and Tunisia are famous for their hot food. In Tunisia, *harisa* is a red chile paste that gets put into nearly everything (page 414). In Algeria, *dirsa* sauce also uses chiles and makes for some pretty spicy dishes. One class of preparation in Algeria is known by the sobriquet "the sauce that dances," implying that the food is so spicy hot that it dances in your mouth. In one of the poorest places in Africa comes some of the hottest food, namely Ethiopia. An Ethiopian national dish is *doro wat* with *berbere* (pages 141 and 417). This is a lemon-marinated chicken stewed with onions and spices, including turmeric, cardamom, fenugreek, gingerroot, paprika, and chile, and the spice paste called *berbere* is itself seasoned with the entire spice shop. Another fiery Ethiopian dish is their version of steak tartare called *kitfo*, made with a cornucopia of spices. In South Africa, the Cape Malays have their own unique cuisine that is noted for its heat.

After Africa, we make a quick stop in Yemen, where we will taste a few very hot stews—one, a succulent oxtail that you won't forget—before arriving in India where one of the most delicious hot cuisines in the world exists. Indian cuisine is justly famous and here we will find recipes for a variety of spicy-hot dishes from vindaloo to curry to dal. Our hot-food tour continues around the globe, stopping next in Thailand where a dish of *kaeng khiao wan nuea* will wake you up. It's a curry made with beef, green curry paste, chiles, eggplants, and coconut cream. Or you can make *lon kung*, a kind of shrimp hash with chiles, mango, and coconut milk. Malaysia, too, has spicy food as we see in *gado-gado*, a chopped mixed vegetable salad with chile peanut sauce. Indonesian food is spicy and a *lawar* is a dish you won't soon forget.

Once we move to Asia we find some very old cuisines in the central Chinese provinces of Sichuan and Hunan. The Sichuanese are renowned for their cuisine and renowned for their use of chiles—one dish uses over a hundred dried red chiles. Ants Climbing a Tree (page 333) is a dish memorable both for its name and its exquisite tastes. In Korea, I've mentioned the hot pickled cabbage relish called kimchi, but many other dishes of pork, beef, vegetables, or seafood are quite hot and easy to prepare in the American kitchen, especially now with the huge number of Korean Americans to help us.

When I first thought of writing this book I thought of the hottest, most piquant cuisines in the world. I went about identifying those cuisines and then researching, collecting, and writing recipes, testing them, and eating a lot of very hot—almost impossibly hot—food. But by the time I finished cooking and eating more than 300 different dishes from 14 different cuisines, I couldn't say that what was notable about this food was that it was spicy-hot, but that it was delicious. What happened? Well, simply, I got used to the heat. So used to the heat that when my children and girlfriend, who ate so much of this food, eat this food now, we never comment on it. And this is true in the culinary cultures from which all this food emanates. The piquancy is not what is notable. What is notable is that it is flavorful, rich, complex food that is delicious and satisfying. It's all relative to what your taste buds are used to, and when you cook from this book over a period of time you will get used to it, I promise.

A Note About the Recipes

THE RECIPES IN THIS BOOK are authentic—very authentic. If your pantry grows to look like mine you will feel that you could go into the grocery business. Although this book is filled with piquant recipes, it is also about "world cuisine." There is no culture in the world, other than American, that would attempt such a thing. It will seem like madness if a guest should look into your pantry and see jars of *dawadawa*, fermented locust bean, dried shrimps, *kochu'jang*, and *harisa*. And

selecting chiles

The recipes in this book call for a variety of specific chile cultivars, all of which have different levels of heat. I try to give alternatives, but this chart will give you an idea of what you might likely find in your market and how to concoct substitutes.

Weaponized chiles: habanero, Scotch bonnet, African bird

Extremely hot chiles: Thai, bird's eye, finger-type, *rocoto*, *piquín*, *chiltepin*, cayenne, Tabasco, *ají*, de arbol, cherry, cascabel

Very hot chiles: jalapeño, serrano, guajillo, Dundicutt, Kashmiri, yellow

Hot chiles: poblano/ancho, pasilla, Anaheim, California Hot, New Mexico

Not hot chiles: Cubanelle, bell

the number of dried chiles and chile powders I have! Yikes! What all this means is that to make these recipes as if you were cooking in a foreign country you will have to make a definite effort—although not a hard one—to find these food products. If you live in a city with ethnic markets, all the better. But today with the Internet, the world arrives at our door. I've made a rather large effort to identify reliable Internet sources, so I hope you give some of them a try. There is an enormous satisfaction in sending an e-mail to the little West African market in Buffalo, New York, and having your red palm oil show up two weeks later. But I recognize that not everyone is going to make this effort, so I've written the recipes to suggest alternatives or substitutes for hard-to-find items. Remember, though, that some of these substitutes are not at all like the real thing. Luckily, you will not need to buy new equipment. Your existing kitchenware will be more than satisfactory. One thing you might have to buy, if you don't already have it, is a wok. Otherwise, plunge in, impress your friends and family, and enjoy yourself.

If you are interested in learning more about the history and science of the world's hot cuisines, an in-depth bibliography of my sources can be found at http://www.cliffordawright.com/somelikeithot/.

One final and important note: Handling chiles requires care and thoughtfulness. Wash your hands thoroughly afterward with plenty of soap and warm water, and *never* put your fingers near mucus membranes of your body—eyes, mouth, nose, and so on—after handling chiles. Some people's skin can be sensitive to chiles as well, so it may benefit you to wear thin disposable plastic gloves when handling chiles.

startling starters

Starters are like the ignition for the blastoff. They excite people and give them a foresight into what might come. Starters are versatile. They can be served as appetizers, as snacks, as cocktail party bites. The recipes in this chapter are not namby-pamby appetizers to stuff your face with, but are incendiary in their own right. Although all the recipes in this chapter are considered starters, appetizers, meze, or snacks in the cultures they come from, they are so boldly flavored and so delicious that you could easily serve any of them as a main course. They are organized by region, starting with South America and then moving north and then east around the world through all the piquant culinary cultures. Don't know where to start with your starters? Begin with Pepper Shrimp (page 26) and you will become a convert to Jamaican food, to shrimp, to the habanero chile, and to nearly anything else pleasurable, because this will be the best shrimp dish you've ever had. If not indicated otherwise in the recipe, all servings are meant to be appetizer portions.

Quinoa Fritters

This Bolivian recipe is called *bocados de quinua* and is typically served with the famous hot sauce *ají criollo* as an appetizer. They are a great cocktail party bite, as guests can eat them with their fingers. This recipe is from Maria Baez Kijac's *The South American Table* (The Harvard Common Press, 2003), and I've changed it only very slightly. Five or six tablespoons of raw quinoa will give you one cup cooked quinoa as called for in this recipe.

1 tablespoon vegetable oil

4 scallions, white and light green parts only, finely chopped

1/2 teaspoon hot paprika

1 tablespoon finely chopped fresh parsley leaves

1 tablespoon finely chopped fresh coriander (cilantro) leaves

1 cup cooked quinoa

1/4 cup unbleached all-purpose flour

1/2 teaspoon salt

1/4 teaspoon freshly ground white pepper

1/2 teaspoon cayenne pepper

1/4 cup freshly grated Parmesan cheese

2 large eggs, lightly beaten

6 to 8 cups vegetable oil, for frying

1 cup Peruvian Creole Sauce (*ají criollo*, page 409)

1. In a small skillet, heat the vegetable oil over medium heat. Add the scallions and paprika and cook until soft, 1 minute, stirring. Remove from the heat and stir in the parsley and coriander. Transfer to a bowl and mix in the cooked quinoa. Add the flour, salt, white pepper, cayenne pepper, Parmesan cheese, and eggs and mix well. The "dough" will be a thick, gooey batter. Refrigerate for 15 minutes.

2. Preheat the frying oil to 350°F in a deep-fryer or an 8-inch saucepan fitted with a basket insert. Drop heaping teaspoonfuls of the quinoa mixture into the hot oil, being careful not to crowd the fritters (you will probably need to cook two or three batches). Cook until golden, about 2 minutes, then remove with a slotted spoon to paper towels to drain. Keep the fritters warm in the oven while you cook the remaining batches. Serve hot with the creole sauce.

MAKES ABOUT 36 FRITTERS FOR 4 TO 6 SERVINGS

Meat-Stuffed Red Rocoto Chiles

This Peruvian preparation called *rocotos rellenos* is blistering, as the *rocoto* chile is one of the hottest on earth. The *rocoto* chile is *Capsicum pubescens*, a native South American chile, unique in that it has black seeds. In Peru an expression about them, *llevanta muertos*, "raise the dead," will give you some idea about their heat. The city of Arequipa is famous for its *rocotos rellenos*. Unless you have special ordered or you grow your own *rocoto* chiles, you will have to use the large red jalapeño chiles that are more commonly found in the market. This preparation is a favorite since it's so flavorful.

FOR THE CHILES

1 tablespoon salt

3/4 cup red wine vinegar

36 fresh red *rocoto* chiles or large fresh red jalapeño chiles (about 2 pounds)

FOR THE STUFFING

1/4 cup unsalted butter

1 medium-size onion, finely chopped

2 large garlic cloves, finely chopped

1 tablespoon *Ají Panca en Pasta* (page 405)

1/2 pound ground beef

1/4 pound ground pork

Salt and freshly ground black pepper to taste

2 large green jalapeño chiles, seeded and finely chopped

1/4 cup chopped pecans

1 1/2 teaspoons unbleached all-purpose flour

1/2 cup beef broth (homemade or canned)

2 tablespoons heavy cream

FOR THE SAUCE

3 tablespoons extra-virgin olive oil

2 tablespoons finely chopped garlic

3 tablespoons tomato paste or 3/4 cup tomato puree

1/2 cup dry white wine

FOR FINISHING THE PREPARATION

6 small potatoes (about 1 pound), cooked, peeled, and sliced 1/2 inch thick

3/4 cup shredded mozzarella cheese

1/2 cup grated Parmesan cheese

1. To prepare the chiles, bring a large saucepan of water mixed with the salt and vinegar to a boil. Plunge the chiles in the boiling water and leave for 1 minute. Remove with a skimmer and let sit for 10 minutes. (Plunge again into the boiling water two more times if using *rocoto* chiles.) Make a slit in the chile near the stem end with a paring knife and run it down three-quarters of the length of the chile. Remove the seeds carefully by cutting them away from the white "veins" that the seeds attach themselves to with the tip of a small paring knife and discard.

2. To make the stuffing, in a medium-size skillet, melt the butter over medium-high heat, then cook the onion and garlic until soft, about 3 minutes, stirring. Add the *ají panca en pasta*, beef, and pork, season with salt and pepper, and stir to mix well and break up the meat. Cook until it turns color, 2 to 3 minutes. Add the chopped chiles, pecans, and flour and stir. Then add the broth and cream and cook 1 minute. Mix thoroughly and set aside.

3. Prepare the sauce by heating the olive oil in a medium-size skillet over medium-high heat and cook the garlic until sizzling, about 1 minute. Add the tomato paste or puree and wine and stir to blend. Leave it to cook over medium-high heat until the wine nearly evaporates, about 5 minutes, stirring occasionally.

4. Preheat the oven to 350°F. Carefully stuff the whole chiles with the meat mixture. Pour the tomato sauce on the bottom of a baking dish and place the stuffed chiles on top of the tomato sauce, alternating layers of chiles with the cooked potatoes. Cover all of it with the mozzarella and Parmesan cheese. Bake until the cheese melts, 20 to 25 minutes, and serve immediately.

MAKES 12 APPETIZER SERVINGS OR 6 MAIN-COURSE SERVINGS

the home of the chile

The original home of the chile is thought by many to be, not in Mexico, but in an area of South America bounded by the mountains of southern Brazil to the east, Bolivia on the west, and Paraguay and northern Argentina to the south.

the chiles

All the chiles, from the mild bell pepper to the blazing orange hot of the habanero chile, are species of the genus *Capsicum*.

The first of the cultivated species is *Capsicum annuum*, the most widely cultivated and economically important species. This species includes bell and other sweet peppers as well as nearly all the varieties of hot chiles sold in the United States, including the jalapeño, serrano, poblano, Anaheim, New Mexico, and guajillo, and all the finger-type chiles (except the Tabasco chile). Various chile blends such as chili powder and paprika are also made from this species.

The second of the cultivated species is *C. frutescens*, originally from South America. It is today mostly grown in lowland tropical America, to a lesser extent in southeastern Asia, and in West Africa, and it is the chile most commonly used in West African cooking. Of all the *C. frutescens* cultivars, only the Tabasco chile is grown outside the tropics, especially in Louisiana.

The third of the cultivated species is *C. chinense*, grown in tropical America and most commonly in the Amazon, where its home is believed to be. *Chinense* means China, of course, but the term is actually a misnomer since this chile originates in the Amazon basin. The best known and most common *C. chinense* available in U.S. markets is the orange-colored habanero chile, also the hottest chile on the market.

The fourth of the cultivated species is *C. baccatum*, and it is cultivated mostly in Bolivia and rarely outside of South America.

The fifth species is *C. pubescens*, a highland species grown in the Andes.

Potatoes with Creamy Cheese Sauce

This famous Peruvian dish is called *papas a la Huancaínas* because it originated in the Andean region of Huancayo. It is believed to be originally a native American Indian dish. In Bolivia and Peru, a special chile powder called *ají limo* is used to spice up this preparation. Cayenne pepper makes a more than acceptable substitute here. Sometimes *ají* can be found in Mexican markets. One can use whole dried *ajís* in this preparation, or whole dried red chiles of any kind, in place of the fresh chiles, if using, in which case you break them in half, shake the seeds out, and soak them in olive or vegetable oil until soft. Some South American cooks also use an herb called *palillo* to make a more yellow dish. The roots of the Peruvian *palillo* turn food yellow; it is a different plant from the Mexican *palillo*.

2 pounds medium-size Yukon gold or Yellow Finn potatoes

³/₄ pound white cheese (such as Mexican *queso cotija, queso fresco, queso ranchero,* farmer's cheese, or cow's milk feta cheese)

One 12-ounce can evaporated milk

1 large garlic clove, crushed

One ¹/₄-inch-thick slice from the center of a medium-size onion

3 tablespoons vegetable oil

3 tablespoons ground yellow chile (*ají limo*) or 4 tablespoons cayenne pepper or 5 fresh yellow chiles (*ají amarillo*) or 1¹/₂ habanero chiles, finely chopped

FOR THE GARNISH

1 head Boston or butter lettuce, leaves separated and wiped clean with paper towels

3 large eggs, hard-boiled, quartered or sliced

10 black olives, pitted and cut in half

1. Place the whole potatoes in a large saucepan and cover with cold water. Bring to just below a boil over medium heat, 20 to 25 minutes, then continue cooking until tender, when a skewer pressed into the thickest part of the potato glides in easily, another 20 to 25 minutes. Drain, peel, and slice the potatoes about ¹/₂ inch thick.

2. Meanwhile, in a saucepan, melt the cheese with the evaporated milk, garlic, onion, vegetable oil, and chile over medium heat, stirring in a figure-eight pattern until the sauce is creamy and smooth, about 8 minutes. Arrange the lettuce leaves on a serving plate, lay the sliced potatoes on top of the lettuce, and spoon the cheese sauce over the potatoes to cover. Garnish with eggs and black olives. Serve at room temperature.

MAKES 8 APPETIZER SERVINGS

starting starters

the chiles of south america

The chile originated in South America. Although all five cultivated species of chile are found in South America, along with many wild species, most of the cultivated chiles used for culinary purposes in South America are commonly called *ají* (pronounced ah-ee), the Arawak name that Columbus encountered in the Caribbean and that he described in his diaries. When the conquistadors arrived in South America, they called the chiles they encountered there by their Arawak name *ají* and not the name used by the Incas, *uchu*. In South America, the Indians called chiles *uchu*, and the fact that they are now called *ají* by all segments of the population shows that the Arawak word traveled with the Spanish as they expanded into South America. Nearly all of these South American *ajís* (chiles) are of the species *Capsicum baccatum*, unlike in Mexico where most of the chiles are *C. annuum*. There are a good many chiles, and here are some of them, none of which you will encounter in supermarkets in the United States at this time, although they are available through the Internet. The color descriptions refer to the chile in its mature stage of growth.

Ají amarillo, also called *ají mirasol*, is the "yellow chile" of Peru, their most common chile (*C. baccatum* var. *pendulum*) that can grow to about five inches long and is of a medium-hot pungency. There are two main types, the *kellu-uchu* (*ají amarillo cusqueño*) and the *puca-uchu* (*uchu* is the Quecha word for chile in Peru). These chiles are best replaced with the yellow chile of *C. annuum* that is called the *güero* chile in Mexico and the U.S. or the banana or "yellow chile," all of which are generic terms for any yellow chile. *Ají ayucllo* is a small, oval, and bright orange chile of undetermined species. *Ají cacho de cabra* is a long, thin, and very hot chile used in table salsas in Chile (the country). *Ají cereza* is a "cherry" chile that is about one inch in diameter, very pungent, and deep red in color that is either *C. chinense* or *C. baccatum*. *Ají charapa* is a round red or yellow Peruvian wild chile harvested about 1/4 inch in diameter and very pungent.

Ají chivato is a tiny round chile grown in Colombia and used in salsas. *Ají de montaña* is a widely cultivated finger-type chile grown in Bolivia, Peru, Ecuador, and Argentina that is sometimes called "finger chile." It is about three inches long and comes in a variety of colors. They may also be packed in brine and sold as *ají entero* in South American markets. *Ají limo* is a very small and elongated chile of the species *C. frutescens* that is very pungent and grows on the northern coast of Peru and is used mostly in salsas. *Ají mono* is the "monkey" chile that grows in the Peruvian jungles to five inches long and is bright red. It is very pungent and believed to be *C. baccatum*. *Ají norteño* is a chile thought to be *C. baccatum* that grows in the northern coastal valleys of Peru. It has a medium pungency and is eaten fresh with seafood. *Ají panca* is a Peruvian chile that grows to about five inches long and is deep red to purple in color and is thought to be *C. frutescens*. *Ají pinguita de mono* means "little monkey penis chile" and is a wild and semicultivated chile found in Peru's central valley of Chanchamayo. *Ají verde* is a mild chile with thick flesh and lime green skin that is used in Chile to make salsas. *Ají yaquitania* is the name in Brazil of a chile of the species *C. chinense*. There are dozens more chiles used in South America. The habanero chile is also used in South America, in Brazil, and in the Amazon basin, where some think its ancestral home is. *Rocoto* (or *locoto*) is a Peruvian chile of the *C. pubescens* species. It is a very hot chile with thick walls and black seeds. It is cultivated throughout the Andes and matures to a variety of colors. *Malagueta* is a Brazilian chile (*C. frutescens* or *C. chinense*) related to the Tabasco chile or the habanero chile. It has nothing to do with the West African spice of the same name, which is grains of paradise. There are many more chiles known in a variety of Indian languages as well as Spanish and Portuguese, some cultivated and more wild.

mexican cheeses

Mexican cheeses, which in general are not very sophisticated, are readily found in super-markets in the western part of the United States and, increasingly, everywhere. They all seem very similar, and they are. *Queso añejo* (or *cotija*) is a very dry, salty, white cheese that is usually crumbled over food. You can substitute domestic feta cheese, which is made from cow's milk rather than sheep's milk as in Greece. *Queso asadero* is a spun-curd cheese, as is mozzarella, which is made in the same way Armenian string cheese is in that the final product is braided. The name means "broiler cheese," and it is common in the Mexican state of Oaxaca. This cheese melts well and forms strings. Substitute mild Monterey Jack or domestic Muenster cheese. *Queso Chihuahua* is a cheese from Chihuahua originally made by the Mennonite community. It is a mild, pale yellow cheese with a high fat content that melts well. Substitute mild white cheddar, Monterey Jack, or domestic Muenster cheese. *Queso panela* is a semisoft cow's milk cheese that is white, smooth, and rubbery. Substitute domestic packaged hard mozzarella. *Queso fresco* is the most common Mexican cheese, and it is used for everything from stuffing chiles to topping tostadas. It crumbles and melts well. *Queso ranchero* is a cream-colored cow's milk cheese sold dry or semihard. Substitute either an Argentinian Parmesan or an Italian semihard Pecorino Sarde. *Queso mocorito* is a cheese from Sonora that resembles Muenster in meltability.

Chile con Queso

This preparation from Chihuahua and Sonora in Mexico is nothing but "chiles and cheese," but what a combination! The first time I had something like it was in a Oaxacan restaurant in Los Angeles. What makes it so appealing is that the blistering hot chiles are moderated by the bland cheeses, making for a delightful appetizer. The cheeses used are *queso Chihuahua* and *queso asadero*, both of which can be purchased in many supermarkets in the United States. You can replace both with a mixture of mild white cheddar and white Jack cheeses. The process of blistering the jalapeño chiles might seem like a lot of work, but the way I do it makes it rather simple. I take the flat rack out of my roasting pan and arrange the chiles on it, and then place the rack over the stove burner until the bottom sides of the chiles are completely blackened. Then I turn them over with tongs and do the other side. If you can grill the chiles, all the better; it will be an even better taste.

30 fresh green jalapeño chiles

1/4 cup vegetable oil

1 medium-size onion, thinly sliced

1 ripe medium-size tomato, peeled, seeded, and coarsely chopped

3/4 cup light cream

1/2 pound mixed Mexican *queso Chihuahua* and *queso asadero* or mixed mild white cheddar and Monterey Jack cheese, diced

Salt to taste

1. Place the chiles on a flat rack from your roasting pan and then place the rack over a burner and turn the heat on to high. Blister the chiles black on all sides, moving the rack and turning the chiles when necessary. Alternatively, you can grill the chiles. Remove the chiles and, when cool enough to handle, rub off as much blackened skin as you can. Cut in half and remove the seeds, then slice into thin strips and set aside.

2. In a medium-size skillet, heat the vegetable oil over medium heat, then cook the onion until it is translucent, about 7 minutes, stirring. Add the chile strips and tomato to the skillet, cover, and cook until soft, about 8 minutes, stirring occasionally. Add the cream and cook another 2 minutes. Stir in the cheese until it melts. Season with salt and serve.

MAKES 6 SERVINGS

starting starters

Soft Tacos of Smoky Shredded Pork

This recipe from Oaxaca in Mexico, called *tacos de picadillo oaxaqueño*, is adapted from cookbook author Rick Bayless, who recommends that the meat be chopped and not ground. This filling could go into tamales or enchiladas, but putting it on soft corn tortillas for tacos is excellent. If you have never heard of or used canned chipotle chiles in adobo, you will be surprised to find them in all supermarkets with other canned goods.

1½ pounds boneless pork shoulder, trimmed of fat and cut into 2-inch cubes

5 large garlic cloves, 2 finely chopped and 3 left whole with their skin

1 large white onion, chopped

1¼ pounds ripe tomatoes

3 canned chipotle chiles in adobo

½ cup slivered almonds

2½ tablespoons pork lard

Salt to taste

½ teaspoon ground cinnamon

Freshly ground black pepper to taste

⅛ teaspoon ground cloves

½ cup golden raisins

16 corn tortillas

½ cup crumbled Mexican *queso panela* or other Mexican cheese or farmer's cheese

Red Sauce (optional, page 410)

1. Place the pork in a 3-quart saucepan with the chopped garlic and half the onion and cover just barely with salted water. Bring to a boil over medium heat, skim the foam off the top, reduce the heat to medium-low, and simmer, partially covered, until very tender, about 1½ hours. Cool the meat in the broth, then remove and shred the meat using two forks.

2. Heat an ungreased cast-iron skillet over medium-high heat, then cook the unpeeled garlic until soft, about 15 minutes, turning occasionally. Remove the garlic and peel. Set aside.

3. Preheat the broiler. Arrange the tomatoes in a broiling pan and roast about 4 inches under the broiler flame or heating element until the skin is blackened, about 6 minutes. Turn and roast the other side until blackened, about another 4 minutes. Remove the tomatoes and set aside. Place the almonds under the broiler on a small metal tray until they are lightly browned, 1 to 2 minutes. Set aside. Cool both the tomatoes and almonds. Once the tomatoes are cool, peel, and collect all

peeling chiles

I am always torn between what I prefer and the time I have. I prefer to peel chiles by holding them over a burner flame until the peel chars and blackens. But then I will have to give my attention to the process and clean up any mess I've made. So, alternatively, I will place the chiles in a baking dish and roast them in the oven for 30 minutes at 425°F, then peel them. The downside of the oven method is that the chiles get cooked too much.

the tomato juices in the pan. Place the tomatoes in a food processor and pulse with the canned chipotle chiles and soft cooked garlic until a medium-fine puree.

4. In a heavy 3-quart saucepan, melt 1 tablespoon lard over medium-high heat, add the tomato puree, and cook until it thickens, about 5 minutes, stirring. Turn the heat off, season with salt, and set aside until needed.

5. In a 12-inch nonstick skillet, heat the remaining $1^1/_2$ tablespoons lard over medium-high heat. Once the lard starts to smoke, add the shredded meat and the remaining onion. Cook until the pork is crispy and golden, 12 to 14 minutes, stirring frequently and scraping the brown bits up. Sprinkle with cinnamon, pepper, cloves, and raisins, then pour in the tomato puree. Reduce the heat to low and simmer until all the liquid has evaporated, about 5 minutes, stirring occasionally. Add the almonds to the meat and correct the seasoning.

6. Place the corn tortillas in a kitchen towel and wrap them up. Place the wrapped tortillas in the steamer portion of a steamer with 2 inches of water in the bottom portion and bring to a boil, keeping the top tightly covered. Once it reaches a boil, turn it off and let the tortillas sit for 15 minutes. To serve, hold a tortilla in your hand and fill with the cheese and shredded meat. Top with Red Sauce if you like.

MAKES 6 TO 8 APPETIZER SERVINGS OR 4 MAIN-COURSE SERVINGS

startling starters

Soft Tacos of Pork and Chile-Sesame Seed Sauce

This appetizer is known by its Nahuatl name in Oaxaca and Guerrero in Mexico, *pizatl en chitextli*. In Mexican culinary vernacular, an ancho chile is the name of the fresh variety; once dried it's called a *mulato*. But these chile names can become quite confused: for instance, some packagers in southern California sell pasilla/ancho chiles as if they were the same thing, though they're not. In any case, this is a delicious and not-too-hot preparation that should be served as soon as it is cooked. Dried shrimp can be found in some supermarkets in the southwestern United States as well as in Latino and Asian markets throughout the country and on the Internet. Serve with warm corn tortillas on the side for diners to make their own soft tacos.

2 tablespoons pork lard

2 pounds boneless pork loin, excess fat removed, cut into ³/₄-inch cubes

1 fresh pasilla chile, roasted, seeded, and chopped

1 fresh poblano chile or jalapeño chile, roasted, seeded, and chopped

1 dried ancho (*mulato*) chile, soaked in tepid water for 30 minutes, seeded, and chopped

1 chipotle chile in adobo, chopped

1 ounce (about 3 tablespoons) sesame seeds, toasted in a toaster oven until light brown

3 ounces (about 1 cup) dried shrimp, soaked in water for 10 minutes and drained

³/₄ cup water

¹/₂ teaspoon dried oregano

Salt to taste

¹/₂ cup sour cream

16 corn tortillas, warmed

1. In a large skillet, melt 1 tablespoon lard over high heat, then cook the pork until crispy brown and some fat is rendered, without stirring or turning it for 4 minutes. Turn and let cook another 1 to 2 minutes. Reduce the heat to low and simmer gently for 4 minutes, then turn the heat off, leaving the pork in the skillet.

2. Meanwhile, in a medium-size skillet, melt the remaining lard over medium heat. Cook the pasilla, poblano, ancho, and chipotle chiles until they soften, about 3 minutes, stirring.

3. In a mortar, crush the toasted sesame seeds with a pestle and set aside, or grind them in a spice mill. Crush the shrimp in the mortar, or run in a food processor until crumbly, and incorporate them into the sesame seeds. Place the sesame seeds and dried shrimp into the skillet with the chiles and add the water. Add oregano, season with salt, and cook on medium heat until the liquid has evaporated, about 8 minutes.

4. Turn the heat under the pork to high, and once it starts to sizzle, reduce the heat to low, pour the sauce over the pork, and continue to cook over low heat until there is no liquid left and the meat is succulent and tender, about 10 minutes, stirring. If the sauce is getting too thick, add a few tablespoons of water. Add the sour cream, stir it in well so it is blended, and serve immediately with the corn tortillas.

MAKES 8 SERVINGS

Sopes with Potatoes and Chorizo Sausage

A Mexican *sope*, also called a *gordita garnacha* or *picada*, is not a soup but a kind of thick tortilla with a lip and an indentation where toppings can rest. *Sopes* are made from *masa harina*, a fine corn flour, in the same way as a tortilla, but they are thicker and about 3 1/2 inches in diameter, and may or may not be round. *Sopes* are sold by the name *garnacha* in some supermarkets and in Latino markets. If you can't find them, you can use two corn tortillas stacked on top of each other. This recipe is one kind of *sope* among many. I first had something like this, called *sopes con papas con chorizos*, in a Mexican restaurant in California. The refried beans called for in this recipe are best if homemade, but they can also come out of a can.

1/2 pound waxy new potatoes, such as Red Bliss

1 tablespoon pork lard

3 chorizo sausage links (about 1/2 pound), casings removed and crumbled

3 chipotle chiles in adobo, chopped

6 *sopes*

1/2 cup refried beans

1 small onion, finely chopped

1/2 cup crumbled Mexican *queso fresco* or farmer's cheese

1.	Place the potatoes in a saucepan with water to cover and bring to a boil over medium heat, then cook until tender but firm, about 20 minutes. Drain, cool, and peel. Dice the potatoes small and set aside.

2.	In a skillet, melt the lard over medium-high heat and cook the chorizo until cooked and the fat is rendered, stirring occasionally while you break it up further with a wooden spoon, about 8 minutes. Add the potatoes and the chipotle chiles, and cook until the potatoes have browned a bit, about 8 minutes, stirring occasionally and scraping the bottom of the skillet with a spatula.

3.	Preheat the oven to 350°F. Arrange the *sopes* on a baking tray and fill the indented side of the *sopes* with about 1 heaping tablespoon of refried beans. Divide the chorizo and potato mixture between the 6 *sopes*, sprinkle 2 teaspoons of chopped onion on each, and top each with a heaping tablespoon of cheese. Place in the oven and bake until the cheese is completely melted, about 10 minutes. Serve immediately.

MAKES 6 SERVINGS

Garnachas

A garnacha, also called a *sope*, is a kind of *antojito* or appetizer that is in the same family as the *gordita* from the Yucatán. *Garnachas* are tartlets made of fine corn flour known as *masa harina* that are fried in oil and filled with a variety of ingredients such as the shredded pork of this recipe or black bean paste and ground beef. These appetizers from Veracruz are called *garnachas de Rinconada*. The word *garnacha* is the root of our word "nacho."

1¼ pounds ripe tomatoes

1 pound boneless pork butt or shoulder, cut into 1-inch cubes

1 medium-size boiling potato

1 large onion, finely chopped

7 large garlic cloves, 4 lightly crushed and 3 mashed in a mortar with 1 teaspoon salt

Salt to taste

2 chipotle chiles in adobo

¼ cup water

½ teaspoon ground cumin

¼ teaspoon ground cloves

¼ teaspoon allspice

Freshly ground black pepper to taste

¼ cup vegetable oil

24 corn tortillas

1. Preheat the oven to 450°F. Place the tomatoes in a roasting pan and roast until blackened, about 45 minutes. Remove and, when cool, peel and chop. Set aside until needed.

2. Place the pork in a saucepan with the whole potato, one-third of the onion, the four lightly crushed garlic cloves, and a little salt and bring to a near boil. Reduce the heat to low and simmer, partially covered, until the potato can be pierced with a skewer and has a slight resistance, about 40 minutes. Remove the potato, peel, and when it is cool cut into tiny dice and set aside. Continue cooking the pork until it is tender and can be shredded with a fork, about $1^{1}/4$ hours more. Let cool in the saucepan. Remove the pork and shred, pulling apart the meat with two forks.

3. Meanwhile, put the mashed garlic and one-third of the onion in a blender with the chipotle chiles and tomatoes. Then add the water, cumin, cloves, allspice, and salt and pepper and blend until smooth. Transfer the sauce to a small saucepan with the shredded pork and heat over low heat until savory and dense, about 45 minutes, making sure it is not bubbling too vigorously.

4. In a cast-iron skillet, heat the vegetable oil over medium heat, then fry the tortillas until still soft but getting crispy, about 1 minute, turning once with tongs. Place the tortillas on platters and spoon some sauce over them. Sprinkle just a few drops of hot oil from the skillet over each, then sprinkle some of the last third of the chopped onion, the potato, and finally a few more drops of oil over each. Serve immediately.

MAKES 24 *GARNACHAS* TO SERVE 8 APPETIZER PORTIONS

féroce d'avocat

The name of this hot crab appetizer that is popular in the French Caribbean islands of Martinique and Guadeloupe literally means "ferocious avocado" (not ferocious lawyer). The avocado, sometimes referred to as an alligator pear, adds a rich taste. One can also use salt cod instead of crab, but crab seems to have a natural affinity for avocado. It is made by blending mashed avocado with tapioca (cassava flour) and forming it into balls with the crabs and a flavoring of shallots, green onions, garlic, Scotch bonnet chile, vegetable oil, vinegar, and lime juice.

Firecrackers

*I*n the late 1980s and early 1990s, American chefs were finding inspiration in the cooking of the American Southwest, and lots of hot sauces and chiles were being used in new and interesting ways. I was living in Cambridge, Massachusetts, at the time and a restaurant opened called the Cottonwood Café, with lots of Navaho themes in its decor and invented dishes that I liked. I had something like this recipe there, although I have no idea who made it up. I remember that their version was rolled in blue corn flour before frying. These appetizers are very popular now, and many restaurants and bars sell them at happy hour. They derive from a Mexican preparation.

12 large green jalapeño chiles

4 ounces Monterey Jack cheese, cut into 1-inch-long ¼-inch-thick sticks

6 cups vegetable oil, for frying

All-purpose flour or finely ground blue corn flour, for dredging

2 large eggs, beaten

Salt to taste

1. Preheat the oven to 450°F. Arrange the chiles on a baking tray and roast until the skins become crinkly, about 25 minutes. Remove from the oven and, once they are cool enough to handle, peel and slit the peppers lengthwise with a small paring knife and remove the seeds. Stuff the peppers with the cheese, securing the opening with a toothpick if necessary.

2. Preheat the frying oil to 360°F in a deep-fryer or an 8-inch saucepan fitted with a basket insert. Dredge the chiles in the flour, then dip them in the egg, and back in the flour again. Cook the stuffed chiles in batches without crowding the fryer until golden, 3 to 4 minutes. Drain, sprinkle with salt, and serve immediately.

MAKES 6 SERVINGS

Sopaipillas

In 1971 I was going to school at Colorado State University in Fort Collins, and near my house was a little joint that served Tex-Mex food, although later I realized it must have really been New Mexico–Mex or maybe even Colorado-Mex, if there is such a thing. On the menu was an item called a *sopaipilla* that was some flattened dough that was shaped like a beaver tail, deep-fried, and then sprinkled with beans and chiles or cheese and chiles. There was also a sweet version with drizzled honey. I remember that I said "Blast off!" when I took the first bite. It was extremely hot and extremely good. If you want to serve these as cocktail bites, cut each one in half.

FOR THE SOPAIPILLAS
2 cups unbleached all-purpose flour

1 teaspoon salt

1 teaspoon baking powder

1 teaspoon vegetable oil

1/2 cup lukewarm water

1/4 cup whole milk, at room temperature

6 to 8 cups vegetable oil, for frying

1 cup shredded Mexican *queso asadero* or white cheddar cheese

1 cup shredded Monterey Jack cheese

6 fresh green serrano chiles, finely chopped

1. In a large bowl, stir together the flour, salt, and baking powder. Pour in the vegetable oil and work it in with your fingers. Add the water and milk and continue to work it into the flour until a sticky dough forms. Turn out the dough onto a well-floured counter and knead for 1 minute, until soft and pliable and not sticky. Cover with a damp kitchen towel and let rest 30 minutes. Divide the dough into 4 balls, cover again, and let rest 30 minutes.

2. Preheat the oven to 350°F. On a floured surface, roll out each ball into an oval about 1/4 inch thick at the most. Preheat the frying oil to 360°F in a deep-fryer or an 8-inch saucepan fitted with a basket insert. Fry the pieces of dough, 1 or 2 at a time, until they puff up, 30 seconds to 1 minute, spooning some oil over the tops, then turn and cook until very light golden, 2 to 3 minutes. Remove from the oil and place on a baking tray.

3. In a bowl, toss the cheeses and chiles together. Place the mixture on top and place in the oven until the cheese melts, about 3 minutes. Serve immediately.

MAKES 4 APPETIZER SERVINGS OR 8 COCKTAIL SERVINGS

starting starters

Batter-Fried Calamari with Habanero Aïoli

This American Southwest–inspired preparation is one of the most wonderful appetizers you'll ever have—although you probably wouldn't have it in New Mexico, as squid-eaters tend to be coastal. The secret here is to not over-fry the squid. It may not seem like enough time, but 1½ minutes at the most is right.

FOR THE AÏOLI
2 large egg yolks

2 large garlic cloves, chopped

1 habanero chile, stem removed

½ cup olive oil

½ cup vegetable oil

1 teaspoon white wine vinegar

Salt and freshly ground black pepper to taste

FOR THE BATTER
1 large egg

1 teaspoon cayenne pepper

Pinch of salt

½ cup all-purpose flour

FOR THE SQUID
2 pounds cleaned squid rings and tentacles

6 to 8 cups vegetable oil, for frying

2 lemons, each cut in thirds

1.   To make the aïoli, place the egg yolks in a food processor with the garlic and habanero chile and run for 30 seconds. While the machine is running, slowly drizzle in the olive and vegetable oils in a very thin stream. Once the mayonnaise is formed, stir in the vinegar and salt and pepper. Refrigerate for 30 minutes before using.

2.   Make the frying batter by beating the egg in a bowl with the cayenne pepper and salt. Incorporate the flour and then thin with water until almost liquid.

3.   Rinse and drain the squid and toss with the batter. Preheat the frying oil to 360°F in a deep-fryer or an 8-inch saucepan fitted with a basket insert. Drain the squid from the batter slightly and deep-fry in batches until light golden and crispy, about 1½ minutes. Drain on paper towels and serve immediately with lemon wedges, salt, and aïoli.

MAKES 6 SERVINGS

Tuna Falafel with Cajun-Style Oyster and Cilantro Mayonnaise

I remember exactly how this recipe came about because I had just returned from Egypt, where I had fallen in love with their version of falafel, the traditional Middle Eastern fried chickpea patties, which they called *ta'amiyya*. At the same time I was considering writing a small book on tuna, and since I also love Cajun food and I love oysters . . . well here you go, falafel with tuna instead of beans. The mayonnaise is a cayenne-hot luscious dipping sauce for the fried tuna patties.

FOR THE MAYONNAISE

1 tablespoon unsalted butter

4 scallions, white parts only, finely chopped

1 tablespoon very finely chopped celery

1 bay leaf

2¹/₂ tablespoons very finely chopped fresh coriander (cilantro) leaves

1 tablespoon Cliff's Cajun Seasoning (page 412)

3 oysters, shucked

1 small egg or 2 egg yolks

1¹/₄ cups vegetable oil

1 tablespoon apple cider vinegar

FOR THE TUNA FALAFEL

1 pound fresh tuna, ground in a food processor

¹/₂ teaspoon salt

1 tablespoon very finely chopped garlic

2¹/₂ tablespoons very finely chopped scallions, white and green parts

1¹/₂ tablespoons very finely chopped fresh coriander

1¹/₂ tablespoons very finely chopped fresh parsley

¹/₂ teaspoon ground cumin

¹/₈ teaspoon cayenne pepper

1¹/₂ teaspoons sesame seeds

6 to 8 cups olive oil, for frying

¹/₂ cup bread crumbs

1. To make the mayonnaise, in a small skillet, melt the butter over medium heat, then cook the scallions, celery, bay leaf, and coriander for 2 minutes, stirring. Reduce the heat to low and add the Cajun seasoning and oysters. Cook for 5 minutes, stirring. Transfer to a bowl to cool. Discard the bay leaf.

2. Put the oyster mixture and the egg in a food processor. Blend for 30 seconds, then slowly pour in the vegetable oil in a thin, steady stream while it continues to blend. It will take about 5 minutes for all the oil to pour out of the

starting starters

21

measuring cup. Add the vinegar and blend for a few seconds. Transfer to a serving bowl and refrigerate for 1 hour before using.

3.   To make the falafel, in a medium-size bowl, mix the tuna, salt, garlic, scallions, coriander, parsley, cumin, cayenne pepper, and sesame seeds. With wet hands, form into 2-inch-diameter hockey-puck shapes. Set aside in the refrigerator for 1 hour.

4.   Preheat the frying oil to 360°F in a deep-fryer or an 8-inch saucepan fitted with a basket insert. Roll the tuna patties in the bread crumbs and deep-fry in two batches until brown and crisp, about 2^1/$_2$ minutes. Drain on absorbent paper towels and serve with the mayonnaise.

MAKES 8 PATTIES TO SERVE 4

Hot Crab Dip

Now here's a dip that will keep a party hopping and hot. You can tell your guests that this is a typical Cajun party dip served at everything from beer-swilling shindigs to family gatherings. The recipe is adapted from one by Suzanne LeMaire and it is temperature-hot *and* chile-hot. One uses crackers or tart shells for scooping up the dip, although the Frito's corn chips called Scoops that are made especially for dipping are very sinful. But celery or carrot sticks are equally nice, and then you can eat more of the dip and not feel so fat.

^{1}/$_2$ pound cream cheese	2 teaspoons garlic powder
^{1}/$_2$ cup (1 stick) unsalted butter	2 teaspoons cayenne pepper
1 pound crabmeat, picked over	2 teaspoons salt
1 small onion, finely chopped	2 teaspoons freshly ground white pepper
2 teaspoons Tabasco sauce	

In a double boiler over medium-high heat, melt the cream cheese and butter, stirring. Once the mixture has become homogeneous, reduce the heat to medium-low, add the crabmeat, onion, Tabasco, garlic powder, cayenne pepper, salt, and pepper, and stir until the dip is heated through, about 5 minutes. Add additional seasoning to your taste and serve hot.

MAKES 3 CUPS

Cajun Barbecued Pork Back Ribs

Pork is king in Louisiana. The pig was first brought to Louisiana by Europeans arriving via the Mississippi. In rural Cajun country west of New Orleans, even today every part of the pig is used. Ham is considered the choicest part. Andouille is a spicy smoked pork sausage. Gratons are pork cracklings cut into small squares and seasoned with chile pepper, pepper, and salt. Ponce is pig's stomach that can be stuffed and smoked and then cooked étouffée style in brown gravy. Boudin is a unique sausage made of pork, liver, bell peppers, green onions, cooked rice, and spices that comes as blanc or rouge (made with pig's blood). But then we come to back ribs, a cut made for Cajun-style long cooking until the meat is soft and can be pulled right off the bone. These back ribs can be accompanied with white rice, cornbread, hot yeast rolls, or coleslaw.

FOR THE SPICE MIX
1 tablespoon hot paprika

3 tablespoons cayenne pepper

1/2 teaspoon red pepper flakes

1 tablespoon garlic powder

2 teaspoons dried oregano

2 teaspoons dried thyme

1/2 teaspoon salt

1/2 teaspoon freshly ground white pepper

1/2 teaspoon ground cumin

1/4 teaspoon nutmeg

FOR THE RIBS
4 pounds pork back ribs

1 cup pork lard (optional)

1. Prepare a hot charcoal fire, and when the coals are glowing, push them to one side of the grill and let the fire die down until the heat is medium; or preheat a gas grill on medium for 15 minutes. Alternatively, preheat the oven to 250°F.

2. Combine the spice mix, then rub all the surfaces of the ribs with it. Place the ribs on the grill on the opposite side from where the coals are, cover, and slow barbecue until tender, about 5 hours, turning the ribs every 15 minutes and uncovering the barbecue if they seem to be blackening. Add coals when necessary, probably 6 to 7 coals every hour. If desired, baste with the pork lard. If you are cooking in the oven, place on a rack in a roasting pan and cook until crusty on the outside and the meat can be pulled off with your fingers, about 5 hours. If the ribs are blackening prematurely, reduce the heat to 225°F.

MAKES 4 SERVINGS

Bayou Cajun Popcorn

Although one can spice up some popping corn and call it Cajun popcorn, the "real" Cajun popcorn is breaded or batter-fried crayfish, or Gulf shrimp, which are spicy hot. This idea of deep-frying crayfish or shrimp in a coating of spiced bread crumbs is an old idea, but the name "Cajun popcorn" seems to be new. The name does not appear earlier than 1990 as far as I can tell—no matter. They make a wonderful appetizer and should be served with cold beer. My suggestion of Tony Chachere's Creole Seasoning is not a recommendation by me of one brand over another but recognition of the fact that most Cajuns consider it to be a natural table condiment. If you use fresh whole shrimp in this recipe, remember that 3 pounds with their heads and shells will yield about 1½ pounds shelled shrimp.

6 to 8 cups vegetable oil, for frying

1½ cups corn flour

2 tablespoons finely chopped fresh parsley leaves

1 tablespoon cayenne pepper

½ teaspoon salt

½ teaspoon freshly ground black pepper

3 eggs

½ cup whole milk

1½ pounds shelled crayfish tails or shelled medium-size shrimp

Tony Chachere's Creole Seasoning or Cliff's Cajun Seasoning (page 412)

1. Preheat the oil to 360°F in a deep-fryer or an 8-inch saucepan fitted with a basket insert.

2. In a medium-size bowl, mix the corn flour, parsley, cayenne, salt, and pepper. In another medium-size bowl, beat the eggs with the milk. Dip the crayfish tails in the egg and milk mixture, then dredge in the flour mixture. Vigorously shake the excess flour off, drop in the oil, and cook the crayfish tails until golden, about 1½ minutes. Remember to not crowd the fryer, so cook in 3 or 4 batches. As the seafood finishes frying, drain on a paper towel–lined platter. Sprinkle with as much of the seasoning as you want and serve hot.

MAKES 4 TO 6 SERVINGS

Coconut Shrimp

This popular Caribbean appetizer must be a restaurant invention. I have no idea where it originated, but variations of coconut shrimp appear in Jamaica and other Caribbean islands, especially in tourist restaurants, and in the Florida Keys and in other areas of Florida. It also appears in several guises as a southern dish from New Orleans to Tennessee to Georgia. This is the Jamaican version, and it is very hot and nutty in taste. This recipe is adapted from Lucinda Scala Quinn's *Jamaican Cooking* (Macmillan, 1997) and from a version that I had in a restaurant in Key Largo.

Juice of 1 lime

1 cup plus 1 tablespoon vegetable oil

1 tablespoon orange blossom honey

1 tablespoon dark rum

1 Scotch bonnet chile or habanero chile, finely chopped

1 teaspoon salt, or more to your taste

2 large egg whites

$^1/_2$ teaspoon Worcestershire sauce

$1^1/_2$ cups dried shredded unsweetened coconut

2 pounds fresh medium-size shrimp with their heads or 1 pound defrosted headless medium-size shrimp, heads and/or shells removed

1. Put the lime juice, 1 tablespoon of the vegetable oil, honey, rum, chile, and $^1/_2$ teaspoon salt in a blender and blend until smooth. Transfer to a small serving bowl.

2. In a small bowl, beat the egg whites, Worcestershire sauce, and the remaining $^1/_2$ teaspoon salt and beat until it is very frothy but not completely stiff. Spread the coconut on a plate. Dip each shrimp in the egg white mixture, then roll in the coconut. Arrange on a platter and refrigerate the shrimp for 30 minutes.

3. In a large skillet, heat the remaining 1 cup vegetable oil over high heat until it is smoking, then cook the shrimp until golden brown on one side, about 1 minute, making sure they don't touch each other in the skillet. You may need to cook in batches. Turn them over one at a time, quickly, and cook until the other side is golden brown, 1 to $1^1/_2$ minutes. Remove and drain on a paper towel–lined platter. Serve the shrimp with the dipping sauce.

MAKES 6 SERVINGS

starting starters

Pepper Shrimp

This is so extraordinary that I'm worried I might start using too many superlatives to encourage you to make it. Everyone who has tasted this dish has told me that it is the best shrimp dish they've ever had. In the small village of Middle Quarters near the Black River in Jamaica, ladies wearing bandanas by the side of the road sell plastic bags of an orange-red food that they call pepper shrimp. It's a simple dish—freshwater shrimp boiled in a salted brine laced with Scotch bonnet chiles. On the northern coast, one might find them sold in one of the roadside pork pits where jerk pork is also sold. Pepper shrimp can be prepared either as in this recipe or by steaming the shrimp with a little water instead of the oil. The best shrimp to use are jumbo shrimp of 12 count to the pound.

1 cup vegetable oil

6 large garlic cloves, finely chopped

6 Scotch bonnet chiles or habanero chiles, very finely chopped

4 pounds fresh jumbo shrimp with their heads, heads and shells left on, or 2 pounds defrosted headless shrimp, deveined, but with their shells left on

1 teaspoon salt

1^1/$_2$ tablespoons white wine vinegar

In a large casserole or skillet, heat the vegetable oil over medium-high heat with the garlic and chiles until beginning to sizzle, about 1 minute. Add the shrimp and salt and cook until they turn orange-red on both sides, about 3 minutes, turning once. Add the vinegar and cook until they are cooked through, 3 minutes. Remove the shrimp and its marinade to a bowl and toss well. Let cool, then place in a zippered-top freezer bag, and refrigerate for 6 hours. Serve at room temperature.

MAKES 6 TO 8 SERVINGS

Jerk Shrimp

The entire story of jerk is told elsewhere (page 133) so I'll just tell you a little about doing jerk with shrimp. First, it's a favorite as an appetizer, although fine as an entrée. Second, it's just incendiary and over-the-top—but still you can't stop eating it. Third, jerk shrimp is just about the best little morsel to serve up at a party that you can imagine, so have plenty of beer and napkins on hand. Remember that shrimp cook very quickly, and there is nothing more unappetizing than overcooked, rubbery shrimp—so pay attention.

FOR THE JERK SEASONING

1 bunch scallions, white and light green parts only, chopped

One 3-inch piece fresh ginger, peeled and finely chopped

10 large garlic cloves, finely chopped

8 habanero chiles, finely chopped

1/2 bunch fresh coriander (cilantro), leaves only, chopped

2 1/2 tablespoons freshly ground black pepper

1 tablespoon ground nutmeg

1 tablespoon ground allspice

3 tablespoons dried thyme

6 dry bay leaves

1 cup peanut oil

1 cup soy sauce

FOR THE SHRIMP

Twelve 10-inch wooden skewers, soaked in water for 30 minutes

4 pounds fresh shrimp with their heads, heads left on, shells removed, or 2 pounds defrosted headless shrimp, shells removed and saved for making broth

Salt to taste

1. Place the jerk seasoning ingredients in a blender and blend until smooth.

2. Skewer the shrimp lengthwise, about 8 to a skewer, and season with salt. Place the skewers on a tray and cover with the jerk marinade, turning a few times so both sides are coated. Leave to marinate in the refrigerator for 2 hours, turning once.

3. Prepare a hot charcoal fire or preheat a gas grill on high for 15 minutes. Place the shrimp skewers directly on the grilling grate's hottest section and grill until orange and firm, 4 to 8 minutes, depending on the distance from the fire, the heat of the fire, and the size of the shrimp, turning once. Serve immediately.

MAKES 6 SERVINGS

starting starters

Shark and Bake

This is a dish from Trinidad and Tobago that is famous at the roadside stands at Maracas Bay in Trinidad. The spicy shark is deep-fried and wrapped in deep-fried bread—just heavenly! The fried bread pieces, called bakes, are also known as floats and can be made with a yeasted dough, too. If shark isn't available, use swordfish. Pickapeppa Sauce is a commercial hot sauce from Jamaica that is likely to be sold in your local supermarket. Lemon pepper is a pepper blend that you will also find in the supermarket along with other seasoning salts and peppers.

FOR THE BAKES
4 cups unbleached all-purpose flour

2 teaspoons salt

2 teaspoons baking powder

2 teaspoons vegetable oil

1 cup lukewarm water

$1/2$ cup whole milk, at room temperature

FOR THE SHARK
1 pound shark fillet, cut into 6 pieces

$1/4$ cup fresh lime juice

3 large garlic cloves, very finely chopped

2 tablespoons finely chopped fresh thyme leaves

$1/4$ teaspoon salt

$1/4$ teaspoon lemon pepper

1 tablespoon finely chopped fresh chives

2 Scotch bonnet chiles or habanero chiles, very finely chopped

$1/4$ cup unbleached all-purpose flour

3 cups vegetable oil, for frying

FOR THE GARNISHES
1 ripe tomato, chopped

$1/2$ small onion, chopped

$1/2$ cucumber, peeled, seeded, and sliced

Pickapeppa Sauce

Lettuce leaves

1. To prepare the bakes, in a large bowl, sift together the flour, salt, and baking powder. Pour in the 2 teaspoons vegetable oil and work it in with your fingers. Add the water and milk and continue to work it into the flour until a sticky dough forms. Turn the dough onto a well-floured counter and knead for 1 minute, until soft and pliable and not sticky. Cover with a damp kitchen towel and let rest 30 minutes. Divide the dough into 12 balls, cover again, and let rest 30 minutes.

2. Toss the shark with the lime juice. In a bowl, mix the garlic, thyme, salt, lemon pepper, chives, and chiles. Add the flour and toss well. Dredge the fish well on all sides in the seasoned flour.

3.   In a cast-iron skillet, heat the frying oil over medium heat. Roll each of the bakes out until 3 to 4 inches long and $1/4$ inch thick. Fry the bakes in batches until golden on both sides and puffed up, about 6 minutes. Remove to a paper towel–lined platter and cool while you continue cooking the rest of the bakes.

4.   Increase the heat of the oil to medium-high, allowing several minutes for it to reach that temperature. Shake the excess flour off the shark and fry on both sides until golden and firm, 4 to 6 minutes, turning several times. Remove from the oil and drain on paper towels. Cut the bakes in half lengthwise, place the cooked shark inside along with as many and as much of the garnishes as you wish.

MAKES 4 SERVINGS

Stamp and Go

This colorfully named Jamaican "fast food" is a typical roadside snack of salt cod fritters. Jamaicans call salt cod "saltfish" and therefore this preparation is also known as saltfish fritters. The dish is called Stamp and Go because, I've been told, it is a quickly eaten snack Jamaicans pick up for the bumpy bus trips around the island. But I believe that it derives from the slang of eighteenth-century British sailors. The phrase was a command given to English sailors to perform certain duties—to step out at the capstan or to haul in a line. The sailors would sometimes sing the command as they worked. Of course, it may also be derived from the word *stampee*, a counterfeit coin circulated in the British West Indies that was described in W. Bullock's 1797 *Naval Chronicles* as "Negro money," so this snack was "pay and go."

STAMP AND GO

Upon being given an order by their superiors, British sailors would sing the command as they worked, as in Patrick O'Brian's novel *Master and Commander* when the sailors sing:

—old Harte, —old Harte

The red-faced son of a dry French fart

Hey ho, stamp and go

Stamp and go, stamp and go

1/4 pound salt cod, soaked in cold water to cover for 2 days, changing the water twice a day, drained and dried

1/4 cup unbleached all-purpose flour

1/4 cup water

2 large eggs, separated, whites beaten to form peaks

1/4 cup finely chopped onions

1 garlic clove, finely chopped

1 tablespoon chopped fresh chives

1 tablespoon finely chopped habanero chile

1 teaspoon salt, or more to your taste

1/2 teaspoon hot paprika

1/2 teaspoon dried thyme

FOR THE SAUCE

2 tablespoons vegetable oil

1 large tomato, peeled, seeded, and finely chopped

1 medium-size onion, finely chopped

1 1/2 scallions, finely chopped

2 large garlic cloves, finely chopped

1 habanero chile, finely chopped

1/2 cup malt vinegar

FOR FRYING

6 to 8 cups vegetable oil, for frying

1. Place the salt cod in a small saucepan and cover with water. Bring to a gentle boil over medium heat, about 15 minutes, then reduce the heat to low and cook until it shreds, about 5 minutes. Turn off the heat and let it cool slightly in the water. Remove and drain, patting dry with paper towels. Shred the salt cod with 2 forks and set aside in a bowl. Add the flour and water to the salt cod to make a thin batter, stirring until it is smooth. Stir the egg yolks, onion, garlic, chives, chile, salt, paprika, and thyme into the batter and mix well. Fold in the egg whites. Refrigerate until you're ready to cook.

2. Meanwhile, prepare the sauce. In a skillet, heat the vegetable oil over medium-high heat, then cook the tomato, onion, scallions, garlic, and chile until soft, about 4 minutes, stirring. Add the malt vinegar and cook until reduced by half, about 3 minutes, stirring. Transfer to a serving bowl.

3. Preheat the frying oil to 350°F in a deep-fryer or an 8-inch saucepan fitted with a basket insert. Spoon a tablespoon of batter into the oil and cook until crisp and golden on both sides, about 4 minutes, without crowding the fryer, cooking in batches. Drain on paper towels, sprinkle with salt, and serve with the sauce.

MAKES 18 FRITTERS FOR 6 TO 8 SERVINGS

ackee and saltfish

Ackee and Saltfish is considered by some to be the national dish of Jamaica. It is often served as a breakfast dish, even though it is fiery hot from Scotch bonnet chiles. The reason it is so unique a dish, and the reason I don't include a recipe for it, is because the ackee, a bright red fruit, is said to be poisonous if eaten before it matures. For this reason it is illegal to import them into the United States. The ackee's scientific name, *Blighia sapida*, comes from its introduction to Jamaica by the famous Captain Bligh of the HMS *Bounty*. The ackee fruit opens itself when mature and ready to eat, revealing black seeds and yellow fruit. One never opens an ackee and eats it and lives to tell the tale.

Sardines with Chile Puree

This meze from Algeria is called *sardin bi'l-dirsa*. Although *dirsa* is a word used in North Africa in connection with the crushing of grapes by trampling, it is also the name of a hot chile sauce popular in Algeria with grilled or baked fish. It is made like a traditional mayonnaise but without the egg yolks. The most popular preparation for *dirsa* is a dish of gutted, headless grilled sardines, but it is also popular with squid and other fish. If sardines are not available you can use smelts, but even squid is a nice substitute. I call for you to either bake or grill the fish. Grilling them is quite spectacular so you might want to think about getting a grill going and grilling other foods. You can also coat the sardines with the *dirsa* sauce before baking or grilling them.

½ cup chopped fresh red finger-type chiles or jalapeño chiles

4 large garlic cloves

1 teaspoon salt, or more to your taste

Freshly ground black pepper to taste

5 to 6 tablespoons extra-virgin olive oil

8 fresh whole sardines or smelts (about 1 pound), gutted, cleaned, and heads removed

¼ teaspoon ground cumin

1. In a mortar, pound the chiles, garlic, salt, and pepper into a paste. Slowly pound in the olive oil. Set aside.

2. Preheat the oven to 350°F or prepare a hot charcoal fire or preheat a gas grill for 15 minutes on high. Lightly oil a baking pan and bake the sardines until golden, 17 to 18 minutes, or lightly oil the fish and place on a hot grill close to the fire until golden, 4 to 5 minutes a side. Arrange the sardines on a serving platter and coat with the *dirsa* sauce. Sprinkle with the cumin and serve.

MAKES 8 APPETIZER SERVINGS OR 4 MAIN-COURSE SERVINGS

Crispy-Fried Fish Patties with Ata Sauce

I n Nigeria, these already hot fish cakes are served with the even hotter ata sauce that is made of chiles and bell peppers. To start this recipe you will need some cooked cassava, which is boiled for about 40 minutes and then mashed. You can use the same cooking water to poach the fish until flaky, which will take about 6 minutes.

2 cups (about ¾ pound fillet) flaked cooked whitefish (such as cod, sole, fluke, flounder, and halibut)

2 cups (about 1 pound) mashed cooked cassava, yam, or sweet potato

3 tablespoons unsalted butter, melted

1 teaspoon salt

1 teaspoon cayenne pepper

1 large egg, beaten

6 cups vegetable or peanut oil, for frying

1 cup Ata Sauce (page 416)

1. In a medium-size bowl, combine the fish, cassava, butter, salt, and cayenne pepper and blend well, mashing together with a fork. Mix in the egg until completely blended. Form the mixture into patties about 3 inches in diameter with wet hands so it doesn't stick. Arrange the patties on a plate and refrigerate for 30 minutes.

2. Preheat the frying oil to 360°F in a deep-fryer or an 8-inch saucepan fitted with a basket insert. Cook the fish cakes in batches until golden brown, about 4 minutes. Remove from the oil and drain on paper towels. Serve immediately with the ata sauce.

MAKES 4 SERVINGS

Shrimp in Mina Sauce

This dish from Togo, a small, narrow country in West Africa, is a very hot one that uses both dried and fresh shrimp in a sauce called *mina* sauce. *Mina* is the name of one of the two major African languages spoken in the southern part of Togo. French is the official language of the country and the language of commerce. This appetizer or snack is usually served with *Fufu* (page 393).

½ cup peanut oil *or* ¼ cup red palm oil and ¼ cup peanut oil

2¼ pounds ripe tomatoes, cut in half, seeds squeezed out, and grated against the largest holes of a grater

2 medium-size onions, finely chopped

3 habanero chiles, finely chopped

1 ounce dried whole shrimp or 6 ounces smoked shrimp or one 3-ounce can smoked mussels or one 3-ounce can smoked oysters

2 teaspoons salt, or more to your taste

1 teaspoon ground ginger

4 pounds fresh large shrimp with their heads or 2 pounds headless large shrimp, heads and/or shells removed

1. In a large skillet or casserole, heat the peanut oil over low heat for 10 minutes, then add the tomatoes, onions, and chiles and cook until the sauce is slightly dense, 1 to 1½ hours, depending on how liquid your tomatoes were, stirring occasionally.

2. Add the dried shrimp, salt, and ginger and cook for 10 minutes, stirring. Add the shrimp and cook until firm and pink-orange, 5 to 8 minutes, stirring and turning.

MAKES 8 APPETIZER SERVINGS OR 4 MAIN-COURSE SERVINGS

the african chile

There are no native African chiles, all chiles having come from the Americas. But the most frequently used chiles in Africa are either *Capsicum frutescens*, the most common, or *C. chinense*, whose African cultivars are often called the hottest chiles in the world. Any chile called an African chile or an African bird chile will be either of these two species.

the piquant cooking of ethiopia

The population of Ethiopia, the mountainous country occupying most of what is known as the Horn of Africa, is almost evenly divided between Christians and Muslims. This is not always evidenced in Ethiopian food because neither population eats pork and their respective foods are nearly identical. One of the earliest written references to Ethiopia as a source of food is in the second century A.D. book by the Greek writer Athenaeus, where there seems to be a short description of the grain known as teff (see page 400). Of course, the most famous product of Ethiopia is coffee, which appears in Mecca by 1511. It seems clear enough that the chile arrived in Ethiopia with the Portuguese in the sixteenth century, probably from Goa or the Portuguese Atlantic islands and not from the Portuguese in West Africa. It's not known what the pre-Columbian cooking of Ethiopia might have looked like, but it's possible that piquant spices such as black pepper and ajwain were used. It could be that the classical Greek writers who referred to "Ethiopian cumin" may have been talking about ajwain. Once the chile arrived, *berbere*, the essential spice paste for all Ethiopian cooking, most likely arose. Ethiopian cooking is simple, heavily spiced, and based almost entirely on stews, many of which are legume and vegetable stews. Ethiopian food is notable for being spicy—not just spicy-hot from chiles but spicy from a wide variety of different spices.

Kitfo

Kitfo is Ethiopian steak tartare. It is served raw and should be prepared just before serving; therefore, it is made with the finest beef tenderloin. When the meat is truly tartare, or raw, it is called *kitfo tere*, and when it is slightly cooked it is *kitfo lebleb*. The meat should be ground in a food processor until velvety. But the success of this dish, just as with the Arab *kibbe nayya* (see my book *Little Foods of the Mediterranean* [The Harvard Common Press, 2003]), rests upon high-quality very lean tenderloin. The chile powder mixture used in this preparation is called *mitmita* in Ethiopia. For the "ground red chile powder," it would be best to use the tiny *piquín* chiles available through mail order, but you can also use cayenne pepper. Some cooks add cardamom seeds, which do indeed provide an exotic smell and flavor.

some like it hot

34

¼ cup *niter kibbeh* (page 419)	1½ pounds boneless beef tenderloin (filet mignon), all fat and sinews carefully removed and ground in a food processor until smooth and velvety
1½ teaspoons cayenne pepper	
1½ teaspoons ground red chile powder	
1½ teaspoons salt, or more to your taste	2 to 4 *Injera* breads (page 400)

In a 9-inch skillet, melt the *niter kibbeh* over medium heat, then add the cayenne pepper, ground chile powder, and salt. Stir, turn off the heat, and let the spice mixture cool in the skillet. Add the beef and blend in the spiced butter thoroughly by mashing and mixing with a fork. Arrange on a serving platter by smoothing it out with a knife so that it looks like a dip. Serve immediately with *injera*.

MAKES 8 SERVINGS WITH *INJERA*; 4 SERVINGS WITHOUT *INJERA*

Fish Raita

Any Indian dish described as a *raita* is a cool dish with yogurt. But this "cool" dish is also a "hot" dish with yogurt *and* chiles. This preparation, called *maach raita*, would be made with pomfret in India, but I find sole an excellent choice. It has one central bone that you push the meat off of when you are eating. This dish should be served cold.

2 cups water	1 tablespoon sugar
1 tablespoon tamarind paste (see page 329)	Salt to taste
2 pounds sole or flounder fillets	4 fresh green finger-type chiles or 5 jalapeño chiles, finely chopped
2 cups strained yogurt (see page 278)	
1 tablespoon mustard oil	¼ cup finely chopped fresh coriander (cilantro) leaves
1 tablespoon ground yellow mustard seeds	

1. In a large skillet, bring the water to a boil with the tamarind paste, breaking it up as the water begins to boil. Add the fish fillets in one layer after the water has been boiling for a few minutes and cook until the fish is firm and the meat could come away easily from the bone, 6 to 7 minutes.

mustard oil in bengali cooking

Much of the distinctive taste of Bengali food comes from mustard oil. Because of the erucic acid, a crystalline fatty acid, and maybe also the isothiocyanates in mustard oil, it is illegal to be traded as a foodstuff in most western countries, including the European Union and the United States. Indian food shops therefore sell mustard oil with the label "for external use only" to circumvent these laws. You need not take the label seriously, as the amounts you are ever likely to use are not harmful. Mustard oil is used as a cooking fat in India and is not consumed raw. It's possible that the heating of the oil detoxifies it.

2. Meanwhile, whisk the yogurt in a bowl until smooth, then add the mustard oil, ground mustard seeds, sugar, salt, chiles, and coriander. Beat until well blended. Spread several tablespoons over the bottom of a glass or ceramic baking dish and cover with some fish fillets. Continue layering the fish and yogurt until both are used up. Cover with plastic wrap and refrigerate at least 2 hours before serving cold.

MAKES 4 TO 6 SERVINGS

Crispy-Fried Pork Belly with Chile Jam

This Thai dish is called *muu grop* and is made with deep-fried marinated slices of pork belly, otherwise known as fresh raw bacon that has not been cured or smoked. Asian markets usually sell presliced fresh bacon and the tamarind paste, which can also be found on the Internet. The dried whole shrimp are usually sold in the international/Asian section of supermarkets, often packed in small bags that hang with other types of Latino products from a display. If you can't come across raw bacon, then use smoked bacon blanched in boiling water for 5 minutes.

2 cups safflower or sunflower seed oil

2 large shallots, each cut into 4 slices

5 large garlic cloves, 4 split in half lengthwise, 1 whole

2 tablespoons dried whole shrimp

6 dried red de arbol chiles

2 tablespoons palm sugar or brown sugar

1/2-inch cube tamarind paste, dissolved in 2 tablespoons hot water

2 teaspoons Thai fish sauce

1 tablespoon salt, or more to your taste

15 white peppercorns

1/2 bunch fresh coriander (cilantro) sprigs, stems reserved and 1/2 of the remaining leaves, finely chopped

1 pound pork belly (fresh bacon), thinly sliced

1/2 cup distilled vinegar mixed with 1 table-spoon shredded unsweetened coconut

1 small cucumber, peeled, seeded, cut into thirds crosswise, and julienned

1. In a wok, heat the safflower oil over medium heat until nearly smoking. Fry the shallots until browned, 1 to 2 minutes, then remove with a slotted spoon and set aside. Add the 4 split garlic cloves and fry until lightly colored, about 1 minute, then remove with a slotted spoon and set aside with the shallots. Add the shrimp and chiles and cook 30 seconds and remove. Place all the fried items in a food processor and puree until blended, adding a little oil from the wok to make it pastier. Transfer the paste to a small saucepan and bring to a boil, then add the sugar, 1 tablespoon of the tamarind water, and the fish sauce. Reduce the heat to low and simmer until quite thick, about 5 minutes. Set the chile jam aside until needed. Leave the oil in the wok, which you will use later.

2. Place the remaining garlic clove, 1 tablespoon salt, the white peppercorns, and the coriander stems in a mortar and pound until mushy. Arrange the sliced pork belly in a glass or ceramic baking dish and cover with the contents of the mortar, spreading it evenly over all the slices. Marinate at room temperature for 1 hour.

3. Bring water to a boil in a steamer. Place the pork slices in the steamer and steam until brown, 15 minutes. Remove the pork slices and rearrange in the baking dish. Strain the vinegar and pour over the pork slices. Leave the pork at room temperature to dry out, about 1 hour.

4. Preheat the oven to 200°F. Sprinkle the pork with salt and place in the oven until dried out, about 1 hour.

5. Reheat the oil in the wok over medium heat until very hot, but not smoking, 300°F to 325°F. Cook the pork slices until crisp but not dark brown, 3 to 5 minutes. Remove and slice each piece crosswise in 1/2-inch-wide strips.

6. Spread the chile jam on a serving platter and arrange the pork on top. Arrange the cucumber julienne around the edge of the plate, sprinkle the chopped coriander leaves over everything, and serve.

MAKES 4 SERVINGS

Three-Flavor Lobster

This Thai dish is called *goong sam ros* and is made with the very large Black Tiger prawns that weigh about 5 or 6 ounces each. A small 1-pound lobster is perfect in this preparation—and still authentic. I serve this as an appetizer, but typically it would be part of a dinner that centered on rice. The three flavors referred to in the name appear to be lobster, chile, and basil, but in fact the name refers to the three tastes of sweet (sugar), hot (chile), and sour (tamarind water and fish sauce). One does not eat the chiles, although you could.

Two 1-pound live lobsters or 4 fresh extra-colossal Black Tiger shrimp (about 1 pound), with their heads left on and shells removed

1 cup peanut oil

6 large garlic cloves, chopped

1 shallot, thinly sliced

20 dried red de arbol chiles

1 cup lightly packed coarsely chopped fresh basil leaves

2 tablespoons Thai fish sauce

1/4 cup palm sugar or granulated sugar

1/4 cup tamarind water

1/4 cup chopped roasted unsalted cashew nuts

1. Steam the lobster until a little less than fully cooked, about 15 minutes. (If you are using shrimp, go to step 2.) Remove from the steaming pot and, once it is cool enough to handle, crack the shell and remove the meat from all parts, keeping the pieces as intact as you can. Split the tail section in half lengthwise. Set the lobster aside until needed. Reserve 1 tablespoon of the steaming liquid from the bottom of the lobster pot.

2. In a large wok over high heat, heat the peanut oil, then cook the garlic, shallot, chiles, and basil until light brown and crispy, about 4 minutes, stirring frequently. Remove with a skimmer and set aside to drain on paper towels.

3. Add the lobster meat to the wok and cook until firm, 2 to 3 minutes, stirring frequently. Transfer the lobster to a medium-size serving platter. Set aside while you finish the sauce.

4. Discard half of the oil remaining in the wok. Over high heat, add the fish sauce, sugar, tamarind water, and the reserved lobster broth (or 1 tablespoon of water if using shrimp). Cook until the liquid turns syrupy, 4 to 5 minutes, stirring almost constantly. Spoon the sauce (avoiding the oil that has separated if you can) over the fried lobster and sprinkle the top with the fried chile, garlic, shallot, and basil mixture and the cashews. Serve immediately.

MAKES 4 SERVINGS

Lawar

This is one of the famous meals of Bali that appear at every big religious celebration. Only the older, and therefore more experienced, men are allowed to mix the ingredients, as this requires a level of expertise and maturity to achieve the proper balance of ingredients so that no one ingredient is noticeable over the others. This recipe requires that you first prepare two condiments essential in Indonesian cooking. The chile seasoning, called *sambel sere tabia*, and the spice paste, *base be siap*, are not hard to prepare and are used in other preparations.

2 tablespoons vegetable oil

10 shallots, thinly sliced

6 large garlic cloves, thinly sliced

1/2 cup fresh or dried shredded unsweetened coconut

3/4 pound yard-long beans (asparagus beans) or thin green beans, ends trimmed and cut into 1/4-inch pieces

2 fresh large red jalapeño chiles or red finger-type chiles, thinly sliced lengthwise

8 fresh green Thai chiles or 3 green serrano chiles, thinly sliced

1 tablespoon Indonesian Chile Seasoning (page 427)

1/4 cup Indonesian Spice Paste for Chicken (page 426)

1/2 pound boneless chicken breast, finely chopped

1 banana leaf, 1 cornhusk, or aluminum foil cut into a 12-inch square

1 teaspoon fresh lime juice

1 teaspoon salt

1/2 teaspoon freshly ground black pepper

1. In a wok or skillet, heat 1 tablespoon of the vegetable oil over high heat and cook 2 of the shallots until crispy brown and soft, 3 to 4 minutes. Remove and transfer to a paper towel–lined plate and let cool and become crisp in the air.

2. Add the remaining tablespoon of vegetable oil to the wok, then cook the garlic and the remaining 8 shallots until crispy golden brown, about 4 minutes. Remove and set aside to cool.

3. Preheat the oven or a toaster oven to 450°F. Put the coconut in a roasting pan or tray and roast until light golden, about 5 minutes, but keep checking. Remove and let cool.

4. In a large bowl, combine the yard-long beans, roasted coconut, cooked garlic and 8 shallots, red and green chiles, Indonesian chile seasoning, and 2 tablespoons of the Indonesian spice paste and mix well.

5. In a medium-size bowl, toss the chopped chicken with the 2 remaining tablespoons of the Indonesian spice paste and mix well. Place the chicken mixture in the center of the banana leaf and roll up very tightly, twisting the sides in opposite directions to tighten the roll. Fill a steamer pot with water and place the roll in the steamer basket. Turn the heat to high, cover, and steam until cooked through, 20 minutes. Let cool, then remove the meat from its package and break up into a large bowl.

6. Add the bean mixture to the chicken and toss well. Season with lime juice, salt, and pepper, toss again, and transfer to a serving platter. Garnish the top with the remaining crispy fried shallots and serve at room temperature.

MAKES 6 SERVINGS

the piquant cuisine of the indo-malaysian archipelago

The Indo-Malaysian archipelago is where the Spice Islands are, so it's not surprising to find the food spicy. The Gujarati of western India, a seafaring people, had a flourishing trade with the Indonesian archipelago long before the Europeans arrived in the early sixteenth century. Gujarati cuisine was pungent and spicy before the chile, and it had an influence on the cooking of the Indonesians, and the Indonesians on them. Chinese traders who settled in Indonesia also had an influence on the cuisine, and an even greater influence on Malaysian cuisine. The Portuguese also had a presence in Indonesia, since they took the trading post of Malacca in 1511. Some early evidence of the chile in the Indonesian archipelago is the fact that the Dutch, in the early seventeenth century, exported from the previous Portuguese settlement of Pamrukan in eastern Java "Spanish pepper," which seems to be chile. H. N. Ridley in *The Dispersal of Plants Through the World* (Bishen Singh Mahendra Pal Singh, 1990), published in 1930, claims that Arab and Gujarati traders brought the chile to Indonesia by 1540.

The Indonesian archipelago is a huge area represented by many cultures, so generalizing about the cuisine is inherently fraught with problems. This country, not to mention Malaysia, Singapore, New Guinea, and the Philippines, is very diverse. In Indonesia alone there are 13,677 islands, 200 million people, and 300 ethnic groups. Generally, it can be said that rice is the staple food, and although the food is spicy-hot it is not as complex a cuisine as that found in Southeast Asia. People eat many snacks throughout the day, and surprisingly given how the sea surrounds everything, very little seafood is actually eaten. Indo-Malaysians don't eat in courses; rather, dishes are put on the table all at once and are usually eaten at room temperature or warm. Little protein is eaten with meals, but rice is eaten every day. The cooking is hot in most of the archipelago, with some islands having hotter foods than others, and some dishes are extremely hot. For instance, the island of Madura, off the northern coast of Java, has hotter food than Java. Before the introduction of the chile, Indo-Malaysian food was not spicy-hot to the extent it is now. But it did use black pepper and *lada rimba*, jungle pepper, a mouth-numbing spice similar to Sichuan peppercorns. On the island of Lombok, southeast of Bali, the Sasak, a Muslim people, love spicy-hot food (the word *lombok* also means "chile" in Indonesian). Kalimantan, the Indonesian part of Borneo, is also spicy-hot food territory. On the northern part of Sulawesi, one of its peninsulas is inhabited by the Minahasans, who have spicy dishes there as well as on the islands of the Moluccas, the original Spice Islands north of the Banda Sea. The food of the Moluccas, though, is less hot than other parts of Indonesia already mentioned.

In the Philippines, only a small area called Bicol on Luzon has chile-infused fiery food. The rest of the country has mild food influenced by the Spanish.

Seafood Satay

Satay is probably the best known Indonesian dish in America, as one finds it often as an appetizer on restaurant menus. Typically, restaurants will serve it with a peanut sauce. This Indonesian snack is called *sate lilit* and is made with ground red snapper or other whitefish and ground shrimp. It is skewered on a hard spear of lemongrass and then charcoal-grilled, preferably over coconut husks. Fresh shrimp is almost a must for this dish because frozen shrimp will probably contain too much water, affecting the consistency, but give it a try anyway. If the mixture is too moist and will not adhere to the skewer or stalk, flatten it and grill it directly on the grilling grate. The kaffir lime leaves called for are seasonal and available only in Thai markets and through the Internet. A nice dipping sauce to use is the bottled Sriracha sauce available in Thai markets and many supermarkets in the international/Asian section.

3/4 pound red snapper or flounder fillets, skin removed

1 1/2 pounds fresh shrimp with their heads or 3/4 pound headless shrimp, heads and/or shells removed

2 cups fresh or dried shredded unsweetened coconut

1/2 cup Indonesian Spice Paste for Seafood (page 425)

5 kaffir lime leaves, very finely sliced, or 1 tablespoon lime zest

1/2 teaspoon freshly ground black pepper

1 tablespoon salt

7 large green Thai chiles or 2 large green jalapeño chiles, very finely chopped

2 tablespoons palm sugar or brown sugar

3 lemongrass stalks, split lengthwise and cut into 6-inch lengths if very long, or twelve 10-inch wooden skewers

1. Place the fish and shrimp in a food processor and puree until pasty. Add all the other ingredients except the lemongrass and blend again. Refrigerate for 30 minutes.

2. Using your hands, mold a small lemon-sized amount of the seafood mixture around the lemongrass stalk or a double set of wooden skewers. Flatten slightly and set aside.

3. Prepare a hot charcoal fire on one side of the grill or preheat a gas grill on high for 15 minutes, then turn off the burners on one side. Grill the satay skewers until golden brown on the non-fire side of the grill, 10 to 15 minutes, turning occasionally.

MAKES 6 TO 8 SERVINGS

Spicy Beef with Orange Flavor

The best meat to use for this fast-cooking dish is tri-tip sirloin, skirt steak, flank steak, and even meat sold as *carne asada* in supermarkets in the western United States. Sichuan cooks use a fermented glutinous rice wine as part of their seasoning of this dish. It can be purchased in Chinese markets or on the Internet. Fermented rice wine is traditionally made at home and consists of cooked glutinous rice sealed in a jar with wine yeast balls (also sold in Chinese markets), which ferments for a few days in a warm place. You can substitute rice wine or sherry, which work well for this dish although the flavor is different. The dried orange peel used in the recipe is readily found in jars in the spice section of supermarkets, but I prefer making my own. Using the largest holes of a four-sided grater, grate 1 large orange, place the peel in a baking dish or tray, and bake in a 250°F oven for 15 minutes, then turn the heat off and leave for another 15 minutes. The fragrance of the dried orange is remarkable and you will be tempted to use it in your general cooking. The Chinese black vinegar is called Chinkiang vinegar and it is available in Chinese markets or via the Internet. Serve with steamed rice if desired.

¾ pound beef skirt steak, flank steak, or tri-tip sirloin, cut into 1½ x ½ x ⅟₁₆-inch slices

¾ teaspoon salt

2½ cups peanut oil, for frying

½ cup halved and seeded dried red de arbol chiles

1 tablespoon dried orange peel

½ teaspoon ground Sichuan peppercorns

1 teaspoon ground star anise

½ cup beef broth

1½ teaspoons fermented glutinous rice wine or rice wine (*mirin*) or sherry

2 teaspoons sugar

1 teaspoon white vinegar or Chinese black vinegar

½ teaspoon sesame oil

1. In a medium-size bowl, toss the beef with ¼ teaspoon salt and leave for 20 minutes at room temperature.

2. In a wok, heat the frying oil over medium-high heat until about 375°F. Cook the beef for 30 seconds, being careful as it will splatter, then remove with a skimmer and drain.

3. Remove all but 2 tablespoons of oil from the wok. Let the remaining oil heat again over high heat, then stir-fry the chiles, dried orange peel, peppercorns,

It's true for all cooking, but in Chinese cooking in particular it is doubly true that preparation and cooking are two entirely separate procedures. Chinese cooking isn't hard, but the preparation can be exacting and sometimes lengthy. Because Chinese cooking happens so fast, the proper preparation of *every* ingredient needed in the dish is of utmost importance. It's quite possible that you will spend up to 45 minutes preparing the ingredients for a recipe that takes 3 minutes to cook. For that reason, you should read through the Sichuan recipes with a little more care than usual.

and star anise until sizzling and fragrant, about 15 seconds, keeping your head away from the fumes of the chiles. Add the cooked beef, beef broth, rice wine, sugar, and the remaining $^1/_2$ teaspoon salt and stir-fry until the liquid is nearly absorbed, about 4 minutes. When most of the liquid has evaporated, add the vinegar and sesame oil and stir. Serve immediately.

MAKES 4 SERVINGS

Sichuan Headcheese

An old New Yorker probably remembers headcheese from those great delicatessens off the IND where one could find a variety of cold cuts that could be sliced by the counterman for delicious sandwiches with a bit of mustard. The Sichuanese also have a kind of headcheese—that's my name for it, not theirs—as we see in this preparation using beef tendon, a product that can only be found in Asian markets or through specialty butchers. Most Americans, I know, find this dish too strange. But if you like Jell-O, there's no reason why you wouldn't like the texture of this dish. Beef tendon is quite gelatinous and must be cooked for a very long time to make it tender—and it can only be eaten when tender. This is a dish that you either like or don't—there's no middle ground. Because it's so highly seasoned and flavored, it is more acceptable to many palates. The secret to this dish is a simple one: cook it for a really long time in seasoned broth. I've been told to cook it at least 5 hours, but I like to cook it 7 to 8 hours at a gentle boil until tender. Once it solidifies, serve it thinly sliced and cold. Eat with chopsticks and a little soy sauce; it's great, I think.

<hr>

³/₄ pound beef tendon	2 teaspoons red pepper flakes
3 scallions, 1 whole and 2 cut into 1-inch diagonal slices	1 teaspoon rice vinegar
	1 teaspoon sugar
One ¹/₄-inch-thick slice fresh ginger	¹/₂ teaspoon ground Sichuan peppercorns
1 tablespoon rice wine or vermouth	¹/₂ teaspoon salt
1 tablespoon Chile Oil (page 424)	

1. Place the beef tendon in a large saucepan with the whole scallion, ginger, and rice wine and boil until tender, 7 to 8 hours, replenishing the water when necessary.

2. Remove the beef tendon, reserving 1 tablespoon of the cooking water, and cut it into thin slices. Place in a colander and let it drain for a bit. Transfer to a bowl and toss the tendon with the remaining scallions, reserved cooking water, chile oil, red pepper flakes, vinegar, sugar, Sichuan peppercorns, and salt. Transfer to a shallow bowl and let the tendon set into a gelatin in the refrigerator, 3 to 4 hours. It will congeal into one large piece. Remove, slice thinly, and serve.

MAKES 6 SERVINGS

Sichuan-Style Steamed Littleneck Clams

This dish is not a traditional Sichuan dish because clams are not found in the mountain-ringed Sichuan province. But a Sichuanese chef on the East or West Coast of America can certainly make this dish, and hundreds of them do.

2 large garlic cloves, finely chopped

1/2-inch cube fresh ginger, finely chopped

1 scallion, finely chopped

1 tablespoon red pepper flakes

2 tablespoons rice wine (*mirin*) or dry sherry

1/4 cup Chile Oil (page 424)

2 teaspoons sesame oil

64 littleneck clams, washed well

In a bowl, stir together the garlic, ginger, scallion, red pepper flakes, rice wine, chile oil, and sesame oil. Place the clams in a large saucepan or large skillet and pour the sauce over them. Place the cover on the pan, turn the heat to high, and steam the clams until they all open, 4 to 8 minutes. Discard any clams that remain firmly shut. Transfer to a serving bowl and serve.

MAKES 4 SERVINGS

Spicy Beef Slices with Tangerine Peel

This appetizer from Sichuan, called *chen pi niu rou*, demonstrates the Sichuanese ingenuity with using ingredients at hand. Peels are not thrown away because they are useful for flavoring and aroma. Fuchsia Dunlop tells us in her *Land of Plenty* (W. W. Norton, 2003) that this dish is one of the few that actually uses tangerine peel and that it is frequently found on banquet menus. It is a blistering hot dish that will make you sweat like a fountain, but it is enchanting because of the unique taste of the crispy beef and tangerine peel. It might be nice to serve this with some peeled and seeded cucumber sticks.

1 pound flank steak

One 2-inch cube fresh ginger, peeled and lightly crushed

2 scallions, white and green parts, cut into 2-inch pieces

2 teaspoons salt

2 tablespoons rice wine (*mirin*) or vermouth

Peel from 1 tangerine, with no pith

3 cups peanut oil, for frying

1 cup halved and seeded dried red de arbol chiles

2 teaspoons Sichuan peppercorns

1 cup chicken broth (homemade or canned)

1 tablespoon sugar

1 teaspoon soy sauce

1 teaspoon sesame oil

1. Butterfly the steak by slicing it into 2 thin pieces (or ask the butcher to do this). Place the pieces of meat between 2 sheets of wax paper and pound with a mallet until $1/8$ inch thick. Cut into $2^1/2$-inch squares.

2. In a medium-size bowl, toss the beef with the ginger, scallions, 1 teaspoon salt, and 1 tablespoon of the rice wine. Marinate for 1 hour. Meanwhile, soak the tangerine peel in cold water to cover for 1 hour.

3. In a wok, heat the frying oil over high heat until nearly smoking. Separate the beef from the ginger and scallions, discarding the ginger and scallions, and deep-fry the beef slices until they turn color, 15 to 30 seconds. Remove with a skimmer, drain, and set aside to cool a bit. Let the frying oil return to its hot temperature and then fry the beef slices again until crisp and deep brown, 15 to 30 seconds. Remove with a skimmer and drain. Julienne the tangerine peel, saving $1/4$ cup of the soaking water.

4. Remove all but $1/3$ cup of the oil and heat over medium-high heat. When it is hot but not smoking, add the chiles and peppercorns and cook 15 seconds, stirring. Add the tangerine peel and cook until you can smell it, a few seconds, then add the chicken broth, steak, tangerine soaking water, the remaining 1 teaspoon salt, sugar, soy sauce, and the remaining 1 tablespoon rice wine. Bring to a boil, then reduce the heat to medium, and simmer until the stock has evaporated, about 15 minutes, stirring occasionally. Transfer to a serving platter and drizzle the sesame oil over it. Serve at room temperature.

MAKES 4 TO 6 SERVINGS

Seafood Pancake

My first explorations with Korean foods came about when I met my friend Unjoo Lee Byars. She made a wonderful Chive Pancake (page 51) for me, and although this dish, which I encountered at a restaurant, is a seafood pancake, the principal is the same. This dish is called *hae-mool puch'ujon* and is made with three kinds of shellfish. You can use store-bought, previously shucked chopped clams and oysters if you wish, but I think freshly shucked shellfish make a much better final product. The powdered sesame seeds called for are best made by toasting the seeds in a small ungreased cast-iron skillet until light brown, then grinding them in a spice mill. You can grind them in a mortar, too. The non-glutinous rice flour can be found in Korean or Japanese markets, whole foods stores, and via the Internet.

FOR THE DIPPING SAUCE

1/4 cup soy sauce

2 tablespoons ground Korean red chile or 1 1/2 tablespoons ground red chile

2 tablespoons rice vinegar

1 tablespoon finely chopped scallions

2 garlic cloves, crushed

1 teaspoon sugar

2 teaspoons sesame seeds, toasted and powdered

2 teaspoons sesame oil

FOR THE PANCAKES

1/2 cup freshly shucked oysters with their liquid (about 24), chopped

1/2 cup freshly shucked mussels with their liquid (24 to 36), chopped

1/2 cup freshly shucked littleneck clams with their liquid (about 24), chopped

1 large egg

1 1/2 cups all-purpose flour

1/2 cup non-glutinous rice flour

9 tablespoons vegetable oil

1/4 pound scallions, white parts chopped, green parts split lengthwise in quarters and cut into 4-inch lengths

2 ounces baby leek or 1 small leek, trimmed, split lengthwise in quarters, and cut into 4-inch lengths

1. In a small bowl, mix the dipping sauce ingredients until well blended.

2. Prepare the pancakes: strain the chopped shellfish and save the juice. You should have about 1 cup of liquid. If you don't, add enough water until you have 1 cup. In a large bowl, mix the shellfish liquid with the egg and add enough water to make 2 cups. Add the flour and rice flour and mix well until smooth. Add the chopped oysters, mussels, and clams to the batter. Refrigerate until needed.

3.　Preheat the oven on the "warm" setting. In a nonstick skillet or seasoned cast-iron skillet, heat 3 tablespoons of the vegetable oil over medium-low heat (for at least 15 minutes if using cast iron), then pour a large ladleful of the batter in the pan, spreading it thin with the bottom of the ladle or with a spatula until it is about 8 inches in diameter. Immediately scatter a third of the lengths of scallions and leek on top, cover the skillet, and let it cook until the bottom is golden, 4 to 5 minutes. Spoon another slightly smaller ladleful of batter over the pancake, spreading it out if necessary to cover the scallions and leek, cover, and let it cook until almost solid on top, about 4 minutes. Flip the whole pancake with a spatula, cover, and cook until golden brown, about 8 minutes. Remove and set aside, keeping the pancakes warm in the oven as you cook them.

4.　Prepare two more pancakes in the same manner, letting 3 tablespoons of oil heat properly before cooking each pancake. Cut the pancakes into wedges, sprinkle the chopped white part of the scallions over them, and serve with the dipping sauce.

MAKES 4 TO 6 SERVINGS

the first written recipe for mustard

Columella, the first century A.D. Roman agricultural writer, gives what might be the first recipe for prepared mustard: "Carefully cleanse and sift mustard seed, then wash it in cold water and, when it has been well cleaned, leave it in the water for two hours. Next, take it out and, after it has been squeezed in the hands, throw it into a new or thoroughly cleaned mortar and pound it with pestles. When it has been pounded, collect the whole mash in the middle of the mortar and compress it with the flat of the hand. After you have compressed it, scarify it and, after placing a few live coals upon it, pour water mixed with nitre upon it to eliminate any bitterness and paleness. Then immediately lift up the mortar, so that all the moisture may be drained away, and after this add sharp white vinegar and mix it with the pestle, then strain it." Columella goes on to say that if you are serving it to guests you should add pine nuts and almonds to the mixture.

Pan-Fried Stuffed Chiles

This Korean preparation, called *koch'ujon*, is served as a side dish or appetizer with Soy Dipping Sauce (page 428). It sounds as if it must be very hot, being stuffed jalapeños, but the cooking process tones down the chiles significantly. But make no mistake, it's still got a nice reminder of what it is. The recipe is adapted from Hi Soo Shin Hepinstall's *Growing Up in a Korean Kitchen* (Ten Speed Press, 2001).

6 fresh red jalapeño chiles, cut in half lengthwise and seeded

6 fresh green jalapeño chiles, cut in half lengthwise and seeded

3/4 pound medium-firm tofu

1 pound ground beef sirloin

3 large eggs

2 scallions, white and light green parts only, finely chopped

2 large garlic cloves, finely chopped

1 tablespoon rice wine (*mirin*) or vermouth

1 tablespoon sesame oil

1 teaspoon salt, or more to your taste

Freshly ground black pepper to taste

1 cup unbleached all-purpose flour

3 tablespoons vegetable oil

1. Arrange the chiles, cut side up, on a baking tray. Wrap the tofu in paper towels and squeeze out as much liquid as you can. In a large bowl, crumble the tofu and mix with the ground sirloin, 1 egg, scallions, garlic, rice wine, sesame oil, salt, and pepper until well blended. Make twenty-four 1-inch diameter balls with the stuffing and stuff 1 ball into each chile half.

2. Spread the flour on a plate. Beat the remaining 2 eggs in a shallow bowl. In a large nonstick skillet, heat 1 1/2 tablespoons of the vegetable oil over medium-high heat until it is nearly smoking. Dredge half the chiles in the flour, then coat entirely in the egg. Add the chiles to the skillet, stuffed side down, and cook until golden, about 3 minutes. Flatten each chile gently with the back of a spatula. Turn the chiles and cook another 3 minutes. Transfer to a serving platter to keep warm while you cook the next batch, adding the remaining 1 1/2 tablespoons of vegetable oil and remembering to let the additional oil heat up properly. Serve hot or warm.

MAKES 4 TO 6 SERVINGS

Chive Pancake

Chives and scallions are both quite common in Korean cooking and much loved in a variety of dishes. Although you can use the common chives found in the supermarket, a farmers' market would be a good source for the Korean-style chives used in this dish, also called garlic chives or Chinese chives. These are broad-leaved chives with either a garlic or leek flavor to them, depending on the cultivar. This Korean appetizer is called *puch'ujon* and the recipe was given to me by my friend Unjoo Lee Byars. These heavenly pancakes are impossibly abundant with chives and scallions. To make the scallion pancakes one sees so commonly in Korean and Chinese restaurants, simply transpose the amounts of chives and scallions in this recipe.

1 cup unbleached all-purpose flour

2 large eggs

3/4 cup water

1/4 pound chives, cut into 3-inch pieces (about 2 cups)

2 scallions, finely chopped

2 fresh red jalapeño chiles, thinly sliced lengthwise and seeded

1/2 teaspoon salt

3 tablespoons canola or vegetable oil

Korean red chile paste (*koch'ujang*), for garnish

Soy sauce, for garnish

1. In a bowl, stir together the flour, eggs, and water until you have a batter the consistency of a cream soup, stirring all the time until smooth. Add the chives, scallions, jalapeño chiles, and salt and blend well with the batter.

2. In a medium-size cast-iron skillet, heat 1 1/2 tablespoons of the canola oil over medium heat, then pour in half the batter, spread it thin in the skillet, and cook on one side without stirring, flipping, lifting, or looking until golden brown on the bottom, about 7 minutes. Turn with a spatula in one flip and continue cooking until golden on the other side, 6 to 7 minutes. Remove and keep warm. Add the remaining oil to the skillet, let it heat, and cook the remaining pancake. Cut each pancake into quarters and serve with the red chile paste and soy sauce.

MAKES 4 SERVINGS

Spiced Tofu Squares

This preparation, called *tofu jon*, is from my friend Unjoo Lee Byars, who instructs that it is important to have properly drained tofu in order for the preparation to work. Make sure it drains for at least a half hour in a colander, and then pat it dry with paper towels. When you shop for tofu, which is usually sold in plastic tubs, it will be marked for different consistencies, from soft to extra firm. For this dish you want the firmest tofu.

2 scallions, white and light green parts only, split lengthwise and chopped

4 large garlic cloves, finely chopped

1 tablespoon sugar

2 tablespoons ground Korean red chile or 1½ tablespoons ground red chile

2 tablespoons toasted sesame seeds

3 tablespoons soy sauce

2 tablespoons sesame oil

3 tablespoons vegetable or canola oil

16 to 18 ounces extra-firm tofu, cut in 2 x ½-inch pieces, drained in a colander for ½ hour, and patted dry with paper towels

1. In a small bowl, blend together a dressing made of three-quarters of the scallions, the garlic, sugar, red chile, sesame seeds, soy sauce, and sesame oil.

2. In a large nonstick skillet, heat the vegetable oil over medium heat, then cook the tofu pieces until light golden on both sides, about 10 minutes, turning once. Once the tofu pieces have cooked on both sides and while they are still in the skillet, spread about 1 teaspoon of dressing over the top of each piece and cook until it looks melted, about 3 minutes. Remove from the oil and drain. Sprinkle with the remaining scallions and serve.

MAKES 6 SERVINGS

sexy salads

The salads in this chapter are the full-flavored, mouth-burning, fiery salads of the world. For cool salads without chiles that can be eaten as a foil for hot dishes, see the recipes in the Cool Accompaniments chapter, page 385. Some of the salads here are quite amazing. The first time I ate Red Kidney Bean and Quinoa Salad (page 54), I just couldn't get over how good it tasted, and how simple the premise. And Strange-Flavor Chicken (page 66) from Sichuan is a must for salad or cold dish eaters and actually not strange, but wonderful.

Red Kidney Bean and Quinoa Salad

*T*his Peruvian salad, called *ensalada de quinua y frejoles rojos*, uses the famous plant of the Incas, quinoa (*Chenopodium quinoa*), an annual herb native to Andean Peru and Bolivia whose seeds are made into bread or cooked as a grain as in this dish. It is a member of the goosefoot family, as is spinach, and its leaves are often used in the same way. Quinoa (pronounced KEEN-wa) is also used in the making of the local chicha beer. This salad makes a nice accompaniment to many dishes and is also excellent as an appetizer.

1 cup (about $1/2$ pound) dried red kidney beans

1 teaspoon salt, or more to your taste

1 tablespoon red wine vinegar

$1/2$ teaspoon freshly ground black pepper

1 cup fresh corn kernels

$3/4$ cup (about 6 ounces) quinoa

$1/2$ cup chopped red bell peppers

$1/2$ cup chopped fresh yellow chiles (*ají amarillo*) or yellow *güero* chiles or 2 teaspoons very finely chopped habanero chile, seeded

$1/4$ cup finely chopped fresh coriander (cilantro) leaves

3 tablespoons finely chopped celery

$1/4$ cup fresh lemon juice

$1/3$ cup extra-virgin olive oil

1 teaspoon ground cumin

1. Place the red kidney beans in a medium-size saucepan and cover with water by several inches. Bring to a boil, salt well, then cook until tender, about $1^1/4$ hours. Drain and transfer to a large bowl while still hot and toss with the vinegar, 1 teaspoon salt, and black pepper.

2. Bring another medium-size saucepan of water to a boil and cook the corn until tender. Drain, cool, and toss with the beans.

3. Place the quinoa in a strainer and rinse it well. Bring a medium-size saucepan of salted water to a boil, then cook the quinoa for 10 minutes. Drain through a strainer and rinse. Place the strainer over a saucepan of boiling water, making sure the quinoa doesn't touch the water. Cover the quinoa with a kitchen towel, place a large lid over the towel, and steam for 10 minutes. Remove from the saucepan and let it cool.

4. Transfer the quinoa to the bowl with the beans and corn and toss with the red bell pepper, chiles, coriander, celery, lemon juice, olive oil, and cumin. Taste and add more salt if desired. Serve at room temperature.

MAKES 4 SERVINGS

pink peppercorns

Pink peppercorns, contrary to their name, are not pungent at all and are not pepper-corns, but are rather sweet and used in combination with chiles in some South American cooking. The Incas knew them as a medicinal plant known as *mulli*, which became *molle* with the Spanish. Pink peppercorns are not ripe pepper fruits but are the small aromatic berries of the mulli tree, a pungent-smelling tree with drooping branches that is indige-nous to Peru and Ecuador. Juan de Velasco writes in *Historia del reino de Quito* that the tree was "an entire pharmacy" that was used to cure a "thousand illnesses." The Incas used the berries to make aromatic drinks. They are now being grown in California and are used in mixes with white and black peppercorns. Today, pink peppercorns are mostly grown on the French island of Reunion in the Indian Ocean.

Carrot Salad with Cayenne

This carrot salad from Algeria, called *salatat al-jazar*, can be made in a number of ways, with a number of added vegetables such as diced green bell peppers. It can also be made hotter by adding fresh chiles, or you could easily use twice as much cayenne pepper as I call for. Vegetable salads are very popular in North Africa as meze and one will find a great variety there.

2 quarts water

12 large garlic cloves, crushed

1 pound small thin carrots, peeled

2 teaspoons extra-virgin olive oil

2 tablespoons fresh lemon juice

¹/₂ teaspoon hot paprika

¹/₂ teaspoon cayenne pepper

³/₄ teaspoon ground cumin

1 tablespoon finely chopped fresh coriander (cilantro) leaves, plus more for garnish

1.   Bring the water to a boil in a large saucepan with the garlic and cook the carrots until very tender, about 20 minutes. Drain and cool. Discard the garlic.

2.   Cut the carrots in half lengthwise. Place the carrots in a bowl and toss gently with the olive oil, lemon juice, paprika, cayenne pepper, cumin, and coriander. Refrigerate until needed, but serve at room temperature garnished with coriander leaves.

MAKES 4 SERVINGS

Green Bell Pepper and Sardine Salad

In Tunisia, this salad would be served as a meze along with other dishes. It is called *hrus*, and you eat it by picking up the salad with pieces of flatbread rather than with utensils. It makes a very nice party appetizer that way. It also works well as an accompaniment to other hot Tunisian preparations, such as Swordfish in the "Sauce that Dances" (page 270).

4 green bell peppers (about 1¼ pounds), cored and seeded

3 fresh green jalapeño chiles, stemmed and seeded

6 tablespoons extra-virgin olive oil

½ teaspoon freshly ground caraway seeds

3 large garlic cloves, very finely chopped

Salt to taste

10 imported black olives, pitted

1 tablespoon capers, chopped if large

One 3½-ounce can imported Moroccan sardines in chiles or any canned sardine in oil

1.   Place the bell and chile peppers in a food processor and pulse until mushy. Transfer to a strainer and leave to drain for 30 minutes.

2.   In a bowl, mix the pepper mixture with the olive oil, caraway, garlic, and salt. Arrange on a serving platter and garnish with the olives, capers, and sardines. Serve at room temperature with flatbread.

MAKES 6 SERVINGS

the piquant cuisine of north africa

The most interesting thing about the use of chiles in North Africa is how limited it is. Only Algerians and Tunisians enjoy the heat of the chile. To the west of them, Moroccans eat very spicy and sweet food, but not any of the "hot" spices such as chile in any notable degree. To the east, the Libyans and Egyptians hardly use any chiles, and when they do it is in moderation. To the south are the nomadic tribes of the Sahara, who eat plain and bland food, except in the southern reaches of sub-Saharan Africa, where the chile influence of West Africa is felt in some preparations made in southern Mali and Niger.

It is a mystery how the chile arrived in North Africa, but the three possibilities hold equal weight. The first is that the chile was brought by the Spanish from the Americas after passing through Seville along the North African coast. The second possibility is that the chile seeds came from West Africa where they had earlier been brought by the Portuguese and traveled north along the long established trans-Saharan trade route, accompanying the usual goods of gold, salt, slaves, and grains of paradise. The third possibility is that the chile came from the east. We know the chile went to Goa with the Portuguese at an early date and was being exported in some small amount from there. It's possible that the chile arrived in the spice markets of Alexandria and Aleppo along with black pepper, cloves, and ginger and that it was then bought by North African traders.

Salad of Pureed Red Bell Pepper and Chile

This Tunisian *turshy* of red bell pepper and chiles is quite different than the Levantine one of the same name, which is basically pickled turnip slices. This is traditionally eaten with pieces of warmed Arabic flatbread and can be served as a meze, salad, or side dish with grilled foods. To roast the bell peppers, arrange them in a baking dish and place in a 425°F oven until blistered black, about 35 minutes, turning to make sure all sides blacken.

1¹/₂ pounds red bell peppers (about 6), roasted, skins removed, cored, seeded, and chopped

3 fresh red finger-type chiles or 5 fresh red jalapeño chiles, stemmed, seeded, and chopped

6 large garlic cloves

1 tablespoon ground coriander

Juice of 1 lemon

1¹/₂ teaspoons salt, or more to your taste

Arabic flatbread, warmed, for garnish

Place the bell peppers, chiles, and garlic in a food processor and blend until thoroughly pureed. Transfer to a strainer and let drain for 10 minutes. Transfer to a bowl and stir in the coriander, lemon juice, and salt. Taste and add more salt if desired. Serve at room temperature with the flatbread.

MAKES 4 SERVINGS

Eggplant Salad with Currants

This preparation from Yemen, called *salatat al-badhinjan*, can be served as a salad or as a meze. Either way you will get the fullest flavor when it is served the day after being cooked, so that the flavors have a chance to meld. If your tomatoes are not juicy, add 1/2 cup to 1 cup water in step 2. Also, if you like, serve with a drizzle of olive oil. I'm always surprised at the reaction I get from this salad—people just love it.

1 large eggplant (about 1 1/2 pounds), cut into 3/4-inch cubes

1 teaspoon salt

6 tablespoons extra-virgin olive oil

2 medium-size onions, finely chopped

1 1/2 pounds ripe juicy tomatoes, peeled, seeded, and coarsely chopped

1 1/2 teaspoons ground allspice

1 1/2 teaspoons ground cumin

1 teaspoon cayenne pepper

5 large garlic cloves, finely chopped

1/4 cup currants

3 tablespoons finely chopped fresh mint leaves

3 tablespoons finely chopped fresh coriander (cilantro) leaves

Salt and freshly ground black pepper to taste

1. Lay the eggplant pieces on some paper towels and sprinkle with salt. Leave them to drain of their bitter juices for 30 minutes, then pat dry with paper towels.

2. In a large skillet, heat 4 tablespoons of the olive oil over medium-high heat, then cook the onions until soft and yellow, 5 to 6 minutes, stirring. Add the tomatoes, allspice, cumin, and cayenne pepper and cook until soft, 5 to 10 minutes, stirring. Add the garlic and currants, stir, and transfer to a bowl.

3. Add the remaining 2 tablespoons olive oil to the skillet and heat over medium-high heat, then brown the eggplant until tender, gently scraping up the pieces with a spatula and turning, 10 to 12 minutes.

4. Add the tomato mixture to the eggplant, then add the mint and coriander and toss gently to mix. Season with salt and pepper. Turn the heat off, cover, and let come to room temperature. If time allows, chill for 1 day in the refrigerator and serve at room temperature.

MAKES 6 SERVINGS

sexy salads

Crispy Fish Salad with Mango

This Thai fish salad, called *yam pla dook fuu*, is a real winner that everyone likes. Maybe it's because of the two-step cooking of the fish that makes it crispy. Or maybe people just love the addition of mango and peanuts. In any case, it is a refreshing salad. Fresh bird's eye chiles may be sold under the name *piquín* chiles in large supermarkets and Latino markets, particularly in the Southwest. In Thailand, bird's-eye chiles are known as *prik kee nu* or "mouse-dropping chiles" and Thai chiles are known as *prik kee fa* or "sky-pointing chiles."

1/2 pound firm white-fleshed fish fillet, such as catfish

Salt to taste

2 cups vegetable oil, for frying

1 shallot, thinly sliced

1 celery stalk, julienned into 1-inch lengths

2 tablespoons roasted peanuts, coarsely crushed

1/2 small, very firm green mango, julienned or shredded

1 tablespoon Thai fish sauce

2 tablespoons fresh lime juice

1 teaspoon sugar

6 large fresh mint leaves, coarsely chopped

2 tablespoons coarsely chopped fresh coriander (cilantro) leaves

1 teaspoon fresh bird's-eye chiles, whole, or 12 fresh green Thai chiles, thinly sliced, or 5 fresh green serrano chiles, thinly sliced

---

1. Preheat the oven to 400°F. Pat the fish dry with a paper towel. Season with salt and place on a rack in a roasting pan. Bake until cooked through, 15 minutes. Remove from the oven and cool. Place the fish in a food processor with a pinch of salt and blend until finely shredded but not pureed.

2. In a wok, heat the frying oil until very hot and almost smoking. Add 1/2 cup of the fish mixture and cook until it puffs up and turns golden brown, 1 to 2 minutes. Turn carefully and cook the other side until golden brown, 1 to 2 minutes. (It may not be necessary to turn them if you have made them thin enough.) Remove and set aside while you continue to cook the remaining fish.

3. In a bowl, break the fried fish patties into pieces. Toss gently and carefully with the shallot, celery, peanuts, mango, fish sauce, lime juice, sugar, mint, coriander, chiles, and salt to taste. Arrange on a serving platter and let sit 15 minutes. Serve cool or at room temperature.

MAKES 4 SERVINGS

some like it hot

# Shrimp and Banana-Stalk Chile Salad

Prik yuak are a kind of yellow-colored Thai chile whose name means "banana-stalk" chile. The yellow chiles most commonly found in supermarkets (and they're not *that* common) are either the Hungarian wax variety (also called banana chiles), which you can use but are not really hot enough, or the so-called "yellow chiles," which are smaller, hotter Tabasco-like chiles, also called *güero* chiles, that are better suited for this preparation. If you can find neither, then use bright red jalapeño chiles. As with all Thai salads, make sure you achieve the proper balance of flavor by not emphasizing one ingredient over another.

---

1 teaspoon safflower oil

1/2 shallot or small red onion, thinly sliced

10 yellow banana chiles or 10 other yellow chiles or 8 red jalapeño chiles

1 teaspoon palm sugar, light brown sugar, or granulated sugar

1 tablespoon Thai fish sauce

1 teaspoon fresh lime juice

1/4 pound small cooked shrimp, chopped

2 tablespoons coconut cream (see page 90)

2 tablespoons fresh coriander (cilantro) leaves

1. In a small skillet, heat the safflower oil over medium-high heat, then cook the shallot until browned on the edges, about 4 minutes, stirring. Remove and spread on some paper towels to cool.

2. Preheat the oven to 425°F. Place the chiles in a baking dish and roast until the skin blisters black, about 20 minutes. Remove the chiles, put them in a paper bag to steam, and, when cool enough to handle, peel off the skin and remove the seeds. Slice the bigger pieces in half.

3. In a small bowl, dissolve the sugar in the Thai fish sauce and lime juice. In a larger bowl, toss the chiles with the shrimp, then toss again with the fish sauce mixture. Transfer to a plate, drizzle with the coconut cream, and sprinkle the shallot and coriander leaves on top. Serve at room temperature.

MAKES 4 SMALL SERVINGS

sexy salads

Squid and Chile Salad

Yam pla meuk is probably the most common seafood salad in Thailand, as squid is plentiful and inexpensive. *Pla meuk* literally means "ink fish," in reference to the squid. Some cooks add Chinese celery to the salad, but remember that no one ingredient should overpower the squid. It is preferable to use large squids, one or two to the pound. These are more likely to be found at fish stores than at supermarkets, but they are sometimes sold as "calamari steaks" in the frozen food sections of supermarkets. If you cannot get those, then use the regular squid you are likely to find, scoring them with a knife if you like, which is merely a decorative affectation.

5 large garlic cloves

40 fresh or dried bird's-eye chiles or 20 fresh green Thai chiles or 8 fresh green serrano chiles

1/4 cup fresh lime juice

1/4 cup Thai fish sauce

1/4 cup white vinegar

1 pound large squid, cleaned, scored diagonally at an angle, cut into 1-inch lengths, tentacles cut into 1-inch lengths

1-inch cube fresh ginger, peeled and very thinly sliced

1 lemongrass stalk, tough outer portions removed, thinly sliced

1 scallion, thinly sliced

2 shallots, thinly sliced

12 fresh red Thai chiles or 5 red serrano chiles or 3 red finger-type chiles, julienned lengthwise

1/4 cup loosely packed and coarsely chopped fresh coriander (cilantro) leaves

1/2 cup loosely packed and coarsely chopped fresh mint leaves

4 large lettuce leaves

1. In a mortar, pound the garlic and the green chiles into a paste. Whisk in the lime juice and fish sauce to form a dressing. Set aside.

2. Bring a medium-size saucepan of lightly salted water with the vinegar to a boil. Drop the squid and its tentacles into the boiling water and parboil for no more than 4 to 5 minutes. Drain and set aside.

3. In a medium-size bowl, toss the squid with the ginger, lemongrass, scallion, shallots, red chiles, coriander, and mint. Pour the dressing over the squid and toss again. Arrange some lettuce leaves on a plate or platter and cover with the squid salad. Serve cold or cool.

MAKES 4 TO 6 SERVINGS

Gado Gado

This recipe for tossed vegetable salad with chile peanut sauce is from Malay cuisine, but it is very popular in Indonesia, too, where the sauce is known as *saus kacang*. This recipe is adapted from Dato' Tunku Mukminah Jiwa and the Malay kitchen of the Federal Hotel in Kuala Lumpur. You may be very tempted to use peanut butter instead of the whole peanuts I call for, but think "peanuts turned into sauce" rather than something coming from a jar. It is better and no more work. Remember that skinned, roasted, and unsalted peanuts are easily found in supermarkets.

FOR THE PEANUT SAUCE

1 tablespoon tamarind paste

2 cups warm water

1 tablespoon vegetable oil

3 shallots, chopped

8 dried red de arbol chiles, broken in half and soaked in water until needed

2 fresh red jalapeño chiles, quartered

1 cup roasted, skinned, and unsalted peanuts or ¹/₂ cup peanut butter

1 teaspoon soy sauce

2 kaffir lime leaves, crumpled in your hands, or ¹/₂ teaspoon lime zest

1 tablespoon palm sugar or brown sugar, or more to your taste

1 teaspoon salt, or more to your taste

FOR THE VEGETABLES

¹/₄ pound yard-long beans (asparagus beans) or thin green beans, ends trimmed and cut into 2-inch pieces

¹/₄ pound bean sprouts

¹/₄ pound green cabbage or kale, chopped

¹/₄ pound water spinach or spinach, chopped

1. To make the peanut sauce, in a medium-size bowl, steep the tamarind paste in the water until needed.

2. In a wok, heat the vegetable oil over medium-high heat, then cook the shallots and dried and fresh chiles until the shallots are golden, about 4 minutes, stirring and tossing frequently. Remove and place in a blender with the peanuts and blend for a few seconds.

3. Place the tamarind and its water in the blender and puree until smooth. Put the contents of the blender back into the wok along with the soy sauce, lime leaves, sugar, and salt. Bring to a boil. Continue boiling until thick and syrupy, adding a little water if necessary to keep it fluid, 2 to 3 minutes. Taste and add more sugar and salt if desired. Let the mixture cool in the wok and set aside until it is needed.

4. To prepare the vegetables, bring a large saucepan of water to a boil and blanch each vegetable in succession, removing each with a skimmer as it finishes cooking: yard-long beans for 4 minutes, bean sprouts for 1 minute, cabbage for 4 minutes, and spinach for 30 seconds. Make sure you don't overcook any of the vegetables. Assemble the vegetables on a serving plate or platter. Top with the peanut sauce and serve.

MAKES 6 SERVINGS

WATER SPINACH

Water spinach (*Ipomoea aquatica* Forsk.) is a tropical perennial water plant with delicious edible green leaves that are highly prized in the Chinese cooking of Malaysia and elsewhere in Southeast Asia. Although it is related to the American sweet potato, the roots are not eaten that often. Also known as *kangkung*, the leaves are used in soups, curries, and stir-fries and are eaten boiled and steamed, too. The youngest leaves and shoots are eaten in salads. The only place it grows well in the United States is Florida, where it is considered a weed, although some farmers might begin cultivating it for farmers' markets. Regular spinach can be substituted for it.

Poached Chicken Salad in Red Chile Oil Sauce

T his is a Sichuan appetizer called *hong you ji kuai*, which combines hotness with salty soy sauce and a sweetness from the sugar. The chicken is usually diced, as are the scallions. Chongqing chickens, named for the second city of Sichuan, are unique in that they are white-skinned and nearly white-fleshed, with black bones—a completely unique chicken. Many Sichuanese consider these black-boned chickens to be especially nourishing. One can also make this dish with rabbit. The dressing used here is also used for a vegetable dish featuring a popular perennial herb in China and Vietnam called chameleon plant (*Houttuynia cordata*).

16 scallions, 12 with white parts only and 4 with white and green parts, sliced into ¹/₂-inch lengths

1-inch cube fresh ginger, peeled

1¹/₄ pounds whole chicken breast on the bone

1 teaspoon salt, or more to your taste

3 tablespoons soy sauce

2 teaspoons sugar

6 tablespoons Chile Oil (page 424)

1 tablespoon red pepper flakes

1 teaspoon sesame oil

1. Bring a large pot of water to a boil with the 12 scallion bulbs and ginger. Place the chicken in the pot and return to a near boil, then as soon as it almost bubbles, turn the heat off and cover the pot. Once the broth is at room temperature, after about 2 hours, remove the chicken from the pot and remove the bone and skin and discard them. Slice the chicken into smaller than bite-size cubes and let cool completely.

2. In a bowl, toss the chicken with the 4 remaining sliced scallions and season with salt. Meanwhile, in a small bowl, stir the soy sauce and sugar together until the sugar dissolves. Stir the chile oil and red pepper flakes together and then stir them into the soy sauce along with the sesame oil. Pour this sauce over the chicken and toss thoroughly so that everything is glistening. Transfer the chicken salad to a serving platter and serve at room temperature.

MAKES 4 SERVINGS

sexy salads

Strange-Flavor Chicken

This Sichuan chicken salad is often served as an appetizer or snack. It is called *guai wei ji si*, which actually means "strange-flavor chicken." But its other name—for a very slightly different variation—is bang bang chicken (sometimes called bon bon chicken on Chinese-American menus), which originated in the village of Hanyang Ba, near the town of Leshan south of Chengdu in Sichuan, according to Fuchsia Dunlop in her book *Land of Plenty* (W. W. Norton, 2003). This village was famed for its free-range chickens, and street vendors there would sell the chicken in a spicy sauce as a snack. It became known as bang bang because of the sound of the cudgel used to hammer the heavy cleaver through the bones of the chicken. This dish is called "strange-flavor" because it has salty, sweet, sour, nutty, hot, and numbing flavors as described by classic Sichuanese culinary terminology. It is garnished with scallions, but you could use cucumbers, too. You will need to poach a chicken first, so read the directions on page 65.

---

1 pound cooked boneless chicken breast meat with its skin

12 scallions, white and light green parts only, cut into 1½-inch lengths and slivered lengthwise

1½ tablespoons light soy sauce

1½ teaspoons Chinese black vinegar or red wine vinegar

1 tablespoon sugar

1 teaspoon salt

3 tablespoons tahini, blended well

1 tablespoon sesame oil

2 tablespoons Chile Oil (page 424), blended with 1 teaspoon red pepper flakes

1 teaspoon ground toasted Sichuan peppercorns

1 tablespoon toasted sesame seeds

---

1.   Pound the chicken with the side of a cleaver several times to break down the tissue. Tear the chicken into shreds with your fingers. Arrange the scallions on a serving plate, then scatter the shredded chicken on top.

2.   In a small bowl, stir together the soy sauce, vinegar, sugar, and salt until dissolved. Stir in the tahini to make a smooth sauce. Add the sesame oil, chile oil with pepper flakes, and Sichuan peppercorns and mix well. Pour the sauce over the chicken and, when you are ready to serve, sprinkle with the sesame seeds. Serve cool or at room temperature.

MAKES 4 SERVINGS

the hot spices:
sichuan peppercorns

Sichuan peppercorns, also called fagara (incorrectly, according to Fuchsia Dunlop, author of *The Land of Plenty* [W. W. Norton, 2003]), anise pepper, or Chinese pepper, is the red-brown dried berry of a Chinese variety of the small prickly ash tree. Its pungency resides in the pericarp of the berry, and that shell or husk that is pinkish red in color and slightly knobby is what is sold as the spice, not the seeds. It has a pronounced spicy-woody aroma and a numbing, rather than a sharp or bitter, taste. This spice, used almost exclusively in Chinese cooking, is also used in the mix known as "Chinese five spice," which you will see in your supermarket. The most celebrated Sichuan peppercorn comes from Hanyuan province in mountainous western Sichuan. In the Han period (202 B.C.– c. A.D. 220), Sichuan peppercorns were used as part of the mix used to make the mud walls of the residences of the imperial concubines. As a result, the houses became known as pepper houses (*jiao fang*), a term that survived into the late imperial era. Apparently this custom arose not just because of the fragrance, but also because it was a symbol of fertility. Sichuan peppercorns may be hard to find, since their import has been banned since 1968 in the United States because of a canker they carry that is harmful to citrus trees. The ban had never been enforced until about 2002.

Spicy Cucumbers

This Sichuan appetizer, called *qiang huang gua*, is very easy to prepare, as the cucumbers don't actually have to be cooked. It is a flavorful dish that appears on banquet tables. This recipe is adapted from *Madame Wong's Long-Life Chinese Cookbook* (NTC Publishing Group, 1977).

1 pound small pickling cucumbers, quartered lengthwise

1 tablespoon salt

2 tablespoons plus 1/2 teaspoon sugar

One 1 1/2-inch cube fresh ginger, peeled and julienned

1 fresh red finger-type chile or red jalapeño chile, julienned

1/2 cup sesame oil

4 dried red de arbol chiles, halved and seeded

1 teaspoon Sichuan peppercorns

1 1/2 tablespoons Chinese black vinegar or red wine vinegar

2 tablespoons soy sauce

1. Sprinkle the cucumbers with the salt and 2 tablespoons sugar, toss lightly, and set aside for 20 minutes. Rinse the cucumber in cold water, drain, and with your hands squeeze more liquid out. Arrange the cucumbers in a ceramic or glass baking dish, cut side down, and sprinkle the ginger and fresh chile on top.

2. In a wok or saucepan, heat the sesame oil over medium-high heat, then stir-fry the dried chiles until dark but not black, about 15 seconds. Add the Sichuan peppercorns and cook for 15 seconds. Immediately pour this mixture over the cucumbers. In a small bowl, mix together the remaining sugar, the vinegar, and soy sauce. Pour over the cucumbers and marinate overnight. Serve cold.

MAKES 4 TO 6 SERVINGS

Daikon Salad

This very refreshing Korean salad is called *moo-oo-sanchae* and is best made a few hours before you want to eat it so that the radish can become softer and more palatable. It is served cold as an appetizer, side dish, or salad and is especially good in the summer with grilled foods. This recipe is from my friend Unjoo Lee Byars. *Moo* is the Korean word for white radish, known as daikon in Japanese.

³/₄ pound white radish (daikon), peeled and julienned into 2 x ¹/₄-inch strips

2 small garlic cloves, finely chopped

5 tablespoons barley vinegar or apple cider vinegar

2 Persian cucumbers, peel left on and julienned into 2 x ¹/₄-inch strips, or 1 small regular cucumber, peeled, seeded, and julienned into 2 x ¹/₄-inch strips

3 tablespoons ground Korean red chile or 2 tablespoons ground red chile

1 tablespoon salt, or more to your taste

3 tablespoons sesame oil

2 tablespoons sugar

1 teaspoon soy sauce

6 oysters (optional), freshly shucked and cut in half, with their liquid

In a medium-size bowl, toss all the ingredients together until they are well mixed. Let marinate in the refrigerator for 2 hours before serving. Serve at room temperature or slightly cool.

MAKES 4 TO 6 SERVINGS

Cold Spicy Noodle Salad with Asian Pear and Cucumber

I n Korean homes, families usually eat communally. That is, foods are served on plates that people pass around family style, although they each eat from an individual, deep bowl of rice. This simple preparation, called *naeng myun* (or *nang-myon*), is made with Korean-style starch noodles, in this case made from mung bean and sweet potato starch. They are green in color and the same size as vermicelli and sold in packages labeled "Oriental-style starch noodle." One good brand is made by the Korean firm Hanmi, Inc., and is available in Korean markets. In its place you can use bean noodles that are usually sold in the international/Asian section of American supermarkets. The red chile paste can be found in Korean markets or on the Internet. This preparation is a kind of Korean bachelor's dish since it is so easy to make, nutritious, and delicious. Noodle dishes are always eaten at the end of a Korean meal as a kind of food to fill you up when the rest of the food has been light. In my friend Unjoo's family, her mother, Lucy, drapes the long noodles over a chopstick to arrange them very neatly in rows in the serving bowl, but, Unjoo warns, you need the help of five people in the kitchen to do this exacting work. In traditionally large Korean families, that was not hard to do. This recipe yields lots of servings so feel free to cut it in half, although the leftovers are perfectly fine.

³/₄ pound Oriental-style starch noodles	1 tablespoon vegetable oil
¹/₄ cup white vinegar	1 Persian cucumber or ¹/₂ regular cucumber, seeded and julienned
3 tablespoons rice vinegar	
¹/₄ cup red Korean chile paste (*koch'ujang*)	1 large Asian pear, peeled and julienned

1. Bring a large pot of unsalted water to a rolling boil, then cook the pasta until almost tender, about 7 minutes, or follow the package instructions. Drain the pasta in a colander and cool with cold water sprayed on it. Dump a tray of ice cubes on top to further chill the noodles.

2. Snip the strands of noodles into smaller pieces with kitchen scissors into a bowl. Toss with the white vinegar and rice vinegar. Toss again with the red chile paste and vegetable oil. You may find it easiest to do this tossing with your hands.

Transfer the noodles to a large serving bowl or platter, place the julienned cucumber and pear on top, and serve.

MAKES 8 SERVINGS

Soybean Sprout Salad

This cool Korean dish is called *kong na mool moo chim*. This recipe comes from my friend Unjoo Lee Byars, who used soybean sprouts when she made it for me but says that any sprouts will do. Every Korean cook will admonish you not to lift the lid while cooking the soybean sprouts because they will then smell fishy. This salad is usually served as an appetizer or side dish.

1/2 pound soybean sprouts, rinsed and drained

1 cup water

2 teaspoons salt

1 tablespoon soy sauce

2 tablespoons sesame oil

1 tablespoon ground Korean red chile or 2 teaspoons ground red chile

1 large garlic clove, finely chopped

1 tablespoon toasted sesame seeds

1. Place the sprouts in a medium-size saucepan with the water and 1 teaspoon salt and bring to a boil. Reduce the heat to medium, cover, and cook until they soften, about 15 minutes, without ever looking under the lid. Drain well, and once they are cool squeeze out any excess water.

2. In a medium-size bowl, stir together the soy sauce, sesame oil, chile, the remaining 1 teaspoon salt, garlic, and sesame seeds. Add the sprouts and toss with your hands, mixing well. Serve cool or at room temperature.

MAKES 2 TO 3 SERVINGS

searing
soups

There is a belief that as easy as soups appear, they are actually hard to make. There's some truth to that notion, but it is a little misplaced. I think that everyone loves soups, but that we become quite casual and inattentive when we make them, as if we don't need to pay attention to their elements and their taste with as much rigor as when we prepare other food. Thus, they don't always come out as good as they should. The recipes in this chapter are from around the world, are very hot and very satisfying, and most are very forgiving. I know that Cow Foot Soup from Jamaica (page 79) may sound unappetizing, but these more unusual ones are far more delicious than they sound, so give them a try, too. Soups play an important role in most of our hot cuisines. Most of the soups in this chapter are substantial and searing, so eat slowly.

Mountain Soup

This Peruvian soup is called *chupe serrano*, which means something like "high-lands soup." *Serrano* also gives its name to a chile. In the Andes, cooks would use ulluco, a familiar tuber in Colombia, Ecuador, Peru, and Bolivia, where it is known as the poor man's potato. Depending on where you live, your supermarket might call cassava by its other names, yucca or manioc. This soup, a sort of Andean version of minestrone, is richly colored and very flavorful without being heavy.

2 tablespoons vegetable oil

1 small onion, chopped

4 large garlic cloves, crushed in a mortar

4 fresh red *rocoto* chiles or 6 large fresh red jalapeño chiles, finely chopped

1 tablespoon *Ají Panca en Pasta* (page 405)

1 medium-size tomato, peeled, seeded, and chopped

2 teaspoons salt, or more to your taste

1 teaspoon freshly ground black pepper, or more to your taste

1/2 cup chicken broth (homemade or canned)

31/2 cups water

1/2 pound pumpkin or any winter squash, peeled and diced

3/4 cup diced cassava

1 medium-size carrot, peeled and diced

1 sprig mint

1/2 teaspoon dried oregano

1/4 cup medium-grain rice

1/4 cup fresh or frozen peas

1/2 pound white potatoes, peeled and diced

3/4 cup fresh fava beans (from about 1 pound of pods) or dried fava beans, peeled (if dried, soak overnight, then boil for 10 minutes to remove peel)

1 ear of corn, husked and cut into 1-inch slices

1 cup evaporated milk

2 large eggs, lightly beaten

3 ounces farmer's cheese or Mexican *queso fresco* or ricotta or domestic feta, diced

1. In a stew pot or casserole, heat the vegetable oil over medium-high heat, then cook the onion until soft, about 6 minutes, stirring. Add the garlic, chiles, *ají panca en pasta*, tomato, salt, and pepper and cook for 1 minute, stirring so it is well blended. Add the chicken broth, water, pumpkin, cassava, carrot,

ULLUCO

A tuber popular among the Incas was ulluco (*Ullucus tuberosus*), which was a major source of carbohydrates in many Andean lands. This earthy, slightly mucilaginous vegetable has a thin skin of different colors, with white or pale yellow flesh. It grows at elevations between 6,000 and 12,000 feet. In Bolivia, this tuber is called *papalisa* and is used in a fiery stew called *ajiaco de ollucos*. Ulloco is still a staple food for many people in the Andes.

mint, and oregano. Bring to a boil, stir, and reduce the heat to low. Simmer, covered, for 20 minutes.

2. Add the rice, peas, potatoes, and fava beans and continue to simmer, covered, for 10 minutes. Add the corn and simmer until tender, 10 to 15 minutes more. Pour in the milk and beaten eggs slowly, stirring constantly. Add the cheese, cook for 2 minutes, and serve hot.

MAKES 6 SERVINGS

Shrimp Soup with Rice and Poached Eggs

T his *chupe de camarones* (shrimp soup) is a quite substantial and very delicious soup from Peru that is popular in the springtime. I don't want you to be misled, so realize that there is a bit of work with this recipe—very rewarding work, to be sure—as you will need to steam the potatoes and poach the eggs. If you are using fresh shrimp and they have some of their coral attached you can use it in the soup, which will enrich it nicely. To skin the fava beans, plunge the shelled beans into boiling water for 5 minutes, then drain, cool a bit, and pinch the skin off at the seam.

2¹/₂ quarts water

2 pounds fresh large shrimp with their heads or 1 pound headless shrimp, heads and coral, if any, and/or shells removed and saved

1¹/₂ tablespoons salt, or more to your taste

¹/₄ cup vegetable oil

1 medium-size onion, chopped

3 large garlic cloves, finely chopped

2 ripe tomatoes (about ¹/₂ pound), peeled, seeded, and chopped

1¹/₂ teaspoons ketchup

2 tablespoons *Ají Panca en Pasta* (page 405)

¹/₈ teaspoon ground cumin

¹/₂ teaspoon freshly ground black pepper

4 small Yukon gold potatoes (about 10 ounces), peeled

¹/₂ cup medium-grain rice

³/₄ pound shelled fresh fava beans, skinned

³/₄ pound fresh or frozen peas

1 ear of corn, husked and cut into 4 segments

4 large eggs

¹/₃ cup evaporated milk

1 teaspoon dried oregano

3 ounces farmer's cheese or Mexican *queso fresco* or ricotta or domestic feta, crumbled

¹/₂ cup *Rocoto* Chile Sauce (page 407)

1. In a large saucepan, bring 2 quarts of the water to a boil with the shrimp heads and/or shells. Add 1¹/₂ tablespoons salt, reduce the heat to medium, and cook until a rich broth results, about 1 hour. Strain the broth and reserve.

2. In a large stockpot, heat the vegetable oil over medium-high heat and cook the onion, garlic, and tomatoes until soft, about 5 minutes, stirring. Add the ketchup, *ají panca en pasta*, shrimp corai (if any and if using fresh shrimp), cumin, pepper, and a little salt to taste and stir to mix well. Reduce the heat to medium and cook until mushy and gooey, about 8 minutes, stirring. Add the reserved shrimp broth and bring to a boil over high heat. Boil for 15 minutes, turn the heat off, and set aside.

3. Place the potatoes in the top part of a double boiler or steamer with a little salt. Turn the heat to high and cook until tender, about 30 minutes. Turn the heat off and leave until needed.

4. Bring the contents of the stockpot to a boil and add the rice, fava beans, peas, and corn. Reduce the heat to medium and cook until tender, 15 to 20 minutes.

5. In a medium-size skillet or saucepan, bring the remaining 2 cups water to a simmer. Stir the water in one direction to create a whirlpool, then quickly and carefully crack the eggs into the water and poach them until the whites set, keeping the water gently twirling. You should be able to cook all the eggs at one time, but if you feel you can't, cook 2 at a time. Remove the eggs from the water with a slotted spoon and set aside in a shallow bowl filled with a few tablespoons of hot water.

6. Add the shrimp, milk, and oregano to the stockpot and cook until the shrimp turn orange-pink, 2 to 3 minutes. Serve by placing ¹/₄ of the cheese and 1 potato in an individual soup bowl. Ladle the soup into the bowl and place a poached egg on top. Spoon a dollop of the chile sauce into the bowl. Serve immediately.

MAKES 4 SERVINGS PLUS LEFTOVERS

Shrimp Soup from Rinconada

This recipe, called *sopa de camaron rinconada*, is adapted from Patricia Quintana's *The Taste of Mexico* (Stewart, Tabori & Chang, 1986). Rinconada is a small village between Veracruz and Xalapa, and this soup is sold at food stands there as a breakfast soup. It's downright ambrosial and is great with warmed-up corn tortillas. The epazote called for may be hard to find; don't worry about it if you can't get it because this soup is incredible anyway. I usually serve this for dinner with corn tortillas and beer.

3 pounds fresh shrimp with their heads, heads left on several shrimp, the remainder removed and saved, shells removed and saved, *or* 1¹/₂ pounds headless shrimp, heads and/or shells removed and saved

2 quarts water

¹/₃ cup extra-virgin olive oil

2 medium-size white onions, cut in half and thinly sliced

3 large tomatoes, cut in half, seeds squeezed out, and grated against the largest holes of a grater

2 large fresh green jalapeño chiles, sliced

Salt to taste

2 leafy sprigs epazote (see page 361) or fresh coriander (cilantro) (optional)

1 lime, quartered

1. Place the shrimp heads, if using, and the shrimp shells in a large saucepan and cover with the water. Bring to a boil, then reduce the heat to low, and simmer for 1 hour. Strain and save the broth, discarding the shells and heads.

2. In a large saucepan, heat the olive oil over medium-high heat. Cook the onions until soft and slightly golden, about 8 minutes, stirring. Add the tomatoes, reduce the heat to medium, and cook slowly until the liquid from the tomatoes is mostly evaporated, 18 to 20 minutes, stirring occasionally. Add the chiles and shrimp broth and bring to a boil over high heat. Season with salt.

3. Add the shrimp and epazote, if using. Reduce the heat slightly and cook uncovered, with the soup barely bubbling, until the shrimp are orange-red and firm, 10 to 12 minutes. Reduce the heat more if the soup is bubbling too much. Serve with a wedge of lime.

MAKES 4 SERVINGS

Cream of Avocado Soup

his *sopa de aguacate* is from Atlixco, an area of Mexico where many avocados grow. It's creamy smooth, very flavorful, and not too hot; a nice dish to serve before chicken, pork, or salmon. For a spicier soup, you can add a small, finely chopped habanero chile. Some Mexicans eat this soup cold, like a gazpacho, but I think it's much better hot.

3 large ripe avocados, peeled, seeded, and diced

1½ cups heavy cream

¼ cup dry sherry

1 tablespoon fresh lime juice

1 tablespoon pureed or grated onions

2 garlic cloves, ground in a mortar with 1 teaspoon salt until mushy

1 teaspoon freshly ground dried ancho chile or ½ teaspoon chile powder

1 tablespoon salt

1 teaspoon freshly ground white pepper

6 cups chicken broth (homemade or canned)

3 corn tortillas, quartered and fried in oil until crisp

Fresh coriander (cilantro) leaves, for garnish

1.   Place the avocados in a blender with the cream, sherry, lime juice, onion, and garlic and blend at high speed for 30 seconds. Season with the ancho chile, 1 teaspoon salt, and white pepper.

2.   Bring the chicken broth to a boil in a large saucepan over high heat. Reduce the heat to low and, once the broth is only simmering, add the avocado puree. Whisk the soup until smooth, taste, and add the remaining 2 teaspoons salt if desired. Serve hot, garnished with the tortilla pieces and coriander leaves.

MAKES 8 SERVINGS

Shrimp Bisque

This bisque is adapted from a recipe by Taunt Nit of Forked Island, Louisiana, who says that it is sometimes called "white shrimp stew." Make sure the milk never comes to a boil; otherwise, it may curdle. If it does then you can correct it somewhat by blending in some *beurre manié*, a blend of equal parts of soft butter and flour, to thicken it again. You can serve this with cornbread or oyster crackers. Crab or lobster may be substituted for the shrimp.

5 tablespoons unsalted butter

1 small onion, finely chopped

1 celery stalk, finely chopped

2 1/2 pounds fresh shrimp with their heads or 1 1/4 pounds headless shrimp, heads and/or tails removed and saved for another purpose, or 3/4 pound raw shelled shrimp

1/4 cup unbleached all-purpose flour

1 quart whole milk

1 1/2 teaspoons salt

2 teaspoons Tabasco sauce

1 teaspoon hot paprika

1/2 teaspoon freshly ground white pepper

2 teaspoons fresh lemon juice

In a large saucepan, melt the butter over medium-high heat, then cook the onion and celery until the onion is soft, about 5 minutes, stirring. Add the shrimp and cook for 2 minutes, stirring frequently. Stir in the flour and, once it is blended in, pour in the milk in a slow stream, whisking gently all the time. Add the salt, Tabasco sauce, paprika, white pepper, and lemon juice. Bring to just below a boil, then reduce the heat to medium, and simmer 5 minutes. Serve immediately.

MAKES 4 TO 6 SERVINGS

Cow Foot Soup

This typically Jamaican soup is far better tasting than sounding. The cow foot is used for flavoring the beans in the soup. You can ask for one at a butcher shop or look in Asian markets. This has a fantastic flavor, spicy with Scotch bonnet chile that eventually melts away into the unctuous sauce. In Jamaica, fava beans are called butter beans. Incidentally, Jamaicans also call allspice berries pimentos, which they're not. Cow foot soup is considered an antidote to a hangover, and Jamaican men believe it is an aphrodisiac. Some Jamaicans like to cook Dumplings (page 000) with this soup, placing them under the cover about 20 minutes before the dish is finished, but I find the soup rich and satisfying enough without the dumplings.

1 beef foot (about 2 pounds), preferably split

2 medium-size onions, chopped

4 large garlic cloves, ground in a mortar with 2 teaspoons salt

1/2 teaspoon ground allspice

Freshly ground black pepper to taste

3 cups dried fava beans

1/2 teaspoon dried thyme

1 whole Scotch bonnet chile or habanero chile with its stem, crushed

Salt to taste

Place the beef foot in a 3- or 4-quart pot or casserole and cover with the onions, mashed garlic, allspice, and pepper. Pour enough water in to come within an inch of the rim and bring to a boil over high heat. Reduce the heat to medium-low and boil gently for 1 hour. Add the fava beans, thyme, and chile and stir. Cook until the beans are tender and the beef foot is falling apart, adding water as needed so the broth remains about an inch from the top, about 3¹/₂ more hours. Stir occasionally. Remove and discard the foot and season the soup with salt. Serve immediately.

MAKES 4 SERVINGS

Fiery Semolina Ball Soup

This stunning soup from Tunisia is made with a large type of couscous called *sidir*. Although this totally North African–style ball of semolina is known as *muhammas* in Tunisia and *burkukis* in Algeria, it is sold in America in Middle Eastern markets with the label "moghrabiye" (or "toasted pasta ball"), which, curiously, is what they call these balls in Syria—far from the home of couscous. Toasted pasta balls are also available through the Internet. This recipe is based on the one served to me by Hechmi Hammami, the executive chef of the Abou Nawas Hotel in Tunis, who used *qadid*, a spiced lamb jerky, for his flavoring. Although it is a hot soup, one can also say it's intriguingly delicate.

1/2 teaspoon caraway seeds

5 large garlic cloves, peeled

1 teaspoon salt

1/4 cup extra-virgin olive oil

2 tablespoons tomato paste dissolved in 1 cup water

1 tablespoon *Harisa* (page 414)

1/2 teaspoon freshly ground black pepper

6 cups water

1/2 pound (about 1/2 cup) toasted pasta balls

1 tablespoon capers, rinsed

1 Preserved Lemon (page 415), cut into small dice without the peel

1 tablespoon finely chopped fresh mint leaves (optional)

1. Grind the caraway seeds in a mortar, then pound in the garlic and salt until the mixture is a paste.

2. In a large nonreactive casserole or saucepan, heat the olive oil over high heat and add the tomato paste dissolved in water, the *harisa*, black pepper, and the garlic-caraway paste. It will sizzle violently for a second so remember to keep your face away. Reduce the heat to medium, stir well to mix, cover, and cook for 5 minutes, stirring a few times.

3. Add the water, pasta balls, capers, and preserved lemon and simmer, uncovered, until the pasta balls are soft but not mushy, about 20 minutes. Sprinkle on the mint, if using. Serve immediately.

MAKES 4 SERVINGS

Vermicelli and Turmeric Soup

Vermicelli means "little worms" in Italian and the vermicelli of Tunisia is called *duwayda*, which means "inchworm" in Arabic. In this spicy hot preparation called *duwayda zarra'*, which means "farmer-style vermicelli," the pasta is indeed broken into one-inch lengths. This soup is a typical midday winter lunch dish in rural Tunisia.

1/2 cup extra-virgin olive oil

1 medium-size onion, finely chopped

2 tablespoons tomato paste dissolved in 1 cup water

3 bay leaves

1/2 teaspoon ground turmeric

1 tablespoon hot paprika

1/2 teaspoon cayenne pepper

1/2 teaspoon freshly ground black pepper

2 tablespoons finely chopped celery leaves with a little stalk

Salt to taste

5 cups water

6 to 8 ounces vermicelli, broken into 1-inch lengths

1. In a large casserole, heat the olive oil over medium-high heat, and cook the onion until soft, about 4 minutes, stirring frequently. Add the tomato paste dissolved in water to the casserole, along with the bay leaves, turmeric, paprika, cayenne pepper, black pepper, celery leaves and stalk, and salt. Reduce the heat to medium and cook 4 to 5 minutes, stirring.

2. Add the water and vermicelli to the casserole and cook over a medium heat until the pasta is soft, about 25 minutes, stirring occasionally. Remove and discard bay leaves. Serve immediately.

MAKES 4 SERVINGS

searing soups

Fish Soup Piquant

This is a fish soup or stew, *maraqat al-hut*, made in the Mediterranean seaport of Sfax in Tunisia. It is traditional for the feast of the breaking of the Ramadan fast. The most common and popular fish at the Sfax fish market are grouper, usually chosen for this stew, and scorpionfish, annular bream, hake, and red gurnard. Whatever fish you choose should ideally be local and fresh. Choose two from the following suggestions: grouper, porgy (scup), red snapper, redfish (ocean perch), ocean pout, cod, haddock, wolffish (ocean catfish), and hake. Of course, if your fish store doesn't have these then choose two that they do have that are medium to firm fleshed (ask the fishmonger). The broth can be eaten separately from the fish with grilled, toasted, or fried bread or with macaroni cooked in the broth. Or the diners can serve themselves a piece of fish to be put into the soup bowl with the broth.

6 large garlic cloves, peeled

2 teaspoons cumin seeds

1/2 teaspoon salt

1/2 cup extra-virgin olive oil

1 medium-size onion, chopped

1 tablespoon tomato paste

8 1/2 cups water

1/2 teaspoon *Harisa* (page 414)

1 tablespoon hot paprika

1 teaspoon cayenne pepper

1/2 teaspoon freshly ground black pepper

2 fresh green finger-type chiles or 3 green jalapeño chiles, stemmed and seeded

2 celery stalks, chopped

3 carrots, sliced

Pinch of saffron threads, crumbled

10 sprigs parsley, tied in cheesecloth

1 bay leaf

Salt to taste

1 1/2 to 3 pounds mixed fish fillets

1 lemon, quartered, or 1 Preserved Lemon (page 415), quartered

1. In a mortar, pound the garlic, cumin, and salt until you have a paste. Set aside.

2. In a large stockpot or casserole, heat the olive oil over high heat and cook the onion until softened, 1 to 2 minutes, stirring.

3. Meanwhile, dissolve the tomato paste in 1/2 cup of the water and add to the stockpot along with the *harisa*, paprika, cayenne pepper, black pepper, and garlic paste. Add 4 cups of the water and cook on high heat for 10 minutes.

4. Add the remaining 4 cups water, the chiles, celery, carrots, saffron, parsley, and bay leaf and season with salt. Reduce the heat to medium-low and simmer for 30 minutes. Strain the broth through a fine-mesh strainer, discarding the vegetables. Return the broth to the stockpot.

5. Bring the broth to a furious boil over high heat. Add the fish and cook for 15 minutes. Remove the fish from the stockpot. Serve the broth as a first-course soup and the fish separately as a second course with regular or preserved lemon quarters, keeping it warm in a low oven.

MAKES 4 SERVINGS

europeans meet the chile

The first European encounter with the chile occurred on New Year's Day, 1493. It occurred shortly after the *Santa Maria* ran aground and volunteers, who couldn't be accommodated by the *Niña*, established a fort called Navidad on Hispaniola, the first settlement in the New World. Near the fort, on January 1, 1493, Columbus wrote in his journal that "the pepper which the local Indians used as spice is more abundant and more valuable than either black or melegueta pepper." Later he recorded in his letter to Luis de Sant' Angel that in the mountains of the islands of the Caribbean the Indians endured the winter cold with "the help of meats which they eat with many and extremely hot spices." Two weeks later on the other end of Hispaniola, around Samana Bay, he recorded that there is much *ají* (the Arawak word for chile), that he found it stronger than black pepper, and that the locals would not eat anything without it.

Chickpea Cumin Velouté

When I first had this soup, made for me years ago by an Algerian friend, I just couldn't associate it with the Algerian food with which I was already familiar. Partly this was because of the fact that it was a velouté, a French concept. My friend told me that the French had indeed heavily influenced the cuisine of Algeria, but more in terms of method and technique than in flavor, and that this soup was a good example of that. That's why this soup can be eaten either with the chickpeas left whole or creamy as in this recipe, the way I like it. This simple soup, said to be a favorite of Algerian dock workers, is healthy, filling, and has a nice spicy flavor.

3 cups canned chickpeas, drained

1 garlic clove, crushed

1/4 cup extra-virgin olive oil

1 teaspoon ground cumin

1 teaspoon hot paprika

1 teaspoon *Harisa* (page 414)

1 tablespoon tomato paste

Salt and freshly ground black pepper to taste

1 quart water

1. In a medium-size saucepan, cover the chickpeas with water by an inch and bring to a boil, then reduce the heat to medium-low and cook 1 hour to make them more tender. Drain, remove as much of their white skins as possible, and set aside.

2. Put the garlic, olive oil, cumin, paprika, *harisa*, tomato paste, salt, and black pepper in a large saucepan or stockpot. Turn the heat to medium, bring to a simmer, and simmer for 5 minutes, stirring occasionally. Pour in the water and bring to a boil. Add the chickpeas and cook for 15 minutes.

3. Remove the chickpeas with a skimmer and puree them in a food processor until smooth. Return the chickpeas to the soup and stir to blend. Heat for a few minutes and serve immediately.

MAKES 4 SERVINGS

Pepper Soup

This simple Gambian soup from West Africa is said to be able to heal someone with a common cold. No kidding! It is very hot in flavor and will clear up your sinuses instantly. In Gambia, and Ghana, too, where they eat this soup, they also add *utazi* or *ukasi*, a bitter-tasting pale green leaf usually used very sparingly for flavoring pepper soups. For seasoning salt, any supermarket seasoning salt will do, but I think the best of them is Knorr's Aromat, which incidentally is popular in West Africa. It is very nice to spoon in some cooked rice right before serving. Try it with white rice or Rice Pilaf (page 396) if desired. This recipe is adapted from one by a Gambian couple named Ebrima and Kiki Touray.

1 pound chicken thighs on the bone, skin removed and cut into 4 pieces

8 cups water

1 tablespoon freshly ground black pepper

1 tablespoon ground red chile or cayenne pepper

1 tablespoon seasoning salt

1/2 teaspoon garlic salt

1 chicken bouillon cube

One 6-ounce can tomato paste

1. Place the chicken in a large pot and add the water. Bring to just below a boil over high heat, making sure the water never comes to a boil and is only shimmering. After the heat has been on high for 10 minutes, add the black pepper, red chile, seasoning salt, garlic salt, and chicken bouillon cube. Reduce the heat to low and cook at a simmer until there are about 3 cups of broth left, about 1 1/2 hours. At no time should the broth be boiling.

2. Add the tomato paste and stir it in until blended. Cook until the broth is fully blended and slightly thicker, about 10 minutes. Serve immediately.

MAKES 4 SERVINGS

searing soups

the hot spices: mustard seed

When speaking of the spice mustard, one is referring to the seeds of the plant and not the leaves, which are used as a vegetable. Four species of mustard, a member of the cabbage family, are recognized in commercial growing: white or yellow mustard, brown mustard, black mustard, and Ethiopian mustard, but these designations are often confused. The taste of mustard is quite sharp and fiery. The pungency of mustard seed is due to an essential volatile oil—which is not present in the living seed or in dry milled powder, but forms when the crushed seed is mixed with water—called an isothiocyanate. This is also the main ingredient in horseradish, wasabi, arugula, and cress, all of which belong to the same plant family. Isothiocyanates are highly toxic and are used in chemical weaponry. When mixed with water, an enzyme then causes a glucoside (a bitter substance chemically related to sugar) to react with the water, and the hot taste of mustard emerges.

The center of origin of black mustard, common in central and southern Europe, is thought to be Asia Minor and Iran, while white mustard is thought to have originated in the eastern Mediterranean. Mustard or brown mustard is thought to have originated in the Central Asia and Himalaya region, migrating to three secondary centers in India, China, and the Caucasus.

Mustard is one of the oldest spices, with evidence of its use in Sanskrit as well as Sumerian records dating to 3000 B.C., as well as being mentioned frequently in the Bible. In a compilation of Assyrian herbals from the second to first millennium, a variety of mustards are included and called *hadappânu*. The "grain of mustard seed" spoken of in the Gospels of the New Testament is thought by some scholars to be black mustard.

In 334 B.C., Darius III of Persia sent Alexander the Great a bag of sesame seeds, symbolizing the vast number of his army. Alexander in turn sent him a bag of mustard seeds, signifying not only the number but also the powerful energy of his soldiers. The Roman naturalist Pliny described mustard as a medicinal plant and noted that it "has so pungent a flavor that it burns like fire."

In the Middle Ages, there was a kind of drink known as "must" in England that was made from "mustseed," which later transformed into the present day "mustard," a word that comes from the Latin *mustum ardens*, via the Old French. Another theory on the origin of the word proposes that in 1382 Philip the Bold, Duke of Burgundy, granted to the town of Dijon, which has always been known for its mustard, armorial bearings with the motto *Moult Me Tarde*. The arms and motto were adopted as a trademark by the makers of mustard, the motto being shortened to *moult-tarde*, which became the French word *moutarde* and then the English "mustard."

Pigeon Pea and Chile Soup

This soup, from the Indian state of Andhra Pradesh, is a kind of *rasam*, a type of soup popular in south India. It's called *nimmkaiya charu* and uses pigeon peas, a legume probably native to Africa that migrated to India in prehistoric times. The Portuguese took it to the New World. It is a familiar pulse in the tropics and has always been associated with poor people. This soup is certainly not poor, though, as it is spicy hot and very satisfying in winter. Pigeon peas are most likely to be found in whole foods markets, and certainly in Indian markets. In the United States, pigeon peas are grown only as a forage crop for animals. In their place you can use split green peas. The curry leaves, black mustard seeds, and asafoetida can only be found at Indian markets and through the Internet.

1 cup dried pigeon peas or split green peas

$1/2$ teaspoon ground turmeric

3 dried red de arbol chiles

1 teaspoon coriander seeds

1 teaspoon yellow split peas or red lentils

$1/2$ teaspoon black peppercorns

$1/2$ teaspoon cumin seeds

Pinch of asafoetida

1 teaspoon black mustard seeds

2 ripe tomatoes (about $3/4$ pound), cut in half, seeds squeezed out, and grated against the largest holes of a grater

3 fresh green finger-type chiles or 4 green jalapeño chiles, seeded and chopped

1 teaspoon salt

Juice from $1/2$ lemon

4 curry leaves

1. Bring a saucepan of water to a boil and cook the pigeon peas with $1/8$ teaspoon of the turmeric until almost tender, about 15 minutes, stirring frequently. Drain, saving $3/4$ cup of the water, and set aside.

2. Preheat the oven to 450°F. Lay the dried red chiles, coriander seeds, yellow split peas, peppercorns, cumin seeds, and asafoetida on a baking tray, then roast dry until crispy, about 3 minutes. Grind coarsely in a spice mill or mortar and set this spice mix aside. Place the mustard seeds in the pan and roast them too until a few begin to crackle and pop, about 4 minutes. Set them aside separately from the spice mix.

3. In a saucepan, bring 2 cups of water to a boil and add the remaining turmeric, the tomatoes, and the green chiles. Once the water returns to a boil, reduce the heat to medium-low, and cook until slightly reduced, about 15 minutes. Add the spice mix and salt, reduce the heat to low, and cook 10 minutes, stirring occasionally. Add the reserved pigeon peas and water, plus another ¹/₄ cup of water, and leave it to simmer gently until very tender, about 20 minutes. Remove from the heat and pour in the lemon juice. Serve very hot garnished with fresh curry leaves and fried mustard seeds.

MAKES 6 SERVINGS

Hot and Sour Shrimp Soup

This dish, known as *tom yam gung* (also transliterated in several other ways), is a very hot shrimp soup that appears on many restaurant menus both in Thailand and in the West and literally means "boil mix shrimp." It is a simple, light soup from the central and southern regions of Thailand, where freshly caught shrimp are plentiful. It tastes very fresh from four main flavors—hot, sour, sweet, and salty. This soup can be made with ingredients other than shrimp, such as chicken, fish, or mushrooms. Some cooks use a combination of fresh and dried chiles in this soup, usually a good amount of *prik kee nu* (literally, "mouse-dropping chiles," also known as scuds or bird's-eye chiles) and fresh chiles such as *prik kee fa* (literally, "sky-pointing chiles"), known in the United States as Thai chiles. There are several things you need to pay attention to when making this soup in order for it to be memorable. First, use fresh shrimp with their heads and cook the shrimp as briefly as possible (if using defrosted shrimp the same rule applies). Second, use fresh ingredients if possible. And third, don't let the lime juice boil.

1 pound fresh jumbo shrimp with their heads, heads and shells removed and reserved, or ¹/₂ pound (about 10) headless jumbo shrimp, shells removed and reserved

4 cups lightly salted water

25 dried bird's-eye chiles or 3 dried red de arbol chiles

2 tablespoons Thai fish sauce

2 lemongrass stalks, tough outer portion removed and finely chopped or thinly sliced

1 tablespoon finely chopped fresh galangal or ginger

3 kaffir lime leaves or lemon leaves, thinly sliced, or 1 teaspoon lime zest

3 tablespoons fresh lime juice

4 tablespoons coarsely chopped fresh coriander (cilantro) leaves

10 fresh or canned straw mushrooms

thai chiles in thailand

According to Christine Jacquat, author of *Plants from the Markets of Thailand* (Duang Kamol, 1990), the chiles of Thailand, all of which are the same name for *Capsicum frutescens* L., the South American native, are *prik kee nu, khree, deeplee, kheenok, prik kee nok, pa-kaeo, prik, prik dae, prik tae, prik nok, ma-ra-tee, mue-saa-see-suu, mue-saa-pho,* and *mak phet.*

1. Rinse the heads and/or shells of the shrimp. Place the heads and/or shells in a medium-size saucepan and pour the water over them. Bring to a boil, then reduce the heat to low, and simmer for 20 minutes. If using fresh shrimp heads, small rivulets of orange-colored oil from the tomalley will rise to the surface—this is where so much flavor resides. Strain the broth through a strainer, pressing out the liquid from the heads and/or shells with the back of a wooden spoon. Return the broth to a clean large saucepan. Slightly bruise the bird's-eye chiles in a mortar with a pestle. (This is not necessary if using dried red de arbol chiles.)

2. Bring the shrimp broth to a boil and season with 1 tablespoon of the fish sauce. Add the bird's-eye chiles, lemongrass, galangal, and lime leaves to the broth. Stir, cook 1 minute, then add the shrimp and cook on medium-high for 2 minutes, then reduce the heat to low and simmer until they turn pink-orange and are firm, another 2 minutes.

3. Meanwhile, in a soup tureen, stir together the remaining 1 tablespoon fish sauce, the bruised chiles, lime juice, and coriander. Pour the soup into the tureen and stir. Add the straw mushrooms and let sit 2 minutes. Serve hot.

MAKES 4 SERVINGS

searing soups

coconut milk and coconut cream

You will encounter these two ingredients in this book and they may seem utterly mystifying. They are both very simple and can be made at home. Coconut cream, or thick coconut milk, refers to the liquid left over from the first pressing of grated or shredded coconut that has steeped in boiling water. When this thick coconut milk is refrigerated, a very thick liquid, almost a solid, rises to the top, and this is called coconut cream. Coconut milk, or thin coconut milk, is the liquid left over after repeated pressings of the same coconut gratings with more boiling water. Although it is best to make these varieties of coconut milk with freshly shredded coconut, you can also use dried unsweetened shredded coconut, usually available at Indian markets (the shredded coconut found in supermarkets often tends to be sweetened). Many supermarkets now sell canned coconut milk, which is not as good a product as freshly made—the canned product uses preservatives and flour as a thickener and its taste is a little "off"—but you can still use it without harming the overall taste of the dish. The canned product can be used as a substitute for both thick and thin coconut milk. To make two cups of coconut milk, soak two cups of shredded coconut in three cups boiling water. This same amount will produce about a quarter cup of coconut cream. Both must be refrigerated and will go bad if not frozen after several days.

Coconut Chicken Soup

This refreshing yet rich northern Thai soup is called *tom kha gai*. It is quite easy to prepare and much of the flavor comes from the garnish that is stirred with the soup after it is cooked: the fresh lime juice, the chiles, the coriander leaves, and the *nam prik pao*, a roasted chile curry paste that can be bought in most supermarkets (for a homemade version, see page 423).

2 cups coconut milk (see box at left)

6 thin slices fresh galangal or 4 slices ginger

2 lemongrass stalks, tender parts only, chopped and crushed in a mortar

5 fresh kaffir lime leaves, torn in half, or 1 tablespoon lime zest

³/₄ pound boneless and skinless chicken breast, thinly sliced

5 tablespoons Thai fish sauce

2 tablespoons palm sugar or granulated sugar

¹/₂ cup fresh lime juice

1 teaspoon Red Curry Paste (page 423)

¹/₄ cup coarsely chopped fresh coriander (cilantro) leaves

25 fresh green bird's-eye chiles or 15 fresh green Thai chiles or 8 green serrano chiles, crushed in a mortar

1. In a wok or large saucepan, combine 1 cup of the coconut milk with the galangal, lemongrass, and lime leaves and bring to a boil. Add the chicken, fish sauce, and sugar, reduce the heat to medium, and simmer until the chicken is white and firm, about 4 minutes. Add the remaining 1 cup coconut milk and heat to just below boiling, about 3 minutes.

2. Divide the lime juice and curry paste into individual serving bowls and ladle the soup over them. Garnish each bowl with the coriander leaves and crushed chile peppers. Serve immediately.

MAKES 4 SERVINGS

searing soups

Thai Mushroom and Chile Soup

Tom kaeng het is one among many types of mushroom soups that Thai cooks make. There are numerous edible fungi in Thailand, and many of them would be completely intimidating and unfamiliar to an American. Your best choice is to use oyster mushrooms and wood's ear mushrooms, both of which are readily available in American supermarkets (as is fish sauce), and they taste good and distinctive. If your market has them, use fresh lemon basil leaves for the garnish, as they provide a delicate and fragrant touch.

1/4 cup dried bird's-eye chiles or dried red de arbol chiles, chopped or crumbled

2 tablespoons chopped lemongrass, tender part only

1/2 teaspoon salt

1 cup water

3 whole salted anchovies or 6 anchovy fillets

3 cups vegetable broth (homemade or canned)

3 ounces oyster mushrooms, coarsely chopped

2 ounces wood's ear mushrooms, coarsely chopped

2 tablespoons Thai fish sauce

1/2 cup coarsely chopped loosely packed fresh basil leaves

4 to 6 thin slices fresh ginger

1. In a mortar, pound the chiles, lemongrass, and salt until a paste. Bring the water to a boil with the salted anchovies and, once they break down completely and there is only 1/4 cup of liquid remaining, turn off the heat and strain, saving the liquid.

2. In a saucepan, bring the vegetable broth to a boil with the anchovy liquid and the chile mixture. Add the mushrooms and fish sauce, reduce the heat to low, and simmer until the mushrooms are tender, about 10 minutes. Remove from the heat and serve garnished with some basil and a slice of ginger.

MAKES 4 TO 6 SERVINGS

 # Beef and Chile Soup

Tripe lovers, this is for you! Others need not apply. This hot clear soup from Issaan, or northeastern Thailand, is called *jael houen*. The beef tripe used in this dish is the paunch or rumen, the smooth-surfaced first stomach, of a ruminant, a cud-chewing animal. It is not the more commonly found honeycomb tripe, or second stomach, that is usually found in the market. But, as I have a local supermarket in California that sometimes carries it, you might find it, too. Likely you will need to order it through a good butcher or shop for it at a Chinese, Thai, or Southeast Asian market. It needs to be parboiled until soft first, which may take four to seven hours, and then the "skin" can be peeled off. When you chew it, it should melt in your mouth—keep in mind that that is a lot of precooking. Ideally, you can precook the tripe a previous day and finish this dish on the day you want to serve it. Thai cooks use a variety of leafy greens in this soup, especially morning glory, a kind of swamp spinach, but regular spinach is perfect here.

2 tablespoons jasmine rice or long-grain rice

1 pound cooked beef tripe (cooked 4 to 7 hours), cut into 1 x 1/4-inch strips

1 pound beef round (London broil), cut into 1 x 1/4-inch slices

6 cups water

One 1-inch cube fresh ginger, peeled and thinly sliced

3 lemongrass stalks, tender parts only, chopped and lightly pounded in a mortar

5 kaffir lime leaves, very thinly sliced, or 2 teaspoons lime zest

1/4 cup Thai fish sauce

1 tablespoon beef broth (homemade or canned) or broth from the cooked tripe

1 small shallot, thinly sliced

2 tablespoons red chile flakes

1/4 cup fresh lime juice

1 cup torn loosely packed fresh basil leaves

2 cups chopped spinach with no heavy stems

2 tablespoons chopped fresh coriander (cilantro) leaves

2 scallions, thinly sliced on the bias

1. Preheat a small cast-iron skillet over medium-high heat, then dry roast the rice in the skillet until light brown, about 2 minutes, stirring. Remove and let cool, then grind it to a coarse powder in a spice mill.

2. In a large saucepan, combine the cooked tripe, beef round, water, ginger, lemongrass, and lime leaves and turn the heat to medium-low. Once it is bubbling, in about 30 minutes, continue to simmer until the beef is tender, about another 30 minutes.

searing soups

3. Turn the heat to high, bring the soup to a boil, and add the fish sauce and beef broth. Remove from the heat and add the shallot, rice powder, chile flakes, and lime juice. Stir and let sit 5 minutes. Place the basil and spinach in individual bowls, ladle the soup over it, and garnish with coriander and scallions. Serve immediately.

MAKES 6 SERVINGS

the hot spices: galangal

Galangal, of which there are two kinds, greater galangal and lesser galangal, are in the same family as ginger. The part of the plant most used for spicing is the rhizome or root stock that is very much like ginger. Some cooks liken the taste of galangal to a mixture of ginger, black pepper, and sour lemon. It is used both fresh and dried. The dried form tends to be "spicier" and more pungent. Galangal is used especially in the cooking of the Indonesian archipelago and the Malay peninsula, including southern Thailand and to a lesser extent in the rest of Indochina. Galangal probably originated in southern China and traveled to Indochina, Thailand, Malaysia, and Indonesia, where it is cultivated today. The English word "galangal" derives from the Arabic name for the plant, *khulunjan*, which in turn may be a mutation of the Chinese *liang-kiang*, meaning "mild ginger." Galangal seems to have anti-emetic properties and is so used in local medicinal treatments.

Lesser galangal is less pungent than greater galangal and is used in the same cuisines. As it is only used in Malesian cuisine (the cuisine of Malaysia, Singapore, and Indonesia), it is nearly impossible to find it other than in expatriate communities or in Thai markets.

Coconut Milk Seafood Soup with Rice Noodles

T his mixed seafood stew from Malaysia is called *laksa lemak* and is often eaten as a breakfast food. But it is not usually made in the home or in restaurants. Many Malays will tell you that the best *laksa* is made at the countless open-air cafés or at the street-food carts run by itinerant vendors. A major flavor in the soup comes from the laksa leaf, which is also known as Vietnamese or holy mint and is a plant from the buckwheat family. Some writers tell us that laksa leaf is also called marsh pepper, knotweed, or Vietnamese coriander and is water pepper. Alan Davidson in his *Oxford Companion to Food* (Oxford University Press, 1999) argues that the name of the dish refers not to the herb but to the noodles, derives from the Persian word for noodles, and arrived with Muslim traders perhaps as early as the fourteenth century. The herb *laksa* does have a unique taste that is replaced here with coriander, although you should first search local Vietnamese or Thai markets as they will sometimes carry it.

This is a classic dish from the Nonya cuisine of Malaysia, the cuisine that results from the blending of Chinese wok cooking with the local spices of the Malays. The name came about when Chinese traders and merchants began to arrive in the Malay peninsula in the early seventeenth century and married Malay women who were known as Nonya, denoting a woman of prominent social standing. These women spoke a patois of Chinese and Malay and began to experiment with a culinary blend of Chinese and Malay cooking in Penang, Malacca, and Singapore that came to be known as Nonya cooking. Some cooks like to add thin strips of omelet to the garnishes (step 6 on page 337). The flavors of this soup are typical of what you would find in Singapore, southern Malaysia, and Sarawak in eastern Malaysia, which have coconut-based curry soups versus the clear tamarind sourish *laksa* you find in Penang in northern Malaysia. This version probably originated in Malacca, as one can see some Indian influences in the curry-like broth. Traditionally, the soup is eaten with chopsticks and a large Chinese-type soup spoon. You may find the fishcakes called for in the recipe in your supermarket shelved with other refrigerated Asian items like tofu.

5 tablespoons peanut oil

1 pound fresh large shrimp with their heads or 1/2 pound headless shrimp, heads and/or shells removed, drained, and saved for making broth

10 cups water and more as needed

2 tablespoons salt, or more to your taste

6 dried red de arbol chiles, broken in half

1 large fresh red finger-type chile or 2 red jalapeño chiles, chopped

2 tablespoons dried whole shrimp or 2 tablespoons shrimp paste (*blacan*)

6 shallots, chopped

One 2-inch cube fresh or brined galangal, peeled and chopped, or one 1-inch cube fresh ginger, peeled and chopped, or 1 teaspoon ground ginger

6 macadamia nuts

2 lemongrass stalks, tough outer portion removed and tender part chopped

1 teaspoon ground turmeric

1 tablespoon ground coriander

6 cups coconut milk (see page 90)

Freshly ground black pepper to taste

One 14-ounce package prepared fishcakes (see page 433), sliced into strips, or 14 ounces imitation crabmeat

6 ounces fresh crabmeat, picked over

3/4 pound rice vermicelli

1/2 pound fresh bean sprouts, tails pulled off if desired, washed well and drained

1 cucumber, peeled, seeded, and cut into matchsticks

1 small bunch fresh coriander (cilantro) leaves, leaves removed and cut into fine strips

1/2 recipe Sambal Ulek (page 425)

3 fresh limes, cut in half

1.　In a large saucepan, heat 1 tablespoon of the peanut oil over medium-high heat, then add the shrimp heads and/or shells and cook until they turn pink-orange, stirring. Add 10 cups water and 1 tablespoon of the salt, bring to a boil, then reduce the heat to low and simmer, covered, until reduced by one-third, about 1 hour. Strain the broth and reserve, discarding the shells and heads.

2.　Meanwhile, in a small skillet, heat 1 tablespoon of the oil over medium-high heat, then cook the shrimp until they turn pink-orange, about 2 minutes, salting as they cook and tossing and stirring. Remove the shrimp and set aside. Add 2 tablespoons water to the skillet to deglaze it and pour into the shrimp broth.

3.　Soak the dried chiles and dried shrimp in hot water for 10 minutes. Drain, but save the water. Put the chiles, dried shrimp, shallots, galangal, macadamia nuts, and lemongrass in a blender and run for a few seconds, then add about 1/2 cup of the chile and shrimp soaking water to allow the blades to twirl and blend until a smooth puree.

4. In a large, heavy stockpot or large wok, heat the remaining 3 tablespoons oil over medium-high heat, then cook the pureed mixture from the blender until bubbling and fragrant, about 3 minutes, stirring. Add the turmeric and coriander and stir-fry for a minute longer. Add the reserved shrimp broth, bring to a boil, then reduce the heat to low and simmer, uncovered, for 30 minutes.

5. Add the coconut milk, season with 1 tablespoon or more of salt and pepper, then add the sliced fishcakes and fresh crabmeat and increase the heat so the broth is just shimmering. Let it simmer while you prepare the rice vermicelli.

6. Meanwhile, bring 2 quarts of water to a boil, and then pour it over the rice vermicelli in a bowl and leave the noodles to soak for 10 minutes. Drain and add the vermicelli to the soup.

7. Place a ladleful or more of the soup into large individual bowls and top each with bean sprouts, cucumber strips, a couple of shrimp, and some coriander leaves. Serve the sambal on the side with halved limes.

MAKES 6 TO 8 SERVINGS

sichuan chile paste

There are two kinds of Sichuan chile pastes called for in the Sichuan recipes in this book. The first is chile paste (*lajiao jiang*) and the second is chile bean paste (*dou ban jinag*). The first one, chile paste, is made with mashed chiles and garlic and has the consistency of a thick sauce. The second, chile bean paste, is a fermented paste made from chiles, beans, garlic, and other ingredients, for example, sesame seeds. In Sichuan, there are different varieties of these two basic pastes. Although these two chile pastes are available on the Internet, you may be surprised to find jars of them being sold in your local supermarket in the international/Asian section. Many of these products will be shelved near the hoisin sauce and soy sauce, and many are imported by a Taiwanese company. They may be labeled "Szechwan chili sauce with garlic" or "hot chili paste with garlic" or "hot chile bean paste." If you can't find the ones with beans, add a little miso to the "Szechwan chili sauce with garlic" jar. You can also make a reasonable mock version of it for yourself and keep it in the refrigerator. It's certainly not hard to do. In a wok, heat 2 tablespoons of vegetable oil over high heat, then stir-fry 4 finely chopped garlic cloves, a 1-inch cube of finely chopped fresh ginger, and half of an onion, also finely chopped, all for about 20 seconds. Add 1 cup of finely chopped fresh red chiles and 1/4 cup of Chinese black vinegar (also called Chinkiang vinegar), reduce the heat to medium-low, and simmer until dense, about 15 minutes, stirring occasionally. Add 2 tablespoons rice wine and some salt, cook another 5 minutes, then let it cool. Place in a blender and run until smooth, then jar or bottle it and store in the refrigerator.

Daikon and Pork Soup

This soup is typically served at the end of the meal in order to cleanse the palate of the rich tastes of the main dishes. Fuchsia Dunlop tells us in *Land of Plenty* (W. W. Norton, 2003) that the name of this soup is *lian guo tang* and means something like "even the soup in the cooking pot." She speculates that it may refer to the fact that the soup pot was brought to the table to finish the meal. Generally, a soup at the end of the meal will not be very salty, and the radish and pork will be lifted out of the broth. This dish is searing hot and will certainly cleanse your palate—and probably more.

2 quarts water

1 pound boneless pork butt or shoulder, in 1 piece

One 1-inch cube fresh ginger

2 scallions, halved lengthwise

1 teaspoon Sichuan peppercorns

3 tablespoons peanut oil

1 cup halved and seeded dried red de arbol chiles

3 tablespoons Sichuan chile bean paste (see box at left)

2 tablespoon soy sauce

1 tablespoon Chile Oil (page 424)

1/2 teaspoon red chile flakes

1 pound daikon, cut into 2-inch pieces and thinly sliced

Salt and freshly ground black pepper to taste (optional)

1. In a large saucepan, bring the water to a boil over high heat and add the pork. After a few minutes, skim the foam from the pot and add the ginger, 3 scallion halves, and 1/2 teaspoon of the Sichuan peppercorns. Reduce the heat to medium and simmer until the pork is almost cooked, about 20 minutes. Remove the pork and set aside to cool. Strain the broth, removing all solid particles, and reserve the liquid. Finely chop the remaining 1/2 scallion and set aside for the garnish.

2. In a wok, heat the peanut oil over medium heat, then add the chiles and remaining 1/2 teaspoon Sichuan peppercorns and stir-fry until a little darker, about 30 seconds. Remove with a skimmer and set aside. Add the chile bean paste and stir-fry for 1 minute, until the oil is deep red. Transfer to a medium-size bowl.

3. Add the chiles to the bowl with the chile paste, along with the soy sauce, chile oil, and red chile flakes, and mix well. Divide this mixture among 6 soup bowls. Slice the pork into very thin slices.

4. Return the broth to a boil over high heat, add the daikon, reduce the heat to low, and simmer until tender, about 12 minutes. Add the pork and simmer for 2 minutes. Season with salt and pepper if desired. Ladle the soup into the bowls, garnish with the remaining chopped ¹/₂ scallion, and serve hot.

MAKES 6 SERVINGS

Sichuan Firepot

The Sichuan firepot is a popular and communal dish that you will encounter in the restaurants of Chengdu and in many Sichuan restaurants in America. The firepot, or hotpot, is a fondue-like pot or wok filled with an oily, rich red broth bobbing with fiery chiles that sits in the center of the table. Arranged around the firepot are small plates of different ingredients, from vegetables to offal. Diners select the food they want to eat and place it in the broth to cook, removing the cooked food with their chopsticks and dipping it in a seasoned sesame oil and garlic dip. In Chongqing, a restaurant might offer the following items as food to be dipped: beef tripe, cow's throat tendons (*huang hou*), squid, crucian carp, hairtail fish (*dai yu*), eels, loaches (*ni qiu*), poultry gizzards, sliced pig's kidneys, smoked bacon, Sichuanese cured sausage (*xiang gu*), rabbit's kidneys, rabbit's stomachs, fatty beef, goose intestines, pig's intestines, pig's brains, crispy pork, meatballs, tender beef, various mushrooms, white seaweed, lettuce stems, lotus roots, winter melon, bamboo shoots, potatoes, sheet seaweed, yam jelly, sweet potato noodles, cauliflower, jellied duck's blood, wood ear fungus, bean curd skin, bean sprouts, Chinese cabbage, water spinach, lily buds, rice jelly, duck tongues, frogs, and chicken kidneys.

Place the pot in the center of the table using a fondue burner. Give every diner a small rice bowl and chopsticks. It might be easiest to make the broth the day before. If you decide to use chicken breast and pork tenderloin for dipping, you will want to partially freeze them so that you can slice them paper thin. Remember that when you are eating, the ingredients should be thinly sliced or small enough so that no ingredient takes longer than 30 seconds to cook.

FOR THE BROTH

4 quarts water

2 pounds beef bones, with meat on them

1 pound chicken wings

One 2-inch piece fresh ginger, peeled and cut in half

3 scallions, cut in half

FOR THE FIREPOT

1/4 cup fermented black beans (see page 433)

6 tablespoons rice wine

1/2 cup peanut oil

2/3 cup dried red chiles, halved and seeded

2/3 cup rendered beef fat, duck fat, or pork lard or a combination of two or more

1/2 cup Sichuan chile bean paste (see page 98)

One 1-inch cube fresh ginger, finely chopped

1 tablespoon sugar

5 teaspoons salt

2 teaspoons Sichuan peppercorns

FOR THE DIPPING SAUCE

1 head of garlic, cloves separated, peeled, and finely chopped

3 tablespoons sesame oil

6 tablespoons peanut oil

1/2 teaspoon salt

FOR THE FOODS TO BE COOKED (CHOOSE AT LEAST 5)

1/2 pound boneless pork tenderloin, very thinly sliced

1/2 pound boneless chicken breasts, very thinly sliced

1/2 pound cooked Chinese sausages, sliced

1/2 pound extra firm tofu, cut into small cubes

1/2 pound shiitake mushrooms, cut in half or quarters if large

1/2 pound small button mushrooms

1/2 pound sliced turnips

1/2 pound sliced daikon

1/2 pound cauliflower, cut into small florets

1/2 pound broccoli, cut into small florets

1/2 pound veal brain, sliced

1/2 pound squid, cut into bite-sized rings

1/2 pound medium-size shrimp, shelled

1. To make the broth, place the water, beef bones, chicken wings, ginger, and scallions in a large stockpot and bring to a boil. Reduce the heat to low and simmer for at least 4 hours. Strain through a cheesecloth-lined sieve and discard the bones, meat, and vegetables. Refrigerate the broth until needed.

2. Prepare the firepot. In a food processor, mash the black beans with 1 tablespoon of the rice wine until a smooth paste. Set aside.

3. In a large wok, heat 3 tablespoons of the peanut oil over medium heat until it is nearly smoking, then stir-fry the chiles until crisp and fragrant but not too darkened, 20 to 30 seconds. Remove the chiles with a slotted spoon and set aside. Discard the oil in the wok and wipe clean with a paper towel.

4. In the wok, melt the beef fat over low heat. Increase the heat to medium and, when the fat begins to smoke, add the chile bean paste and cook until the paste is sizzling gently and is a rich red, about 1 minute, stirring constantly. Add the reserved black bean paste and ginger and continue to cook for another minute, stirring and breaking up and blending the beans into the sauce. Pour in $1^{1}/_{2}$ quarts of the reserved broth, saving the remaining broth to replenish the firepot when serving. Bring the broth to a boil over high heat. Add the sugar, the remaining 5 tablespoons rice wine, and the salt and stir. Add the chiles and Sichuan peppercorns, reduce the heat to medium-low, and simmer for 20 minutes.

5. Meanwhile, prepare the dipping sauce. In a small serving bowl, stir together the chopped garlic, sesame oil, peanut oil, and salt.

6. Transfer the boiling broth to the fondue pot and place on a burner in the center of the table. Cover the fondue pot and allow the broth to return to a boil before starting to cook the food. As the liquid evaporates, add some more broth. Place the various foods to be cooked in the pot and cook 15 to 45 seconds, depending on the ingredient.

MAKES 6 SERVINGS

Spicy Chicken and Potato Stew

This bright red and inviting soupy stew is called *dak jo lim* in Korean and is a wonderful wintertime dish. The stew cooks slowly until the chicken is very tender and falling off the bone. For this reason, it is important that if you are using a young chicken, the broth must never come to a boil. The Korean red chile paste (*koch'ujang*) can be found in Korean markets or via the Internet.

2¹/₂ pounds chicken breast, leg, and thigh on the bone, skin removed, cut up into fist-size pieces, and rinsed

2 teaspoons salt

1 tablespoon freshly ground black pepper

1 tablespoon sake or rice wine (*mirin*) or vermouth

¹/₄ cup ground Korean red chile or 2¹/₂ tablespoons cayenne pepper

¹/₄ cup Korean red chile paste (*koch'ujang*)

5 large garlic cloves, finely chopped

1 tablespoon soy sauce

2 quarts water

2 large boiling potatoes (about 1 pound), peeled and cut into chunks

2 carrots, cut into large pieces

1 medium-size onion, sliced ¹/₃ inch thick

3 scallions, sliced on the bias in ¹/₂-inch slices

2 fresh green jalapeño chiles, sliced on the bias

1. In a large glass or ceramic bowl, toss the chicken pieces in the salt, 2 teaspoons of the black pepper, and sake and leave to marinate for 15 minutes. In a small bowl, mix together the ground Korean red chile, Korean red chile paste, garlic, soy sauce, and the remaining 1 teaspoon black pepper.

2. Put the chicken into a large pot, cover with the water, and bring to a near boil over high heat. Pour the chile mixture over the chicken and stir to mix. Reduce the heat to low and cook the chicken, uncovered, until nearly falling off the bone, about 2 hours, without ever letting the broth come to a boil. The broth should only be shimmering on top.

3. Add the potatoes, carrots, and onion and cook until tender, about another hour. Add the scallions and chiles and cook another 5 minutes. Serve immediately.

MAKES 6 SERVINGS

searing soups

Korean Clam Soup

This simple preparation is called *jo gae gook* in Korean. It involves almost nothing to make and yet it is beautiful to look at and its tastes are hot and straightforward. This is a recipe I would recommend to someone who has never made Korean food, because it's very easy and tastes very Korean and will be as good as anything you could order in a Korean restaurant.

1 quart water

10 small littleneck or Manila clams, cleaned

2 teaspoons salt

1¹/₂ teaspoons ground Korean red chile or 1 teaspoon ground red chile

3 ounces firm tofu, diced

1 scallion, white and green parts, cut on the bias in ¹/₄-inch slices

1 fresh red jalapeño chile, chopped

Pour the water into a pot with the clams. Bring to a boil, reduce the heat to medium, and, just after the clams open up, take them out with a slotted spoon. Discard any clams that remain firmly shut. Add the salt, ground chile, tofu, and scallion to the broth, and cook for another minute. Put the clams back in the pot and heat for 1 minute. Serve garnished with the fresh chopped chile.

MAKES 2 TO 4 SERVINGS

KOREAN RED CHILE

This flaky dried red chile powder is ubiquitous in Korean cooking, and it can be bought in Korean markets and via the Internet. But this chile mixture, which is bright red and mildly hot, is so similar to a particular kind of Mexican chili powder that you might be able to get away with this substitution. The one I'm thinking of is made with equal parts dried ground pasilla chile, New Mexico Hot (a kind of Anaheim chile), and California chile (another kind of Anaheim chile), and should say so on the label ingredients.

 # Crab and Miso Soup

This is a very satisfying soup and I imagine it would be perfect on a cold day in the late fall. I use the Japanese word *miso* in the name of this recipe for the fermented soybean paste that is used because it is more familiar to us, but in this Korean soup, called *toenjang jiege keh*, the same fermented product is known as *toenjang* in Korean. One can find it in Korean markets, but the Japanese miso may be more readily available in supermarkets. This recipe comes from Kwangju, where cooks like salty and spicy hot food. To prepare the crab, clip off the big claws, wash the crab, turn it over so the bottom is facing up, and pull out the gills and inner viscera and discard. Wash the crab again and crack the claws. Serve the soup in individual bowls with rice on the side if desired.

2 cups water

2 tablespoons miso (fermented soybean paste, *toenjang*)

1/2 pound firm tofu, cut into 1/2-inch cubes

1 tablespoon ground Korean red chile or 2 teaspoons cayenne pepper

One 1/8-inch slice fresh ginger

1 small onion, thinly sliced

2 large garlic cloves, crushed

2 live blue crabs or 1 Dungeness crab (about 1 3/4 pounds), prepared for cooking as described above

1 small zucchini, peeled and cut into 1/8-inch-thick slices

2 teaspoons salt

1 fresh red jalapeño chile, sliced

1. Put the water and miso in a saucepan and turn the heat to low. Cover and simmer until blended, about 10 minutes, stirring occasionally. Add the tofu and cook 5 more minutes.

2. Add the chile, ginger, onion, garlic, crabs, zucchini, and salt and bring to a boil over high heat. Turn with a spoon several times to blend the ingredients, being careful not to break the tofu. Cover, reduce the heat to low, and simmer until the crabs are cooked through and the vegetables are soft, 25 to 30 minutes. Garnish with the fresh red chile and serve hot.

MAKES 4 SERVINGS

searing soups

Noodle Soup with Seafood and Kimchi

This Korean recipe, given to me by my friend Unjoo Lee Byars, is called *oh jingoe gook soo*. The noodles you use in this dish should be very thin vermicelli-style Asian noodles made from mung bean flour. Usually they are sold in the international/Asian section of supermarkets, and the label might say "bean threads." Remember that this dish gets served immediately after cooking. If you wait, you will no longer have a soup because the noodles will absorb all the broth. The imitation crabmeat called for in this dish might seem ridiculous for someone concerned with the authentic, but Unjoo assures me that the use of imitation crabmeat, a processed product made from pollack, is popular and common in Korea because it is much less expensive than real crab. The dried anchovies can be found in Asian markets and on the Internet.

7 cups water

16 dried anchovies

1/4 cup kimchi, liquid squeezed out and chopped

3 large garlic cloves, finely chopped

1 tablespoon ground Korean red chile or 2 teaspoons ground red chile

5 small squid (about 6 ounces), cleaned and sliced into rings with their tentacles

2 bunches (4 1/2 ounces) Asian vermicelli noodles

1/2 medium-size onion, cut into 1/4-inch slices

4 scallions, diagonally sliced into 1-inch pieces

4 shiitake mushrooms, halved

1/4 pound imitation crabmeat, sliced diagonally into 1/2-inch pieces

6 headless medium-size shrimp, shells removed

1 teaspoon soy sauce

2 teaspoons salt

1 teaspoon freshly ground black pepper

1. Bring the water to a boil in a large saucepan over high heat with the dried anchovies, then reduce the heat to medium and simmer for 10 minutes.

2. Add the kimchi, garlic, and chile and cook for 1 minute, then add the squid and bring to a boil. Add the noodles, onion, scallions, mushrooms, imitation crabmeat, and shrimp and boil until the noodles are cooked, about 5 minutes. Sprinkle with soy sauce, salt, and pepper and serve.

MAKES 4 SERVINGS

electrifying eggs

Even eggs get the hot treatment in super-spicy cuisines of the world. One might think that this couldn't possibly work, but try these recipes and you will be won over to the delectable tastes of eggs cooked with spices. Many people have already tasted Huevos Rancheros (page 109) for breakfast, but these recipes are definitely not just for breakfast. In various cuisines egg dishes are eaten for midday meals, appetizers, snacks, and dinners. Just try the Indian Chile Eggs (page 115) and you will see how satisfying these are at any time of the day.

Chorizo Sausage with Scrambled Eggs

This Mexican dish is one of my favorite egg dishes. You can easily eat this as a light dinner as well as for breakfast. Many people like to eat these eggs with their hands, by layering the eggs in the warm tortilla and rolling it up. The Mexican cheeses called for here may seem hard to find, but they are increasingly being sold in many supermarkets these days—just look for them. Of course, they are also available via the Internet.

1 tablespoon corn oil

1 pound chorizo sausage, casings removed and crumbled

1 small onion, finely chopped

1 large ripe tomato, peeled, seeded, and chopped

2 fresh green jalapeño chiles, finely chopped

8 large eggs

Salt to taste

1/2 cup crumbled Mexican *queso fresco*, *queso panela*, or farmer's cheese (optional)

4 warm flour tortillas

1. In a large nonstick skillet, heat the corn oil over medium heat, then cook the sausage until well done, about 10 minutes, breaking up the lumps of meat with a wooden spoon as you stir and toss. Remove the sausage with a slotted spoon and pour off all but 1 or 2 tablespoons of the remaining fat. Add the onion, tomato, and chiles and cook until the onion softens, 6 to 8 minutes, stirring. Return the sausage to the skillet.

2. Meanwhile, in a bowl, beat the eggs very lightly with some salt, so that the yolks and whites are just combined, then pour into the skillet and cook over medium heat, stirring occasionally, until the eggs have set and are between wet and dry, about 5 minutes. Transfer to a serving platter, sprinkle the cheese over the top, and serve immediately with tortillas.

MAKES 4 SERVINGS

Huevos Rancheros

I n Mexican cooking, *rancheros* refers to a dish prepared ranch style, which means, generally, country style, farmhouse style, or rustic. Huevos rancheros are always served with refried beans, a slice of orange, and corn tortillas. The chiles used in this dish will depend on who is making it. So, for instance, in the Yucatán you are likely to find it made with the superhot habanero chile, while serrano or chipotle chiles may be used elsewhere. I like to use canned chipotle chiles because I'm fond of the adobo sauce they come in, or serrano chiles for their taste and color. The tortillas used should be slightly stale, so if you don't have any stale ones, take some fresh or frozen ones out and leave them exposed to the air as you start preparing the recipe.

1 tablespoon lard or unsalted butter

1¹/₂ pounds ripe plum tomatoes, peeled, seeded, and coarsely chopped

3 chipotle chiles in adobo, chopped, or 6 fresh green serrano chiles, chopped

¹/₂ small onion, chopped

1 large garlic clove, finely chopped

¹/₂ teaspoon salt, or more to your taste

¹/₄ cup vegetable oil

4 stale corn tortillas

8 large eggs

Freshly ground black pepper to taste

¹/₄ cup crumbled Mexican *queso fresco*, *queso ranchero*, or farmer's cheese

1 tablespoon finely chopped fresh parsley leaves (optional)

1. In a medium-size skillet, heat the lard over medium-high heat, then add the tomatoes, chiles, onion, and garlic and cook for 5 minutes, stirring. Season with salt and set aside, keeping it warm.

2. In a 12-inch nonstick skillet, heat the vegetable oil over medium-high heat until nearly smoking, then cook the tortillas only until they are soft, about 3 seconds a side, turning once with tongs. As they finish cooking, pat them with paper towels, then wrap in aluminum foil to keep warm.

3. Reduce the heat under the large skillet to medium-low, giving it 5 minutes to reach that lower temperature. Break the eggs into the skillet and cook sunny-side up, or let them cook a minute and then break them up by stirring with a wooden spoon. Season with salt and pepper.

the piquant cuisine of mexico

Before Columbus, a number of great Indian civilizations existed in Mexico. The Mayan civilization was one of the great world civilizations with a highly accurate calendar, hieroglyphic writing, knowledge of mathematics, and the beginnings of stone architecture. Other civilizations were the Toltec, the Olmec, the Mixtec in Oaxaca and the related Zapotecs. The Aztec civilization was perhaps the greatest that dominated central Mexico at the time of the Spanish conquest. Their civilization was based on advanced agriculture, universal education, stone wheels, weaving, sculpture, metalwork, music, engineering, and picture writing.

By 1521 Hernán Cortés had conquered Mexico for the Spanish Crown. The Spanish had set out from Cuba, where they already knew the chile by the name *ají*. In Mexico, they discovered that the chile was called *chilli*, a Nahuatl word and the root of our word "chile."

Archaeologists have found wild chile seeds in human settlements in the desert valley of Tehuacán, 150 miles south of Mexico City, dating to 7000 B.C. But by 5200 B.C. Indians were cultivating chiles.

Our knowledge of the food of the Aztecs at the time of the conquest of Mexico in the sixteenth century derives from chronicles such as Bernardino de Sahagún's *Historia general de las cosas de la nueva españa* (*General History of the Things of New Spain*), a treasure trove of culinary anthropology. He tells of sauce made with red chiles and tomatoes and thickened with ground pumpkinseeds and called *pipián*, as it is still known today. A variety of casseroles also contained chiles, such as one made of whitefish with yellow chile and tomatoes and another with a dark fish made with red chile and tomatoes and ground squash seeds, "which is very good to eat." He also tells us that for the festival of the jaguar god Tezcatlipoca the Aztecs stuffed tamales with beans

4. Place 1 tortilla on each of 4 plates. Top each tortilla with 2 fried eggs, then spoon the sauce over the tortillas and whites of the eggs, leaving the yolk exposed (if you have made sunny-side-up eggs). Sprinkle the top with the crumbled cheese and parsley, if using. Serve immediately.

and chiles, while celebrations of the fire god Huehueteotl featured shrimp and chile sauce tamales.

Bernal Díaz del Castillo, in his *Historia verdadera de la conquista de la nueva españa (True History of the Conquest of New Spain)*, describes how the meals of the Aztec emperor Moctezuma II (this is how it is properly spelled) were served with great solemnity, and how his cooks had more than 30 ways of cooking 300 dishes for him and more than a thousand dishes for his guards. Díaz does mention that the Aztecs were cannibalistic and ate their victims with *chilmole* sauce, a sauce made from tomatoes, chiles, onions, and salt. In the sixteenth century, the friar Bartolomé de las Casas made this observation about the Mexicans: "without the chile [the Mexicans], don't believe that they are eating."

There is hardly a savory dish in the Mexican repertoire that does not contain chiles of some kind in some proportion. The number of chiles used in Mexican cooking is hard to enumerate because there are hundreds of cultivars and their names change from region to region. But it should be emphasized that chile is used for flavor and not solely for heat in Mexico. A chef who used too much chile in his preparation would not be considered a good chef.

The northern states, Baja California, Sonora, Chihuahua, Durango, Coahuila, Nuevo León, and Tamaulipas, have food that most Americans associate with Mexican food. The southern states of Guerrero, Oaxaca, Tabasco, and Chiapas, as well as the states of the Yucatán, have the hottest food in Mexico. Chiles now form part of the Mexican national identity, captured in the popular refrain: *Yo soy somo el chile verde, picante pero sabroso* ("I am like the green chile, hot but tasty").

variation After removing the eggs from the skillet, add a tablespoon of lard to the empty skillet and let it melt over medium-low heat. Cook $1/2$ pound crumbled chorizo sausage until the fat is rendered. Sprinkle the sausage over the eggs, then top with the sauce, cheese, and parsley.

MAKES 4 SERVINGS

Fiery Eggs with Chile Puree

One could probably write a small book on the egg dishes of North Africa—there are so many of them. This Tunisian preparation popular in Gabes, a coastal town that was once the terminus for the medieval trans-Saharan trade, is called *'ujja bi'l-hrus*, eggs with *hrus* (pronounced hroos). *Hrus* can be three things: a spice mix made from preserved onions, dried chiles, rose petals, and cinnamon; a salad of sweet peppers and hot chiles, tuna, olives, capers, garlic, and caraway seeds; or a puree of sweet and hot chiles, as in this dish.

2 green bell peppers, roasted, peeled, and seeded

2 fresh green or red finger-type chiles or 3 green or red jalapeño chiles, roasted, peeled, and seeded

1/2 cup extra-virgin olive oil

1/4 cup tomato paste dissolved in 1 cup water

1 tablespoon hot paprika

2 tablespoons *Harisa* (page 414)

1 tablespoon caraway seeds

Salt and freshly ground black pepper to taste

2 cups water

8 large eggs

1.   Pound the bell peppers and chiles together in a mortar with a pestle, or puree in a food processor or blender until green and soupy, about 30 seconds. Set aside.

2.   In a large skillet, heat the olive oil over high heat, then add the pepper puree, tomato paste dissolved in water, paprika, *harisa*, and caraway seeds. Season with salt and pepper. Pour in the water and, when it reaches a boil, reduce the heat to medium-low and cook until it reduces in consistency, about 10 minutes. Then increase the heat to medium for another 10 minutes.

3.   Carefully crack the eggs into the skillet, without breaking the yolks, and cook in the sauce over medium heat until they set, about 15 minutes. Season with salt and serve.

MAKES 4 SERVINGS

Fiery Eggs with Merguez Sausage

This eye-opener from Tunisia is called *'ujja bi'l-mirqaz* and is made with the famous merguez sausage which is at last being made in this country. (God bless these Tunisians because this sausage is fantastic.) The dish is a winter specialty of Zarzis, on the coast south of Djerba, where they typically scramble the eggs. I have also eaten this dish with sunny-side-up eggs, a very nice way of preparing it and the method I use here. In Djerba, they serve it with tiny local black olives and a side plate of mild Berber-style *harisa*, but with no de arbol chiles. Today a number of excellent merguez sausages are made in the U.S. and Canada, and you can order them easily on the Internet if you can't find them in your local gourmet shop.

6 tablespoons extra-virgin olive oil

3 cups canned or freshly crushed or finely chopped tomatoes (about 1 pound)

1 green bell pepper, cored and thinly sliced

1 tablespoon *Harisa* (page 414)

2 large garlic cloves, sliced

1/2 teaspoon freshly ground caraway seeds

1/2 teaspoon cayenne pepper

Salt and freshly ground black pepper to taste

1 cup water

1/4 pound merguez sausage, cut into 1-inch pieces

4 large eggs

1. Put 4 tablespoons of the olive oil, the tomatoes, bell pepper, *harisa*, garlic, caraway, cayenne pepper, salt and black pepper, and water in a medium-size saucepan and turn the heat to medium-high. Cook until well blended and fragrant, about 45 minutes, stirring frequently so it doesn't stick and adding a little water if the juices evaporate too quickly.

2. Add the sausage and continue cooking until they are cooked through, about 30 minutes. Meanwhile, heat the remaining 2 tablespoons olive oil in a nonstick skillet and fry the eggs sunny side up. Transfer the eggs to a round serving platter and surround and cover slightly with the sausage and sauce. Serve immediately.

MAKES 2 TO 4 SERVINGS

electrifying eggs

The Sheik's Brains

This curiously named dish said to come from the coastal town of Bejaïa in Algeria is called *mukh al-shayk*, which literally means "brains of the sheik." (Sheik is pronounced "shake," *not* "sheek.") But it's not clear whether it means that this scrambled egg dish, which has no brains in it, is meant to resemble cooked brains (it does) or whether it is named after a sheik who was not fond of brains and made the dish with scrambled eggs instead. Or maybe the sheik had no brains. In any case, it's delicious and very easy to prepare. Typically, it is served as a lunch dish, but it makes a fine, if unusual, meze, too. A similar dish is prepared in neighboring Tunisia, but they season it differently using *harisa*, paprika, and caraway. Remember that the heat is very low for this preparation; that's why the eggs can cook for 15 minutes and still remain wet. It will resemble a pudding more than anything else.

8 large eggs

2 teaspoons finely ground dried red *piquín* chiles or cayenne pepper

¹/₂ teaspoon salt, or more to your taste

¹/₄ cup extra-virgin olive oil

2 heads garlic (about 25 cloves), cloves separated, peeled, and left whole

1 medium-size cooked potato, peeled and finely diced

1. In a bowl, beat the eggs until frothy with the ground chile and salt.

2. In a 12-inch nonstick skillet, heat the olive oil with the garlic over very low heat, and let the cloves cook gently, but not so they turn color, about 10 minutes, stirring occasionally. Pour in the eggs and potato and cook, stirring constantly until the eggs are soft, velvety, and slightly wet, about 15 minutes. Serve immediately.

MAKES 4 SERVINGS

Indian Chile Eggs

This scrambled egg dish in the style of the Parsi of India is known as *akuri* or *akoori*. The Parsis are an old Zoroastrian community located in the western part of India, especially around Mumbai, who were originally from Persia, hence their name. They revere, but do not worship, fire, and maybe that is evidenced in this dish with its own kind of fire. Clarified butter does not need to be store bought. You can easily make it at home by melting some butter and spooning off and discarding the while milk solids separate from the yellow butter. Store the clarified butter in the refrigerator. Serve as a light lunch dish or an appetizer with chapatis or Naan (page 398).

6 large eggs

$1/2$ teaspoon ground cumin

Salt and freshly ground black pepper to taste

2 tablespoons clarified butter (*ghee*)

3 fresh green finger-type chiles or 4 green jalapeño chiles, seeded and finely chopped

6 scallions, chopped

1 teaspoon grated fresh ginger

1 large ripe tomato, peeled, seeded, and chopped

2 tablespoons finely chopped fresh coriander (cilantro) leaves

$1/8$ teaspoon ground turmeric

1 medium-size tomato, cut into wedges, for garnish

Fresh coriander (cilantro) leaves, for garnish

1. In a medium-size bowl, beat the eggs with the cumin and salt and pepper. In a large nonstick skillet, melt the clarified butter over medium heat, then cook the chiles, scallions, and ginger until soft, about 3 minutes, stirring. Add the tomato, coriander, and turmeric and cook for 2 minutes, stirring.

2. Add the eggs and cook on medium heat until congealed but not dry, about 3 minutes, lifting them gently and turning them with a rubber spatula. Once they have congealed, transfer them to a serving platter and garnish with the tomato wedges and coriander leaves. Serve immediately.

MAKES 4 TO 6 SERVINGS

electrifying eggs

Tofu and Eggs in Pounded Fried Chiles

This Indonesian dish is called *balado tahu telor*. It's an interesting and unlikely preparation because you end up deep-frying the hard-boiled eggs, which I bet you've never done before. The eggs and the cubes of tofu look similar at that point and they are both very spicy hot because of how much chile you use. This recipe is adapted from an Indonesian cook named Rudy Supratman. When hard-boiling the eggs, undercook them slightly by placing the eggs in boiling water for 9 minutes and not longer. Cool them as soon as they come out of the boiling water.

6 to 8 cups vegetable or peanut oil, for frying

8 hard-boiled eggs, shells removed

One 14-ounce block firm tofu, cut into 8 cubes

10 fresh red finger-type chiles or 13 red jalapeño chiles, chopped

5 shallots, chopped

4 large garlic cloves, chopped

$^1\!/_2$ teaspoon shrimp paste

3 tablespoons vegetable oil

3 ounces headless medium-size shrimp, shells removed

1 large juicy tomato, peeled and cut into 8 pieces

1 teaspoon salt, or more to your taste

2 teaspoons palm sugar or granulated sugar

1.   Preheat the frying oil to 360°F in a deep fryer or an 8-inch saucepan with a basket insert. Deep-fry the hard-boiled eggs until golden brown, 3 to 4 minutes. Remove and drain on a paper towel–lined plate. Deep-fry the tofu until golden brown, about 5 minutes, and drain on paper towels.

2.   In a food processor, puree the chiles, shallots, garlic, and shrimp paste, but not too finely.

3.   In a wok, heat the 3 tablespoons vegetable oil over high heat, then cook the chile paste until sizzling and mushy, stirring, about 3 minutes. Add the shrimp and cook until they turn pink-orange, 1 to 2 minutes. Add the deep-fried eggs and tofu, cook 1 minute, then add the tomato, salt, and sugar and cook for another 3 minutes, stir-frying constantly. If the tomato is not juicy, add $^1\!/_4$ cup water. Serve hot or warm.

MAKES 4 SERVINGS

hot chicks, wicked ducks, and one killer rabbit

The fiery cuisines of the world sure know how to make chickens dance. In this chapter you're going to find some incredible stuff. The recipes here will open your eyes to some intriguing, delicious, and incendiary chicken dishes. And the duck! I'm crazy about duck—I think it's close to my favorite food—and when I'm at a restaurant I always seek out the duck dishes. There's only one rabbit recipe here—a great meat and a great taste. Well, as always in this book, we start in the west and we move east. Get that roll of paper towels and start cookin'. Try that Chongqing Spicy Chicken (page 156) and then you know you will have crossed to the other side.

Piquant Shredded Chicken in Creamy Walnut and Chile Sauce

*I*n the *cocina aymara*, the cuisine of the Aymara Indians in Andean Peru, the potato is the most important food, appearing in every dish they make. This Peruvian dish is called *ají de gallina*, which means "chicken chile" and is a classic dish made in Chiclayo. The preparation has an uncanny resemblance to a famous dish of the Middle East called Circassian chicken, a shredded chicken cooked with a creamy walnut sauce (see pages 308–309 in my *A Mediterranean Feast*).

3 pounds bone-in chicken breast

8 Yukon gold potatoes (about 1½ pounds)

4 slices of white bread, crusts removed

1 cup shelled walnut halves

One 12-ounce can evaporated milk

1 tablespoon extra-virgin olive oil

3 tablespoons safflower oil

1 medium-size onion, finely chopped

2 large garlic cloves, crushed

½ teaspoon ground cumin

3 tablespoons ground red chile

3 tablespoons cayenne pepper

2 fresh red jalapeño chiles, finely chopped

1 tablespoon salt

2 teaspoons freshly ground black pepper

1 cup freshly grated Parmesan cheese

2 cups white rice

2 large hard-boiled eggs, sliced, for garnish

Finely chopped fresh parsley leaves, for garnish

1. Place the chicken in a large casserole with the potatoes and cover with water. Bring to just below a boil, then reduce the heat and simmer until the chicken is cooked through and you are able to pull it apart with your fingers, about 2 hours, making sure the water *never* boils. Remove the chicken from the broth and let cool. Leave the potatoes in the broth for another 20 minutes on low heat. Remove the meat from the chicken bones. Discard the bones and skin, shred the chicken meat with two forks, and set aside. Remove the potatoes, peel, and slice ½ inch thick. Reserve 3 cups of the broth.

2. In a blender, puree the bread, walnuts, and evaporated milk until creamy.

the piquant cuisine of
south america

There are two major areas where one finds piquant cooking in South America. The first is Peru and Bolivia, and the second is Amazonian Brazil from Bahia and including parts of Guyana. The former is the oldest culinary region in the world to use chiles.

Agriculture in South America is several thousand years old, but it was with the beginnings of the Inca empire in Peru in the early fifteenth century that agriculture became quite sophisticated. At the time of the Spanish conquest the Incas had domesticated 70 crops. One of the early commentators on the Incas was Bernabé Cobo, whose *Historia de nuevo mundo* (translated as *History of the Inca Empire*; University of Texas, 1979) describes one chile dish called *locro*, a thick stew made with corn kernals, potatoes, *ajís* (chiles), meat, and beans. Fernando de Santillan, in *Relación del origen, descendencia, política y gobierno de los Incas*, which he wrote right after the Conquest, says that the food of the Incas "is maize and chile and greens, they never eat meat or anything of substance, except for some fish for those who are near the coast. . . ." Another early writer, and half Incan himself, was Garicilaso de le Vega, who noted in his *Royal Commentaries of the Incas* (Orion, 1961) that chiles were the favorite fruit of the Indians, who ate them with everything they cooked, "whether stewed, boiled, or roasted." Garicilaso de la Vega tells us that the Incas raised three varieties: the *rócot uchu*, "thick pepper" (*C. baccatum*), a second variety that de la Vega forgot the name of except that it was used exclusively by the royal household, and a third type called *chinchi uchu*, which "resembles exactly a cherry with its stalk" and is today's *rocoto* chile.

The highlands of Bolivia were also an area of intensive culinary chile. The two most important Indian groups were the Quechuas and the Aymaras. The Aymaras were located around Lake Titicaca in the province of La Paz, while the Quechuas were found in the southern part of the Bolivian highlands. Both peoples used chiles extensively in foods that were mostly made up of potatoes, quinoa, squash, beans, and corn.

There seems to be a pronounced separation in cultures that determines who uses chile in South America. For the most part, native Indians use more chiles than immigrants, *mestizos* (mixed race people), or those of European descent. Certain local cuisines are fiery hot and quite famous for that. For instance, Arequipa, a city in southern Peru whose houses are built of white volcanic stone, has a reputation for some of the hottest food in South America. The word *arequipeño* indicates not only a dish from Arequipa but also that the dish is very hot.

3. In a casserole (you can use the one you poached the chicken in after cleaning it), heat the olive oil and safflower oil over medium-high heat, then cook the onion, garlic, cumin, ground red chile, cayenne pepper, fresh chiles, salt, and pepper until the oil separates and is bubbling, about 3 minutes, stirring. Add the bread and walnut cream, bring to a boil, reduce the heat to low, then cook until dense, about 5 minutes, stirring constantly.

4. Add the reserved shredded chicken, 2 cups of the reserved broth, and the Parmesan cheese and stir over medium heat until a soft, creamy consistency, about 10 minutes, adding more broth if the sauce is getting too thick. You want to keep the creamy consistency.

5. Arrange the boiled potatoes and white rice next to each other on 6 to 8 individual plates. Spread the shredded chicken on one side, flattening it to cover the plate rather than mounding it. Garnish with the sliced eggs and parsley and serve.

MAKES 6 TO 8 SERVINGS

Chicken Stew with Black Beer and Green Rice

This thick dark Peruvian stew is called *aguadito de pollo*. It is unique in its use of black beer and pureed coriander leaves, which turn the broth black. It's also quite spicy from both the chopped fresh yellow chile, called *ají amarillo*, and the chile paste made from softened dried *ají panca*. As these Peruvian chiles are only available in specialized groceries and through the Internet, I make some suggestions for substitutes. This stew is hearty and filling, as it contains not only the chicken and spices but also rice, potatoes, bell pepper, and peas.

10$^1/_4$ cups water

One 3$^1/_2$-pound chicken, backbone, neck, and wings removed and reserved, the remaining parts cut into 8 pieces

2 tablespoons plus 2 teaspoons salt, or more to your taste

1 small leek, white and green parts, split lengthwise and quartered

6 celery stalks, quartered

$^3/_4$ cup chopped fresh coriander (cilantro) leaves

$^1/_2$ cup vegetable oil

2 teaspoons ground cumin

2 teaspoons freshly ground black pepper, or more to your taste

2 large garlic cloves, crushed

1 medium-size onion, chopped

$^1/_4$ cup *Aji Panca en Pasta* (page 405)

$^1/_4$ cup finely chopped fresh yellow chiles (*aji amarillo*) or 5 tablespoons yellow *güero* chiles or 6 tablespoons red jalapeño chiles or 2 tablespoons habanero chiles

1 tablespoon hot paprika

1$^1/_4$ pounds small Yukon gold potatoes, peeled and cut into halves

$^1/_2$ cup black beer (such as Guinness)

1 red bell pepper, cored and thinly sliced

$^3/_4$ cup fresh or frozen peas

1 cup medium-grain rice

1. Pour 10 cups water into a large pot and add the backbone, neck, and wings of the chicken along with 2 tablespoons salt, the leek, and celery. Bring to just below a boil over high heat, then reduce the heat to low and simmer for 2 hours. Pour through a strainer and reserve 7 cups of broth, setting aside the remainder. Discard the bones and vegetables. Meanwhile, puree the coriander leaves and the remaining $^1/_4$ cup water in a blender until homogeneous. Set aside.

2. In a large skillet, heat the vegetable oil over medium-high heat. Season the chicken pieces by rolling them in a pan filled with the cumin, 1 teaspoon salt, and $^1/_2$ teaspoon pepper. Cook the chicken until deep golden on both sides, 10 to 15 minutes in all, turning occasionally. Remove and set aside, covered.

3. Add the garlic, onion, *ají panca en pasta*, and fresh chiles to the skillet. Stir to blend, then add the pureed coriander, paprika, the remaining 1 teaspoon salt, and the remaining 1$^1/_2$ teaspoons pepper. Transfer the mixture from the skillet to a deep casserole and add the reserved chicken broth, the potatoes, and black beer. Bring to a near boil over medium-high heat. Reduce the heat to medium-low, cook 5 minutes, then add the reserved chicken pieces, bell pepper, and peas and cook for 10 minutes more (the heat can be turned off at this point and the stew can sit for a few hours until you are ready to finish it).

4. Raise the heat to medium-high and bring the stew to just below a boil, then add the rice and mix well. Reduce the heat to low, cover, and cook until the rice is nearly done, about 10 minutes. Add more broth to keep the stew from drying out. It should have the consistency of a thick soup. Serve hot.

MAKES 6 SERVINGS

Picante de Pollo

*I*n Bolivia, from where this dish hails, it's also known as *sajta*. This preparation is quite definitive of Bolivian cooking and is usually made as part of an even larger feast of *picante mixto*, mixed piquant foods prepared for special occasions and festivities. Some of these other dishes are *picante de lengua*, stuffed potatoes, paste torts, and chile salsas. You can also add coriander seeds and paprika to this and serve it with tomato salad and rice, or *chuño phuti* (dried potato) instead of the potato. Personally, I like to serve this with a combination of boiled Yellow Finn and Peruvian purple potatoes and Fried Cassava (page 390) on the side.

3 large garlic cloves, peeled

One 4-pound chicken, cut into 6 parts

1 large white onion, cut in half and thinly sliced

1 large tomato, peeled, seeded, and finely chopped

4 large fresh red *rocoto* chiles or 8 red jalapeño chiles, seeded and finely chopped

1 cup fresh or frozen peas or 1/4 small cabbage, cut into strips

1/4 cup ground *aji mirasol* or 3 tablespoons cayenne pepper

1 teaspoon ground cumin

1 teaspoon dried oregano

1 tablespoon salt

1/2 teaspoon freshly ground black pepper

2 tablespoons olive oil or vegetable oil

3 cups chicken broth (homemade or canned), dark beer, or water

6 small boiling potatoes, cooked until tender and peeled

1/2 cup finely chopped fresh parsley leaves, for garnish

1. Preheat the oven to 400°F. Place the garlic cloves on an ungreased baking tray and roast until golden, about 8 minutes. Remove and chop finely.

2.   In a large casserole, arrange the chicken pieces on the bottom and cover with the onion, tomato, fresh chiles, peas, ground chile, cumin, oregano, salt, black pepper, and olive oil. Pour the broth over all the ingredients.

3.   Bring the broth to a near boil, then reduce the heat to low and simmer, almost completely covered, until the chicken is nearly falling off the bone, about 2

mole

Mole must be one of the most famous of Mexican foods. In the United States, it is usually thought of as a kind of dark chile–chocolate sauce, which is quite unfortunate, because it is much, much more than that. To counter the idea that mole is a chocolaty sauce, remember that the most famous mole is guacamole, which literally means "avocado sauce." Is mole a sauce or the name of the dish? For Rick Bayless, author of *Authentic Mexican* (William Morrow, 1987) and other cookbooks, they are one and the same. After guacamole, the most famous mole is mole poblano, a mole from Pueblo that is very complex and, frankly, baroque. This makes sense when we think of the Spanish influence on Mexican cooking, which coincided with the Baroque period. Mole poblano is made with dried chiles, nuts, seeds, vegetables, spices, and a little bit of chocolate. The use of chocolate in savory dishes also appears in Spain and Spanish Bourbon–ruled Sicily in the seventeenth century. There are many moles and, in fact, Oaxaca is known as the *lugar de sietes moles*, place of seven moles (see page 126). Moles are characterized by using pulverized nuts, seeds, and chiles as a thickening agent for sauces. It is a very time-consuming and complex preparation, and I've tried to simplify it in my recipe (page 126).

When the Spanish arrived in Mexico they encountered the Aztecs, who had a stew or sauce called *molli*, which soon became known as mole. Jesuit priest Bernabé Cobo (1580–1657) describes 40 different shapes and colors of chiles in his *Historia de nuevo mundo*, first published in 1653. He notes that they are used to make sauces, one of which was called *locro*, which was similar to the mole sauce in Mexico that brought "tears to the eyes of those not accustomed to eating it." The traditional story of the origin of moles as we know them smacks of apocrypha, but that's okay—it makes a great story. Supposedly, mole was created by Sister Andrea de la Asunción for a hours, stirring occasionally and gently, pushing the onion down into the broth, and making sure the broth *never* comes to a boil. Remove to a serving platter. Serve with the boiled potatoes and spoon some broth over the chicken and potatoes. Sprinkle the chopped parsley on top and serve.

MAKES 4 TO 5 SERVINGS

seventeenth-century bishop visiting the Santa Rosa Convent in Puebla de los Angeles, or it was asked of Sister Andrea by Bishop Fernández de Santa Cruz for the visiting viceroy of New Spain, Don Tomás Antonio de la Cerda y Aragón, around 1680. Although Bernabé Cobo described something that sounds like mole and Sister Andrea has her legend, the first recorded mole recipe appears in a book published in Mexico City in 1831 called *Novisimo arte de cocina-o-Escelente coleccion de las mejores recetas*.

There are some other origin stories, but what makes them important is not their truth or falsity but the fact that mole is perceived to be such an important part of Mexican culture. One innovative study, undertaken by anthropologist Professor Judith Friedlander of the New School University in New York, tried to trace mole by looking at its ingredients in her study *Being Indian in Hueyapan: A Study of Forced Identity in Contemporary Mexico* (Bedford/St. Martin's, 1975). She notes that most of the ingredients of a mole come from the Old World. The only New World products are the chiles and chocolate (and turkey, if making it traditionally), and the Nahautl word *molli* (sauce). As the dish was traditionally served for religious celebrations when priests were in their converting mode, Friedlander concludes that moles were introduced to Indian communities by Spanish missionaries. This conclusion assumes that the conquistadors destroyed local culture and did not give credit to native traditions, which is more or less true. The counterargument is that the blending of chiles to create complex flavors was clearly a pre-Columbian culinary technique and one that the Spanish learned from the Indians. There is yet another interpretation: given the complexity and ostentatiousness of a mole, it must be a creation of the Baroque-era cooks of New Spain. There is probably an element of truth in all of these explanations.

Tablecloth Stainer

This dish, called *manchamantel*, is associated with Oaxaca and means "tablecloth stainer." In Oaxaca, they say there are seven moles: this one, *mole negro* (a black mole, rich and chocolaty), *mole coloradito* (dark and spicy), *mole verde* (a green mole made with fresh herbs), *mole amarillo* (an everyday mole that is very hot and "yellow," although the color is actually orange), *mole rojo* or *colorado* (a spicy red mole), and *mole chichilo* (a dark and smoky mole). This is a scrumptious meal. The combination of fruit and chiles may confuse your taste buds at first, but then slowly you become accustomed to the flavors. The banana is cooked peel and all, and it is all edible once everything is cooked. Serve with white rice and fried zucchini and forget about the tablecloth—it will become stained.

³/₄ pound ripe tomatoes

2 onions, 1 medium-size, 1 large, both quartered

7 large garlic cloves, 4 peeled and 3 unpeeled

5 fresh poblano chiles (see page xxv)

One large Cornish game hen or 1 young fryer chicken (about 2 pounds), cut up into 8 pieces and skin removed

1 pound pork shoulder, cubed

1 carrot, quartered

1 bouquet garni tied in cheesecloth, consisting of 5 sprigs parsley, 5 sprigs thyme, and 1 bay leaf

2 tablespoons pork lard or bacon fat

¹/₂ cup blanched whole or slivered almonds

¹/₂ cinnamon stick, slightly crushed

2 whole cloves

5 whole peppercorns

Two ¹/₂-inch-thick slices French or Italian bread

Salt to taste

¹/₄ teaspoon sugar

1 tablespoon lime juice

1 large Granny Smith apple, peeled, cored, and chopped

1 banana, peel left on and cut into slices

2 slices fresh pineapple, peeled and cut into triangles

1. Preheat the oven to 450°F. Put the tomatoes, quartered large onion, and 3 unpeeled garlic cloves in a baking dish or tray and roast until all are blistered and blackened, about 30 minutes. Put the poblano chiles in another baking dish and roast them, too, until the skin is blistered and blackened, about 40 minutes. Remove both baking dishes and peel the skin off the tomatoes and garlic. Place the tomatoes, onion, and garlic in a blender and puree briefly. Place the chiles in a paper bag for 15 minutes to steam them a little bit, then remove their peels and seeds.

2.　In a large casserole or stockpot, place the game hen and pork with the quartered medium-size onion, carrot, 4 peeled garlic cloves, and the bouquet garni and cover with water. Bring to just below a boil over high heat, then reduce the heat to low and simmer until the meat is white and firm, about 45 minutes. Remove the game hen and pork. Remove the meat from the game hen and cube it, then set aside with the pork. Save 2 cups of the cooking liquid. Clean the casserole, which you will need in step 4.

3.　In a large skillet, heat 1 tablespoon lard over medium heat, then cook the almonds, cinnamon, cloves, and peppercorns until the almonds begin to turn light brown, about 5 minutes. Using a slotted spoon, transfer the contents of the skillet to the blender with the tomatoes. Cook the bread slices in the remaining fat in the skillet until crispy, then remove to the blender. Add the chiles to the blender along with 1 cup of the game hen poaching liquid and blend until smooth, stopping and scraping down the sides when necessary, adding only enough liquid from the poaching game hen and pork to make the blades twirl.

4.　Add the remaining lard to the casserole and heat over high heat until almost smoking. Add the pureed sauce and cook until smooth and dense, stirring occasionally, about 5 minutes. Season with salt, sugar, and lime juice and stir. Add the game hen and pork to the casserole with the apple, banana, and pineapple and cook until some of the banana peels start falling apart, about 30 minutes, adding poaching liquid when necessary to keep the sauce smooth and gravy-like, not dense and not saucy. Serve immediately.

MAKES 8 SERVINGS

the hot spices: clove

Cloves are the unopened flower buds of a small evergreen tree native to the North Moluccas (Indonesia) that was cultivated on the islands of Ternate, Tidore, Bacan and the west coast of Halmahera in today's Indonesia. Interestingly, however, cloves do not play a major role in the spicing of contemporary Indonesian cuisine. The taste of cloves is fiery, burning, and very aromatic. It is the most important of the "flower spices," those spices that eventually open into flowers. The clove tree can grow to 50 feet in height and thrives in a tropical maritime environment. The buds are gathered before the corolla has become detached and when the petals, still compact and unopened, form a round head above the calyx. The English name *clove* derives from the Latin *clavus*, meaning "nail," since the clove looks like one.

The earliest references to cloves are in ancient Chinese literature of the Han period in the third century B.C. Jill Norman in her *The Complete Book of Spices* (Viking Studio, 1991) tells us that courtiers and officers of state were required to have a few cloves in their mouths when addressing the emperor to keep their breaths sweet. In the first century A.D., Pliny, the most important of the Roman authors on the natural world, describes cloves and mentions that they are imported in Rome for their aroma. Their culinary use was never mentioned in early or late Roman writing except for an oblique reference in the fifth century work by the Greek physician Paul of Aegina, who said cloves were reputed to be "aromatic, sour, bitterish, hot and dry in the third degree, excellent in relishes." Al-Idrisi (1099–c. 1180), an Arab and the royal court geographer of the Norman king of Sicily Roger II, wrote in his geographical encyclopedia about the growing, harvesting, and processing of cloves. From the eighth century onward, cloves were regularly imported into Europe.

From the early sixteenth century the Portuguese controlled the trade in cloves until the Dutch took the Moluccas in 1605. They restricted the cultivation of clove trees to one island, the island of Pemba, and were successful in monopolizing the clove trade. But in 1770 the French smuggled seedlings to Mauritius, and from there plantations were eventually established on Zanzibar and Madagascar, two of today's largest exporters. Other contemporary producers are India (the largest producer), Sri Lanka, Malaysia, and Grenada.

Cloves are used in many cuisines today, especially in China and Sri Lanka, and are used extensively in the Mogul cuisine of northern India. In the Middle East and North Africa, Arab cooks use cloves in various spice mixes.

Chicken in Adobo Sauce

The Mexican adobo sauce, so called because it always has vinegar, is a blended sauce of dried chiles soaked in chicken broth and mixed with roasted onions, tomatoes, garlic, and vinegar. It can be used in a variety of dishes, so if there is any left over, save it for something else. In this preparation the chicken pieces swim in an ocean of adobo sauce, and when you pull the tender meat off the bone swirl each bite into the sauce before eating. This dish is nice served with Shredded Cabbage Salad (page 388), white rice, and some warmed corn tortillas.

3 medium-size tomatoes (about 1 pound)

1 medium-size onion

1 cup boiling chicken broth (homemade or canned)

4 dried ancho chiles, seeded, stemmed, and broken into smaller pieces

3 dried guajillo chiles or 4 dried red de arbol chiles, seeded, stemmed, and broken into smaller pieces

2 large garlic cloves

1 tablespoon apple cider vinegar

1 teaspoon sugar

1/2 teaspoon ground coriander

1/4 teaspoon ground cinnamon

1/4 teaspoon ground cloves

4 teaspoons salt

2 teaspoons freshly ground black pepper

4 tablespoons pork lard or bacon fat

One 3 1/2-pound chicken, cut into 8 pieces and skin removed

1. Preheat the oven to 450°F. Place the tomatoes and onion on a baking tray and roast them until they blacken, about 25 minutes for the tomatoes and 40 minutes for the onion. Remove the skin from the tomatoes. Cut up both into smaller pieces and place in a bowl. Reduce the heat of the oven to 350°F.

2. In a bowl, pour the chicken broth over the dried chiles and let soak for 30 minutes, keeping a weight such as a smaller bowl on top to keep the chiles submerged. Place the chiles and their soaking liquid in a blender and puree at high speed for about 1 minute. Add the roasted tomatoes and onion along with the garlic, vinegar, sugar, coriander, cinnamon, cloves, salt, and black pepper. Blend until it is a thick puree.

3. In a large skillet, melt 1 tablespoon lard over medium heat, then cook the puree, uncovered, for 5 minutes, stirring frequently and lowering the heat a bit if it is splattering. Remove from heat and set aside, covered to keep the sauce warm.

4.   Meanwhile, in another large skillet, melt the remaining 3 tablespoons lard over medium heat, then cook the chicken pieces until golden brown, 12 to 14 minutes, turning once with a spatula and scraping up any sticking bits. Transfer the pieces to a large shallow casserole that you can bring to the table, arranging the pieces in one layer. Pour the reserved adobo sauce over them, making sure all the pieces are coated and covered with sauce. Cover the casserole and bake for 45 minutes. Uncover and bake until the chicken can be pulled off the bone with a fork and the sauce is bubbling, about 15 minutes, basting once. Serve immediately.

MAKES 4 TO 6 SERVINGS

 # Enchiladas Verdes

Enchilada comes from the Spanish verb *enchilar*, which basically means to get chile all over something. An enchilada is something "en-chilied." What this means practically for this recipe is that you will dip the tortilla into the chile sauce. In this "green" version of enchilada, the green color comes from tomatillos and green chiles, while the red version, *enchilada rojo*, is made with tomatoes, red chiles, and chorizo sausage. The one technique that is a little tricky in this preparation is the quick pre-frying of the tortillas. The reason this is done, besides adding some nice flavor, is to make the tortillas softer for rolling and less likely to crack.

9 cups water

1 pound (9 to 12) tomatillos, husked

3 small onions, quartered

8 large garlic cloves, crushed

8 fresh green serrano chiles

Leaves from 15 sprigs fresh coriander (cilantro)

1 teaspoon salt

1¼ pounds whole bone-in chicken breasts

½ teaspoon dried thyme

2 bay leaves

¼ cup crème fraîche or sour cream

¼ cup vegetable oil, or more if needed

12 corn tortillas

FOR THE GARNISH

⅓ cup crumbled Mexican *queso añejo*, mild white cheddar, Monterey Jack, or domestic feta

¼ cup crème fraîche or sour cream

2 slices of a medium-size onion, separated into rings

6 radishes, sliced

making enchiladas

Enchiladas are chile-smeared tortillas, literally, for the Spanish word derives from *enchilar*, to "en-chile" or "to get chile all over it." In Mexico, enchiladas are usually not baked as they are eaten fresh and quickly, and lean more toward warm in temperature than the piping-hot style found in Mexican-American restaurants. Enchiladas probably were born of the necessity and desire to use up nearly stale tortillas. There are several methods for making enchiladas. In the first method, an almost stale tortilla is dipped into a raw chile-tomato sauce and then fried quickly in a skillet until leathery, but not dried-out crisp. Fresh tortillas won't work because they will absorb too much sauce and fall apart. If too stale, they will not absorb enough sauce and be tough. In the second method the enchilada is fried before being dipped into a cooked sauce. In the last method the tortilla is not fried at all, but is simply rolled and served with whatever sauce and stuffing are being used. The tortilla should be cooked so that when you are rolling them they do not crack. A well-seasoned cast-iron pan is ideal for cooking the tortillas. When you dip the tortillas into the chile-tomato sauce, make sure the sauce is quite light and liquidy, otherwise the chunks of tomato and chile that adhere to the tortilla may burn when you cook them.

1. Bring 6 cups of the water to a boil in a large saucepan and add the tomatillos, 1 small quartered onion, 3 garlic cloves, and 4 serrano chiles. Reduce the heat to medium and simmer until the tomatillos are soft, about 30 minutes. Drain, saving some of the cooking water, and transfer the vegetables to a blender. Add another small quartered onion, 2 garlic cloves, the remaining chiles, and the coriander to the blender. Blend until smooth, about 2 minutes, adding just enough of the reserved cooking water so the blades of the blender can twirl. Set aside. Place the tomatillo sauce in a skillet or saucepan with $1/2$ teaspoon salt and heat over low heat, covered.

2. Place the chicken breasts in a saucepan filled with the remaining 3 cups of water, along with three-quarters of the remaining small onion, the remaining $1/2$ teaspoon salt, thyme, bay leaves, and the remaining 3 garlic cloves. Finely chop the reserved quarter of onion and set aside. Bring to just below a boil over high heat, and before the water starts bubbling reduce the heat to medium and poach the chicken until firm, about 12 minutes. Let cool in the broth. Remove and discard the bay leaves. Remove the chicken from the saucepan, pull the meat off the bones, discard the skin and bones, and shred the chicken into small pieces. Place the chicken in a skillet or saucepan and keep warm over low heat. Stir in the crème fraîche and the reserved chopped onion. Turn the heat off and cover to keep warm.

3. In a heavy well-seasoned skillet or a cast-iron skillet, heat the vegetable oil over medium-high heat, then cook the tortillas one at a time until soft, about 3 seconds per side. Remove with tongs and set aside on paper towels to drain. Replenish the oil in the skillet if need be to cook the remaining tortillas.

4. Preheat the oven to 350°F. Pour 1 cup of the tomatillo sauce on a dinner plate and lay a tortilla in the sauce. Fill the center with about 2 tablespoons of the chicken stuffing, then roll up and arrange in a baking dish. Continue filling and rolling the remaining tortillas. Pour the remaining sauce over the top of the enchiladas. Cover the baking dish with aluminum foil and bake until heated through, about 10 minutes. Remove from the oven, sprinkle with cheese, crème fraîche, and garnish with onion rings and radishes. Serve immediately.

MAKES 6 SERVINGS

Opelousas Baked Chicken

I came across this recipe on the Web, posted by someone who wrote that "the secret to this very famous Opelousas dish is in the seasoning and in the long, slow basting process." She recommended serving it with "Cajun rice dressing, petit pois, candied yams, a green salad, and French bread." You could also serve this with rice and green beans. I've adapted the recipe a bit, adding some measurements that weren't in the original. The use of Tony Chachere's Creole Seasoning is typical in Cajun cooking, and one finds it being called for often in many Cajun recipes. You can also use my homemade Cajun spice mix. The chili powder called for is the commercial spice blend known as "chili powder" used in a lot of Southwestern cooking.

4 chicken breast fryer halves with ribs attached (about 3¼ pounds)	1 cup vegetable oil
	1 cup water
¼ cup Tony Chachere's Creole Seasoning or Cliff's Cajun Seasoning (page 412)	2 tablespoons hot paprika
	1 tablespoon chili powder

1. Dredge the chicken in the Creole seasoning, rubbing it into all sides. Place the chicken in a baking dish and pour the vegetable oil and water over it. Sprinkle with the paprika and chili powder.

2. Preheat the oven to 250°F. Place the chicken in the oven and bake until a deep dark brown, basting every 30 minutes, 4½ to 5 hours. Serve immediately, with some of the liquid from the baking dish as a dipping sauce.

MAKES 4 SERVINGS

Jerk Chicken

One story about the origins of jerk attributes its invention as a means of preserving the meat of wild hogs on Jamaica. The Maroons, descendants of slaves of the Spanish and British who had escaped into the rugged interior of the Blue Mountains known as Cockpit country, are said to have pit-barbecued the hog meat slathered in spices and marinating liquids. By 1739 treaties granted the Maroons land and some self-government, and soon after that at island markets they started selling jerked pork and chicken. Today roadside barbecues along the highway that runs from Montego Bay to Ochos Rios sell jerked dishes in billowing clouds of flavored smoke. Many a travel and food writer will recommend that the best place to have jerk in Jamaica is at Boston Bay, near Port Antonio. The secret to jerk, and every jerk man will claim a secret, is a long marinade, slow cooking, and abundant use of the dried berry of the small and aromatic tropical tree known by the misnomer pimento tree, better known as allspice. The branches of the tree are sometimes used as an aromatic wood in the *patas* or grill stands where the jerk is barbecued. Although every part of the chicken can be used, you must remember to pay close attention to the breasts, as they can dry out if not properly cooked. Serve with Rice and Peas (page 362) and a green salad.

FOR THE JERK MARINADE

2 tablespoons ground allspice

2 tablespoons dried thyme

1 tablespoon cayenne pepper

1 tablespoon freshly ground black pepper

1 tablespoon dried sage

1 1/2 teaspoons ground nutmeg

1 1/2 teaspoons ground cinnamon

2 tablespoons salt

6 large garlic cloves

One 1-inch cube fresh ginger

1 tablespoon sugar

1/2 bunch fresh coriander (cilantro), leaves only

1/4 cup soy sauce

3/4 cup fresh lime juice

1/2 cup fresh orange juice

1/4 cup peanut oil

2 cups chopped scallions

4 Scotch bonnet or habanero chiles, stemmed

FOR THE CHICKEN

6 pounds mixed chicken breasts, thighs, and legs

3 bay leaves (optional)

1.   Place all the ingredients for the jerk marinade in a blender and puree until smooth.

2.   In a large bowl, toss the chicken pieces with the marinade. Divide the chicken pieces and marinade between 2 heavy-duty zippered-top plastic bags. Seal the bags, pressing out the excess air, and let the chicken marinate in the refrigerator, turning the bags over several times, for at least 6 hours and up to 2 days.

3.   Prepare a charcoal fire on one side of the grill or preheat a gas grill on high for 15 minutes, then turn off one set of burners. If using a charcoal grill, toss 3 bay leaves on the coals if desired. Grill the chicken away from the fire, in batches if necessary, and cover if possible, until golden brown with bits of blackened skin, about 1 1/2 hours, turning every now and then and basting with leftover jerk marinade. During the last 30 minutes of cooking keep the chicken breasts skin side up so the meat is farther away from the heat source, and stop basting. If the chicken pieces are blackening too quickly, it means your fire is too hot and you should either keep the cover open, push the coals further away, or lower one of the gas burners. Transfer the jerk chicken to a platter and serve.

MAKES 8 TO 10 SERVINGS

Poulet Yassa

Probably the best known of the West African dishes, *poulet yassa* is a preparation from the Casamance region north of Dakar in Senegal. It is a true specialty, in which chicken is marinated in onions and lemon juice, then grilled, then stewed with lots of chiles, and it never fails to appear on restaurant menus. In Africa, chickens and Guinea fowl are tough and therefore you will see the use of overnight marinades as in this recipe. Here I instruct you to either grill the chicken or bake it in the oven. *Poulet yassa* is good with a cool salad, and the best drink to accompany it is ginger beer, mint tea, or beer. For real authenticity use the fermented locust bean (see page 185). But the Maggi Sauce, readily available in supermarkets, is equally authentic, as this Swiss-produced condiment is quite popular in West Africa. Serve with Rice Pilaf (page 396), couscous, or *Fufu* (page 393).

One 3½-pound chicken, cut into 8 pieces, skin removed if desired

4 pounds yellow onions, chopped

1 head of garlic, cloves separated, peeled, and chopped

¼ cup apple cider vinegar

½ cup fresh lemon juice

1 fermented locust bean paste ball (*dawadawa*) or 1 tablespoon Maggi Sauce or 1 tablespoon soy sauce

1 small bay leaf, crumbled

¼ cup prepared mustard

2 fresh green jalapeño chiles, finely chopped

3 habanero chiles or 5 fresh cherry chiles or 15 fresh red finger-type chiles, finely chopped

2 dried red de arbol chiles, crumbled

2 teaspoons freshly ground black pepper

¼ cup peanut oil

¼ small cabbage, cut into small chunks

1 carrot, diced

2 teaspoons salt, or more to your taste

1.   In a large ceramic or glass bowl, toss the chicken with the onions, garlic, vinegar, lemon juice, fermented locust bean paste ball, bay leaf, mustard, fresh green chiles, habanero chiles, dried red chiles, and black pepper. Marinate overnight in the refrigerator.

2.   Prepare a hot charcoal fire on one side of the grill or preheat a gas grill on medium for 15 minutes. Remove the chicken from the marinade, scraping off the onion pieces and reserving the marinade. Place the chicken on the cool part of the grill, away from the fire, and grill slowly with the hood down until crispy golden brown and firm to the touch, about 1 hour. Keep checking because the heat of the grill is quite variable. Alternatively, preheat the oven to 325°F. Place the chicken in a baking dish and bake until golden brown, about 1^1/$_2$ hours. Remove the chicken and set aside, keeping the pieces warm.

3.   Meanwhile, place the onions in a strainer and set over a bowl to separate the liquid from the solid pieces, saving both. In a large casserole or stockpot, heat the peanut oil over medium-high heat, then cook the onions until golden, 10 to 12 minutes, stirring. Add the reserved liquid marinade to the casserole along with the cabbage and carrot and bring to a boil, then reduce the heat to medium-low, season with the salt, and cook 10 minutes. Add the reserved chicken, cover, and simmer over low heat until the chicken is tender, about 10 minutes. Serve hot.

MAKES 6 SERVINGS

the hot spices:
grains of paradise

Grains of paradise, also called malagueta pepper and, in West Africa, Guinea pepper, is related to cardamom. It is a hot, spicy spice of seeds that are brownish red in color with a slight hint of lemon. The plant grows to eight feet and has showy pink or yellow trumpet-shaped flowers and long leaves. The brown seeds are the spice and are formed in the pulp of a sour, pear-shaped orange fruit. Grains of paradise is native to West Africa and got its name during the Middle Ages in Italy because of its high value as an ersatz black pepper in times of black pepper scarcity or when pepper prices went too high, and also because its country of origin was not known by consumers. The first known reference to grains of paradise is 1214, at a festival held at Treviso in the Veneto of Italy, where 12 noble ladies and their attendants defended a sham fortress attacked by knights who fought with fruits, flowers, perfumes, and spices, including grains of paradise. Although the spice is mostly used in West Africa, it does find its way into some North African spice mixes and even an American beer, Samuel Adams Summer Ale.

Chicken Cooked in Hell

No, they don't call it that in Cameroon, a Central African country on the Gulf of Guinea with nearly two hundred different ethnic groups and customs. Cameroonian food is generally very hot, and this recipe is blast-off hot. I developed it from a description by Georges Collinet, a Cameroonian radio presenter and host of National Public Radio's *Afropop Worldwide*. The name of the dish, *folon*, which comes from his area of Cameroon, is also the name of the mineral-rich vegetable used in the dish, known as bitterleaf. Varieties of bitterleaf are eaten throughout Africa, and real *folon* leaf is probably unavailable in North America. Some African markets in the U.S. might carry it, especially for Nigerian cooks, who use a variety of it, too, in their food. Bitterleaf has a slightly viscous property, and although some African cookbooks for Americans will recommend using spinach in its place, collard greens or kale are actually better choices. The peanut butter used in so much African cooking is not actually "peanut butter" but is the paste of ground peanuts. That might not sound like something different, but you will get an earthier taste by using an organic peanut butter rather than Skippy. Serve this dish with yams, fried plantains, rice, cassava, or all of the above. And as Georges Collinet recommends: "Drink a good, strong beer with your *folon*."

4 tablespoons peanut oil

3 medium-size onions, 1 thinly sliced, 1 cut into eighths, and 1 chopped

3 quarts water

1 pound fresh collard greens or kale, thick stems removed

3 bone-in chicken breast halves, skin removed

1/2 pound fresh peanut butter

3 medium-size tomatoes, cut in half, seeds squeezed out, and grated against the largest holes of a grater

2 1/2 pounds fresh large shrimp with their heads or 1 1/4 pounds headless shrimp, heads and/or shells removed, or 1 1/4 pounds dried fish, such as stockfish or African dried fish (see page 431)

2 habanero chiles, finely chopped

Salt and fresh ground black pepper to taste

1. In a medium-size skillet, heat 2 tablespoons of the peanut oil over medium heat, then cook the sliced onion, separating its rings as it cooks, until golden brown, about 12 minutes, stirring and turning frequently. Remove, spread out on a paper towel–lined plate, and set aside.

2. Bring the water to a boil in a large saucepan and boil the collard greens for 30 minutes. Add the chicken and the onion cut into eighths and cook until it returns to a near boil, but not more than 5 minutes. Remove the chicken with a slotted spoon, pat dry with a paper towel, and set aside. Remove the greens with a slotted spoon, and cut them into small pieces, and set aside. Reserve 3 cups of the broth. In a medium-size bowl, mix 1 cup of the broth with the peanut butter so that it becomes more liquid and easier to handle, and set aside.

3. In a large skillet, heat the remaining 2 tablespoons peanut oil over medium-high heat, then cook the chicken pieces on all sides until golden brown, about 5 minutes. Remove the chicken, cut each breast in half with a heavy chef's knife, and set aside.

4. Add the chopped onion and the tomatoes to the skillet and cook over medium-high heat until the liquid of the tomatoes is mostly evaporated, about 3 minutes, stirring occasionally. Add the peanut butter mixture and cook over medium-low heat for 20 minutes, stirring often so that it doesn't stick, and adding $^1/_2$ cup increments of the remaining reserved broth to keep the sauce creamy. Add the collard greens, shrimp, chiles, and salt and pepper and stir to blend well. Add the chicken, increase the heat to medium, and cook, partially covered, until the chicken is cooked through and the shrimp are firm and orange-pink, turning occasionally, 15 minutes. If the sauce is bubbling too vigorously, reduce the heat to low. Transfer to a serving platter or individual plates and serve with the fried onions reserved from step 1 scattered on top.

MAKES 4 TO 5 SERVINGS

Egusi Stew

I n Nigeria, watermelon seed, or generically any edible melon seed, goes by the name *egusi* in Yoruba and *agusi* in Hausa. In this stew, the melon seeds are ground and give the dish a unique color and flavor. In place of melon seeds, pumpkinseeds work quite well. Any combination of crab, shrimp, and smoked fish can also be used in place of the shrimp. Smoked oysters from a can and beef can be used in place of the chicken. Red palm oil is that very distinctive African cooking oil that makes African food taste African. It can be bought in West African markets and some Latino markets, especially those with Brazilian clientele, as well as on the Internet. It is very much worth the effort to find red palm oil—you'll love it. This is always a well-received stew, and you can accompany it with Cassava Ball Fritters (page 364) and Sweet Puff-Puffs (page 392).

½ cup *egusi* (melon) seeds or pumpkinseeds

One 3-pound chicken, cut into 8 pieces

Salt to taste

⅓ cup red palm oil *or* ⅓ cup walnut oil mixed with ¾ teaspoon hot paprika

2½ pounds ripe tomatoes, cut in half, seeds squeezed out, and grated against the largest holes of a grater

1 small onion, chopped

2 habanero chiles, stemmed and halved

2 tablespoons tomato paste

¾ cup water

2½ pounds fresh shrimp with their heads or 1¼ pounds headless shrimp, heads and/or shells removed

1 pound fresh spinach, with heavy stems, chopped

1. Put the seeds in a food processor and blend for 30 seconds until powdery. Set aside.

2. Salt the chicken. In a large casserole, heat the red palm oil over medium-high heat for 4 to 5 minutes. Brown the chicken pieces on both sides, about 6 minutes in all.

3. Place the tomatoes, onion, and habanero chiles in the food processor and blend for about 30 seconds or until smooth. Dissolve the tomato paste in the tomato mixture and pour over the chicken. Reduce the heat to low, cover partially, and cook until the chicken can be pulled off the bone with a tug of a fork, about 1¼ hours, turning the chicken occasionally.

4. Add the water and shrimp and continue simmering for 10 minutes.

5. Add the spinach and the reserved ground seeds and continue to simmer for 10 minutes more. Serve immediately.

MAKES 6 SERVINGS

hot chicks, wicked ducks, and one killer rabbit

the food of nigeria

Nigerian foods rely heavily on starchy root vegetables such as cassava and yams and green vegetables such as bitterleaf, okra, spinach, and other African plants. The cooking also relies on meat, and in Nigeria goat is popular, but also chicken and fish prepared with legumes such as peanuts. The Hausa people of northern Nigeria like spicy-hot meat kebabs. In Hausa, one of the languages of Nigeria, *yaji* is a word for a spice mix with chiles. The name derives from the name of the ruler of fourteenth-century Kano called "the hot-tempered one." An expression in Hausa, *komai ya yi zafi, ya yi sauki* (everything that gets hot will cool down), refers not only to temperature heat but chile heat as well. In southern Nigeria, the Ibo people love stews of fish, shrimp, crab, lobster, rice, and vegetables. In the central part of the country, the Yoruba people enjoy stewed meats that they serve with mashed yams or cassava.

Cape Malay Chicken Curry

The Cape Malay community of South Africa is the only culture in South Africa that actually has hot-spicy food in its cuisine. Cape Malay cooking is transplanted and transformed from its original home in the Indo-Malaysian archipelago as it was influenced by Indians. It all sounds so complicated, and it is. But luckily, this recipe isn't. It is adapted from Cass Abrahams's *Cass Abrahams Cooks Cape Malay: Food from Africa* (Metz Press, 2000).

4 tablespoons Cape Malay *Garam Masala* (page 420)

1½ cups unbleached all-purpose flour

Salt and freshly ground black pepper to taste

2¼ pounds boneless chicken breasts, cut into 1-inch cubes

2 tablespoons vegetable oil

3 tablespoons unsalted butter

2 large onions, thinly sliced

2 teaspoons cumin seeds

2 teaspoons fennel seeds

1 bay leaf

1 pound ripe tomatoes, peeled, seeded, and chopped

1 teaspoon ground turmeric

1 teaspoon crushed garlic

3 fresh green finger-type chiles or 4 green jalapeño chiles, seeded and finely chopped

2 cups whole-milk plain yogurt

1. In a medium-size bowl, mix together 3 tablespoons of the *garam masala*, the flour, and salt and pepper. Toss the chicken in this mixture, shaking off the excess.

2. In a casserole, heat the vegetable oil with the butter over medium-high heat and, once the butter has melted and is sizzling, cook the chicken breasts on both sides until lightly browned, 4 to 5 minutes. Remove the chicken and set aside.

3. Add the onions, cumin seeds, fennel seeds, and bay leaf to the skillet and cook until the onions are soft and translucent, about 5 minutes, stirring. Add the tomatoes, the remaining 1 tablespoon garam masala, the turmeric, garlic, and chiles. Cook until the sauce is thick, about 30 minutes, stirring occasionally. Return the chicken to the skillet, reduce the heat to low, and cook until the chicken is firm when poked with your finger, about 15 minutes. Add the yogurt and heat, but don't let it come to a boil or it will curdle. Serve immediately.

MAKES 6 SERVINGS

Doro Wat

T his chicken stew could probably be considered the national dish of Ethiopia. It is richly flavored not only with spices but also with onions. You can use either regular yellow onions or sweet onions, if you like the contrast between spicy and sweet. This is a long-cooking stew, and on top of that there are two items that need to be prepared before you start the stew, so keep that in mind as you plan. Since there is so much finely chopped onion in this stew you may want to use a food processor. If you do, make sure you chop the onions by pulsing the machine. This recipe is adapted from the African Studies Center at the University of Pennsylvania. Serve with lots of *Injera* (page 400).

One 3½-pound chicken, cut into 8 serving pieces, skin and fat removed, scored all over

Juice of 1 lemon

1 cup white wine

4 large onions (about 4 pounds), finely chopped

¼ cup *niter kebbeh* (page 419)

6 tablespoons *Berbere* (page 417)

10 large garlic cloves, finely chopped

2 teaspoons finely chopped fresh ginger

½ teaspoon ground fenugreek

½ teaspoon ground cardamom

¼ teaspoon ground nutmeg

¼ teaspoon ground cumin

1 tablespoon cayenne pepper

2 tablespoons hot paprika

½ cup water

6 hard-boiled eggs, shelled

1 tablespoon salt

2 teaspoons freshly ground black pepper

1. Place the chicken pieces in a large ceramic or glass bowl or baking dish and marinate with the lemon juice and wine for 6 hours in the refrigerator.

2. Place the onions in a large casserole such as a Dutch oven or cast-iron stew pot, and cook without any fat or liquid over high heat until they start to sizzle. Reduce the heat to low and cook until there is no liquid left and the onions are pale yellow, about 1 hour, stirring occasionally.

3. Add the *niter kebbeh* and cook until it has melted, stirring. Add the *berbere*, garlic, and ginger and cook 30 minutes, stirring frequently. Add the fenugreek, cardamom, nutmeg, cumin, cayenne pepper, and paprika and stir to blend well. Remove the chicken from the marinade, pat dry with paper towels, and submerge in the sauce, turning the pieces until coated on all sides. Add the water, cover, and simmer until tender, about 1½ hours.

4. Meanwhile, pierce the hard-boiled eggs with the tines of a fork or a corn-cob holder, piercing approximately ¼ inch into the egg all over the surface, but not into the yolk. After the chicken has cooked, add the eggs, turning them gently in the sauce. Season with salt and pepper, cover, and cook for ½ hour more. Serve immediately.

MAKES 4 TO 6 SERVINGS

Chicken Kurma

This dish, from the Indian state of Andhra Pradesh, is very hot, as is most of the food from this region. *Kurma* was originally a Mogul dish (see page 145) and was not so hot spicy as just spicy. Although usually thought of as a northern dish, when *kurma* is made in the south a paste from fresh coconut and raw cashews might be used to replace the traditional yogurt or cream used in the north. Serve with plain Rice Pilaf (page 396).

One 1-inch cube fresh ginger, peeled

3 large garlic cloves

4 tablespoons vegetable oil

1 pound onions, chopped

3 fresh green finger-type chiles or 4 green jalapeño chiles, seeded and finely chopped

2 teaspoons salt

1/2 teaspoon ground turmeric

1 teaspoon *garam masala* made from equal parts cloves, cinnamon, cardamom, and caraway (see page 309)

1 teaspoon ground coriander

2 pounds bone-in chicken breast and thighs, skin removed

1/2 pound Stabilized Yogurt (page 278), whipped until smooth

1/2 cup water

1/3 cup shredded dried unsweetened coconut

1/2 teaspoon freshly ground black pepper

1 tablespoon finely chopped fresh coriander (cilantro) leaves

1 tablespoon finely chopped fresh mint leaves

1. Pound the ginger and garlic in a mortar until mushy. Alternatively, use a food processor. In a casserole, heat the vegetable oil over medium-high heat, then cook the onions until golden, about 15 minutes, stirring occasionally. Meanwhile, mix the ginger-garlic paste, the chiles, salt, turmeric, *garam masala*, and coriander in a bowl, then spread this on the chicken and marinate for 10 minutes.

2. Add the chicken pieces to the onions in the casserole and cook 10 minutes, turning occasionally. Add the yogurt and water and stir well. Cook for 5 minutes, then add the coconut, black pepper, coriander leaves, and mint leaves. Cover, reduce the heat to low, and cook until the chicken is very tender, 15 to 20 minutes. Serve hot.

MAKES 4 SERVINGS

hot chicks, wicked ducks, and one killer rabbit

Chile Chicken with Coconut and Cashews

This chicken preparation is known as a *pandhra rassa*, "white chicken curry," and is part of Maharashtrian cuisine. The preparation, which can also be made with mutton, is a specialty of Kohlapur, a southwestern city in the state of Maharashtra. Lower-caste Maharashtrians are meat eaters, and their cuisine also includes subtly flavored vegetable dishes as well as aromatic, spicy hot meat and fish curries. All non-vegetarian and vegetarian dishes are eaten with boiled rice or with *bhakris*, which are soft rotis made of rice flour. Special rice poori bread called *vada* and *amboli*, which are pancakes made of fermented rice, black gram (*urad dal*), and semolina, are also eaten as a part of the main meal. This dish is served with the poori bread called *tikoni puris* (page 399). The red chile seeds called for in this recipe can usually be gathered loose from the bottom of a bag of dried red chiles you would have bought for your pantry. Or you can break some dried chiles in half and shake the seeds out.

1 cup shredded dried unsweetened coconut	3 tablespoons clarified butter or peanut oil
2 ounces fresh ginger, peeled	1 cinnamon stick
12 large garlic cloves	3 dried red de arbol chiles
2 pounds boneless chicken breast and thigh, skin removed and cut into large pieces	3 fresh red finger-type chiles or 4 red jalapeño chiles, chopped, seeds reserved
1½ teaspoons cumin seeds	2 tablespoons unsalted cashew nuts
1½ tablespoons poppy seeds	2 tablespoons raisins
1½ tablespoons coriander seeds	2 medium-size onions, finely chopped
2 teaspoons dried red chile seeds	½ cup Stabilized Yogurt (page 278)
Seeds from 8 cardamom pods	Salt to taste
12 whole cloves	½ cup coconut milk (see page 90)
¾ cup water	

1. Place the coconut in a food processor and blend until almost powdery. Remove and set aside. Place the ginger and garlic in the food processor and blend until it forms a paste, stopping and scraping down the sides if necessary.

2. In a large baking dish, rub the chicken pieces with the ginger-garlic paste and set aside to marinate for about an hour. In a spice mill, or using a mortar and pestle, finely grind the cumin seeds, poppy seeds, coriander seeds, red chile seeds, cardamom seeds, and 8 of the cloves. Remove to a bowl and mix together with the powdery coconut and stir in the water to make a paste. This is the masala paste.

3. In a large, heavy casserole, heat 1 tablespoon clarified butter over medium-high heat, then add the cinnamon, dry and fresh red chiles, cashew nuts, raisins, and the remaining 4 cloves and cook until the nuts are golden brown, 2 to 3 minutes, stirring. Add the chicken and cook until lightly browned, about 5 minutes. Reduce the heat to low, cover, and cook until the chicken is half done, about 20 minutes. Remove the chicken from the casserole with a slotted spoon and set aside.

4. Raise the heat to medium-high, add the remaining 2 tablespoons clarified butter to the casserole along with the onions, and cook until the onions are translucent, about 8 minutes, stirring. Add the reserved masala paste and cook for 3 minutes, stirring. Reduce the heat to low, add the yogurt and salt to taste, and cook for 2 minutes, stirring. Return the chicken to the casserole along with the coconut milk and simmer, uncovered, until tender, 20 to 30 minutes, stirring occasionally. Bring to a near boil, stir well, and turn the heat off. Serve immediately.

MAKES 4 SERVINGS

the cuisine of
andhra pradesh

Andhra Pradesh is a large Indian state in the southern part of the subcontinent with a coastline on the Bay of Bengal. Some say that the cuisine of Andhra Pradesh is the spiciest and hottest of all Indian cuisine and that the city of Guntur has the hottest food in this state. There are two important elements to the cuisine. The first is the original Hindu cuisine of Andhra, and the second derives from the Muslim influence of the Mogul era as represented most importantly in Hyderabadi cuisine, the capital of the state. It is the original Hindu cuisine that can be said to be red hot.

Although the cuisine is not vegetarian, vegetables play a big role in the food of Andhra Pradesh and are prepared with a variety of different *masalas* (the sauce/gravy or basis to a gravy), which lend different flavors to the same vegetable. Traditional Andhra meat cookery is also spicy and unique. Lamb is the most widely used meat in Hyderabadi cooking, which is a rich and aromatic cuisine that liberally uses exotic spices and clarified butter (ghee). Nuts and dried fruits are also used prominently in the food. Lamb or vegetable *biryanis* are one of the most distinct Hyderabadi foods.

the indian way of eating

Indians eat differently than Westerners. In the West we tend to eat in courses, while in India the different dishes, and there may be many, are placed in small individual dishes and arranged on a tray along with rice, breads of various kinds, pickles, chutneys, and other relishes.

Baked Chicken in Spicy Yogurt Gravy

This preparation is really nice, very easy, and not too hot. It's a preparation from northern India with influences from the Moguls, as we can tell by the use of yogurt. The chicken bakes until it falls off the bone, and it's great served with Rice Pilaf (page 396).

1/4 cup blanched whole or slivered almonds

1/2 cup shredded dried unsweetened coconut or fresh coconut

3 large garlic cloves

One 1-inch cube fresh ginger, peeled

1 teaspoon ground red chile or cayenne pepper

1 cup Stabilized Yogurt (page 278)

Juice of 1 lemon

1 large ripe tomato, peeled and chopped

2 pinches of saffron, crumbled

One 3-pound fryer chicken, separated into 2 breasts, 2 thighs, 2 legs, and 2 wings

1/4 cup clarified butter (*ghee*)

2 large onions, thinly sliced

Salt to taste

1. Place the almonds, coconut, garlic, ginger, and chile in a blender and grind. If the blade doesn't turn properly to blend, add a little yogurt until it does. Add the remaining yogurt, the lemon juice, tomato, and saffron and blend until smooth. Transfer to a large ceramic or glass baking dish, add the chicken, and toss to coat. Cover with plastic wrap and let marinate in the refrigerator for 2 to 4 hours.

2. Preheat the oven to 325°F. In a heavy casserole, melt the clarified butter over medium-high heat, add the onions, and cook until golden, about 15 minutes, stirring. Add the chicken and its marinade. Season with salt, cover, and bring to a gentle simmer over medium heat, but don't let the broth boil. Seal the casserole with aluminum foil and replace the lid. Bake in the oven until the chicken is tender and the meat can be pulled off the bone with a fork, 1¹/₂ hours. Remove and serve.

MAKES 6 SERVINGS

maharashtrian cuisine

Mumbai (formerly Bombay), the capital of the Indian state of Maharashtra, has been described as the place where North India meets South India. Mumbai has its own cuisine, heavily favoring street foods such as *vada pav*, a fried potato patty in a bun, and *pav bhaji*, a kind of fast food made from mixed mashed vegetables served with bread liberally fried in butter. There are Muslim-style kebabs, tandoori chicken, and fish. Although Maharashtrians use chiles in their cooking, they don't do so with the same kind of abandon as elsewhere in India.

On the Deccan Plateau, the heart of Maharashtra, large areas are arid and barren, and therefore the cooking sees a lot of pulses and grains. The cooking is also simple; for example, many dals are just boiled together with salt, turmeric, and one or two other ingredients. Peanuts and cashews are widely used in vegetable dishes, and peanut oil is the main cooking medium. The upper castes have a spicy mostly vegetarian diet, while others castes are more meat eaters. Grated coconuts spice many kinds of dishes. Rice is a staple food, as is *bhakri*, a thick roti (unleavened bread) made from millet, sorghum, rice, wheat, or corn that is typically eaten as a workingman's meal with pickles, raw onions, and chiles. The sweets of Maharashtra are quite numerous and include *puran poli*, which is roti stuffed with a sweet mixture of cane sugar and gram flour, and *shreekhand*, a sort of thick yogurt sweet dish flavored with cardamom powder and saffron and served with hot poori bread.

Chicken in Green Coconut Sauce

This dish from Goa, called chicken *xacuti* or *xhacuti* or *shakuti*, is really quite hot. It is also labor intensive, and it would be best for you to have everything prepared before you begin cooking. Once it is cooking, though, it can remain relatively unattended. This recipe uses "thin" coconut milk and "thick" coconut milk. Thin coconut milk can be made by following the instructions in the method. Thick coconut milk (also called coconut cream) can also be homemade, but when I am lazy or pressed for time I usually use canned coconut milk, which is thick already and works perfectly fine. See page 90 for more on coconut milk. The chicken will be tender, nearly falling off the bone, and the sauce is a piquant and greenish blend of chiles, onions, and coconut. It is best eaten with a Raita (page 396) and Rice Pilaf (page 396).

FOR THE SPICE MIX

15 dried red de arbol chiles, stemmed and seeded, or 3 tablespoons ground red chile or cayenne pepper

10 black peppercorns or ¹/₂ teaspoon freshly ground black pepper

2 tablespoons coriander seeds

6 whole cloves or ¹/₂ teaspoon ground cloves

One ¹/₂-inch piece cinnamon stick or ¹/₂ teaspoon ground cinnamon

¹/₂ whole nutmeg seed or ¹/₂ teaspoon ground nutmeg

2 teaspoons aniseeds

1 tablespoon poppy seeds

1 teaspoon ground turmeric

FOR THE CHICKEN AND SAUCE

2 cups shredded dried unsweetened coconut

3 cups boiling water

6 tablespoons clarified butter (*ghee*)

10 medium-size onions, 2 sliced ¹/₄ inch thick, 4 finely chopped, and 4 quartered

¹/₄ cup diced fresh coconut

6 fresh green finger-type chiles or 8 green jalapeño chiles, finely chopped

One 3-pound chicken, cut into 6 pieces

Salt to taste

1 cup coconut cream (see page 90) or canned coconut milk

Juice from 2 limes

2 tablespoons finely chopped fresh coriander (cilantro) leaves

1. To make the spice mix, place the red chiles, black peppercorns, coriander seeds, cloves, cinnamon stick, nutmeg, aniseeds, and poppy seeds in a spice mill and grind until a powder. Stir in the turmeric.

2. To make the chicken and sauce, place the shredded coconut in a 1-quart measuring cup or bowl, pour the boiling water over it, and let sit until needed. Once this is strained, it is the coconut milk.

3. Preheat the oven to 450°F. Place 2 tablespoons of the clarified butter in a roasting pan and melt it in the oven. Add the sliced onions and the diced coconut to the roasting pan and roast until the onions are golden and the coconut is light brown, about 10 minutes. Remove the onions and coconut and finely grind them in a blender until smooth, stopping and scraping the sides when necessary. Do not add water.

4. In a large skillet or casserole, melt the remaining 4 tablespoons clarified butter over medium-high heat, then cook the chopped onions and fresh chiles until the onions are light golden and soft, about 8 minutes, stirring occasionally. Add the chicken to the skillet and brown on all sides, about 5 minutes. Add the spice mix and salt and cook for 1 minute, distributing the spices around the skillet and on the chicken pieces. Pour the thin coconut milk through a strainer and add to the chicken, reduce the heat to very low, partially cover, and simmer gently, without letting the liquid come to a boil, until the chicken is tender, about 1³/₄ hours, turning the chicken pieces now and then.

5. Add the quartered onions and the diced roasted coconut and onion blend. (To incorporate the onion and coconut blend into the sauce it may be easier to momentarily remove the chicken pieces and then return them to the skillet.) Simmer the quartered onions in the sauce for 5 minutes, then add the thick coconut cream. Mix well, then check the seasoning and add salt if necessary. Cook on low heat until the sauce is thickened, about 45 minutes. Pour the lime juice over the chicken and sprinkle with coriander leaves. Serve immediately.

MAKES 6 SERVINGS

Stir-Fried Ground Chicken with Basil and Fried Eggs

Pad bai or *Phàt bai kà-phrao* (also *pad bai ga-prow*) is a kind of hash that can be made with either chicken or shrimp. It is stir-fried with hot basil and uses Thai chiles, shallots, garlic, fish sauce, and vegetables if desired. Hot basil is a peppery basil, but you can use whatever is available. If you decide to add vegetables, some nice choices are snow peas, eggplant, and bok choy. Some people like to slide a fried egg, cooked over medium-hard, on top of the dish, which is the way I like it. Serve this over rice.

8 large garlic cloves, chopped

4 shallots, chopped

25 fresh green Thai chiles or 8 large fresh green jalapeño chiles, sliced

25 fresh red Thai chiles or 8 large fresh red jalapeño chiles, sliced

1 teaspoon green peppercorns

3 tablespoons peanut oil

1 pound ground chicken

1/4 cup Thai fish sauce

2 tablespoons palm sugar or granulated sugar

1 cup loosely packed fresh hot basil leaves or regular basil leaves

4 large eggs

1. Place the garlic, shallots, green and red chiles, and peppercorns in a food processor and blend until very finely chopped. Transfer to a mortar and pound until a paste, in batches if necessary. Set aside.

2. In a wok, heat 2 tablespoons of the peanut oil over high heat, then add the chile paste and cook 1 minute, stirring. Add the chicken, Thai fish sauce, and sugar and cook until reduced and there is very little liquid left, 10 to 15 minutes, stirring. Add the basil leaves and cook 1 minute, stirring. Transfer the chicken to a serving platter and spread it out.

3. Meanwhile, heat the remaining 1 tablespoon peanut oil in a nonstick skillet. Crack the eggs into the pan. Cook until firm, then flip over and continue cooking until cooked medium. Slide the eggs on top of the chicken and serve immediately.

MAKES 4 SERVINGS

thai chiles in the supermarket

Many Thai cooks have assured me that the tiny Thai chiles sold in supermarkets in this country today, and especially in southern California, are not the ones used in Thailand. They are the same cultivar but they are just not as hot. Another confusion is that the chiles sold as "Thai chiles" in American supermarkets, which are about 1½ inches long and ¼ inch thick, are also a name used for the small bird's-eye chiles called "mouse-dropping chiles" in Thailand. My nomenclature is based on what you will find in the market, whether it is correct or not.

Stir-Fried Chicken with Impressive Chile

This Thai stir-fry is called *kai pad prik haeng* or *kai pad bai gra prao*, a chicken dish with indeed an impressive amount of chile. The most important thing to remember when you make this is that cooking the chiles can be dangerous (well, not *really* dangerous, but rather alarming). The chiles go into the hot wok without any other food for about a minute and will release, in vapor form, the active ingredient of capsaicin into the air, which can irritate your throat, lungs, and eyes. If you did this every day you would simply get use to it, but as a novice you should be aware of this possibility. Turn the vent hood on full blast, pull your head back away from the wok, hold your breath, and close your eyes as you add the chiles. After about 10 seconds, open your eyes and proceed as normal. After all this you are probably wondering what this dish will taste like. In a word—*hot*; therefore you always eat it with steamed rice.

1 cup unsalted peanuts	½ pound yard-long beans (asparagus beans) or green beans, cut into 1-inch lengths
2 tablespoons peanut oil	
6 large garlic cloves, thinly sliced	1 teaspoon palm sugar, light brown sugar, or granulated sugar
⅔ cup crumbled dried red de arbol chiles	
	3 tablespoons light soy sauce
1 pound boneless chicken breast, cut in half lengthwise and thinly sliced crosswise	¼ cup Thai fish sauce
	1¼ cups chicken broth (homemade or canned)

1.　In a wok, dry roast the peanuts over medium heat until they begin to turn golden, about 2 minutes. Remove, chop, and set aside. Increase the heat to high for a few minutes, then add the peanut oil. Let the oil heat, then cook the garlic until golden and slightly crispy, 30 to 60 seconds. Remove the garlic with a skimmer and drain on paper towels.

2.　Leave the heat on high and, after a minute or so, add the chiles and cook for 1 minute, stirring quickly and constantly. Add the chicken and cook until it turns color, about 2 minutes, stirring and tossing almost constantly. Add the yard-long beans, sugar, and reserved peanuts one after the other quickly in succession, stirring, then add the soy sauce, fish sauce, and chicken broth. Cover and cook 5 minutes, stirring occasionally. Uncover and continue cooking until the liquid has been absorbed and evaporated, about another 5 minutes. Add the garlic, cover, and cook until done, 1 to 2 minutes. Serve immediately.

MAKES 4 TO 6 SERVINGS

Chicken Adobo with Hot and Tangy Coconut Sauce

This Filipino dish from Bicol, a province on the southern island of Luzon, which has a significant Muslim population, has an obvious Spanish influence as we see by the fact that it is called adobo, a reference to the vinegar used in poaching the chicken. But the Muslim Indian influence—and the piquant influence—is also evident in that this is very much like a curry and it is hot, but not too much. The area of Bicol is the only area of the Philippines that has chile-hot cooking. Serve with steamed rice.

1 pound boneless chicken thighs, cut into 1-inch pieces

1 small bay leaf

1 teaspoon freshly grated ginger

2 tablespoons soy sauce

3 large garlic cloves, finely chopped

1/2 cup rice vinegar

2 yellow banana chiles or 7 yellow *güero* chiles or 4 green jalapeño chiles or 1/2 habanero chile, finely chopped

1 1/2 teaspoons black peppercorns

3 tablespoons vegetable oil

1/2 cup coconut cream (see page 90) or canned coconut milk

1. Put the chicken, bay leaf, ginger, soy sauce, garlic, vinegar, chiles, and peppercorns into a stockpot or heavy saucepan and turn the heat to high. Once the liquid starts to bubble, reduce the heat to low and simmer until the chicken is firm, about 15 minutes. Drain and set the chicken aside. Reserve the poaching liquid.

2. In a large wok or skillet, heat the vegetable oil over medium-high heat, then cook the chicken until golden brown, about 3 minutes, tossing and turning. Add the reserved poaching liquid to the wok and scrape any bits clinging to the wok down into the broth. Bring to a near boil, then reduce the heat to low and simmer until the liquid is reduced to about 1/4 cup, about 25 minutes. Add the coconut cream, raise the heat to medium, and stir for 2 to 3 minutes. Serve hot.

MAKES 4 SERVINGS

 # Kung Pao Chicken

Although this is one of the most famous Chinese dishes, appearing on every Chinese restaurant menu in America and assumed to be a Sichuan preparation, it is actually a dish from one of China's least known provinces. Guizhou is a backward and poor province bordering Sichuan to the northeast. Kung pao (*gong bao*) chicken is a spicy dish made with diced chicken, peanuts, and chile peppers, but as for the rest of Guizhou cuisine, one writer declared that it "is awash with mediocrity." The dish is said to be named after a late Qing dynasty (late nineteenth century) *gong bao* or court official of Sichuan named Ding Baozhen. During Communist China's Cultural Revolution kung pao chicken suffered for being associated with the imperial past and was renamed. In kung pao chicken all the ingredients are cut in harmony, and the cubed chicken is complemented by small chunks of scallion. Serve this dish with steamed rice.

1 pound boneless, skinless chicken breast, cut into 1/2-inch cubes

3 tablespoons soy sauce

5 1/2 teaspoons cornstarch

1 1/2 tablespoons water

1 tablespoon rice wine (*mirin*) or vermouth

1 tablespoon sugar

1/2 teaspoon salt

1/2 teaspoon sesame oil

3 cups vegetable oil, for frying

3/4 cup dried red de arbol chiles, seeded and halved

1/2 cup unsalted roasted peanuts

One 1 1/4-inch-thick slice fresh ginger, peeled and julienned

1 large garlic clove, thinly sliced

2 scallions, cut into 1/2-inch pieces

1.　In a medium-size bowl, toss the chicken with 1 tablespoon of the soy sauce, 4 1/2 teaspoons of the cornstarch, and the water and marinate for 30 minutes. In another bowl, mix together the remaining 2 tablespoons soy sauce, the rice wine, sugar, the remaining 1 teaspoon cornstarch, the salt, and sesame oil and set aside.

2.　In a large wok, heat the frying oil over high heat, then cook the chicken until golden, about 1 minute. Remove with a skimmer and drain. Remove all but 1 1/2 tablespoons oil from the wok, reserving at least 2 tablespoons from what you remove, then let the remaining oil heat over high heat again. Cook the dried chiles until they darken a bit but do not turn black, about 30 seconds, stirring. Remove with a skimmer and set aside.

3.　Add 1 tablespoon of the reserved oil to the wok, heat over high heat, and cook the peanuts until they turn golden, about 1 minute. Remove and set aside to cool. Add the remaining 1 tablespoon oil to the wok and let it heat, then cook the ginger, garlic, scallions, and chicken about 1 minute, stir-frying rapidly. Stir in the reserved sauce of soy and rice wine, tossing and stirring until it is well mixed with the other ingredients, about 1 minute, then add the peanuts and stir again. Serve immediately.

MAKES 4 SERVINGS

Sichuan Peppery Chicken

This brightly colored dish is traditionally made with the meat from chicken legs, but I find that using chicken thighs is much less work, and the taste is identical. The dark-fleshed meat becomes golden-purple when it is cooked and it contrasts with the brilliant green or red of the bell pepper. This is a very hot dish and, therefore, you will want to eat it with steamed rice.

Thick pastes made of chiles and beans are called *lajiao jiang*, and they represent a whole class of cooking condiments. You can find them in Chinese groceries and many supermarkets, with "hot chile paste with garlic" written on the label. The Sichuanese use a hot bean paste, too, which they call *ladouban jiang*. Fuchsia Dunlop, in her book *The Land of Plenty* (W. W. Norton, 2003), tells us that people from Sichuan have a reputation for being a little spicy themselves, and local women are even known as "spice girls" (*la mei zi*). "The spicy local diet is so notorious that Chinese people will invariably ask outsiders on their way to Sichuan whether or not they are 'afraid of chile heat (*pa la*),'" she tells us.

1 pound boneless, skinless chicken thighs, cut into ¹/₂-inch cubes

1 egg white, beaten until frothy

2 teaspoons cornstarch

2 teaspoons soy sauce

3 cups peanut oil, for frying

8 fresh red finger-type or jalapeño chiles, seeded and chopped

1 green or red bell pepper, seeded and cut into ³/₄-inch squares

1 scallion, white part only, finely chopped

1 teaspoon finely chopped fresh ginger

1 large garlic clove, finely chopped

1 tablespoon Sichuan chile bean paste (page 98)

2 dried red de arbol chiles

¹/₄ teaspoon ground Sichuan peppercorns

1¹/₂ teaspoons rice wine (*mirin*) or vermouth

1 teaspoon sugar

1 teaspoon sesame oil

1 teaspoon water

¹/₂ teaspoon white vinegar

1. Place the chicken in a medium-size glass or ceramic bowl with the egg white, 1¹/₂ teaspoons of the cornstarch, and 1 teaspoon of the soy sauce. Marinate for 20 to 30 minutes.

2. In a large wok, heat the frying oil over medium heat to about 250°F. Dip the chicken in the hot oil until it turns color, about 15 seconds, then remove the chicken with a skimmer and set aside. Remove all but 3 tablespoons of oil from the wok and raise the heat to medium-high. Cook the fresh red chiles, bell pepper, scallion, ginger, and garlic until fragrant, about 1 minute, stirring. Remove from the wok and set aside with the chicken.

3. Add the chile bean paste and cook until fragrant, about 10 seconds, breaking it up and stirring, then add the dried red chiles and Sichuan peppercorns and stir. Add the chicken, reserved bell pepper mixture, rice wine, the remaining 1 teaspoon soy sauce, the sugar, sesame oil, water, vinegar, and the remaining $1/2$ teaspoon cornstarch. Stir several times, then cook over medium-high heat until the chicken is cooked through and the bell pepper is softer but still crunchy, about 5 minutes, stirring. Serve immediately.

MAKES 2 TO 4 SERVINGS

Chongqing Spicy Chicken

*I*n Sichuan province, Chongqing's cuisine reflects a peasant heritage even though it is a major industrial city at the junction of the Kialing and Yangtze rivers, because it has attracted migrants from the surrounding rural countryside for generations. It is said that Chongqing's cuisine is hotter than elsewhere in Sichuan. This dish came recommended, and the moment I saw it arrive at our table in the brightly lit Sam Luk Restaurant, at 655 Jackson Street in San Francisco, I knew I must learn how to make it. When our dish came—it's simply called chicken with chiles in Chinese, *la zi ji*—it was covered with about a hundred bright red chiles. I'm not exaggerating—it looked intimidating. My daughter Dyala was with me, and she is as an adventurous an eater as I am and also particularly fond of Sichuan food. Although the restaurant billed itself as the "only authentic Szechwan restaurant in the heart of Chinatown," I knew that to get "authentic" would be an effort. Before we even ordered I went through my usual pantomime with the owner and waiter to convey the idea that "we may look like Americans but we eat like Sichuanese." This insistence isn't always successful, but at the Sam Luk it was and we had some amazing food that I'm pretty sure the other American customers were not privy to.

Although this is a simple dish in its cooking, the tricky part is the chicken. American supermarkets don't sell the wings cut up the way you need them for this preparation. So you will have to buy chicken wings, preferably from a quite young bird, and cut each wing into 4 to 5 pieces. The dish we had at the Sam Luk had crunchy golden chicken pieces so tender that you could eat the bones as well. I've not been able to reproduce that in my home kitchen because I don't have access to young chickens, but you can get the tastes exactly right by buying supermarket chicken wings and following this recipe. Although this preparation uses an impossible amount of chiles, diners usually pick out the chicken with their chopsticks and not the chiles. Even so, the dish can only be described as incendiary.

2 pounds chicken wings, cut into 1-inch pieces

1 tablespoon rice wine (*mirin*) or vermouth

2 teaspoons soy sauce

1 1/2 cups rice flour or unbleached all-purpose flour for dredging

4 cups peanut oil, for frying

2 large garlic cloves, thinly sliced

One 1/2-inch cube fresh ginger, peeled and thinly sliced

2 ounces dried red de arbol chiles (about 2 cups), seeded and halved

1 tablespoon Sichuan peppercorns

3 scallions, white and light green parts only, cut into thirds

1 teaspoon salt, or more to your taste

1/2 teaspoon sugar

2 teaspoons sesame oil

1. Toss the chicken in a large glass or ceramic bowl with the rice wine and soy sauce and marinate for 30 minutes.

2. In a large wok, heat the frying oil to 300°F over medium heat. Drain the chicken and toss with the flour until lightly coated, shaking off any excess flour in a colander. Cook the chicken in 3 batches until golden brown and a little crispy, 7 to 8 minutes. Remove with a skimmer and set aside.

3. Remove all but 3 tablespoons of peanut oil from the wok and heat over medium heat. Add the garlic and ginger and cook, stirring, until they start to turn color, about 20 seconds. Add the chiles and Sichuan peppercorns and cook 20 seconds, stirring, making sure the chiles don't turn black. Remove the wok from the heat if they look like they are turning black. Return the chicken to the wok, add the scallions, and stir. Season with salt to taste and sugar, stir, and toss until the chicken is well coated. Remove from the heat and stir in the sesame oil. Serve immediately.

MAKES 4 SERVINGS

hot chicks, wicked ducks, and one killer rabbit

Braised Chicken in Hot Chile Paste

This Korean dish is called *tak koch'ujang bokkum* and comes from the southwestern towns of Kwangju and Chongju, where people are quite fond of salty and fiery foods made with lots of chiles. This dish *should* taste salty and spicy hot. As in most cooking in East Asia, saltiness derives from the soy sauce more than from salt. The amount of sugar sounds excessive, but it isn't—it balances the chile paste quite harmoniously. Some cooks leave the meat on the bone, but I wrote this recipe so that it is entirely boneless. The recipe is based on a similar dish I ate at the Sa Rit Gol restaurant in Koreatown in Los Angeles. The Korean red chile paste and Korean red chile are available in Korean markets and via the Internet. Serve with steamed rice.

1/4 cup sugar

3 large garlic cloves, finely chopped

1 scallion, finely chopped

1 tablespoon ground Korean red chile or 2 teaspoons ground red chile

1 tablespoon finely chopped fresh ginger

5 tablespoons Korean red chile paste

2 tablespoons soy sauce

2 tablespoons sesame oil

2 tablespoons toasted sesame seeds

2 1/2 pounds chicken parts (breasts, thighs, legs, and wings), bones, skin and fat removed and cut up into bite-size pieces

1/2 cup water

1. In a large bowl, mix together the sugar, garlic, scallion, ground Korean red chile, ginger, Korean red chile paste, soy sauce, sesame oil, and sesame seeds. Toss with the pieces of chicken and marinate for 2 hours in the refrigerator.

2. In a large saucepan or wok, bring the water to a boil, then add the chicken and its marinade. Reduce the heat to low, cover, and simmer until the chicken is cooked through and the sauce is dense and the liquid is nearly evaporated, about 30 minutes, stirring once in a while. Serve immediately.

MAKES 4 SERVINGS

Jamaican Roast Duck with Lime Sauce

Jamaican cooks, and Caribbean cooks in general, love to mix citrus juices into their marinades and sauces. This was an extraordinary recipe when I first tested it. I just didn't expect how wickedly good and hot it would be. My kids and I ate it up like there was no tomorrow and just loved it, and I would make it often if I didn't have too much other stuff to do in my life. It is an excellent dish to serve as an introduction to how spicy-hot Jamaican food can be.

One 5-pound duck, large pieces of fat pulled off, neck and giblets reserved

1 carrot, coarsely chopped

1 celery stalk with leaves, coarsely chopped

1 medium-size onion, coarsely chopped

1 cup water

Salt and freshly ground black pepper to taste

2 Scotch bonnet chiles or habanero chiles, finely chopped

1/2 teaspoon dried thyme

2 limes

1/2 cup dry white wine

1/2 cup chicken broth (homemade or canned)

1/4 cup sugar

3 tablespoons white wine vinegar

1 teaspoon cornstarch blended with
1 teaspoon water

1. Preheat the oven to 375°F. Rinse the duck and dry it thoroughly, then chop the neck and giblets coarsely and place them in a large roasting pan. Add the carrot, celery, and onion to the pan. Place a rack in the pan and pour the water in. Sprinkle the duck inside and out with salt and black pepper, chiles, and thyme. Prick the skin of the duck all over with the prongs of a corncob holder or the tip of a small paring knife to allow the fat to run out when it roasts. Truss the duck by tying the legs together with kitchen twine and bending the wing tips into or under the duck. Place the duck in the roasting pan, breast side down. Roast for 30 minutes, then remove the duck from the pan and spoon or pour off the accumulated fat. Return the duck to the roasting pan on its side and roast another 30 minutes. Again remove the pan from the oven and remove as much fat as you can.

2. Raise the oven temperature to 400°F. Turn the duck to its other side and roast another 30 minutes. Remove from the oven again, pour off the fat, return the duck to the roasting pan, breast side up, and roast until golden brown, 30 to 40 minutes.

3. Meanwhile, remove the zest of the limes with a vegetable peeler or paring knife and cut it into julienne strips. Squeeze the limes and set the juice aside. Bring a small saucepan of water to a boil and cook the lime zest for 1 minute. Remove, drain, and set aside.

4. Transfer the duck to a serving platter and cover with aluminum foil to keep it warm while you continue the preparation. The contents of the roasting pan will be mostly black. Pour off the remaining fat from the roasting pan, then place the pan on a stove burner over medium heat and add the white wine to deglaze the pan, stirring to loosen any bits and pieces. Add the chicken broth.

5. In another small saucepan, bring the sugar and vinegar to a boil. Cook over high heat until the mixture is lightly caramelized, watching carefully so it does not burn. Immediately pour the vinegar mixture into the roasting pan and bring to a boil. Add 2 tablespoons of reserved lime juice. along with the cornstarch mixture and cook until the sauce returns to a boil. Taste and add salt, pepper, and additional lime juice if desired. Stir in the lime zest. Carve the duck into 6 portions, spoon the sauce over it, and serve.

MAKES 6 SERVINGS

the cuisine of kerala

Kerala, the home of the Malabar Coast and the home of black pepper, is in the far south-western portion of India. There are five distinct groups of people in the state of Kerala, including an ancient community of Syrian Christians. The Muslims of Kerala are called Moplahs and are descendants of Arab traders who married local Kerala women. The Arab influence is seen in the *biryanis* and in the ground wheat and meat porridge called *aleesa*, which comes from the Arabic word *harisa*. The Moplah cooking of north Kerala is thought to be similar to Yemeni cooking, because there were many Yemenis among the original Arab traders. The Moplahs use chile, but their food is not outrageously hot. The other ethnic groups are the Thiyas; the Nampoothiris, who are the brahmins of Kerala; and the Nairs, who are descended from the original warrior class of Kerala. Their famous and distinctive dish is *avial* (page 312), a spicy vegetable stew.

Spicy Duck Curry

This preparation from the Indian state of Kerala is a fine way to make a duck, and simple, too. The dish is tricky, and I wouldn't fool around with this recipe, as the tastes are well balanced. I am very fond of duck and like to save the fat for cooking purposes and the skin for tossing with rice.

3 tablespoons vegetable oil

1 large onion, thinly sliced

3 large garlic cloves, crushed

3 fresh green finger-type chiles or 5 green jalapeño chiles, seeded and finely chopped

2 tablespoons ground coriander

1 teaspoon ground turmeric

1/2 teaspoon ground cumin

1 teaspoon cayenne pepper

One 1-inch cube fresh ginger, peeled and finely chopped

One 5-pound duck, wings removed and saved for another purpose, split in half lengthwise, and cut into 2 legs, and the remaining duck cut into 2-inch-wide pieces, and fat removed

Salt to taste

1/2 cup water

1 cup coconut cream (see page 90) or canned coconut milk

1/4 cup fresh lemon juice

1. In a large casserole, heat the vegetable oil over medium-high heat, then cook the onion until yellow and soft, about 8 minutes, stirring. Add the garlic, chiles, coriander, turmeric, cumin, cayenne pepper, and ginger. Cook until sticky on the bottom of the casserole, about 1 minute. Add the duck, salt, and water. Bring to a near boil, then reduce the heat to very low, using a heat diffuser if necessary, and cook partially covered until the duck is very tender, about 5 hours.

2. Skim off excess fat and save for another purpose if you like. Add the coconut cream. Stir and cook at a simmer, uncovered, for 10 minutes. Remove from the heat and stir in the lemon juice. Serve immediately.

MAKES 5 SERVINGS

hot chicks, wicked ducks, and killer rabbits

the hot spices: black pepper

Black pepper is economically and gastronomically the world's most important spice. It is a very pungent spice as a result of a volatile oil called alkaloid piperine. The pepper plant is a perennial vine with dark green leaves and spikes of white flowers that become clusters of green berries, which turn red as they ripen. When the berries are harvested while green berries, this is the product known as green peppercorns. Black peppercorns are the sun-dried unripe berries, while white peppercorns are simply black peppercorns with their outer skins rubbed off. The harvesting of black peppercorns occurs as the berries are turning red, but before they are completely ripe. The harvesters leave the peppercorns on mats to dry and ferment in the sun, which must be done with haste to avoid mold. As the berries dry, they turn black. Because the pungency of black peppercorns mostly resides in the pericarp (the outer skin), black peppercorns are stronger in pungency than white peppercorns. Red peppercorns are very rare and Gernot Katzner, a thermochemist formerly with the University of Graz who has made an extensive study of spices, says that as far as he knows it is marketed by only one firm in the world, an Indian firm in Kerala. When you see "red peppercorns" or "pink peppercorns" being sold, these are not related to pepper but are a different plant entirely (see page 55).

Black pepper is native to the monsoon forests of the Malabar Coast in southwest India, in today's state of Kerala. It has been grown and used for millennia, and the wild form has not yet been unambiguously identified. It is first mentioned, and mentioned frequently, by old Sanskrit medical writers. In the sixteenth century, when the Portuguese were first actively engaged in the pepper trade, the typical pepper orchard in Kerala consisted of a small plot of land located in a hollow where moisture and shade were available in abundance. The orchard was first planted with trees such as areca-nuts, mangoes, or betel-palms, upon which the vines of the pepper plant could be trained.

They were planted in June at the onset of the monsoon season. The pepper plant would shoot up, twining itself around the existing trees, and with careful watering and manuring, would bear first fruit in three years. The plant would flower the following May, and by December the berries began to change color and were ready for harvesting. This was done with care since the berries were fragile. After they were picked, the berries were spread on the ground to dry in the sun and turn black and shriveled. After a month's storage they were ready for the buyer as black peppercorns.

The trade in black pepper can be traced to the earliest civilizations. Scientists examining the mummy of Ramses II (d. 1225 B.C.) discovered black peppercorns lodged in his nostrils and abdomen, apparently used as part of the mummification process. This can only mean that there was a trade in spices between Egypt and India. The Roman naturalist Pliny describes black pepper at length and with great detail, and it is often mentioned by Roman writers in the Augustan age. Pliny was not impressed with black pepper as a spice and thought "it is remarkable that the use of pepper has come so much in favor [as it] has nothing to recommend it in either fruit or berry. To think that its only pleasing quality is pungency and that we go all the way to India to get this!" It is also reported that the Visigothic king Alaric (c. 370–410) demanded from Rome as part of the city's ransom 3,000 pounds of pepper. Cosmas Indicopleutes, a sixth-century A.D. merchant, wrote *Topographia Christiana* in 548, describing the importance of the spice trade in Ceylon. He visited Malabar and related how pepper was harvested in the hill country and how it was processed and marketed. In 1101, after the conquest of Caesarea in Turkey by the Genovese, each soldier was rewarded with two pounds of pepper as part of his booty. The European demand for pepper was ostensibly the impetus for the Age of Discovery.

Rabbit in Adobo Sauce

For stews such as this Peruvian *adobo de conejo*, I usually cut up the rabbit into eight pieces. Split the rabbit down the middle, then cut off the forequarters and hindquarters, then cut the body into four pieces. Your butcher can also do this for you. Corn (maize) is an old ingredient in the cooking of the Incas. According to Inca mythology, Mama Huaco, sister and wife of the first Inca, was responsible for the origin of maize. She is said to have brought ears of corn out of the cave of Pacaritambo, the legendary place from which the eight founding Incas were said to have emerged. For this reason, maize was also called "cave seeds." Serve this with black beans and white rice.

8 large garlic cloves

1 teaspoon salt

2 tablespoons *Ají Panca en Pasta* (page 405)

1 tablespoon ground *ají mirasol* chile or cayenne pepper

1/2 teaspoon ground cumin

1 teaspoon freshly ground black pepper

1 cup white wine vinegar

1 rabbit (about 2 3/4 pounds), cut into 8 pieces

2 tablespoons vegetable oil

1 cup cooked corn kernels

1 pound cassava, peeled, boiled, and cut into smaller pieces

1/2 recipe Peruvian Creole Sauce (page 409)

1.   In a mortar, pound the garlic with the salt until mushy, then transfer to a bowl. Stir in the *ají panca en pasta*, ground chile, cumin, black pepper, and vinegar and mix well. Place the rabbit pieces in a ceramic or glass baking dish, pour the marinade over the rabbit, cover with plastic wrap, and marinate in the refrigerator for 4 hours.

2.   Remove the meat from the marinade, reserving the marinade. In a large skillet, heat the vegetable oil over high heat, then cook the rabbit pieces until slightly golden on all sides, about 3 minutes, turning with tongs. Reduce the heat to low, add the reserved marinade, and simmer, covered, until tender, about 2 hours. The sauce remaining should not be liquidy. If it is, remove the rabbit pieces and keep warm while you reduce the remaining liquid over high heat until the sauce is slightly syrupy. Place the rabbit on a serving platter and scatter the corn and cassava around. Serve immediately with the creole sauce on the side.

MAKES 4 TO 6 SERVINGS

blazing beef
and incendiary
lamb

Beef is most popular in the South and Central American piquant cuisines, where both stew beef and tender sirloins get a hot treatment. There's an amazing taste behind a rich, juicy skirt steak covered with a blazing tomatillo sauce (see page 170). It's complex, delicious, and very satisfying. The beef stews, many of which come from Africa, simmer slowly, breaking down the connective tissue that provides all stews with their flavor, and the meat percolates in searingly hot chile-infused sauces and gravies. Some recipes, such as the Cayenne Oxtail Stew (page 194), seem so simple that you will wonder how so much flavor emerges.

Among our 14-odd super-hot cuisines, there is no doubt that the mecca of spicy lamb cookery is found in

North Africa and on the Indian subcontinent. Lamb cookery is found elsewhere, of course, and it's quite good, too. But when I think of a dreamy lamb dish that will blow my top, I'm often thinking of some incredibly flavored Mogul dish from Rajasthan (see page 210) or a piquant lamb with *harisa* from Tunisia (see page 204). As far as the actual lamb goes, there is a lot of hype about Australian and New Zealand lamb. It's okay, but the best lamb is American lamb and you should ask for it. Goat is not a meat eaten very much by Americans except by those of Latin or Caribbean descent. But goat is a delicious meat and well suited for long simmering in stews, so I've included two goat recipes so you can give it a try.

Lomo Saltado

The first time I ate the famous Peruvian *lomo saltado* I was quite surprised at how good it tasted. A quick glance at the ingredients list doesn't portend the experience to come. By all means make this dish, which is a Peruvian favorite whose name literally means "jumped sirloin," a reference to the stir-fry technique in which the pieces of meat are tossed vigorously in the pan. The dish may very well have originated with nineteenth-century Chinese immigrants to Peru. In fact, many recipes for *lomo saltado* call for soy sauce to be added, as I have done here. Remember that in this preparation you do not want the vegetables to be too soft. They should be slightly crunchy, and the meat should be rare to medium-rare, so pay attention to the timing.

6 to 8 cups vegetable oil, for frying

2 pounds Idaho baking potatoes, peeled and cut into thin French fries and dried thoroughly with paper towels

3 large garlic cloves, finely chopped

1 tablespoon finely chopped fresh *ají limo* chile or 2 teaspoons finely chopped habanero chile

2 pounds beef tenderloin or skirt steak, cut into 1/2-inch strips

1/4 teaspoon ground cumin

2 teaspoons salt

1 1/4 teaspoons freshly ground black pepper

2 medium-size red onions, cut in half and sliced 1/4 inch thick

2 teaspoons red wine vinegar

1 1/2 pounds ripe tomatoes, peeled, seeded, and cut into 6 wedges

3 fresh *ají amarillo* chiles or 4 yellow chiles or 6 red jalapeño chiles, seeded and very thinly sliced lengthwise

6 tablespoons soy sauce

2 tablespoons finely chopped fresh coriander (cilantro) leaves

1. Preheat the frying oil to 350°F in a deep fryer or an 8-inch saucepan fitted with a basket insert. Cook the French fries until light golden, 5 to 6 minutes. Remove from the oil, transfer to a paper towel–lined platter, and let cool completely. Turn the frying oil to 360°F, as you will fry the French fries one more time in step 5.

2. In a wok (preferably) or large skillet, heat 1 tablespoon oil from the frying oil over medium-high heat, swirling the oil to coat the wok, then cook the garlic and *ají limo* chile until sizzling and turning color, about 15 seconds. Increase the heat to high, add the beef, and cook until it browns, about 2 minutes, tossing

almost constantly. Add the cumin, 1 teaspoon of the salt, and $1/2$ teaspoon of the pepper and toss again. Remove the meat with a skimmer and set aside in a bowl.

3.   Add 1 tablespoon oil from the frying oil to the wok and let it heat over high heat, then cook the onions until approaching soft but still crunchy, about 2 minutes, tossing constantly. Season with half of the remaining salt and pepper, add 1 teaspoon of the vinegar, and cook until the vinegar evaporates, about 30 seconds, tossing. Remove the onions from the wok and set aside with the meat.

4.   Add 1 tablespoon oil from the frying oil to the wok, then cook the tomatoes as you did the onions, until softer but crunchy, about 2 minutes, then add the remaining salt and pepper. Add the remaining 1 teaspoon vinegar, cooking until it and some of the tomato liquid evaporates, about 1 minute, tossing. Remove the tomatoes from the wok and set aside with the meat and onions.

5.   Re-fry the potatoes until golden, about 2 minutes. Drain and set aside.

6.   Add 1 tablespoon oil from the frying oil to the wok and heat over high heat. Return the beef, onions, and tomatoes to the hot wok, add the *ají amarillo* chiles and soy sauce, and cook until heated through over high heat, 30 seconds to 2 minutes, tossing. Add the French fries, mix it all together carefully, tossing, and cook until hot, about 1 minute. Toss with the coriander leaves and serve.

MAKES 6 SERVINGS

Piquant Beef Picadillo

T his Bolivian dish is called *saisi* or *saice* and is a kind of *picadillo* that is popular throughout Latin America. A *picadillo* is made with finely diced meat seasoned with onions, chiles, and herbs. The final meat preparation is very spicy but is offset by the bland potatoes and rice. Typically it is also served with *chuño phuti*, freeze-dried potatoes, which are available in South American markets. The chile used in this dish is *ají limo*, a chile found on the northern coast of Peru that is very pungent and is rust colored when dried and ground. It is a chile of the species *Capsicum frutescens*, the same species as Tabasco chile, of which the entire U.S. crop goes into the making of the famous Tabasco sauce.

1/2 pound boneless beef chuck, cut into 1/4-inch cubes

1/4 cup vegetable oil

1/2 cup fresh or frozen peas

1 medium-size white onion, finely chopped

1/2 cup finely chopped peeled tomato

1/4 cup ground *ají limo* chile or cayenne pepper

1/4 teaspoon ground cumin

1/2 teaspoon dried oregano

1/4 cup finely chopped fresh parsley leaves

1/2 teaspoon freshly ground black pepper

1 1/2 teaspoons salt

1 1/2 cups chicken broth (homemade or canned) or cold water, plus more as needed

4 cooked boiling potatoes (about 1 pound), peeled

1 cup cooked white rice

4 *chuño phuti* (optional)

1 tablespoon finely chopped fresh parsley leaves

1. In a casserole or stockpot, combine the beef with the vegetable oil, peas, onion, tomato, chile, cumin, oregano, parsley, black pepper, salt, and broth. Bring to a boil, then reduce the heat to low and simmer, uncovered, until the beef is tender, about 2 hours, stirring occasionally. Add broth so the stew remains juicy, but neither liquidy nor syrupy.

2. In 4 individual bowls, place 1 potato, a large spoonful of steamed rice or *chuño phuti*, if using, and some of the sauce. Ladle the stew into the bowl, sprinkle with the chopped parsley, and serve.

MAKES 4 SERVINGS

blazing beef and incendiary lamb

the piquant restaurants of peru and bolivia

Maria Baez Kijac, in her comprehensive introduction to the cuisines of South America, *The South American Table* (The Harvard Common Press, 2003), says that the real flavor of the Andes is found in the *picanterías*, small restaurants where very hot dishes are the specialty. Their name derives from the fact that the food served is very piquant, a result of the abundant use of *ajís*, as the very hot chile of the Andes are known. These special restaurants seem to congregate in the outskirts of cities, probably because of their clientele, peasant newcomers from the countryside seeking work in the cities. They attract a variety of people, though, especially on weekends, when a pig might be roasted or in the early morning hours by partygoers seeking culinary relief from their hangovers. Some of the most famous, in terms of their adherence to traditional cooking, are in Arequipa, a colonial city in southern Peru. The food is prepared in cauldrons with enormous amounts of *rocoto* chiles, one of the most piquant chiles anywhere. Very hot food—hotter than in Peru according to Maria—is also found in Bolivia. Elsewhere in South America, excepting Bahia in Brazil, one does not encounter piquant cuisine, although one may stumble on a piquant dish now and then and hot table sauces are popular.

Grilled Skirt Steak with Green Tomatillo Sauce

This northern Mexican dish popular in Monterey and Sonora is called *ranchero al carbón con salsa verde*, which means "charcoal grilled country-style steak with green sauce." This is a very simple, yet very delicious, way of preparing skirt steak (called *arrachera* in Mexico) that you can do on a grill in the summer or in a cast-iron skillet in the winter. Green sauces are usually made with tomatillos and chiles. Tomatillos are increasingly available in supermarkets, both canned and fresh, and certainly anywhere where there is a Mexican-American population.

3/4 pound tomatillos, husks removed and washed

1/2 small onion, chopped

3 fresh green serrano chiles, chopped

2 tablespoons finely chopped fresh coriander (cilantro) leaves

Salt to taste

Juice of 1 lime

1 pound beef skirt steak, cut into 3-inch lengths

Freshly ground black pepper to taste

4 large flour tortillas, warmed

Crumbled Mexican *queso fresco*, for garnish

1. Bring a medium-size saucepan of salted water to a boil and cook the tomatillos until they start to become tender, about 8 minutes. Drain, place in a food processor, and puree briefly until a little chunky. Add the onion, serrano chiles, and coriander leaves and blend again. Pour into a bowl, season with salt, and let stand 1/2 hour before using.

2. Meanwhile, prepare a hot charcoal fire or preheat a gas grill on high for 15 minutes, or preheat a ridged cast-iron skillet or griddle over high heat for 10 minutes. Pour the lime juice over the steak and let rest for 10 minutes. Sprinkle salt and pepper on both sides of the steak and grill until rare or medium-rare, 6 to 8 minutes, then remove and slice into 1/4-inch-thick slices, cutting with the grain.

3. You can serve everything separately and let diners construct their own taco or you can prepare the tacos yourself. Hold a tortilla in one hand and layer some steak on it, then spoon some salsa verde over the steak and sprinkle some crumbled cheese on top. Serve immediately.

MAKES 4 SERVINGS

TOMATILLOS

Tomatillos are not a kind of tomato, but are a husked fruit related to the Cape gooseberry. They are used mostly in central Mexico, and their Nahautl name is *tómatl*. They have green fruits smaller than tomatoes that are covered with a thin paperlike husk. They are also known as husk tomato and Mexican ground-cherry. When the tomatillo is unripe their fruit is tart and used in Mexican *salsa verde*, served with a variety of foods such as enchiladas, tostadas, tacos, and stuffed chiles. The ripe fruits are sweeter and used in preserves. More and more supermarkets now carry them, so it's worth your while asking for them. They are also sold in cans.

blazing beef and incendiary lamb

Ranchero Steaks with Chipotle Chile Sauce

*T*he country-style steaks called *ranchero* steaks are thin Mexican-style beefsteaks that are cut from the top loin and typical of Sonoran country cooking. One could also use the more expensive skirt steak. A Mexican butcher will sell *ranchero* steaks that are pounded very thin and used for pan-frying. In order to properly brown the steaks, don't crowd them in the pan; cook them in batches. These steaks are nice served with warm flour tortillas.

3/4 pound fresh tomatillos, husks removed and washed

2 large garlic cloves

3 canned chipotle chiles

2 tablespoons water

1/2 teaspoon salt

Freshly ground black pepper to taste

Vegetable oil, for frying

1 1/2 pounds thin steaks (see above), cut into 8 pieces and pounded 1/8 inch thin

1. Preheat the oven to 450°F. Arrange the tomatillos and garlic on a baking tray and roast until the skin blackens, 20 to 25 minutes. Remove from the oven and place the tomatillos and garlic in a blender with the chipotle chiles, water, salt, and pepper. Blend until very smooth.

2. Meanwhile, preheat a large cast-iron skillet rubbed with just a film of vegetable oil over high heat for 10 minutes, then cook the steaks one at a time until crispy brown on both sides, about 3 minutes in all. Remove and set aside, keeping them warm as you cook the remainder. Serve the steaks with a thin layer of chipotle chile sauce spooned over them and the remaining sauce served on the side.

MAKES 4 TO 6 SERVINGS

Flank Steak with Poblano Chile Strips

This recipe, called *res con rajas de chile poblano*, is a much hotter steak dish than the two previous ones. *Rajas* means "strips," which gives you an idea of how everything is cut. I particularly like this recipe because the cream is so enticing spiked with the chile flavors. I adapted this recipe from Karen Hersh Graber, an American food writer living in Mexico. The steak can be accompanied with Green Rice (page 387).

1 pound flank steak, cut into 1/2-inch strips against the grain at a 20-degree angle

Salt and freshly ground black pepper to taste

1 tablespoon unsalted butter

1 tablespoon corn oil

1 medium-size white onion, cut in half and then thinly sliced

4 fresh poblano chiles, roasted, peeled, seeded, and cut into strips

2 large red jalapeño chiles, seeded and sliced lengthwise

1 cup heavy cream

Salt to taste

1. Season the flank steak with salt and pepper. In a large cast-iron skillet, melt the butter with the corn oil over high heat for several minutes so the pan is very hot, then cook the flank steak until brown, making sure the skillet isn't too crowded and that you don't stir too much at first so that a nice crust can form on the meat, 2 to 3 minutes.

2. Add the onion and cook until it is translucent, 4 to 5 minutes. Add the poblano and jalapeño chiles and cook 3 minutes, stirring. Add the cream, season with salt, and cook until the sauce is gravy-like, 3 to 5 minutes. Serve immediately.

MAKES 4 SERVINGS

blazing beef and incendiary lamb

Chanducata

This simple family-style summertime preparation is a recipe from the Mexican state of Michoacan. One glance and you can see why it is popular—it is quick and easy and has great flavor. It's hot, too, so this dish can be eaten on a tostada (a crispy tortilla) or wrapped in a warm, soft flour tortilla.

2 tablespoons extra-virgin olive oil

1 pound ground beef

1 medium-size onion, chopped

4 large garlic cloves, finely chopped

Salt to taste

4 fresh green serrano chiles, finely chopped

1 sprig mint, leaves only, chopped

4 ripe tomatoes (about 1^1/$_2$ pounds), peeled and chopped

2 cups fresh corn kernels (about 2 cobs)

^{1}/$_4$ cup finely chopped fresh coriander (cilantro) leaves

1. In a large skillet, heat the olive oil over medium-high heat, then cook the meat with the onion, garlic, and salt until it has browned, about 10 minutes, stirring occasionally.

2. Add the serrano chiles, mint, tomatoes, corn, and coriander, then cook until all the liquid has evaporated, about 25 minutes, stirring. At the end of the cooking, if the food is sticking to the skillet, add ^{1}/$_4$ cup water, scraping and mixing it up. Serve immediately.

MAKES 4 SERVINGS

Braised Meatballs in Red Chipotle Chile Sauce

This dish from Oaxaca is called *albóndigas con chipotle*, and the meatballs are really closer to quenelles (light dumplings) than meatballs. I like to make this dish during the winter, when the aromas can permeate the house and the tastes are spicy and warming. You will need both a food processor and a blender for this recipe to make it very easy. Serve with Green Rice (page 387) and any kind of salad.

FOR THE MEATBALLS

One 1/2-inch-thick slice stale white country bread (not sourdough), crust removed

Milk for soaking

1 medium-size zucchini, peeled

1 medium-size onion, chopped

3/4 pound ground beef

3/4 pound ground pork

2 large eggs

1/2 teaspoon dried thyme

1/2 teaspoon ground cumin

1 finely crumbled bay leaf

1/4 teaspoon dried marjoram

2 teaspoons salt

FOR THE SAUCE

1 medium-size onion, peeled

4 large garlic cloves

7 canned chipotle chiles in adobo

Two 28-ounce cans peeled plum tomatoes

2 tablespoons lard or unsalted butter

2 fresh green jalapeño chiles, finely chopped

2 teaspoons salt

1. To make the meatballs, place the bread in a bowl of milk and soak until needed. When ready to use, squeeze the liquid out of the bread.

2. Place the zucchini and the chopped onion in a food processor and grind very finely with the metal blade. Remove from the receptacle and change the blade to the plastic blade. Transfer the zucchini and onion to a bowl and mix them with the beef, pork, the soaked and squeezed bread, the eggs, thyme, cumin, bay leaf, marjoram, and salt. Place half the mixture back into the food processor and run the processor until the mixture is very well blended, about 2 minutes. Remove and set aside, then process the second batch. Make 24 golf ball–size meatballs. Place on a tray and refrigerate while you continue working.

3. Preheat the oven to 450°F. To prepare the sauce, place the whole onion and the garlic in the oven until blackened, 20 to 25 minutes. Remove and peel the garlic. Place the onion, garlic, and chipotle chiles with any sauce that clings to them in a blender and run until smooth. Add the tomatoes and their liquid and puree until a smooth tomato sauce. You may have to do this in batches, too.

4. In a large casserole, melt the lard over medium-high heat, then add the tomato sauce and green chiles, season with salt, reduce the heat to medium-low, and simmer until dense, 20 to 25 minutes. Add the meatballs, reduce the heat to low, cover, and cook until the meatballs are cooked through, about 45 minutes. Serve hot.

MAKES 6 SERVINGS

the piquant cooking of the southwestern united states

The cookery of the southwestern United States is directly influenced by Mexican cuisine. But let's remember what the chef and author Rick Bayless says about Mexican cuisine. There are two Mexican cuisines: the first is from and in Mexico and rarely found outside of it, and the second is Mexican American, the same that is the root to the fish tacos of San Diego, the chile verde of Albuquerque, and the chili con carne of Texas. But there are three kinds of Mexican-American cookery. There is Cal-Mex, Tex-Mex, and New Mex–Mex. This last variety uses chiles as a vegetable in sauces rather than merely a spice or condiment, and this distinguishes it from the Tex-Mex cooking of Texas and Arizona. The cooking of the Californios, the Mexican inhabitants of California before its incorporation into the United States, helped lay the foundation for the cooking of the Southwest. These Californios were mestizos and Christianized Indians from Mexico and few were actually settlers from Spain. The first record of the cooking of this population was published in Spanish in 1898 in California. Encarnación Pinedo's *El cocinero español* (selected in *Encarnación's Kitchen*; University of California/Berkeley, 2003) demonstrates the early cooking of the Southwest. But there is also now another kind of Southwestern cooking that was born and finds its home in restaurants: inventions of contemporary chefs.

The beginnings of the piquant cooking of the Southwest probably should be dated by the legend that Juan de Oñate (1554–c. 1617) brought the first chiles to New Mexico from Mexico in 1597. Dave DeWitt, author of *The Chile Pepper Encyclopedia* (William Morrow, 1999), suggests that they may have been introduced to the Pueblo Indians of New Mexico by the Antonio Espejo expedition of 1582–1583. According to one member of the expedition, Baltasar Obregón, "they have no chile, but the natives were given some seed to plant." Another curiosity about Southwest cooking is that it does not fit any traditional conception of cuisine. Because it evolved in a nontraditional way in a rich society of Americans from many places, the cooking is not based on staple ingredients, seasonal ingredients, or traditional ingredients, methods, or heritages. Home cooking, especially in purely Anglo families, tends to be "international eclectic with chiles." Piquant cooking is growing in other parts of the United States, especially in large cities. The influences on this style of cooking are Mexican, Caribbean, and Cajun, but it's likely other influences will make themselves felt as its popularity grows.

Chili con Carne

This chili con carne recipe was first published in my book *Real Stew* (The Harvard Common Press, 2002). It's just great so I'm not going to tweak it at all. Let me reprise here what I said there: chili con carne is not a Mexican dish. It is a classic, defining dish of Texas cooking. A true Texas "bowl of red" contains neither beans nor tomatoes, the purists say. Another element of a true chili is that it is only made with finely diced beef chuck, not ground beef. In Texas one drinks beer with chili con carne. All the chiles mentioned here, by the way, are easily found in Texas and west to California, but perhaps less so in the rest of the country. Serve this chili with cornbread, flour tortillas, or corn tortillas . . . and beer.

2 tablespoons bacon drippings or rendered beef kidney suet

3 pounds boneless beef chuck, trimmed of fat, chopped in a food processor or chopped into 1/4-inch dice, but not ground

4 tablespoons dark chili powder

2 teaspoons granulated garlic

6 dried pasilla chiles or ancho chiles

1 dried New Mexico chile (also called Anaheim, Long Green, or Long Red Chiles)

2 dried guajillo (mirasol) chiles

2 cups cold water

3 cups beef broth (homemade or canned)

2 tablespoons onion powder

2 large garlic cloves, crushed

1 1/2 tablespoons garlic powder

1 teaspoon ground red chile

2 teaspoons cayenne pepper

2 teaspoons freshly ground white pepper

1 tablespoon hot paprika

1 teaspoon salt

1 tablespoon dried oregano

1 tablespoon gently crushed cumin seeds or ground cumin

2 cups lager beer (such as Corona)

4 fresh green serrano chiles, seeded and chopped

2 tablespoons red wine vinegar

2 tablespoons shaved bitter chocolate or unsweetened cocoa powder

1/2 teaspoon Tabasco sauce

1 tablespoon brown sugar

1/4 cup *masa harina* (Mexican corn flour)

1. In a large casserole or Dutch oven, heat the bacon fat over medium-high heat, then brown the meat with 2 tablespoons of the dark chili powder and the granulated garlic, in batches if necessary, about 5 minutes. Turn the heat off and return all the cooked beef to the casserole if you cooked in batches.

2. Place the pasilla, New Mexico, and guajillo chiles in a small saucepan with the 2 cups water, cover, bring to a gentle boil over medium-high heat, reduce the heat to low, and simmer until soft, 20 minutes, covered. Drain, reserving the cooking water. Place the chiles in a food processor with 2 to 4 tablespoons of the reserved cooking water and puree until a smooth paste forms and until there is no evidence of any pieces of pepper skin. Mix the chile puree into the beef, add 2 cups beef broth, and bring to a boil over high heat. Reduce the heat to low, cover, and gently simmer for 30 minutes.

3. Stir the onion powder, crushed garlic, garlic powder, ground red chile, cayenne pepper, white pepper, paprika, salt, oregano, cumin, the remaining 2 tablespoons dark chili powder, beer, and the remaining beef broth into the casserole. Bring to a boil over high heat, then reduce the heat to low and add the serrano chiles, vinegar, chocolate, Tabasco, and brown sugar. Cover and simmer 45 minutes.

4. In a small bowl, stir a ladleful of broth with the *masa harina* until there are no lumps and then pour into the casserole. Stir and cook uncovered on the lowest possible heat, using a heat diffuser if necessary, until the meat is very tender and the gravy is thick, $1^1/_2$ to 2 hours, stirring occasionally so that the mixture doesn't stick. If the chili con carne is too thick, thin it with small amounts of boiling water. Serve immediately, although I like to refrigerate it overnight and serve it the next day after a minute of microwaving.

MAKES 6 SERVINGS

Cajun Meat Loaf

This meat loaf is not like any meat loaf you've had before; it's aromatic and spicy and very appealing. I've been making this recipe for years and have seen it around here and there. But it finally dawned on me that this recipe must have had a source because I hadn't made it up. I figured chef Paul Prudhomme must be responsible and, sure enough, I went to my favorite Cajun cook and found the recipe in his first book, *Chef Paul Prudhomme's Louisiana Kitchen* (William Morrow, 1984). I've adapted it slightly.

FOR THE SPICE MIX

2 whole bay leaves

1 teaspoon salt

1 teaspoon ground cayenne pepper

1 teaspoon freshly ground black pepper

1/2 teaspoon freshly ground white pepper

1/2 teaspoon ground cumin

1/2 teaspoon ground nutmeg

FOR THE MEAT LOAF

1/4 cup unsalted butter

1 medium-large onion, finely chopped

1 celery stalk, finely chopped

1 medium-size green bell pepper, chopped

3 scallions, finely chopped

4 large garlic cloves, finely chopped

1 tablespoon Tabasco sauce

1 tablespoon Worcestershire sauce

1/2 cup evaporated cultured buttermilk

1/2 cup ketchup

1 1/2 pounds ground beef (85 percent lean)

1/2 pound ground pork

2 large eggs, lightly beaten

1 cup fine dry bread crumbs

1. Combine the spice mix ingredients in a small bowl and set aside.

2. To make the meat loaf, in a medium-size saucepan, melt the butter over medium heat. Add the onion, celery, bell pepper, scallions, garlic, Tabasco, Worcestershire, and the spice mix until the mixture starts sticking to the bottom of the saucepan, 6 to 7 minutes, stirring occasionally and scraping the bottom well. Stir in the buttermilk and ketchup and continue cooking for about 2 minutes, stirring occasionally. Remove from the heat and allow the mixture to cool to room temperature in the saucepan.

3. Preheat the oven to 350°F. In a large bowl, mix the ground beef and ground pork until well blended. Spread the meat to cover the bottom of an ungreased 13 x 9-inch baking pan. Add the eggs, the cooked vegetable mixture (remove the bay leaves), and the bread crumbs. Mix by hand until thoroughly combined. In the center of the pan, shape the mixture into a loaf that is about 1 1/2 inches high, 6 inches wide, and 12 inches long. Bake for 25 minutes, then raise the heat to 400°F and continue cooking until the edges are quite blackened and the juices and fat are bubbling vigorously, about 30 minutes longer. Serve immediately.

MAKES 6 SERVINGS

blazing beef and incendiary lamb

Stew Peas

Red kidney beans are called peas in Jamaica, and they are the basis for a variety of stews such as this one. Many food historians suggest that Jamaican food became spicy in the nineteenth century, when Chinese and East Indian workers arrived after the abolition of slavery, bringing with them their spicy cuisine. But it should be remembered that the chile existed in Jamaica before the arrival of Asian immigrants, and it seems to me that the food would have been spicy already. The native chile went into the food with abandon, and this luscious stew—hot as ever—is an example.

$1/2$ pound salt pork or salt beef

2 cups dried red kidney beans

1 pound boneless beef chuck, cut into 1-inch cubes

3 scallions, chopped

3 sprigs thyme

2 cups coconut milk (see page 90)

$1/4$ cup diced pimiento from a jar

3 large garlic cloves, finely chopped

1 large onion, chopped

$1/2$ green bell pepper, cored, seeded, and chopped

1 habanero chile or Scotch bonnet chile, chopped

Salt and freshly ground black pepper to taste

1 recipe Dumplings (page 394)

1.   Bring a small saucepan of water to a boil and drop the salt pork into the water for 5 minutes to remove some of the salt. Remove the salt pork, cool under cold running water, and plunge again into the boiling water for another 5 minutes. Drain, chop, and set aside.

2.   Place the beans, beef, and blanched salt pork in a large stockpot and cover by 1 inch with cold water. Bring to a boil over high heat and, once it reaches a boil, reduce the heat to low and cook, partially covered, for 2 hours or until the water level is below the meat.

3.   Add the scallions, thyme, coconut milk, pimiento, garlic, onion, bell pepper, and habanero chile. Season with salt and pepper and cook until the beans and meat are both very tender, again partially covered, about another 2 hours. The broth should be only slightly bubbling, not boiling, as it cooks. Stir once in a while. Remove the thyme sprigs and discard.

4.   Place the dumplings on top of the stew 20 minutes before you want to serve the stew, cover tightly, and cook for 20 minutes without lifting the lid. Serve immediately.

MAKES 6 SERVINGS

Braised Beef with Capers and Preserved Lemon

I n this Tunisian preparation called *tajin marqa mua'lla*, beef is braised with tomato sauce and spices, and then at the very end of the cooking the spinach is wilted into the casserole. The heat of the chile-flavored beef acquires an additional level of tangy flavor from the preserved lemons and capers. The Arabic name of the dish indicates that it is a ragout made with young vegetables in an earthenware casserole, but you can use any casserole you might have to prepare it. Serve with steamed couscous or Rice Pilaf (page 396).

2 tablespoons extra-virgin olive oil

1 pound beef tri-tip sirloin, cut into $1/2$-inch cubes

$1/2$ pound beef bone, with marrow and some meat on it

1 large onion, chopped

1 teaspoon ground coriander

1 tablespoon cayenne pepper

2 teaspoons salt

3 tablespoons tomato paste dissolved in $1/2$ cup water

3 large fresh green jalapeño chiles, quartered lengthwise

$1^1/2$ pounds spinach, with stems and roots, washed very well

3 ounces capers

1 Preserved Lemon (page 415), quartered

1. In a casserole or stockpot, heat the olive oil over medium-high heat, then brown the beef with the bone, onion, coriander, cayenne pepper, and salt, about 5 minutes, stirring frequently. Pour the tomato paste dissolved in water over the meat. Add the fresh chiles.

2. Reduce the heat to low and simmer, partially covered, until the beef is tender, $1^1/2$ to 2 hours, stirring occasionally. Keep the sauce moistened with water if it is drying out. Remove the beef bone, scoop the marrow out, and add it to the broth. Discard the bone.

3. Add the spinach, capers, and preserved lemon, stir to mix well, and cook until the spinach has wilted, 8 to 10 minutes. Serve immediately.

MAKES 4 SERVINGS

blazing beef and incendiary lamb

Palaver Sauce

This interestingly named dish is, first of all, a stew not a sauce, and is most popular in Ghana and Sierra Leone, where they call it *plasas*. One theory concerning the origin of the name suggests that it derives from *plabba*, coming from the French word *palabre*, meaning an interminable discussion. But both the French word *palabre* and the English word *palaver* derive from the Portuguese word *palavra*, meaning "word" or "speech." According to Webster's dictionary, *palaver* means "a long parley usually between persons of different cultures or levels of sophistication." How this fiery stew of meat and greens came to be named is a mystery. One suggestion is that the stew simmers for a long time, just like a palaver. Another suggestion is hinted at by the fact that some countries, such as Mali, have a palaver tree, a shady spot designated for gathering and hashing out the affairs of the community in each village.

Some cooks add tripe or smoked fish to the palaver sauce. The vegetable typically used in a West African palaver is *ndolé* or bitterleaf, a leafy green vegetable that is widely used in soups and stews in Africa. A dried version may be found in African markets, but any combination of spinach, okra, kale, collards, or turnip greens works very well as a substitute. The *egusi* seed called for in the recipe is powdered melon seed used as a thickener, and it can be replaced with unsalted pumpkinseeds, which are sold as *pepitas* in supermarkets and Latin American groceries. The ground dried shrimp can also be found in Latin American markets and the international section of your supermarket. Palaver Sauce is usually eaten with rice or *Fufu* (page 393). For an authentic African experience, use the habanero chiles instead of the serrano chiles. The red palm oil and African dried fish can only be found in African markets or on the Internet, which is usually how I buy mine. They provide a unique flavor.

1 pound kale, trimmed of heavy central stalks and chopped

1/2 pound okra, sliced thinly

1 pound spinach, heavy stems removed, washed well, and coarsely chopped

1/2 cup red palm oil, *or* 1/2 cup walnut oil mixed with 1 teaspoon paprika

2 pounds beef stew meat, cut into 1-inch pieces

1/2 pound boneless fresh cod, halibut, or haddock fillet

1/2 pound African dried fish or smoked fish, such as haddock, cod, stockfish, or other whitefish, soaked in cold water for 2 hours, bones and skin removed if any

1 large onion, finely chopped

2 pounds ripe tomatoes, cut in half, seeds squeezed out, and grated against the largest holes of a grater

15 fresh green finger-type chiles or 22 green serrano chiles or 3 habanero chiles, finely chopped

1 teaspoon ground red chile or cayenne pepper

Salt to taste

$^1/_2$ cup ground *egusi* seeds (melon seeds) or ground unsalted pumpkinseeds

1 tablespoon finely chopped fresh ginger

1 tablespoon dried ground crayfish or shrimp

1. Bring a large saucepan of lightly salted water to a boil and cook the kale and okra until the kale has wilted, about 4 minutes in all. Add the spinach and once it wilts drain all the vegetables, reserving 2 cups of the water.

2. In a large casserole, heat the red palm oil over medium-high heat, then brown the beef, cooking in batches if necessary to ensure it gets evenly browned, about 7 minutes, stirring. Add the 2 cups of reserved vegetable broth, bring to a boil over high heat, reduce the heat to low, cover, and simmer until tender, about $1^1/_2$ hours.

3. Add the drained vegetables, stir, and cook 15 minutes, covered. Add the fresh and dried fish, onion, tomatoes, fresh chiles, ground red chile, and salt. Cover and simmer until bubbling nicely, about 30 minutes.

4. Add the *egusi* seeds, ginger, and dried ground crayfish. Stir to mix well. Cook over low heat, uncovered, stirring often, until it is a thick saucelike consistency, about 45 minutes. Taste and add more salt if desired. Serve immediately.

MAKES 6 SERVINGS

blazing beef and incendiary lamb

Soupoukanja

This Senegalese dish, also called *soupou-kandia* or *soupi kandia*, is made of okra and meat and literally means "okra sauce" in Wolof, one of the main languages of Senegal in West Africa. The dish is known in Guinea, Mali, Gambia, and Benin, too, where it might be called *superkanja*, *soupi kandia*, *supa kanja*, *supakanja*, or *kanjadaa*. *The Congo Cookbook* (available as an e-book at www.congocookbook.com) suggests that the name may be a combination of the Portuguese word for soup, *sopa*, and a West African language word for okra, *kanja*. *Soupoukanja* can be served with rice, but it is equally good just with some (untraditional) bread to mop up the sauce.

In Casamance, a region of Senegal, okra is abundantly cultivated. It was introduced to the Americas by African slaves coming from the Ivory Coast area of West Africa. They called it *nkruman*, which became, after much transformation, *okra*. Slaves coming from Angola in southwest Africa called okra *ngumbo*, which became *gumbo*, a stew made with okra. The mock tomato called for in this recipe is grown and eaten in Senegal and is also called African scarlet eggplant; it is a plant in the same family as eggplant with orange-red fruit. You can replace it with eggplant, as that would be, despite the name, a closer family member than the tomato. If you can find it, use the white eggplant that looks like a goose egg. The fermented locust bean (see box at right) can only be bought in African markets and through the Internet. Serve the dish with plain rice or *Fufu* (page 393).

1 pound beef stew meat, cut into 1-inch cubes

1 large tomato, quartered

1 quart water

2 cups beef broth (homemade or canned)

1 ounce (about 5 balls) fermented locust beans (*dawadawa*) or 1 tablespoon Maggi Sauce or 1 tablespoon soy sauce

3/4 pound okra

2 large onions, 1 cut in eighths and 1 roughly chopped

3 habanero chiles or 5 cherry chiles or cascabel chiles

One 3-ounce can smoked mussels or oysters, *or* 1 ounce smoked mussels or oysters *and* 2 ounces smoked fish, such as herring, haddock, trout, or albacore tuna

1 mock tomato (*diakhatou*) or 1/2 pound eggplant, peeled and chopped

1/4 cup red palm oil, *or* 1/4 cup walnut oil mixed with 1/2 teaspoon hot paprika

3 ounces tomato paste

2 teaspoons salt, or more to your taste

1. Place the beef and tomato in a stockpot or casserole, cover with the water and beef broth, and bring to a boil over high heat. Boil for 20 minutes. Remove and discard the tomato peels once they loosen.

2. In a food processor or blender, blend the fermented locust beans, okra, onion cut in eighths, and the chiles until a paste forms. If using a blender, add some broth or water from the stew pot so the blades can turn.

3. Transfer the contents of the food processor or blender to the pot along with the chopped onion, the smoked mussels, and mock tomato. Simmer over low heat for 2 hours, stirring occasionally. Add the red palm oil and tomato paste, stir to blend well, and continue cooking until thick and tender, about 1 hour, stirring occasionally. Add the salt, stir, and serve hot.

MAKES 8 SERVINGS

fermented locust beans

This has got to be the most unusual ingredient I've come across in writing this book. Fermented locust beans are used solely in West African cooking. The first time my then 14-year-old son tasted a dish made with them, he said in no uncertain terms that it tasted terrible. I learned later that way, way too much had been used. You use this condiment sparingly. What is it? Fermented locust bean, known and usually sold in African markets in the U.S. as *dawadawa* or *daddawa*, the Hausa names, a language of Nigeria, comes from the West African locust tree, the flat beans of which are fermented by *Bacillus* species in an alkaline fermentation process. *Dawadawa* is a culinary product that enhances or intensifies meatiness in soups and other prepared dishes. It is considered the most important food condiment in the entire West/Central African savanna region. It is called *kimba* in Sierra Leone, *iru* in coastal Nigeria, and *ogili-igala* in Ibo, *nere-nététou* in Senegal, *soumbara* in the Gambia and Burkina Faso, *Soumbala* in Mali, and *kpalugu* in parts of Ghana. The beans have a slightly salty taste and are extremely smelly, although some Americans have actually said there is a vague chocolatelike smell, too. In Africa, they are sold fresh or dried and are mostly used to season soups and stews. In the United States, you are likely to find only the dried version, sold as balls, cakes, or bouillon cubes. African cooks will tell you to use commercial Maggi Sauce as a substitute, and I have also used soy sauce in a pinch and it works fine.

the piquant cooking of west africa

The most likely way the chile was brought to West Africa was by the Portuguese. They had established relations in the Congo by 1482, and the West African coast was dotted with their castles and forts by 1500. African populations readily accepted the new chile, as they were already familiar with hot spices such as cubeb pepper, Ashanti pepper, and grains of paradise, also known as Guinea pepper.

The only written sources for the history of West Africa from the eighth to the fifteenth centuries are Arabic writings. The Arabs were the first foreigners to penetrate Africa. These Arabic sources are all we have as a record of what life was like in the interior of Africa and what people were eating.

At first this Arab exploration was a military penetration, but it soon became commercial and cultural as ties with the Islamizing and Arabizing Berbers became stronger. The Berbers of North Africa, a Muslim but non-Arab people, had long been in contact with sub-Saharan Africa, and they were a major source of information for the Arab scholars.

The first written source on the history of West Africa comes from the geographer Ibn al-Faqih al-Hamadhani, who wrote about 903. The geographic and climatic conditions of a greater portion of West Africa were not conducive for agriculture, so one finds animal husbandry, food collecting, fishing, and hunting as the principal sources of food. All this changed once the Portuguese discovered a sea route around Africa to Asia and once the Spanish discovered America. There was a huge influx of new plants, both from Asia and America, which changed what people ate. Foods that we now associate with Africa—chiles, coconut, maize, sweet potatoes, potatoes, cassava, and pineapple—were all introduced between 1520 and 1540.

In sub-Saharan Africa one finds the most piquant food in West Africa. East, Central, and southern Africa have mostly bland food in comparison, with the following exceptions: The two Congos, Cameroon, and Gabon have piquant foods, and some say the hottest foods in Africa; the former Portuguese colonies of Angola in the southwest and Mozambique in the southeast of the continent are spicy-hot; and in South Africa the Cape Malays have piquant food, although that is an influence of India and the Indo-Malaysian archipelago rather than Africa.

West African cooking refers to the cooking of Senegal, Gambia, Guinea-Bissau, Guinea, Sierra Leone, Mali, Mauritania, Liberia, Ivory Coast, Burkina Faso, Ghana, Togo, Benin, and Nigeria. Very hot cooking is found in all these countries except for Mauritania and most of Mali. The southern portions of all these countries have hotter foods than the northern portions. West African food is based on the stew. Breads are rarely found in West Africa, as they are mostly a European influence. The starches that are found are usually found in stews. Typical among them, and this has been true since before medieval times, are millet and sorghum, although there is also maize, rice, wheat, and beans. From the tenth to the sixteenth centuries the principal grain in West Africa was millet.

Another important food of West Africa is a bland cereal called *fonio* (*Digitaria exilis*). As *fonio* does not require careful cultivation and prospers in years of drought, it was an ideal food for Africans. In European literature it is sometimes called "hungry rice." Wheat was rare and expensive and played a minor role in the diet of West Africans. The most important cooking fats are red palm oil and peanut oil (after the discovery of the New World).

Before the arrival of the Portuguese in West Africa in the fifteenth century there is very little mention of spices in medieval Arabic accounts. The most outstanding reference is by the Arab traveler known as Leo Africanus, who tells of the importation of "Sudan pepper" to Morocco. It seems that this spice was Ashanti pepper or cubeb, a variety noted for its hotness. Ashanti pepper was cultivated in some places on the Guinea coast before the coming of the Portuguese. In 1512, Leo Africanus journeyed from Morocco to Timbuktu, where on the Arawan plateau to the north he was entertained by a prince of the Zanaga tribe, who offered his guests meat "seasoned with herbs and a large quantity of spices imported from Negroland." (Negroland was the English translation of the Arabic name for the western Sudanic region of West Africa, *Bilad al-Sudan*, land of the black man.) This tantalizing description doesn't tell us much, except that it is possible these spices came from the Guinea coast. Some spices were imported from North Africa, we know that from the famous Arab traveler Ibn Battuta's descriptions in the mid-fourteenth century.

Beef Stew with Chiles, Cassava, and Plantains

I n Sierra Leone, where this dish is from, the cook will refer to chiles in Creole (pidgin English) as one of three grades of hotness—small-small pepper, small pepper, and plenty pepper. If the dish is too spicy-hot, the Sherbro people of Sierra Leone have a trick to "cool" the mouth. They pull a burning stick from the fire and pass it back and forth an inch or so from their open mouths to "draw" off the heat.

This hearty one-pot meal is called *ebbeh* and is quite filling with all the root vegetables. *Ebbeh* or *eba* can mean either cassava flour pudding or a kind of African yam. The African yam is not the same thing as the American sweet potato, which is sometimes called a yam. It is a very large, bland root vegetable and is barely sweet. Its closest relative would be the malanga or *ñame* sold in supermarkets serving Caribbean and Latin American populations. Many supermarkets actually carry this item, usually tucked away with their more exotic items. But if you can't find it, it is better to use potato than American yam. And when shopping for ripe plantains, look for those with skin that is mottled black or brown. The proportion in this recipe of meat to vegetables is much more in line with what would be typical in West Africa.

½ pound beef stew meat, cut into 1-inch cubes

¾ pound ripe tomatoes, peeled and seeded

1 large onion, cut into eighths

10 green jalapeño chiles, stemmed

1 pound cassava, peeled and cut into 1-inch cubes

1 pound African yam, malanga, *ñame*, or boiling potatoes, peeled and cut into 1-inch cubes

1 pound ripe plantains or taro, peeled and cut into 1-inch cubes

2 teaspoons salt

½ cup peanut oil

1 pound smoked fish, such as herring, haddock, trout, or albacore, skin and bones removed

1. Place the meat in a stockpot or casserole and cover with water. Bring to a boil, then reduce the heat to medium and simmer briskly for 20 minutes, skimming the foam off.

2. Place the tomatoes, onion, and chiles in a blender and blend until smooth. Add the cubed cassava, yam, plantains, salt, and peanut oil to the pot. Continue cooking over medium heat until the vegetables are very tender, about 3 hours, adding cupfuls of water every time the stew gets very thick. You'll probably use 6 to 8 cups of water.

3. Once the root vegetables and plantains are tender, mash some of the vegetable pieces against the side of the pot to make them more of a thickener. Add the fish to the pot, reduce the heat to low, and continue cooking at a simmer until heated through, well blended, and a thick stew, about 15 minutes. Serve immediately.

MAKES 8 SERVINGS

Sik Sik Wat

T his Ethiopian beef stew made with the spice paste known as *Berbere* (page 417) can be found on the menu of every Ethiopian restaurant, as it is a national dish. Most prepared dishes in Ethiopia are stews, *wat*, and they are always made with *berbere*. Two other unique features of Ethiopian stews are that the initial browning of the onions is not done with any fat (and this method accounts for the unique taste of many stews) and that nearly all stews are eaten on top of *Injera* (page 400), a flat flapjack-type bread made from teff or millet that acts as an edible tablecloth. One visitor to Ethiopia described *wat* as "so fierce that it practically makes the ears bleed." This heat comes from the chile, but before the discovery of the New World chile in 1493 and its arrival in Ethiopia in the mid-sixteenth century most piquancy derived from the long pepper, which is still used in local cooking. Don't forget to make the *injera*, which goes with every Ethiopian meal.

2½ pounds onions, finely chopped

6 tablespoons *niter kebbeh* (page 419)

2 large garlic cloves, finely chopped

One 1-inch piece fresh ginger, peeled and finely chopped

½ teaspoon ground fenugreek

½ teaspoon ground ajwain (optional)

¼ teaspoon ground clove

¼ teaspoon fresh ground allspice

¼ teaspoon ground nutmeg

2 tablespoons cayenne pepper

2 tablespoons hot paprika

3 tablespoons *Berbere* (page 417)

1 cup water

1 cup tomato puree

2 teaspoons salt

3 pounds boneless beef chuck or round, cut into ¾-inch cubes

2 teaspoons freshly ground black pepper

1. In a large cast-iron pot, cook the onions without any fat over medium heat until translucent and soft and most of their liquid has evaporated, 20 to 25 minutes, stirring. Add the *niter kebbeh* and once it melts add the garlic, ginger, fenugreek, ajwain, if using, cloves, allspice, and nutmeg and stir well. Add the cayenne pepper, paprika, and *berbere* and stir for 3 minutes, until the mixture looks like a thick vegetable marmalade. Add the water, tomato puree, and salt and bring the mixture to a near boil over high heat.

2. Add the beef and stir so the meat is covered in the sauce. Cover the pot, reduce the heat to very low, using a heat diffuser if necessary, and simmer until the beef is very tender, about 5 hours. Season with black pepper and serve hot.

MAKES 6 TO 8 SERVINGS

the hot spices: ajwain

Ajwain, also spelled ajowan, is a member of the carrot family and has an astringent quality. It is closely related to caraway and cumin, but its taste is closer to a strong thyme and its seeds look like celery seeds. It is primarily cultivated as an essential oil. It is native to southern India and also grown in Afghanistan, Pakistan, Iran, and Egypt. In cooking it is mostly used to flavor vegetables on the Indian subcontinent, such as in dals, but also appears in the cooking of Yemen and Ethiopia. Most Westerners are not familiar with ajwain and it is available only in Indian groceries or through the Internet. The strong aroma of ajwain can be enhanced by dry-roasting in a cast-iron skillet.

the hot spices: long pepper

Long pepper does indeed have a long and narrow flower. As the tiny long pepper berries grow they fuse into a rodlike structure that resembles the catkins of a willow tree. Long pepper berries are harvested while green and then sun-dried. Long pepper, which originated in the south of Asia on the Dekkan peninsula, is slightly more pungent than black pepper. The Greek naturalist Theophrastus described both long pepper and black pepper in the first century A.D., and in Roman times Pliny reported that long pepper was worth almost four times as much as black pepper and could be adulterated with Alexandrian mustard. The Romans used a lot of both black pepper and long pepper in their cooking. In the anonymous ancient Greek work *Periplus of the Erythraean Sea* (The Hakluyt Society, 1980), the author notes that long pepper was exported from a port near the Ganges. The Arabs introduced long pepper to North Africa in the eighth or ninth century, where it can still be found in some spice mixes. In the Middle Ages, Saladinus of Ascoli, a noted physician and herbalist, listed long pepper among the drugs that should always be kept in stock by apothecaries. In India, long pepper is always used whole, mostly for pickling and preserves. In China, long pepper was mentioned by Ji Han in the fourth century A.D., who said that it came from Westerners, while Su Gong in the seventh century said it was used to flavor foods. Today, long pepper is rarely found outside of the Far East. It has been suggested that long pepper could not face the competition from the arrival of the chile.

Fiery Beef Shank

This Yemeni stew is called *hur'iy*, an Arabic word that means "stewed very well until the meat shreds." And this is exactly what you do. Typically the dish is made with beef foreshank, although oxtail could be used, too. At the end of the cooking there should be just a little syrupy liquid left. An otherwise bland cut of tough meat is simmered with a delectable blend of spices and the resulting stew is complex, interesting, and savory. It's likely that the use of spices in Yemen, a country that sits on the southwestern corner of the Arabian Peninsula, is due to the fact that it has been a transit point for the spice trade for two thousand years. Some of those spices clearly fell into a local pot. Serve this with rice and flatbread.

3 pounds beef shank, cut into 1-inch slices

2 large onions, cut into eighths

12 large garlic cloves, peeled and crushed

3 large tomatoes (about 1¹/₂ pounds), peeled, seeded, and quartered

2 teaspoons freshly ground black pepper

4 dried red de arbol chiles, broken in half

1 teaspoon freshly ground caraway seeds

¹/₄ teaspoon ground saffron

¹/₄ teaspoon ground cardamom

1 teaspoon ground turmeric

2 teaspoons salt

1. Put the shank in a large casserole with barely enough water to cover. Bring slowly to a boil over medium heat, skimming the foam off the surface.

2. Once the water is boiling, add the onions, garlic, tomatoes, black pepper, chiles, caraway seeds, saffron, cardamom, turmeric, and salt. Cover, reduce the heat to low, and simmer until the meat is so tender that it would shred with the gentle tug of a fork, about 5 hours. There should be very little liquid left, but if there is, remove all the contents of the casserole with a slotted spoon, bring the broth to a boil, and boil until only 2 or 3 cups of broth remain. Return everything to the casserole and, once heated, serve immediately.

MAKES 6 SERVINGS

the piquant cooking of yemen

Yemen, the biblical land of the Queen of Sheba, has had a sophisticated and advanced agriculture since early times. In the Middle Ages, Yemeni agricultural was so advanced that it was adopted in the small oasis-like *huertas* of medieval Valencia in Spain. Medieval Yemeni technological expertise in irrigation and hydrology was influential throughout the Mediterranean. We know that hard wheat was an important grain in Yemen in the tenth century A.D. from the detailed writings of al-Hamdani (893?–945?). In the early centuries of the first millennium, Persians had colonies in Yemen, and it is possible they may have influenced the spicing of the foods. The two most important spices being traded by Yemen were black pepper and ginger, both mentioned by the fourteenth-century Arab traveler Ibn Battuta as being bought in Mangalore in India by Persian and Yemeni traders. The Yemenis also traded with Mecca, although it was not a transit trade, and spices arriving from India on their way to the Mediterranean went through Yemen. Today, Yemeni cooking has some similarities with Ethiopian cooking in that one finds many stews that are highly seasoned with chile and fenugreek, which seems to be the favorite spice of the Yemeni cook. Several important spice mixes, pastes, and sauces are used in Yemen to flavor food, such as *hilbah*, made with fresh coriander, black pepper, caraway, black cardamom, dried red chiles, garlic, fenugreek seeds, tomato puree, lemon juice, and sage. *Zhug* is a fiery chile and coriander relish made with lots of spices, and *hawayij*, a spice blend of black pepper, caraway, cardamom, turmeric, and saffron, is used in many stews.

Cayenne Oxtail Stew

This stunning and spicy stew is an all-day affair, best made on a winter day. Stewing is a favorite way of cooking in Yemen and so too is the use of spices and chiles. The history of Yemeni spice use goes back to the time of the Queen of Sheba. In this very long simmering stew, called 'akwa in Arabic, oxtail is used. Oxtail is a very tough meat, and that's why it cooks for so long. 'Akwa is a word that means the thickest part of the tail, which is the part that goes into this stew. The spice blend here is what makes the finished dish so delectable as the stew cooks for a very long time. Serve with Rice Pilaf (page 396), flatbread, and a green salad.

5 pounds oxtail

4 teaspoons black peppercorns

1 tablespoon cayenne pepper

2 teaspoons caraway seeds

1/2 teaspoon cardamom seeds

1/2 teaspoon saffron threads

1 teaspoon ground fenugreek

1 1/2 teaspoons ground turmeric

2 teaspoons salt, or more to your taste

2 large ripe tomatoes (about 1 1/2 pounds), peeled and chopped

2 pounds small white onions, peeled

14 garlic cloves (about 1 head), separated, peeled, and lightly crushed

1. Rinse the oxtail, then place in a large casserole and cover with water. Bring to a gently bubbling boil over medium heat, then reduce the heat to low and skim the foam off the surface until there is very little foam left.

2. Blend the peppercorns, cayenne pepper, caraway seeds, cardamom seeds, and saffron in a spice mill or with a mortar and pestle. Stir the fenugreek, turmeric, and salt into the spice mix. Add the tomatoes, onions, garlic, and spice mix to the oxtail. Bring to a boil, then reduce the heat to very low, cover, and simmer for 3 hours. Uncover and continue to cook until the meat is falling off the bone, another 5 to 6 hours. The stew is done when the meat is falling off the bone and the sauce is much reduced.

MAKES 6 SERVINGS WITH RICE

Beef and Spinach with Peanut and Coconut Sauce

There are a number of versions of this Thai dish called *pra ram long song*, which means something like "Rama doing his ablutions." Chat Mingkwan in *The Best of Regional Thai Cuisine* (Hippocrene, 2002) suggests that Rama—the king of classical Thai mythology—has an emerald green complexion, represented in this dish by the green vegetable morning glory (but I've substituted spinach). He performs his ablutions and emerges fresh, as represented by the now golden-colored curry sauce of coconut and peanut. Serve with steamed rice.

10 dried red de arbol chiles, stems removed, soaked in water for 30 minutes, and drained

4 large garlic cloves, chopped

1 small shallot

2 teaspoons finely chopped coriander (cilantro) roots and/or stems

1 tablespoon finely chopped lemongrass

1 teaspoon finely chopped fresh ginger

1 teaspoon lime zest

1 pound baby spinach leaves

1 1/4 pounds beef round (London broil), cut into 2 x 1/4-inch slices

2 1/2 cups coconut milk (see page 90)

3 tablespoons tamarind water (see page 329)

1/2 cup peanut butter (see page 137)

2 tablespoons Thai fish sauce

2 tablespoons palm sugar or granulated sugar

1 1/2 teaspoons salt

1. Prepare the chile paste by placing the drained chiles, garlic, shallot, coriander, lemongrass, ginger, and lime zest in a food processor and blending until very finely chopped. Transfer to a mortar and pound until a paste forms.

2. Bring a large saucepan of water to a boil and dunk the spinach. Drain immediately and set aside. Blanch the beef in the same water until the top of the water is filled with foam, about 5 minutes, then drain the beef and set aside.

3. In a wok, bring the coconut milk to a boil over high heat and stir in the chile paste, tamarind water, and peanut butter, stirring until well blended. Add the beef slices, fish sauce, sugar, and salt. Reduce the heat to medium and simmer until the beef is tender, about 15 minutes. Arrange the spinach on a platter and spoon the beef over it with some of the sauce. Serve immediately.

MAKES 4 SERVINGS

blazing beef and incendiary lamb

Crying Tiger

Su-Mei Yu, author of *Cracking the Coconut: Classic Thai Home Cooking* (William Morrow, 2000), tells us that this dish of grilled beef with chile dipping sauce called *seua rong hai* is a true Bangkok creation because of its intense flavors. It is called "Crying Tiger" because the chiles should be hot enough to make one howl like a tiger, but balanced with a blend of sweet-salty flavors to lesson the fire. On the other hand, the literal translation is "as the tiger weeps," and it has been suggested that the fat from the beef "weeps" into the red-hot coals of the grill. But I believe that the reference is probably related to the heat of the chiles, which will indeed make you sweat and tear. The dipping sauce is a kind of *nam prik* (page 000), of which there are many varieties that can also be used for grilled Thai sausage, grilled pork, or grilled chicken. This dish is nice accompanied by steamed jasmine rice.

1/4 cup soy sauce

1/4 cup Thai fish sauce

1 tablespoon palm sugar or granulated sugar

1 pound beef rib eye or beef round (London broil), in 1 piece

2 heads garlic

2 teaspoons vegetable oil

1/4 cup dried bird's-eye chiles or dried *piquin* chiles or crumbled dried red de arbol chiles

1/2 teaspoon salt

1 shallot, chopped

1 tablespoon finely chopped fresh coriander (cilantro) leaves

One 1-inch cube fresh galangal or ginger, peeled and chopped

3 tablespoons fresh lime juice

1. In a large bowl, combine the soy sauce, 2 tablespoons of the fish sauce, and the sugar. Mix until the sugar dissolves. Place the steak in the bowl, turn several times, and marinate for 1 hour at room temperature, turning once.

2. Meanwhile, preheat the oven to 400°F. Cut the garlic heads in half so the inside of the cloves are exposed and drizzle with vegetable oil, then wrap in aluminum foil and roast until the insides are soft, 30 minutes. Cool, then squeeze the soft garlic mush into a small bowl and set aside.

3. Prepare a hot charcoal fire or preheat a gas grill on high for 15 minutes.

4. Meanwhile, prepare the dipping sauce. In a small cast-iron skillet, dry-roast the chiles over high heat with a little salt until the chiles begin to blacken, 3 to 4 minutes, shaking the skillet. Remove and cool and add to the bowl with the garlic. Transfer the contents of the bowl to a food processor along with the shallot, coriander leaves, and galangal and puree into a paste. Add the remaining 2 tablespoons fish sauce and lime juice and continue to puree, scraping down the sides when necessary, about 3 minutes of continuous processing. Transfer to a dipping bowl.

5. Place the steak on the grill and cook until the center is medium rare, 8 to 10 minutes, 4 to 5 inches directly above a very hot fire, turning several times. If you are using the rib eye, which is marbled with more fat, it will flare up more than the London broil and char the steak a bit, which is preferred for this dish. Remove the steak from the grill and transfer to a carving or serving platter and let rest 10 minutes. Slice crosswise into thin slices and serve with the dipping sauce.

MAKES 4 SERVINGS

Beef with Green Curry Sauce

T his standard Thai dish, called *gaeng gwiow wan nuea* or *kaeng khiao* (or *keang keow*) *wan nuea*, is best made with fresh homemade green curry paste, but a good version of the paste can also be found in the international/Asian section of the supermarket. Thai curries can be served either as a one-dish meal or with steamed rice and various accompaniments. The difference between coconut cream and coconut milk is that the cream is the skimmed top of the liquid obtained from the first soaking and the milk is from the "whey" or lighter, more watery, part of the first and subsequent soakings. The pea eggplants called for in the recipe are known as *ma-keua puang* and are found in Asian markets and via Internet sources. They can be replaced with either shelled peas or Japanese eggplants.

---

1 pound boneless beef top loin, sliced into 2 x ¹/₄-inch strips

6 tablespoons coconut cream (see page 90)

3 tablespoons Green Curry Paste (page 422)

1¹/₂ cups coconut milk (see page 90)

¹/₂ cup pea eggplant or 6 ounces Japanese eggplant, cut into diagonal offset slices

4 fresh red finger-type chiles or 8 red serrano chiles, julienned lengthwise

¹/₂ cup coarsely chopped and loosely packed fresh basil leaves

2 tablespoons Thai fish sauce

1¹/₂ teaspoons palm sugar or light brown sugar or granulated sugar

1 cup loosely packed whole fresh coriander leaves, for garnish

---

1. Bring a large saucepan of water to a rapid boil and plunge the beef in until the surface is covered with foam, about 5 minutes. Drain and set the meat aside.

2. In a wok, heat the coconut cream over medium heat until it begins to separate, about 1 minute, then add the green curry paste and stir until well blended and aromatic, 2 to 3 minutes. Add the beef to the wok and cook, stirring, until some oil begins to appear on the edges, about 4 minutes. Add the coconut milk and eggplant and cook on medium heat, covered, until the eggplant is tender, about 15 minutes, stirring occasionally. Stir in the red chiles, basil, fish sauce, and sugar and cook, uncovered, for another 1 to 2 minutes so that the basil begins to wilt. Garnish with coriander leaves and serve.

MAKES 4 SERVINGS

Beef in Coconut and Chile Curry

Rendang daging is an example of a style of cooking in Indonesia called *nasi Padang*, "Padang food." It originates from the western Sumatra province and is named after the capital, Padang. The region is inhabited by the Minangkabau, a Muslim people who are known for their buffalo. (For authenticity, you would make this with water buffalo meat.) Even by Indonesian standards, Padang food is quite spicy. *Rendang* is also a popular dish in Malaysia, where it is made for special occasions such as Malaysian New Year or, among Muslims, the Id al-Fitr feast celebrating the breaking of the Ramadan fast. This is an easy dish to make since everything goes into a pot and you cook it with a minimum of fuss. Serve with white rice, one or two vegetables, such as Spicy Cabbage in Coconut Milk (page 315), a variety of sambals (pages 420 and 425), and prawn crackers, which are sold in many different Asian markets and some supermarkets.

4 shallots, coarsely chopped

3 large garlic cloves, chopped

One 1-inch cube fresh ginger, peeled and chopped

3 fresh red finger-type chiles or 4 red jalapeño chiles

2 cups coconut cream (see page 90)

1 1/2 teaspoons salt

1/2 teaspoon ground turmeric

2 teaspoons cayenne pepper or ground red chile

1 teaspoon ground coriander

3 curry leaves (see page 372)

1/2 lemongrass stalk, tough outer portion removed, white tender part only, finely chopped

One 1-inch cube fresh galangal, peeled and chopped, or one 1/2-inch cube fresh ginger, peeled and chopped, or 1/2 teaspoon ground galangal or 1/4 teaspoon ground ginger

1 1/2 pounds beef chuck, cut into 1 x 2-inch strips

1/4 cup tamarind water (see page 329)

1 teaspoon palm sugar or brown sugar

1. Put the shallots, garlic, ginger, fresh chiles, and 1/2 cup of the coconut cream into a blender and puree until smooth.

2. Pour the blender mixture into a wok or stockpot. Pour the remaining coconut cream into the blender, swish it around, and then pour it into the wok. Add the salt, turmeric, cayenne pepper, coriander, curry leaves, lemongrass, and galangal to the wok. Mix well and add the beef. Bring to a boil over high heat, then reduce the heat to medium and add the tamarind water and cook 1 minute. Reduce the heat to low and simmer, uncovered, until the sauce is a thick gravy and almost sticking to the bottom, 3 to 3$^{1}/_{2}$ hours, stirring occasionally. Once the oil of the coconut starts to separate from the gravy, add the sugar, stir, and cook 5 minutes. Serve immediately.

MAKES 4 SERVINGS

Sichuan Shredded Beef and Celery

This blistering hot Sichuanese dish is great, but be careful with the celery, as it is very strong tasting once cooked and could easily dominate the dish if you use more than I call for. The hot soybean paste used in this recipe is sold in jars in the international/Asian section of supermarkets but can be labeled differently, so read the jars closely. Serve with steamed rice.

3 tablespoons Chile Oil (page 424)

3 teaspoons soy sauce

$^{1}/_{8}$ teaspoon baking soda

$^{3}/_{4}$ pound beef sirloin or flank, sliced into strips 1$^{1}/_{2}$ inches long and $^{1}/_{4}$ inch thick

3 cups vegetable oil, for frying

3 celery stalks, trimmed of leaves and the bottom end, julienned

1 leek, white and light green parts only, washed well and cut into 1-inch diagonal slices

4 garlic cloves, slivered

1 tablespoon shredded fresh ginger

4 fresh red jalapeño chiles, seeded and julienned

1 tablespoon Sichuan chile bean paste (see page 98), or 2 teaspoons soybean paste (miso) mixed with 1 teaspoon Korean red chile paste (see page 334), or $^{1}/_{2}$ teaspoon ground red chile

1 teaspoon cornstarch mixed with 1 tablespoon water

1$^{1}/_{2}$ tablespoons white cooking wine, rice wine (mirin), or sake

1 teaspoon rice vinegar or white wine vinegar

1 teaspoon sesame oil

1. In a medium-size bowl, mix 2 tablespoons of the chile oil, 2 teaspoons of the soy sauce, and the baking soda. Marinate the beef in this mixture for 15 minutes.

2. In a wok, heat the frying oil over medium-high heat until nearly smoking. Cook the beef until it turns color, about 30 seconds. Remove with a slotted spoon or skimmer and set aside. Add the celery, leek, and garlic to the wok and, once it is submerged in the oil, cook 1 minute, then remove immediately with a skimmer or slotted spoon and set aside with the beef.

3. Discard all but a film of oil from the wok, add the remaining 1 tablespoon chile oil, and heat for a few minutes. Add the ginger and red chiles and stir-fry until the ginger turns light brown, 1 to 2 minutes. Mix in the bean paste and, once it dissolves, add the reserved beef, celery, leek, and the remaining 1 teaspoon soy sauce. Stir-fry 2 minutes to mix well. Add the cornstarch dissolved in water to thicken the sauce and sprinkle on the wine, vinegar, and sesame oil. Serve immediately.

MAKES 2 SERVINGS WITHOUT RICE OR 4 WITH RICE

Boiled Beef in Fiery Sauce

Part of the Chinese name of this dish, *chuan nan shui zhu niu liu*, is a very misleading "beef boiled in water." In fact, it's quite piquant and full of much more flavor than "water" implies. Fuchsia Dunlop in her *Land of Plenty* (W. W. Norton, 2003) tells us that the dish is said to have originated in the city of Zigong, known as Sichuan's salt capital because it sits in the middle of a salt mining district. This dish is served in a deep bowl and is stewy looking. Serve with rice.

³/₄ pound flank steak, cut against the grain into thin 1 x 2-inch slices

1 teaspoon salt, or more to your taste

1 tablespoon rice wine (*mirin*) or vermouth

10 tablespoons peanut oil

10 dried red de arbol chiles, cut in half and seeded

2 teaspoons Sichuan peppercorns

1 small head celery (about ³/₄ pound), blemished or fibrous outer stalks removed if necessary, each stalk split lengthwise and cut into ¹/₂-inch sticks

4 scallions, white and green parts, cut into ¹/₂-inch pieces

3 tablespoons Sichuan chile bean paste (see page 98)

2 cups chicken broth (homemade or canned)

2 teaspoons soy sauce

3 tablespoons cornstarch mixed with 3 tablespoons water

1. In a medium-size bowl, toss the beef with ¹/₄ teaspoon salt and the rice wine, then leave to marinate while you continue the preparation.

2. In a wok, heat 3 tablespoons of the peanut oil over high heat until it is almost smoking, then cook the chiles and Sichuan peppercorns until the chiles darken, about 15 seconds, stirring constantly. Remove quickly with a skimmer and set aside. Chop the chiles and Sichuan peppercorns and reserve.

3. Reheat the oil remaining in the wok over high heat and, once it is smoking, add the celery, scallions, and ¹/₂ teaspoon of the salt, and cook until they are hot but still crunchy, 1 to 2 minutes, stir-frying constantly. Remove with a skimmer to a large bowl.

4. Add 3 tablespoons of the peanut oil to the wok and heat over high heat until it begins to smoke. Reduce the heat to medium, add the chile bean paste, and stir-fry for 30 seconds. Add the broth, soy sauce, and remaining ³/₄ teaspoon salt and bring to a boil. Add the cornstarch mixture to the beef and stir to coat well. Drop the beef slices into the boiling broth and, once it returns to a boil, cook for 1 minute, stirring constantly to separate the slices of beef. Remove the beef with a skimmer to the bowl with the celery. Pour the remaining sauce over the beef. Sprinkle the reserved chiles and Sichuan peppercorns over the meat.

5. Working quickly, rinse the wok and dry it. Add the remaining 4 tablespoons peanut oil to the wok and heat over high heat until smoking. Pour the contents of the bowl into the wok; they will sizzle dramatically. Cook until heated through, about 1 minute. Serve immediately.

MAKES 4 SERVINGS

what is a de arbol chile?

When you buy whole dried red chiles, the ones about ¹/₄ inch wide and 3 inches long, or jars of red chile flakes in the supermarket, you are buying de arbol chiles. They are a finger-type chile, as are cayenne chiles, whose dried and powdered form is known as cayenne pepper, and I call for them throughout the book. I just want to assure you that there is nothing mysterious or exotic about them—de arbol is just the name of this particular cultivar, and it means "tree chile" in Mexican Spanish, because the bush they grow on resembles a tree.

Lamb and Pumpkin Curry

C urry came to Jamaica with East Indian workers who immigrated there in the late nineteenth century, after the abolition of slavery. They worked on the plantations, and their curries from India were transformed into super-hot dishes such as this Jamaican lamb stew. You will want to eat it with something very bland, such as plantains (see pages 389 and 390) or white rice.

1 pound boneless leg of lamb, cut into 1-inch cubes

2 tablespoons curry powder

Salt to taste

1 teaspoon ground allspice

1 teaspoon freshly ground black pepper

1 teaspoon ground coriander

2 tablespoons vegetable oil

1 medium-size onion, chopped

3 large garlic cloves, finely chopped

2 pounds tomatoes, cut in half, seeds squeezed out, and grated against the largest holes of a grater

1 tablespoon tomato paste

6 ounces diced pumpkin or other winter squash flesh

1 Scotch bonnet chile or habanero chile, finely chopped

1/2 cup beef broth (homemade or canned)

2 sprigs fresh thyme

2 tablespoons finely chopped fresh coriander (cilantro) leaves (optional)

1. In a large bowl, toss the lamb with the curry powder, salt, allspice, black pepper, and ground coriander and leave to marinate in the refrigerator, covered with plastic wrap, for 2 hours.

2. In a large stockpot or casserole, heat the vegetable oil over medium-high heat, then brown the lamb, about 6 minutes, turning and tossing. Add the onion, garlic, tomatoes, and tomato paste and cook for 5 minutes, stirring. Add the pumpkin, Scotch bonnet chile, beef broth, thyme, and coriander leaves, if using, stir well, reduce the heat to low, cover, and simmer, using a heat diffuser if necessary, until the meat is tender and the diced pumpkin is very soft, 2^1/$_2$ to 3 hours. Serve immediately.

MAKES 4 SERVINGS

blazing beef and incendiary lamb

Piquant Ragout of Swiss Chard and Lamb

This stew, called *maraqa al-khudra* in Tunisia, is typical of home cooking in the capital city of Tunis, where it would be cooked for the important midday meal, then reheated for supper. The name means "ragout of vegetables," which gives you an idea that the Swiss chard is more important than the lamb. Some cooks might add other leafy vegetables such as spinach, root vegetables such as turnips, legumes such as haricot beans, and even thistles such as artichokes, cardoons, or golden thistle. Serve with a salad, steamed couscous, warmed Arabic bread, or Rice Pilaf (page 396).

1/2 cup extra-virgin olive oil

1 pound boneless lamb or mutton shoulder, trimmed of all fat and cut into 1-inch cubes

1 1/2 teaspoons *Tabil* (page 415)

Salt and freshly ground black pepper to taste

2 medium-large onions, chopped

1 pound Swiss chard, stalks trimmed and chopped

Leaves from 1 bunch parsley, chopped

2/3 cup cooked chickpeas, drained

2 tablespoons tomato paste

1 tablespoon *Harisa* (page 414) mixed with 1/2 cup water

Juice from 1 lemon

1 1/2 teaspoons freshly ground black pepper

1 1/2 teaspoons ground red chile or cayenne pepper

1. In a medium-size nonreactive casserole, heat the olive oil over high heat. Toss the lamb with the *tabil* and salt and pepper. Brown the meat and onions in the hot oil, about 5 minutes, stirring frequently.

2. Reduce the heat to low and add the Swiss chard and parsley with the water clinging to them from their last rinsing. Cook until this liquid is mostly evaporated, about 10 minutes.

3. Add the chickpeas, tomato paste, *harisa* diluted in the water, lemon juice, black pepper, and ground chile. Mix well, cover, and simmer over very low heat until the meat is very tender, about 2 hours, moistening the ragout with small amounts of water if it is drying out. Serve immediately.

MAKES 4 SERVINGS

Lamb and White Bean Stew

The most important meal of the day in Algeria is the midday meal, when the father returns home from work to eat a dish such as this one with his family. In the modern age, with the growth of large cities and traffic, this doesn't always happen anymore. This stew is made with lamb or often mutton and dried white haricot beans, with lots of onions and tomatoes. It is seasoned in a spicy hot way with cayenne pepper, fresh chiles, and the ubiquitous chile paste called *harisa*. My adaptation of this family-style stew has a ratio of almost two to one, meat to beans, while a typical Algerian cook would use a ratio of four to one, beans to meat. The stew is substantial on its own because of the beans, but this is very nice served with a *salade composée* such as a platter of fresh salad greens, seeded and sliced cucumbers, and ripe tomatoes all chopped up and dressed with a drizzle of extra-virgin olive oil, very finely chopped garlic, a dusting of cayenne, and fresh lemon juice.

1/4 cup extra-virgin olive oil

1 3/4 pounds boneless leg or shoulder of mutton or lamb, cut into 1/2-inch pieces

1 tablespoon salt, or more to your taste

2 teaspoons freshly ground black pepper, or more to your taste

1 teaspoon cayenne pepper

1 tablespoon *Harisa* (page 414)

3 medium-large onions, coarsely chopped

3 large ripe tomatoes (about 1 1/2 pounds), peeled, seeded, and chopped

1 quart water

1 pound (2 cups) dried white haricot beans, soaked in water to cover overnight, drained

1/2 cup finely chopped fresh coriander (cilantro) leaves

1.   In a large stew pot, preferably earthenware, using a heat diffuser if you are using earthenware, heat the olive oil over high heat. Season the meat with the salt, black pepper, and cayenne pepper, then brown it in the pot for 5 to 10 minutes, stirring occasionally. Add the *harisa*, stir, then add the onions and tomatoes, reduce the heat to low, cover, and leave to simmer for 15 minutes.

2.   Add the water, beans, and coriander and bring to a boil over high heat. Reduce the heat to low and let it simmer until the beans are tender, 2 to 2 1/2 hours, stirring occasionally. Add more salt and pepper if desired. Serve immediately.

MAKES 6 TO 8 SERVINGS

blazing beef and incendiary lamb

TÔ

One of the largest population groups in the West African nation of Mali is the Bambara, a subgroup of the Mande people. The Bambara were originally from what is now Burkina Faso, where some still live. The Bambara language is important in Mali because it is both a common language and the language of trade. Most Bambara are rural farmers and in the lowlands their staple crops are millet, sorghum, peanuts, and rice. This preparation is a staple food, and although the name of the dish, *tô* (pronounced "toe"), refers to millet polenta, it also means the entire preparation as represented in this recipe. Fine millet flour is soaked in water until creamy and then boiled in water, stirred continuously until the dough pulls away from the sides of the pot, just as you would make polenta. One can use corn flour in place of millet flour, or combine both. Millet flour can be found in whole foods markets or via the Internet. If you decide to use corn flour, use the Latin American kind that usually says *masa harina* on the package. *Tô* was so ubiquitous among the people of western Sahel in West Africa that one traveler wrote, "the villagers eat *tô*, *tô*, and *tô*." See pages 185 and 431 for more on the fermented locust bean and African dried fish.

1 pound catfish fillet

1 tablespoon peanut oil

2 cups (about 10 ounces) fine millet flour or corn flour

7¼ cups water plus more as needed

3 tablespoons salt, or more to your taste

3 pounds lamb or mutton shoulder, on the bone, cut into pieces

2 medium-size onions, chopped

1 fermented locust bean ball (*dawadawa*) or 1 tablespoon Maggi Sauce or 1 tablespoon soy sauce

½ pound okra, ends trimmed

¼ pound African dried fish or smoked fish (page 431)

¼ cup red palm oil or walnut oil mixed with ½ teaspoon hot paprika

3 habanero chiles or 5 cherry chiles

1.   Prepare a hot charcoal fire or preheat a gas grill on high for 15 minutes or preheat a cast-iron skillet for 15 minutes over high heat. Lightly oil the catfish with half the peanut oil and grill until blackened and flaky, about 10 minutes, or pan-fry until blackened and flaky, about 8 minutes. Remove and set aside.

2.   In a deep bowl, stir the millet flour with 4 cups of water to form a kind of cream. In a large pot, bring the remaining 3¼ cups of water to a boil over medium-high heat, and as soon as you see the first shimmering of bubbles, stir the water

eating *tô* in mali

Dogon country sits on the edge of the Bandiagara Escarpment in the West African nation of Mali. The Dogon are an ancient people guided in their daily lives by a highly complex cosmology. In the hamlet of Koundou, my Dogon guide Ouma Sangara introduced me to my first *tô*. I had just finished several days of hiking and sleeping under the night sky of the African savanna and was now ravenous. Ouma had some *tô* for himself, as it is much too primitive a food for most Western stomachs. It was indeed probably the most primitive food I have ever eaten. It consisted of pounded millet flour mixed with boiling water until it formed a thick green paste like a *fufu*. This big ball of pounded millet sat in a large bowl surrounded by a viscous olive drab sauce made of broth, dried okra, fermented locust bean (*soumbala*), ground baobab, and baobab leaves. I had a few bites to see what it was, each bite bringing out my curiosity and wonder. Ouma ate it like there was no tomorrow along with the other Dogon. The amount in the bowl could have served 50 Westerners and maybe four Dogon.

in one direction to make a whirlpool, then slowly pour the flour liquid into the pot, stirring constantly with a wooden spoon. As soon as the mixture starts to splutter, reduce the heat to low and continue stirring until it is like a polenta with the mixture beginning to stick to the sides of the pot, about 40 minutes. Lightly oil a tray or large baking dish with the remaining peanut oil and pour the polenta into it, spreading evenly. Let the polenta cool and solidify, then cut into whatever shapes you like.

3. In a large stockpot, bring 3 quarts of water to a boil with 3 tablespoons salt, add the lamb, and cook for 15 minutes, skimming the surface of foam a couple of times. Add the onions and fermented locust bean and cook for 45 minutes over medium-high heat so the liquid is boiling.

4. Place the okra in a food processor and blend until mushy, then transfer to the stockpot. Crumble the reserved grilled fish and add to the stew pot with the dried fish. Stir and cook 1 hour at a gentle boil.

5. Reduce the heat to medium, pour in the red palm oil and add the chiles, and simmer until the meat and fish are falling apart, 1 hour. Serve with the millet polenta.

MAKES 6 SERVINGS

blazing beef and incendiary lamb

Saga-Saga

This extraordinary dish, called *saka saka* or *plat saffe*, a Mandingo dish from Guinea that is eaten in Sierra Leone, Mali, and Congo, too, may be difficult to make. I ordered all the African ingredients through the Internet. It's hard to believe I now actually have this stuff in my pantry and recently just "whipped" this up for friends. I have come up with substitute ingredients for you, suggested by African immigrants in this country. Although it calls for cassava leaves, spinach will work fine. *Soumbara* is a dried powder made from the fermented African locust bean (also called *dawadawa*) and is called *néré* fruit (see page 185). Interestingly, Africans suggest using Maggi Sauce, the one made by the Swiss company and available in supermarkets, in its place. The dried fish used in the recipe can also be ordered through the Internet, or you can use any available smoked or dried fish. Dried okra is also called for in many recipes, but replacing it with gumbo filé will work. Serve with rice or sautéed potatoes.

a pirogue on the niger river

Our day started out from Mopti, a big harbor town on the Niger River in the West African nation of Mali where we rented our pirogue, a narrow, flat-bottomed, and long-prowed river craft. We were going to spend the entire day on the river beneath the blazing African sun going downriver, in this case north toward Timbuktu. Our cook was Nafi Wologem, a young Dogon girl who specialized in *saga-saga*. Although *saga-saga* means "mutton-mutton," this dish was going to be made with beef. Nafi had brought her hardwood coals, firepots, and earthenware stew pots on board, where she quickly got the fire going because the *saga-saga* would take hours to prepare. In one pot she began cooking the chopped fresh potato leaves in water, washed first with potassium permanganate. In another pot, Nafi had some beef, tomatoes, eggplant, onion, a little dried fish, and about six habanero chiles stewing in a broth made with Maggi chicken bouillon cubes (called *sunbalini* here) dissolved in water with some lye. She cooked the stew until the broth was much reduced and very thick. Then she would add more water and reduce it again, this going on for a total of about three hours. Then the cooked potato leaves were mixed with the stewed beef and served. The final dish was richly delicious, spicy-hot, and served with tons of rice.

¼ cup red palm oil *or* walnut oil mixed with 1 teaspoon hot paprika

1 pound cassava leaves (see page 390) or spinach leaves, washed and dried very well

1 large onion, chopped

10 scallions, white and light green parts only, chopped

2 large ripe tomatoes (about 1 pound), cut in half, seeds squeezed out, and grated against the largest holes of a grater

1 pound boneless lamb or mutton leg or shoulder, cut into ½-inch cubes

2 teaspoons salt, or more to your taste

1½ teaspoons freshly ground black pepper, or more to your taste

¼ cup water

½ pound boneless red snapper fillet, cut into 4 pieces

¼ pound African dried fish or smoked fish (see page 431)

1 tablespoon African dried okra or 1 tablespoon gumbo filé or 4 large okra pods, ends trimmed and finely chopped

2 habanero chiles or 4 cherry chiles or cascabel chiles, finely chopped

1 fermented locust bean ball (*dawadawa*), pounded in a mortar, or 1 tablespoon Maggi Sauce or 1 tablespoon soy sauce

1. In a large saucepan, heat 2 tablespoons of the red palm oil over low heat, then cook the cassava leaves until wilted, about 15 minutes, stirring occasionally. Chop and set aside.

2. In a large casserole or stockpot, heat the remaining 2 tablespoons oil over medium-high heat, then cook the onion and scallions until soft, about 5 minutes. Add the tomatoes and lamb, season with salt and pepper, reduce the heat to low, cover, and simmer until almost tender, about 45 minutes. Uncover and simmer another 15 minutes. Add the water, fresh fish, dried fish, okra, chiles, and fermented locust bean. Cover and simmer until the sauce is lush and syrupy, about 25 minutes. Add the cassava leaves until heated, about 2 minutes. Serve immediately.

MAKES 4 TO 6 SERVINGS

blazing beef and incendiary lamb

Lamb in Spicy Cardamom and Rose Water–Flavored Yogurt Sauce

This rich dish, called *safed maas*, from Rajasthan belies the stark and arid landscape of this mostly desert state in northwest India. One story attributes its invention to the Kachchwaha family of Jaipur, who were close to the Moguls through marriage. This preparation is not only hot from chiles but also fragrant from coconut, ginger, rose water, and cardamom. A more "royal" version of *safed maas* would marinate the meat in strained yogurt, garlic paste, ginger paste, papaya paste, chile paste, and white pepper and then braise it in a cream sauce made of strained yogurt, chile paste, cashews, melon seeds, and poppy seeds, mace, cinnamon, and cardamom. It should be served with rice and Mustard Greens and Chiles (page 377). Both the white pepper and cardamom should ideally be freshly ground, and the coconut should ideally be fresh.

2 pounds boneless lamb shoulder or lamb top round, excess fat removed, cut into 1-inch cubes

Salt to taste

2 cups Stabilized Yogurt (page 278)

2 teaspoons freshly and finely ground white pepper

1/4 cup cashews or whole blanched almonds

1 ounce fresh coconut flesh (from 1/2 small coconut) or 1 cup dried unsweetened shredded coconut

3 tablespoons vegetable oil

2 tablespoons julienned fresh ginger

3/4 teaspoon freshly and finely ground white cardamom seeds

1/4 cup heavy cream

Juice from 1 lemon

2 teaspoons rose water

4 fresh green finger-type chiles or 5 green jalapeño chiles, seeded and chopped

1. Bring some water to cover the lamb to a boil in a large saucepan, add salt to taste, and boil the lamb for 5 minutes. Drain and rinse the lamb.

2. In a small bowl, whisk the yogurt until smooth, then add the white pepper and mix again. Place the cashews and coconut in a food processor and blend until a paste.

the food of rajasthan

Rajasthan, a large desert state in northwestern India bordering Pakistan, was once a princely state that gave rise to a royal cuisine. The chronicle *Kanhadade-Prabanda* of Padmanabha, written in 1455, describes some of the food served at the table of this ruler. Royal hunts led to the incorporation of meat into the cuisine, although there are also vegetarian Rajasthanis whose food cooked in pure *ghee* is famous. Rajasthani cooking was also influenced by the lifestyles of the desert dwellers, as well as by the Persians via the Mogul Empire. A scarcity of water and lack of fresh green vegetables affected Rajasthani cooking, and food that could be preserved and that didn't require heating was preferred. Pulses such as lentils are staple foods because rice and wheat do not grow well in the desert. Millet and corn are used for making breads and cereals and form the backbone of all Rajasthani food. Because there is not much water, cooks turn to milk, buttermilk, and *ghee* as alternatives. To balance the richness of milk products in the food cooks use spices as aids to digestion, especially asafoetida, ginger, ajwain, fenugreek seeds, dried fenugreek leaves, and aniseed. A regional variation is the use of powdered mango in Maheshwari cooking. The curries of Rajasthan are bright red but are not as spicy as they look.

3. In a large skillet, heat the vegetable oil over medium-high heat, then add the lamb, yogurt, ginger, salt to taste, and $1^1/_2$ cups water. Cover, reduce the heat to low, and simmer until the lamb is tender, $2^1/_2$ to 3 hours, stirring occasionally. When there is about $1^1/_2$ cups of liquid left, add the cashew-coconut mixture and stir for 2 minutes. Sprinkle in the cardamom and stir. Add the cream, lemon juice, rose water, and chiles and stir. Cover the pan and cook over low heat until the sauce is thick and syrupy, about 15 minutes. Serve immediately.

MAKES 4 TO 6 SERVINGS

blazing beef and incendiary lamb

the hot spices: garlic

Garlic, a bulb from the onion family, is probably native to Asia, since Central Asia is the center of diversity of the nearly 700 species of the genus *Allium*. No wild form of garlic has been found. Although known from the earliest times, the pungency of garlic, which diminishes as it cooks, is rarely noted in any writings. It was a well-known and common food to the ancient Egyptians, the Israelites, Romans, and Muslims. From earliest times, the medicinal value of garlic has been widely recognized, and the ancient Greek physician Galen gave it the name *theriaca rusticorum*, "poor man's treacle." The Greek historian Herodotus tells the famous story of how the workers who built the Pyramid of Cheops fed largely on radishes and garlic. Its affect on the breath was noted by Shakespeare, where Bottom says in *A Midsummer Night's Dream*, "And, most dear actors, eat no onions nor garlic, for we are to utter sweet breath. . . ." Today, garlic is used in a variety of forms from fresh to granulated and is popular with most cuisines in the world except northern ones above the 45th to 50th parallel.

Lamb Keema

A lamb keema is a ground lamb dish. If you take the ground lamb and form it into a meatball it is called a kofta, which derives from the cooking of the Arab and Persians who influenced Indian cuisine during the early Mogul period (1526–c. 1650). This dish is from Lucknow in the state of Uttar Pradesh, which is famous for its Muslim-influenced keemas, koftas, and kebabs. I've adapted this recipe from one by Sanjay Kumar and Nivedita Srivastava. Serve with Raita (page 396), Rice Pilaf (page 396), Poori Bread (page 399), or Naan (page 398).

2 pounds ground lamb

4 teaspoons very finely chopped ginger

4 large garlic cloves, pounded in a mortar with 1 teaspoon salt until mushy

5 fresh green finger-type chiles or 6 green jalapeño chiles, seeded and finely chopped

1 large egg

1 tablespoon white wine vinegar

2 tablespoons fresh bread crumbs

2 teaspoons ground cumin

1 teaspoon ground red chile or cayenne pepper

1/4 cup vegetable oil

1 small lemon, thinly sliced, for garnish

3 tablespoons chopped fresh coriander (cilantro) leaves, for garnish

1. In a large bowl, mix the ground lamb, ginger, garlic and salt, chiles, egg, vinegar, bread crumbs, cumin, and ground red chile. Let rest for 30 minutes in the refrigerator.

2. In a large skillet, heat the vegetable oil over high heat, then add the ground meat and cook for 1 minute, stirring. Reduce the heat to low, cover, and cook until browned and tender, 1 hour, stirring occasionally. Remove from the heat, arrange on a serving platter and garnish with the lemon and coriander leaves. Serve immediately.

MAKES 4 SERVINGS

blazing beef and incendiary lamb

Kashmiri Kebab

The kebabs in this preparation are long sausage-like logs of chile-spiced meat mixed with onions. First they are poached in water until firm, and then they are deep fried and finally brushed with clarified butter before being served with raw onions and lemon wedges. It is a delicious meal that I like to serve with rice, Cabbage Curry (page 378), and Naan (page 398).

1 tablespoon cumin seeds

2 pounds ground lamb

2 medium-size onions, coarsely chopped

4 fresh green guajillo (mirasol) chiles or green finger-type chiles or 5 green jalapeño chiles, coarsely chopped

One 1½-inch cube fresh ginger, finely chopped

1½ teaspoons ground red chile or cayenne pepper

1 tablespoon salt

1 teaspoon freshly ground black pepper

1 large egg

2 cups water

6 to 8 cups vegetable oil, for frying

1 lemon, cut into eighths, for garnish

2 medium-size onions, 1 sliced into rings and 1 chopped, for garnish

1 cup whole plain yogurt, for garnish (optional)

1. Place the cumin seeds on a small tray and roast at 450°F in a toaster oven or regular oven until darker, about 3 minutes. Grind the cumin seeds until a powder in a spice mill or mortar and reserve until needed.

2. In a large bowl, mix the lamb, the chopped onions, green chiles, ginger, red chile, the reserved cumin, salt, and pepper with your hands, blending well. Add the egg and blend that in with your hands. Mold the meat into 4 oblong-shaped kebabs, about 8 inches long and 3 inches in diameter.

3. Bring the water to a boil in a shallow pan and add the kebabs. Reduce the heat to low and simmer until the kebabs are firm and slightly browned, about 45 minutes. Remove the kebabs.

4. Preheat the frying oil to 350°F in a deep-fryer or an 8-inch saucepan fitted with a basket insert. Cook the kebabs, one or two at a time depending on the size of the fryer you are using, until a deep brown, about 4 minutes. Serve immediately with the lemon, sliced and chopped onions, and yogurt if desired.

MAKES 4 SERVINGS

Stoba Kabritu

The Dutch Antilles, consisting of the islands of Aruba, Bonaire, and Curaçao, were originally inhabited by the Arawak and Carib Indians. The population today is mixed, a result of the slave trade and immigration by people from India. The population is mostly urban, and the land is not abundant in food, so much needs to be imported. The cuisine on Curaçao can be described as a Creole cuisine, with African, Spanish, Indian, and other influences. Cooks like hot chiles and use them, but not quite with the abandon you would find in Jamaica. This recipe is adapted from Desiree Da Costa Gomez's Web site in the Papiamentu language, a Creole language spoken on Curaçao. It's best to make this dish with goat, but you can also use lamb. Instead of banana one could add a cucumber. This stew can be accompanied with white rice or Dumplings (page 394).

2 tablespoons vegetable oil

2 pounds boneless leg of goat or lamb, cut into 1½-inch cubes

2 medium-size onions, chopped

6 large garlic cloves, finely chopped

1 celery stalk, finely chopped

1 tablespoon finely chopped fresh ginger

3 habanero chiles, finely chopped

1 green bell pepper, chopped

2 medium-size tomatoes, peeled, seeded, and chopped

¼ cup freshly squeezed lime juice

1 teaspoon ground cumin

1 teaspoon curry powder

1 teaspoon ground allspice

2 cups water

1 tablespoon white vinegar

1 banana, diced

¼ cup chopped green olives

1. In a large casserole or heavy stockpot, heat the vegetable oil over medium-high heat, then brown the goat on all sides, 5 to 6 minutes. Remove the meat with a slotted spoon and set aside. Add the onions, garlic, celery, ginger, chiles, and bell pepper to the casserole and cook until the onions are soft, stirring about 5 minutes.

2. Return the goat to the casserole and add the tomatoes, lime juice, cumin, curry powder, allspice, and water. Reduce the heat to low and simmer, partially covered, until the meat is very tender and starts to fall apart, 2 to 2¼ hours. Add the vinegar, banana, and olives and simmer until the banana is cooked through and soft, another 20 to 30 minutes. Serve immediately.

MAKES 6 SERVINGS

blazing beef and incendiary lamb

the piquant cuisine of
the caribbean

There's no argument that the hottest cuisine of the Caribbean is found in Jamaica. There is some piquant food in Trinidad and Tobago, as well as Martinique and Guadalupe, and a dish here and there in places like Cuba or Bermuda and even the Florida Keys. We know the Caribbean has had chiles for a long time because this is where Columbus first encountered the chile. But basically, the hot Caribbean is all about Jamaica, a lush tropical island of steep cloud-shrouded mountains and blue lagoons whose population is mostly descendants of African slaves. Jamaica was first inhabited about A.D. 1000 by Arawak Indians from the Orinoco region of South America. The Caribs were the other important Indian tribe occupying the Caribbean when it was discovered by Europeans. They were cannibals and warlike, very unlike the peaceful Arawaks. The Caribs inhabited Trinidad, the Lesser Antilles, and the eastern part of Puerto Rico. Jessica B. Harris, author of *Sky Juice and Flying Fish: Traditional Caribbean Cooking* (Simon & Schuster, 1991), believes that the Caribs were responsible for the present-day love of hot chile sauces. The Arawaks, too, had chile sauces, such as one called *taumalin* prepared from limes, chiles, and crabmeat. The Spanish had discovered Jamaica and ruled it until 1655, when the British appeared. Through the seventeenth century the economy of Jamaica was based on sugar and slaves. The history of Jamaica through this time is a long history of slave rebellions. The most inspirational rebels were the Maroons, descendants of escaped slaves from the days of Spanish rule. These runaways, called *cimarrones*, lived in the mountains and became famous for outwitting the British.

The main kinds of chiles used in Jamaica, and the Caribbean generally, are bird chiles and Scotch bonnet chiles. All these chiles have different names as you island-hop. In

Trinidad, the Scotch bonnet and its relatives are called Congo peppers, while in Barbados they are bonney peppers. In the French Caribbean islands of Martinique and Guadeloupe, *le derrière de Madame Jacques* is a colloquial name for very hot chiles. In Haiti, they call them *piment bouc* or goat pepper. In Puerto Rico and Cuba the Scotch bonnet chiles are called *rocotillos* and *cachucha*. Some other names of chiles one will encounter in the Caribbean are *Bonda Man'Jacques*, *piment negresse*, lady finger chiles, and *wiri-wiri*.

Although the piquancy of Caribbean cooking is based on the New World chile, the cuisine or style of cooking has its roots in West Africa, with an infusion from India and an overlay of the culinary culture of the original colonial power. The spicy *matoutou crabes*, a traditional Easter dish in the French Antilles, is a direct descendant of Benin's *ago glain*. The Akan people of Ghana made *kenkey* and *dokono*, which became the *conkies* of Barbados and the *dunkanoo* of Jamaica.

There is another very hot Caribbean-related cuisine, although geographically it's in South America. The description Luso-Afro-Brazilian refers to a cuisine that derives from African cooks cooking for Portuguese overlords in Brazil. In Bahia, Brazil, and through the Amazonian Basin and Guyana, cooks prepare a very hot cuisine using the malagueta pepper, another name for the Scotch bonnet chile. The use of this chile is so lavish in Bahia that Margarette de Andrade, author of *Brazilian Cookery: Traditional and Modern* (A Casa do Livro Eldorade, 1975), describes a Bahian hostess serving little sandwiches with a layer of these extraordinary hot chiles added to the filling.

Curry Goat

Anything called curry in Jamaica ultimately derives from the arrival of indentured servants from India who worked on the sugar plantations after the end of slavery in the nineteenth century. It is said that every special party in Jamaica must have curry goat, which is often served with "rice and peas" (rice and beans). This recipe comes from a Jamaican woman, Carmen Sinclair, who serves it also with mango chutney, fried plantains, or boiled green bananas. Some cooks let the browned meat sit overnight before continuing with the preparation. That the goat is an old, tough animal is reflected in the fact that to make a tender goat stew you will need to let the meat stew for 6 to 7 hours.

3¹/₂ pounds goat shoulder on the bone, cut into 3-inch pieces

2 teaspoons salt

Freshly ground black pepper to taste

3 tablespoons curry powder

2 garlic cloves, finely chopped

¹/₂ teaspoon dried thyme

¹/₂ teaspoon ground allspice

Juice of 1 lime

2 ripe tomatoes (about 1 pound), peeled, seeded, and chopped

2 medium-size onions, thinly sliced

2 scallions, chopped

2 Scotch bonnet or habanero chiles, finely chopped

2 tablespoons unsalted butter

¹/₄ cup vegetable oil

2 cups water

¹/₂ cup coconut milk (see page 90)

1. In a large bowl, toss the goat with the salt, black pepper, curry powder, garlic, thyme, and allspice. Toss again with the lime juice, tomatoes, onions, scallions, and chiles and marinate in the refrigerator for 2 hours.

2. In a large casserole, melt the butter with the vegetable oil over medium-high heat. Scrape the marinade ingredients off the goat and reserve. Cook the goat until light brown, about 6 minutes, turning a few times. Pour in the water and coconut milk and bring to a boil. Reduce the heat to low, add the reserved marinade, cover, and simmer until the meat is completely tender and the liquid is reduced, 6 to 7 hours. Serve immediately.

MAKES 4 SERVINGS

piquant pork

Pork figures in all our hot cuisines except Muslim ones, in which pork is not eaten. Some of the most exciting recipes are from South America and Mexico, such as the magnificent Incendiary Pork and Egg Stew (page 220) or the wonderful and easy Carnitas (page 227). If you've never had jerk pork—or you want to try the real thing—see page 233, where you will not only find a taste of Jamaica but one maybe of heaven, too. Don't overlook the Asian pork recipes. They're basically quite easy and once you taste Fish-Fragrant Pork Threads (page 246), you'll never go back.

Incendiary Pork and Egg Stew

This Bolivian dish is called *fritanga* or *fricasé*. You start off by boiling pork ribs until the water evaporates and then you sauté the vegetables in the fat that remains. The pork country ribs called for are very meaty and also not as commonly found in supermarkets as are pork loin spareribs, which I suggest as a substitute. They stew for a long time and then, at the end, a couple of eggs are stirred into the red chile sauce until they are firm. It may seem like an impossible amount of chile, but the dish is meant to be served with very plain boiled white corn and boiled potatoes to offset the heat. Still, there is only so much offsetting that can occur. This dish is hot, hot, hot.

1¼ pounds pork country ribs or 2½ pounds pork loin spareribs

1 to 2 cups water (use 2 cups if using the loin spareribs)

1 medium-size white onion, thinly sliced

1 medium-size ripe tomato, peeled and thinly sliced

1½ teaspoons finely chopped fresh mint leaves

¼ cup finely chopped fresh parsley leaves

1½ teaspoons dried oregano

4 large garlic cloves, finely chopped

¾ teaspoon ground cumin

¼ cup cayenne pepper

½ teaspoon freshly ground black pepper

1½ teaspoons salt

2 cups chicken broth (homemade or canned) or water

½ cup chopped scallions

2 large eggs

1. Place the pork in a stockpot or casserole with the water, bring to a boil over high heat, and leave at a boil until the water evaporates, 15 to 25 minutes. Remove the pork with tongs and set aside. Leave the fat remaining from the pork in the pot and heat over high heat.

2. Add the onion, tomato, mint, parsley, oregano, garlic, cumin, cayenne pepper, black pepper, and salt and cook over high heat until the onion softens, 3 to 4 minutes. Add the reserved pork and the broth and bring to a boil. Reduce the heat to low and simmer until the pork is very tender, using a heat diffuser if necessary, 2 to 2½ hours. Add water as necessary to keep the broth from getting too thick.

3. Add the scallions, stir, and simmer for 5 minutes, then add the eggs and stir a few times until the eggs set, about 4 minutes. Transfer to a deep serving bowl or serve from the pot.

MAKES 4 SERVINGS

Oven-Roasted Pork

This Peruvian recipe for *lechón al horno* should be made with a piglet of about six to seven pounds. In its place a pork butt or shoulder roast will work very nicely. If using the piglet, have the butcher clean it, which is usually a matter of course. Both the piglet and the butt or shoulder will marinate overnight in the refrigerator, so factor that in when you think of making this. The roasting goes very slowly and so you will want to use a pork butt with a nice layer of fat and skin to keep the meat moist through this process. And yes, you are reading the ingredients list correctly— it's 1 *cup* of cayenne pepper. Serve this with baked potatoes or plain rice and a green salad.

One 6½- to 7-pound piglet or 5-pound pork butt with skin

1 lemon, cut in half

¾ cup white wine vinegar

¼ cup vegetable oil

8 large garlic cloves, roasted in a 450°F oven until the peel is crispy, peeled, and mashed

1½ teaspoons dried oregano

¼ cup finely chopped fresh parsley leaves

1 tablespoon dried thyme

1½ teaspoons ground cumin

1 cup cayenne pepper

1½ tablespoons salt

1 teaspoon freshly ground black pepper

1. Rub the pork with the lemon on all its surfaces. In a bowl, mix together the vinegar, vegetable oil, garlic, oregano, parsley, thyme, cumin, cayenne pepper, salt, and pepper until you have a thick marinade paste. Rub the pork with this marinade and leave overnight in the refrigerator.

2. Preheat the oven to 250°F. If using a piglet, make small cuts with a sharp boning knife at all the joints of the shoulder and legs to sever nerves and cartilage to prevent shrinkage as it roasts. You don't need to do this if using pork butt. Place the pork in a roasting pan and pour the marinade over it. Roast until the meat falls away when tugged on with a fork and the marinade paste on the top of the meat is looking slightly crusty, 8 to 9 hours. Remove from the oven and let rest 10 minutes, then cut into 4-inch pieces and serve.

MAKES 6 TO 8 SERVINGS

Little Roast Pig

The Mexican name of this famous preparation from the Yucatán, *cochinita pibil*, almost literally means "little roast pig." *Pibil* is a Mayan word that refers to the traditional oven of the Yucatán, which was a pit lined with stones where a roaring fire was made and a marinated piglet was wrapped in banana or plantain leaves and cooked in a manner similar to a New England clam bake. In this adaptation, I've used a pork butt and roasted it in the oven. Should you want to give pit-barbecuing a try (without actually digging a pit), build a charcoal fire on one side of your grill, place the wrapped pork on the other side, and grill for many hours, replenishing the coals when necessary. Should you want to roast the pork while you are away at work, set the oven to 250°F and place the roast in by 7:00 A.M. It will be tender and done by 7:00 P.M.

One 5-pound pork butt or shoulder with its fat

2 teaspoons salt

FOR THE MARINADE
1/4 cup freshly ground black pepper

1 teaspoon ground cinnamon

1 teaspoon ground cumin

2 teaspoons dried oregano

1 tablespoon ground annatto (*achiote*) seed

3 allspice berries

1/4 teaspoon hot paprika

8 large garlic cloves, chopped

2/3 cup freshly squeezed orange juice, orange rinds reserved

3 habanero chiles, finely chopped

1/4 cup red wine vinegar

FOR THE WRAPPING
1 large onion, sliced, or reserved orange rind halves

Banana leaves, plantain leaves, cornhusks, or aluminum foil

FOR THE SAUCE
1/2 cup very finely chopped onions

3 habanero chiles, very finely chopped

1/2 teaspoon salt

2/3 cup freshly squeezed bitter orange juice *or* 1/3 cup freshly squeezed navel orange juice and 1/3 cup freshly squeezed lime juice

Tortillas for serving

1. Pierce the meat several times with a skewer and rub the salt all over. Combine the marinade ingredients in a small bowl, then coat the pork with the marinade. Place the onion over the meat, then wrap it up with banana leaves. Refrigerate overnight.

2. Preheat the oven to 325°F. Transfer the wrapped pork to a roasting pan and place in the oven to roast until very tender and the meat shreds easily with a fork, 6 to 7 hours. Remove the wrapping from the meat and shred the pork off the bone with two forks. Transfer the meat to a serving platter and spoon the collected juices over it. Serve hot with the sauce and tortillas.

3. To make the sauce, place the onion, habanero chiles, salt, bitter orange or orange-lime juice mix in a blender and run briefly until almost smooth. Transfer to a serving bowl.

MAKES 6 SERVINGS

ANNATTO (*ACHIOTE*) SEED

The small red seeds of the annatto tree (*Bixa orellana*), a small tree or tall shrub that is native to tropical America, are called *achiote*. They are a much used spice for coloring and flavoring food in the Yucatán and southern parts of Mexico as well as parts of the Caribbean. They are often used to color butter, cheese, and ointments yellow. Annatto seed can be found in Latin American markets or on the Internet.

aztec chiles

From Bernardino de Sahagún's *Historia general de las cosas de la Nueva España* (Dastin Export S.L., 2004), written about 1569, we know that chile vendors in the local Aztec markets sold a wide variety of chiles. There were mild red chiles, broad chiles, hot green chiles, yellow chiles, *cuitlachilli*, *tenpilchilli*, and *chichioachilli*. The vendor sold the thick-fleshed water chiles, *conchilli*, smoked chiles, small chiles, tree chiles, thin chiles, and chiles like beetles. He sold green chiles, sharp-pointed red chiles, and chiles from Arzitz-iuacan, Tochmilco, Hauxtepec, Michoacan, Anauc, the Huaxteca, and the Chichameca. Separately he sold strings of chiles, chiles cooked in an *olla* (an earthenware casserole), fish chiles, and white fish chiles. Francisco Hernández, who lived in Mexico from 1570 to 1577 and was the first European to collect living plants, described seven Nahautl-named chiles. They were the *quauhchilli*, or tree chile, which was the smallest and hottest chile and used as a vegetable, not a spice. The *chiltecpintli*, or flea chile was, as its name suggests, tiny. This chile seemed hotter than the one above but lost its heat quickly. The *totcuitlatl* was known as the bird-dropping chile. *Tlilchilli* was a black chile that came in three sizes. *Tzanalchilli* was a very small chile grown in August. *Tonalchilli* was the "heat of the sun" chile because it only fruited in the summer and was the color of the sun. *Tzinquauhyo* was a chile for which there is no agreement on the meaning of its name, perhaps "from the mountain" chile. It was long and thin and red when ripe. The other chiles were the *tzonchilli*, *texochilli*, and *tepochilli*, the *chilcoztli* or yellow chile and *milchilli*, or field chile. According to Amal Naj in *Peppers: A Story of Hot Pursuits* (Vintage, 1993), the Aztecs categorized the chile's pungency as *coco* (hot), *cocopatic* (very hot), *cocopetez-patic* (very, very hot), *cocopetztic* (brilliant hot), *cocopetzquauitl* (extremely hot), and *cocopalatic* (runaway hot). The modern cultivar counterparts of these Aztec chiles are not known.

Pork Adobo

This marinated Peruvian dish is called *adobo de cerdo* and is made with *ají panca en pasta*, a paste made from a Peruvian chile called *ají panca* that grows up to 5 inches long and whose fruit is deep red to purple when ripe. Its pungency is considered mild, or so a Peruvian tells me. One man's mild is another man's fire. This chile will not be found in your supermarkets, so you will need to use the combination I suggest below or order it via the Internet. Serve this with white rice and boiled sweet potatoes, cassava, or white potatoes.

1¼ pounds boneless pork shoulder, cut into ½-inch cubes

½ teaspoon ground annatto (*achiote*) seed

3 large garlic cloves, finely chopped

½ teaspoon ground cumin

1 teaspoon freshly ground black pepper

½ cup white vinegar

1 medium-size onion, halved and cut into ¼-inch slices

¼ cup *Ají Panca en Pasta* (page 405)

2 tablespoons safflower oil

2 teaspoons salt

1. Place the pork in a large bowl with the annatto, half of the garlic, the cumin, and pepper. Toss well, then add the vinegar, onion, and chile paste. Toss and stir again to blend all the ingredients. Cover and marinate in the refrigerator for 24 hours.

2. In a large skillet, heat the safflower oil over medium-high heat, then cook the remaining garlic for a few seconds, until sizzling. Add the pork and its marinade, including the onion. Stir, add the salt and more pepper if desired, stir again, cover, reduce the heat to low, and cook until the pork is tender, about 2 hours, stirring occasionally. Add small amounts of water if necessary to keep the meat from drying out. Serve immediately.

MAKES 4 SERVINGS

Pork with Chipotle Chile Cream Sauce

The mixture of a rich, mild cream with blazing hot smoked jalapeño chiles, which are what chipotle chiles are, is so appealing in taste because, I believe, they balance each other so well. This recipe, called *carne de puerco con chipotle*, is adapted from the *Larousse Mexican Cookbook* (Larousse, 1984) by Sue Style. Serve this with white rice and cooked spinach.

Salt and freshly ground black pepper to taste

1/4 cup finely chopped fresh parsley leaves

1/4 cup finely chopped fresh coriander (cilantro) leaves

2 tablespoons fresh lime juice

1 large garlic clove, finely chopped

2 3/4 pounds pork shoulder in 1 piece

1 tablespoon pork lard or vegetable oil (if needed)

3 canned chipotle chiles in adobo

1 cup crème fraîche or sour cream

1/4 cup shredded Monterey Jack cheese or Mexican *queso asadero*

1/4 cup shredded white cheddar cheese or Mexican *queso blanco*

1. In a small bowl, mix together the salt and pepper, parsley, coriander, lime juice, and garlic. Rub the mixture all over the pork and place in a small or medium-size casserole that will fit the pork relatively snugly. Let marinate for 6 hours in the refrigerator.

2. Pour in enough water to cover the pork by an inch, bring to a boil over high heat, and cook at a boil, uncovered, until the liquid has evaporated and the meat is starting to fry in its own fat, about 1 hour. Cover with water again, bring to a boil again, and continue boiling until the water has evaporated and the pork is tender, about another hour. Add the lard only if there isn't enough fat to fry the pork. Once all the liquid has evaporated, let the pork brown all over in the fat at the bottom of the casserole, about 4 minutes. Remove the meat to a cutting board or platter and let it rest for 10 minutes. Slice the pork off the bone, discard any gristle, excessive fat, and skin and slice the remaining meat into 1/2-inch slices.

3. Meanwhile, preheat the oven to 350°F. In a food processor or blender, blend the chipotle chiles, crème fraîche, and salt to taste together until smooth. Arrange the pork slices in a baking dish and spread the sauce over it. Sprinkle on both cheeses and bake until the cheese is bubbling and melted, about 30 minutes. Serve immediately.

Carnitas

T his absolutely delicious crisp-on-the-outside, succulent-on-the-inside pork dish is traditionally made from the thick meaty cut called pork country ribs or from pork butt. The final result is a small piece of meat that is orange-tinged from chipotle chiles in adobo, soft and succulent from hours of stewing in a flavorful broth, and crispy on the outside after roasting in a hot oven. Carnitas can be eaten as is or—and this is preferable—wrapped in tortillas with guacamole, black beans, and/or white rice. This is a food that you are very likely to find at roadside stands throughout Mexico.

One 7-pound pork butt, cut into 10 large chunks

1 very large onion, quartered

1 tablespoon ground cumin

1 tablespoon ground coriander

1 tablespoon dried oregano

5 chipotle chiles in adobo, chopped, plus 3 tablespoons adobo sauce from the can

2 bay leaves

2 to 3 quarts chicken broth (homemade or canned) or more as needed

1 tablespoon salt

2 tablespoons pork lard or vegetable oil

1. Place the pork in a large stockpot or casserole. Add all the remaining ingredients, except the lard. If the pork is not covered with liquid, add more chicken broth. Cover the pot and bring to a boil over high heat. Reduce the heat to low, uncover, and simmer until the meat pulls apart easily with a fork, about 3 hours. Remove the pork from the broth with a slotted spoon and place on a platter. Allow to cool, then cut into 1-inch cubes.

2. Preheat the oven to 450°F. Place the lard in a baking dish and melt in the oven. Toss the pork in the lard, then roast in the oven, uncovered, until lightly browned and sizzling, about 30 minutes. Remove and serve.

MAKES 8 SERVINGS

piquant pork

Chile Verde

Chile verde could be considered the state dish of New Mexico. New Mexico cooking is distinct from Tex-Mex and from Cal-Mex, but it is redolent with the smells and tastes of the Southwest, especially that combination of pork, New Mexico chiles, and chipotle chiles. This recipe comes from my friend Chris Hardy, whose grandmother is a native of New Mexico. I first published this recipe in my book *Real Stew* (The Harvard Common Press, 2002), and am only fine tuning it here. But my original excitement about making chile verde came from an unknown young man who was standing behind me in line at a supermarket in Santa Monica, California, when I was buying the pork and those beautiful, long, thick green New Mexico chiles (also called Anaheim chiles) needed for the stew. He struck up a conversation by asking if I was going to make chile verde. I was surprised until he told me that he was from New Mexico and missed chile verde. He waxed on about the stew and gave me a few pointers. Serve the stew with little side dishes of chopped onion, chopped coriander leaves (cilantro), sour cream or Mexican *crema*, *padilla*, and *cotija* cheese (see www.caciqueUSA. com), or *queso fresco*, *ricotta salata*, or mild domestic feta cheese to crumble over the top. For accompaniment, white rice, refried black beans cooked with epazote, corn tortillas, and good Mexican beer are all traditional. Some cooks also like to add a little of the sauce from a can of chipotle chiles in adobo.

10 fresh New Mexico chiles

4 tablespoons extra-virgin olive oil

1 large onion, coarsely chopped

4 large garlic cloves, passed through a garlic press or mashed in a mortar

2 pounds lean boneless pork shoulder or butt, as much fat removed as possible, cut into 1-inch cubes

Masa harina (corn flour), for dredging

One 12-ounce bottle of lager beer

1 teaspoon ground cumin

3 tablespoons chopped chipotle chiles in adobo

1 bay leaf

1 tablespoon dried oregano

2 teaspoons salt

2 teaspoons freshly ground black pepper

1/2 cup coarsely chopped fresh coriander (cilantro) leaves

1. Preheat the oven to 450°F. Place the chiles on a baking sheet and roast until the skin blisters and turns black, 25 to 30 minutes, watching them carefully. Remove and place in a paper bag to steam for 10 minutes. Remove and, when cool enough to handle, peel, stem, seed, and cut into strips.

hold the chile, please

2. In a large casserole or Dutch oven, heat 2 tablespoons of the olive oil over medium heat, then cook the onion and garlic until translucent, about 8 minutes, stirring. Remove with a ladle and set aside. Add 1 tablespoon olive oil to the casserole and let it heat up. Dredge the pork in the *masa harina*. Tap off any excess, then brown the pork on all sides over medium heat, cooking in two batches if necessary so the pieces of meat don't touch each other, about 12 minutes for each batch, turning with tongs. Use the remaining 1 tablespoon of olive oil for the second batch. Set the meat aside.

3. Deglaze the bottom of the casserole by pouring in about a quarter of the beer, scraping up the bits on the bottom with a wooden spoon. Once all the crust is picked up, add the remaining beer. Return the onion and garlic and pork to the casserole. Add the cumin and leave to cook on medium-low heat for 10 minutes. Add the reserved New Mexico chiles, chipotle chiles in adobo, bay leaf, and oregano, and season with salt and pepper. Bring to a boil over high heat, reduce the heat to low, cover, and cook until the pork is very tender, about 45 minutes, stirring occasionally. Add the coriander leaves and cook for another 10 minutes, then turn the heat off and let it sit for 5 minutes before serving.

MAKES 4 TO 6 SERVINGS

Andouille Sausage and Lamb Sausage with Cajun-Style Mirliton

*I*n Louisiana, you'll hear a lot about mirliton, a pear-shaped member of the squash family that is better known in the Southwest and elsewhere in the country by its Latin American name, chayote. Chayote is indigenous to Mexico and arrived in Louisiana with the Spanish. In today's Cajun cooking it is a popular vegetable. The andouille sausage is a smoked, highly seasoned pure pork sausage that probably is the most popular sausage in Cajun country. It is widely available now, but you can substitute kielbasa if you need to. The lamb sausage is one of those specialty sausages that are made throughout the country, either by supermarkets, small butcher shops, or certain well-known manufacturers such as Bruce Aidells Sausage Company. Serve this dish with rice.

2 tablespoons unsalted butter

1 large onion, sliced

3 chayotes (mirliton), peeled, seeded, quartered lengthwise, and sliced $1/4$ inch thick

$3/4$ pound lamb sausage

$3/4$ pound andouille sausage or kielbasa

$1/2$ teaspoon cayenne pepper

$1/4$ teaspoon chili powder

$1/4$ teaspoon ground cumin

$1/2$ teaspoon gumbo filé

Salt and freshly ground black pepper to taste

1 cup water

In a large skillet, heat the butter over medium-high heat until it melts, then cook the onion, chayotes, and sausages until the vegetables begin to turn color, about 10 minutes, stirring. Add the cayenne pepper, chili powder, cumin, and gumbo filé. Season with salt and pepper, stir, reduce the heat to low, add the water, and cook until the chayotes and sausage are tender, about 2 hours, covered. Stir occasionally and add small amounts of water if it seems to be drying up. Serve immediately.

MAKES 4 SERVINGS

GUMBO FILÉ

Gumbo filé is a spice used in the Creole and Cajun cooking of Louisiana. It is made from the dried and powdered leaves of sassafras. It is used as a thickening agent in stews and gumbos, and it provides a mild and sort of musty flavor, too. A good brand to look for is Zatarains.

Jamaican Roast Pork

After you taste this you will see why pork is a popular meat in Jamaica. Yes, this is blazingly hot, but the pork is so tender after all the roasting that it just melts away. This preparation is thought to have been influenced by the Spanish, who probably added the tomatoes to the dish. Although you don't have to, pushing the sauce through a food mill until it is smooth is a nice finishing touch. Serve with Fried Plantains (page 389) and plain rice.

One 3-pound boneless pork shoulder

5 large garlic cloves, 3 slivered and 2 finely chopped

3 tablespoons vegetable oil

4 Scotch bonnet chiles or habanero chiles, seeded and chopped

1 green bell pepper, coarsely chopped

1 medium-size onion, coarsely chopped

1 teaspoon ground cumin

1 teaspoon dried oregano

1 teaspoon freshly ground black pepper

$1/2$ teaspoon ground cinnamon

1 bay leaf

$1/2$ cup fresh lime juice

2 cups canned or fresh tomato puree

1. Make slits all over the pork with the tip of a paring knife and stuff them with the slivered garlic. Roll the pork up and tie with kitchen twine if necessary.

2. In a large skillet, heat the vegetable oil over medium-high heat, then cook the chiles, bell pepper, onion, chopped garlic, cumin, oregano, pepper, cinnamon, and bay leaf until the vegetables are soft, about 8 minutes, stirring frequently. Remove the skillet from the heat and stir in the lime juice.

3. Place the pork in a large bowl and pour the marinade over it, turning the meat several times to coat it evenly. Cover with plastic wrap and refrigerate for 2 to 8 hours, turning occasionally.

4. Preheat the oven to 350°F. Scrape the marinade off the pork and reserve in a saucepan. Place the pork in a roasting pan and roast until a meat thermometer registers 165°F, about 1³/₄ hours. Meanwhile, add the tomato puree to the marinade and bring to almost a boil, before it begins to sputter too much, stirring, then reduce the heat to low and simmer for 5 minutes. Remove the bay leaf and pass the sauce through a food mill if desired. Transfer the pork to a serving platter and let stand 10 minutes before slicing. Spoon the sauce over the sliced pork and serve immediately.

MAKES 6 SERVINGS

caribbean hot sauces

Throughout the Caribbean, table sauces made from chiles are very popular and come in a bewildering variety. Jamaicans love their hot sauces, and most Jamaicans either make their own hot sauce for the table or buy any of the great number of bottled hot sauces in the grocery. Pawpaw pepper sauce is a simple, yet very hot and flavorful, sauce that one might find in a typical Jamaican home. It's great on everything and anything, especially, I think, grilled skirt steak. It's a coarse sauce made with finely ground carrots, Scotch bonnet chiles, chayote, and papaya. This mixture is then boiled with brown sugar, vinegar, and water before being jarred. Another Jamaican chile sauce is red devil pepper sauce, brilliantly red and very, very hot. The recipe for it in Jessica B. Harris's delightful *Sky Juice and Flying Fish: Traditional Caribbean Cooking* (Simon & Schuster, 1991) calls for six Scotch bonnet chiles to be blended with three onions, a smidgin of ketchup, allspice, vinegar, and the famous Jamaican Pickapeppa Sauce. Pickapeppa Sauce, made by the company of the same name, is a blend of tomatoes, onions, sugar, cane vinegar, mangoes, raisins, tamarind, and spices. Walkerwood's, another famous company, makes everything from Coconut Run Down Sauce to Firestick Sauce.

But other Caribbean countries have their hot sauces, too. Saba pepper sauce, from Saba, is made with finely chopped chiles, onions, garlic, malt vinegar, salt, and a little olive oil. Sauce Ti-Malice is from Haiti and made with finely chopped onions, lime juice, butter, fresh chiles, and garlic and is used as a marinade. Pepper wine from Aruba is made by marinating chiles in rum and using it to flavor Callaloo (page 302). Mango chile relish from Trinidad is made with unripe mangoes, chiles, garlic, and salt. Sauce Creole from Martinique is made with tomato puree, lime juice, onions, celery, chiles, salt, and pepper and is used with broiled shellfish.

Jerk Pork

I find it surprising how many Americans don't know what jerk pork is, given the popularity of Jamaica as a vacation destination and the island's reggae music. But Jamaicans in this country lament that when you do find it here, the jerk has been jerked out and the flavor has been Americanized into blandness. This recipe is the real thing. It's succulent and very hot—if you love flavorful hot food this is the recipe you must make. The word "jerk" has been traced to an Indian word in the Quechua language of the Indians of Peru, *ch'arki* or *ccharqui*. Today, the word jerk refers to five things. First, a jerk is a kind of air-dried spiced meat. Second, it is the verb of the process of making this air-dried product. Third, it is also the method of marinating a slow-cooked dish of the same name. Fourth, it is the name of the marinade itself. Finally, it is the particular Jamaican dish of slow- and well-cooked spiced marinated meat that results in a smoky, pungent, succulent preparation.

The method of jerk cooking is attributed to the Maroons, runaway slaves who hid in the jungles of Jamaica in the first part of the eighteenth century. Only within the past 75 years has Jamaican jerk cooking become the commercial success it is. The beginning point of a jerk is a complex marinade that always includes the native spice known as allspice that is called pimento (which it is not) in Jamaica. Jerk marinade also always includes a good amount of Scotch bonnet chile and some combination of thyme, scallions, ginger, garlic, and nutmeg. After this point each individual cook will add other ingredients such as sage, cinnamon, nutmeg, cloves, orange juice, lime juice, soy sauce, and coriander. In Jamaica, the meat is cooked with the highly aromatic wood and leaves of the pimento (allspice) tree. You can also use another aromatic wood to cook the meat, such as apple, hickory, birch, pecan, or oak chips, but not mesquite.

Jerk pork can be made with pork loin or tenderloin or with shoulder. I prefer shoulder because it is fattier and juicier, and loin can, if you are not careful, overcook easily. Depending on which cut you choose, the marinating and cooking will be different. If you use pork loin the meat will look white when it is done, and if you use shoulder the meat will be reddish, almost like beef. The trickiest part of the cooking is grilling at a low enough temperature so that it cooks for 2½ to 3 hours and preferably 5 hours. The reason that is difficult to achieve, and for me to specify, is because all grills and grill fires are different and you will end up fiddling a lot with the grill cover. The internal temperature of the pork should be about 135°F for loin and up to 160°F for shoulder and the temperature inside the grill should be about 225°F if you cook it 5 hours. Realistically, you should assume your grill will be too hot and that you should check the pork for doneness in about 2 hours. Just remember one rule of thumb—low, low, low heat. An accurate meat thermometer is very useful here, and if the meat is cooking too quickly set it as far away from the fire as possible and remove the cover. You can serve side dishes from the Cool Accompaniments chapter (page 385), although I like a simple coleslaw.

FOR THE JERK MARINADE

2 tablespoons ground allspice

2 tablespoons dried thyme

1 tablespoon cayenne pepper

1 tablespoon freshly ground black pepper

1 tablespoon dried sage

1¹/₂ teaspoons ground nutmeg

1¹/₂ teaspoons ground cinnamon

2 tablespoons salt

6 large garlic cloves

One 1-inch cube fresh ginger

1 tablespoon sugar

¹/₂ bunch fresh coriander (cilantro), leaves only

¹/₄ cup dark soy sauce

³/₄ cup freshly squeezed lime juice

¹/₂ cup freshly squeezed orange juice

¹/₄ cup peanut oil

2 cups chopped scallions

8 Scotch bonnet chiles or habanero chiles, stemmed and finely chopped

3 pounds boneless pork loin or 4 pounds boneless pork shoulder, cut up into 1-pound chunks and scored in a diamond pattern 1¹/₂ inches apart

1. Place the jerk marinade ingredients in a blender and run until smooth. Place the pork pieces in a large ceramic or glass dish and pour the marinade over the pork, coating well. Cover with plastic wrap and marinate in the refrigerator for 1¹/₂ days. Alternatively, place the meat and its marinade in two plastic zip-lock bags to marinate.

2. Prepare a small, hot charcoal fire, or preheat only one set of burners on a gas grill on low for 15 minutes. Push the coals to one side of the grill, preferably the side with a latched opening so you can add coals occasionally if necessary, and let the fire die down a bit. Place the pork on the side away from the fire, directly on oiled grilling grates or in an aluminum roasting pan, and grill slowly until blackened on the outside and cooked through, with an internal temperature of 135° to 140°F for the pork loin and 155° to 160°F for the pork shoulder, 2¹/₂ to 5 hours, turning and basting with the remaining marinade every 20 minutes. Remove the pork from the grill, let sit 5 minutes, then cut into thin slices and serve.

MAKES 6 TO 8 SERVINGS

Pork Vindaloo

This famous preparation from Goa, the former Portuguese colony in western India, takes its name from the Portuguese, who held Goa for about 450 years. The word *vindaloo* derives from the Portuguese words *vinho* for wine and *alhos* for garlic. Goa's Hindu community would tend to make vindaloo with seafood, while pork is popular with Goa's Christian community. The Christian community uses vinegar in its cooking while the Hindus use tamarind. Some Goan cooks use *feni*, a distilled drink made from coconut sap, in the vinegar sauce. In Goa and all of India, the dried red chiles used are called Kashmiri chiles, because that is where most of them come from. Serve with Rice Pilaf (page 396).

2 pounds boneless pork loin, fat removed and cut into 1-inch cubes

Salt to taste

20 dried red de arbol chiles, broken in half and seeded

10 black peppercorns

8 whole cloves

1 cinnamon stick

1 teaspoon cumin seeds

1 teaspoon coriander seeds

1/2 teaspoon black mustard seeds

1 teaspoon ground turmeric

One 1-inch cube fresh ginger, peeled

6 large garlic cloves

1 teaspoon sugar

1/2 cup apple cider vinegar

2 tablespoons vegetable oil

2 medium-size onions, finely chopped

2 large tomatoes, peeled, seeded, and chopped

6 fresh green finger-type chiles or 8 green jalapeño chiles or 12 green serrano chiles, sliced

3/4 cup coconut milk

1. Sprinkle the pork with salt and set aside in a large bowl. Place the dried chiles, peppercorns, cloves, cinnamon stick, cumin seeds, coriander seeds, mustard seeds, and turmeric in a spice mill and grind to a powder. Transfer the spice mix to a blender with the ginger, garlic, sugar, and vinegar and blend. Pour the mixture over the pork, toss, cover, and marinate in the refrigerator for 4 to 6 hours.

2. In a wok or large skillet, heat the vegetable oil over medium heat, then cook the pork with its marinade for 5 minutes. Add the onions, tomatoes, fresh chiles, and coconut milk. Cover, reduce the heat to low, and cook until the meat is

piquant pork

tender, 30 to 35 minutes, stirring occasionally. If the sauce is liquidy, remove the meat with a skimmer and set aside while you reduce the sauce over high heat until dense, 10 to 15 minutes. Return the meat to the sauce and heat for 3 minutes. Serve immediately.

MAKES 6 SERVINGS

goan cooking

Goa, a small state on the western coast of India, was a Portuguese colony for centuries, and that influence is felt in the cuisine, particularly in the cuisine of the Christian community there. There are many Goan dishes that retain their Portuguese names, such as *recheiado*, *temperado*, *assado*, and *buffado*. Most Goan food, though not all of it, is very hot from chiles. The Goans are also very fond of seafood and coconut milk. In fact, rice, fish, and coconut form the staple ingredients of Goan cooking, as well as vinegar in the Christian community's cooking and tamarind in the Hindu community's cooking.

Bhutan Pork with Bean Threads and Chile

Bhutan is a small, primarily Buddhist, Himalayan country between India and China. The country is under the protectorship of India, and it is from India that the first chiles arrived in Bhutan. They are a favorite ingredient in Bhutanese cuisine. It's thought by some that the chile continued its journey in this direction to arrive in Sichuan, China. Here they add zest to a mellow pork and noodle combination called *fing*. This recipe is adapted from Susanne Waugh, a traveler to Bhutan in the early 1980s who collected recipes. I make this with some frequency because it is rich in chile flavor and also quite easy.

2 ounces bean threads or cellophane noodles

^{1}/2 cup (1 stick) unsalted butter

1 medium-size onion, chopped

1 medium-size tomato, peeled and chopped

1^1/2 pounds pork shoulder, cut into 1-inch cubes

^{1}/2 cup water

3 fresh green finger-type chiles or 4 green jalapeño chiles, seeded and julienned

1^1/2 teaspoons salt, or more to your taste

Freshly ground black pepper to taste

1. Bring a small saucepan filled with water to a boil and cook the bean threads for 2 minutes. Drain and snip into 6-inch lengths with kitchen scissors.

2. In a large saucepan or casserole, melt the butter over medium-high heat, then add the onion, tomato, pork, and water. Bring to just below a boil, then reduce the heat to low and cook, partially covered, until just tender, about 1^1/2 hours. Add the bean threads, chiles, and salt and pepper to taste and simmer until heated through, about 10 minutes.

variation Add 1 pound of bok choy, split lengthwise into quarters or sixths, at the same time you add the pork.

MAKES 6 SERVINGS

piquant pork

why does it burn?

What happens when we taste piquant foods? It comes down to taste buds and the brain and how this is all controlled by genetics. Scientists who study taste recognize that different people have different sensitivities of taste because taste is genetically determined. Fungiform papillae, the structures that contain taste buds, are surrounded by pain neurons. When the taste buds come into contact with capsaicin, the active ingredient that causes the burn when eating chiles, there will be several different reactions depending on the category of person.

Linda Bartoshuk, a professor in the Ear, Nose, and Throat section of the Surgery Department at the Yale University School of Medicine, has conducted studies where she has divided people into three groups, based on those having the fewest fungiform papillae to those having the most. Those with the fewest fungiform papillae are called the non-tasters because they could not taste the bitterness of a taste sample. The medium tasters tasted a medium amount of bitterness, and the super-tasters found the sample intensely bitter. So, too, it will be the super-tasters who experience the most pain from the burn of chile when it is eaten because of the density and proximity of pain receptors. Over time, and with continue eating of chiles, the pain neurons of the super-tasters are turned off, and they become accustomed to the burn. The evolutionary reason for super-tasters might be due to their ability in early human evolution to detect bitterness in poisonous plants and avoid them. On the other hand, the evolutionary advantage of the non-tasters is that they have a wider food world to choose from, on top of which they tend to like bitter or piquant foods that contain phytochemicals, which are proving healthy to eat. (These foods include dark leafy green vegetables that are apparently effective in fighting certain forms of cancer.) Super-tasters are attracted to salt, sweeteners, and fats, all of which are less healthy to eat. But there is an anomaly here: among thin people super-tasters are usually the thinnest and among heavy people super-tasters tend to be the heaviest—and we don't known why this is!

Exposing the tongue to capsaicin does not effect the sense of taste in the long run, although taste buds seem dulled when you are experiencing the burn of chile. The mechanism behind this is not known. In any case, the burn of capsaicin fades slowly, taking about 20 minutes to disappear entirely. If you were to take another mouthful of chile after that 20 minutes had passed, you would discover that your taste buds had been desensitized and that the second bite would not seem as hot as the first. Capsaicin produces no harm to the body, but it does cause the body to react as if it is being harmed. It passes through the body with very little absorption, and for this reason there is meaning to the expression "chile burns twice."

Another physiological phenomenon of eating chiles is called gustatory sweating. When one eats chiles one's face will flush red and one will sweat, almost always on the scalp, nose, and upper and lower lips. After 15 minutes the sweating will subside. This is caused not by their taste, but by the burn effected by the capsaicin. Because there are no taste fibers in the areas affected by sweating, it means that pain fibers are playing a role in the sweating. Scientists also know that sugar and whole milk are effective at reducing the oral burn of capsaicin.

Stir-Fried Spicy Pork

This Thai dish is called *pad het moo tort* and it has an Indian influence, as we see by the use of turmeric. I like to make it with pork tenderloin, but you can use sirloin or spareribs, too. One always serves this very hot dish with steamed rice.

1/2 ounce dried red de arbol chiles (about 35), soaked in tepid water for 5 minutes and chopped

1 tablespoon dried bird's-eye chiles or red chile flakes

20 white peppercorns

10 dried coriander seeds

2 lemongrass stalks, tough outer portions removed and tender inner parts chopped

One 1 1/2-inch-cube fresh ginger, peeled and chopped

2 tablespoons finely chopped fresh coriander (cilantro) leaves

1 shallot, chopped

8 garlic cloves, chopped

1/2 teaspoon shrimp paste or 1/2 teaspoon ground shrimp mixed with 1/2 teaspoon water

1/2 teaspoon lime zest

2 teaspoons ground turmeric

1 cup vegetable or peanut oil

1 1/2 pounds pork tenderloin, sliced into 2 x 1/4-inch strips

2 tablespoons water

1 tablespoon soy sauce

1 tablespoon Thai fish sauce

1/2 chicken bouillon cube

1 teaspoon palm sugar or granulated sugar

10 fresh green serrano chiles, thinly sliced lengthwise

5 kaffir lime leaves, cut into thin strips, or 1 tablespoon lime zest

1 1/2 tablespoons freshly squeezed lime juice

1. In a mortar, pound the two different kinds of dried red chiles, the white peppercorns, and coriander seeds until pasty and ground. Add the lemongrass, ginger, coriander leaves, shallot, garlic, shrimp paste, lime zest, and turmeric and continue pounding until mushy. You can use a blender, but if you do, add 3 tablespoons water to help the blade turn. (Don't add the water called for in step 2 if you do this.)

2. In a wok, heat the vegetable oil over medium-high heat, then cook the pork until it turns color, 2 to 3 minutes. Remove the pork with a slotted spoon and set aside. Discard all but 2 tablespoons of the oil. Reduce the heat to low, add the paste from the mortar, and cook until thick and mushy, 5 minutes, stirring. Return the pork to the wok and cook for 8 minutes heat, stirring occasionally. Add the water, soy sauce, Thai fish sauce, chicken bouillon cube, and sugar and continue cooking 5 minutes, stirring.

3. Add the green serrano chiles and kaffir lime leaves, cover, and stir occasionally until almost dry, about 10 minutes, then add the lime juice, raise the heat to high, and cook 2 minutes. As the chiles cook, pick out the skins that separate from the flesh and discard. Remove immediately from the heat and serve.

MAKES 4 SERVINGS

Red-Cooked Tofu

This fiery dish from Sichuan is called "red-cooked bean curd" (*hongshao dofu*), which is not an allusion to the heat of the chile nor to anything red in the sauce. It simply means it's cooked with soy sauce. There are many dishes like this with a variety of vegetables, all "red-cooked." They don't always have to contain meat, either. What is so pleasant in this dish is the contrast between the bland tofu and the hot chile. It's important that your pork chops have a nice layer of fat because you will use it in diced form to flavor the preparation. Serve with steamed rice.

¹/₄ cup peanut oil

³/₄ pound pork loin or chops with fat, bones removed; fat removed, diced, and reserved; and meat sliced into 3 x ¹/₂-inch strips

3 large garlic cloves, coarsely chopped

One 1-inch cube fresh ginger, peeled and finely chopped

2 tablespoons Sichuan chile paste (see page 98)

1 teaspoon red chile flakes

5 scallions, white and light green parts, cut into 1¹/₂-inch lengths

5 tablespoons soy sauce

¹/₂ pound firm tofu, cut into 12 cubes

Salt to taste (optional)

1 tablespoon cornstarch dissolved in ¹/₂ cup water

1. In a wok, heat the peanut oil over high heat, then cook the diced pork fat until crispy, pressing it against the sides of the wok with the back of a wooden spoon to render more fat. Add the garlic, ginger, chile paste, red chile flakes, and pork slices and stir-fry, tossing constantly, for 30 seconds. Add the scallions and soy sauce and continue cooking for another 30 seconds, tossing and stirring constantly.

2. Add the tofu and season with salt if desired. Bring the liquid in the wok to a boil and cook, uncovered, until mostly evaporated, about 5 minutes, stirring occasionally. Add the cornstarch and water and toss in the wok, cooking until the sauce is syrupy, about 30 seconds. Serve immediately.

MAKES 4 SERVINGS

RED-COOKED IN SICHUAN

Red-cooking in Sichuanese cuisine refers to a method of cooking that proceeds a bit slower than frying and uses soy sauce. The name comes about from the fact that the soy sauce darkens the food being cooked. There will be a remaining sauce or gravy, and some cooks save this sauce to be used as a master sauce for other preparations.

Double-Cooked Stir-Fried Pork

This Sichuan dish often appears as "Szechwan pork" on restaurant menus in America. The name *huiguo rou* means double-cooked, or, literally, "back-in-the-pot" meat. Fuchsia Dunlop in her book *The Land of Plenty* (W. W. Norton, 2003) tells us that this was a ritual meal at meetings of Sichuan's secret societies before they were wiped out by the Communists. Although it is very hot, there is a touch of sweetness in this dish derived from the hoisin sauce. One of the keys to making this preparation successful is to pay attention to the pork needed, namely fresh bacon, which will be sold as pork belly in the markets. Many Asian markets sell presliced pork belly. If you find that, then it only needs a dunking in the boiling water. The pork is indeed cooked twice in this dish. First it is boiled and then it is fried. You will need a very hot fire because the pork belly must fry in its own fat and not stew in its juices. The leeks, too, are important in this dish, as they replace the harder-to-find green garlic (young garlic that has not developed cloves) that is sometimes found in farmers' markets. The final dish will have no sauce, but will be glistening from the reduction of the liquids. Serve with steamed rice.

1 pound pork belly or fatty part of pork butt, in 1 piece

3 tablespoons peanut oil

2 green bell peppers, seeded and cut into 1-inch squares

Salt to taste

6 green garlic bulbs or 6 baby leeks or 3 regular leeks, white and light green parts, split lengthwise, washed well, and sliced into 2-inch pieces

4 large garlic cloves, finely chopped

1 tablespoon Sichuan chile paste (see page 98)

2 tablespoons red chile flakes

2 tablespoons hoisin sauce

1. Place the pork belly in a large saucepan and cover with water. Bring to a boil, then cook 3 minutes. Drain and cool. Slice into $1/4$-inch slices and set aside. If using presliced pork belly, bring a saucepan of water to a boil, plunge the slices of meat in, leave for 30 seconds, and drain and cool.

2. In a wok, heat 1 tablespoon of the peanut oil over high heat, then cook the bell peppers with a little salt for 1 minute. Reduce the heat to medium-high and continue to cook the bell peppers for another minute, tossing and stirring constantly. Remove and set aside. Reduce the heat to medium.

3. Add the green garlic and stir-fry for 2 minutes, stirring and tossing constantly. Remove from the wok and set aside with the peppers.

4. Increase the heat to medium-high, add the remaining 2 tablespoons peanut oil and let it become very hot, and cook about 6 slices of the pork until much of the fat is rendered, about 3 minutes, tossing and stirring frequently and pressing the slices against the side of the wok to render more fat. Add the garlic, chile paste, chile flakes, hoisin sauce, and the rest of the pork and stir-fry, tossing and stirring constantly, until quite dry, 2 to 3 minutes. Return the green garlic and bell peppers to the wok and stir-fry for another 2 minutes. Serve immediately.

MAKES 4 SERVINGS

the piquant cuisine of sichuan

The origins of modern Chinese cuisine can be traced to the Sung dynasty (A.D. 960–1279), when an agricultural revolution made diverse ingredients available to an expanding population. A growing middle class began to appreciate the pleasure of eating, and a culture of gastronomy emerged that saw cooks experimenting with regional ingredients to create a cuisine that went beyond the rigid ideas of classical court cooking.

In order of piquancy, the regions of China with the hottest and spiciest foods are Sichuan, Hunan, Yunnan, and Guizhou. There are other piquant cuisines to some extent in the provinces of Gansu, Shaanxi, Hubei, Xinjiang, and Jiangxi.

The use of chiles in Sichuan is, as with all "hot" cuisines, meant to heighten one's sensations of taste and to open up the palate. The Sichuanese say that their love of the chile is because their climate is so muggy and damp and that eating chiles dispels humidity. Another piquant spice favored by the Sichuanese are Sichuan peppercorns, which provide—as the Chinese say—a numbing rather than a piquant taste.

The chile entered China during the Ming dynasty and was brought by Chinese traders returning from Manila. The chile may also have entered China via the port of Macao, brought by the Portuguese or Spanish. Another possible point of entry for the chile and other New World foods was across the Himalayas from India from their origin point of Portuguese Goa, although this route may not have been active until the early Manchu dynasty in the latter half of the seventeenth century. In any case, the evidence seems to point rather to the east and southeast rather than the west.

The spicy cuisine of Sichuan and its immediate neighboring provinces seems to predate the arrival of the chile. A collection of poems called *Songs of the South* (Foreign Languages Press, 2001), from the ancient state of Ch'u, today's Hunan, testify to the use of pungent spices such as Chinese brown pepper, cassia, artemisia (a kind of sagebrush or wormwood), and water pepper. Texts from the Han Dynasty (202 B.C.–c. A.D. 220) tell us that Hunan had a reputation for highly spiced food. In the fifth century A.D., a historian named Chang Qu noted that the Sichuanese liked spicy-hot and fragrant dishes, the heat coming from Sichuan peppercorns, ginger, and black pepper.

 # Peppery Pork Slices

This rich-tasting dish from Sichuan is easy and quick to prepare. The final result is a glistening dish of golden-colored tofu and pork. Because the pork must be sliced very thin, it may be easier to freeze it partially first and then shave off the slices. This recipe will serve two with rice; you can double the recipe easily, but you will then have to cook the tofu and pork in two batches.

1 large egg white	2 cups vegetable oil, for frying
1½ teaspoons all-purpose flour	¼ pound bok choy hearts (white parts) or Savoy cabbage, cut into ¼-inch slices
½ pound boneless pork loin, cut into 2 x ⅛-inch strips	6 ounces firm tofu, cut into 12 cubes, drained on paper towels for 15 minutes
⅛ teaspoon salt	½ teaspoon Sichuan peppercorns, crushed
1 tablespoon soy sauce	1 tablespoon Sichuan chile bean paste (page 98)
¼ teaspoon sugar	1 tablespoon red chile flakes
½-inch cube fresh ginger, peeled and finely chopped	1 tablespoon Chile Oil (page 424)
1½ teaspoons cornstarch mixed with 1½ teaspoons water	2 teaspoons toasted and ground sesame seeds
¼ cup beef, pork, or chicken broth (homemade or canned)	

1. In a medium-size bowl, beat the egg white until frothy, then whisk in the flour. Add the pork and half the salt and toss until well coated, then set aside. In a small bowl, mix together the soy sauce, sugar, ginger, cornstarch, and broth and set aside.

2. In a wok, heat 1 tablespoon of the vegetable oil over medium-high heat, then stir-fry the bok choy with the remaining salt until wilted and slightly soft, about 1 minute, tossing constantly. Remove and set aside on a serving platter.

3. Add the remaining vegetable oil to the wok and heat over high heat. Cook the tofu cubes until light golden, about 4 minutes. Remove with a skimmer and set aside with the bok choy. Add the pork slices to the wok, stirring to keep them from sticking together, and stir-fry until light golden, 2 to 3 minutes. Remove the pork with a skimmer and drain well.

chiles in sichuan cooking

Dried chiles are used more than fresh ones in Sichuan. The most common type is the facing-heaven chile (*chao tian jiao*), a short, plump, bright red chile that is moderately hot and fragrant. "Seven-star" chile (*qi xing jiao*) is so named because the chiles grow in bunches of seven. In Chongqing and eastern Sichuan, thinner, pointier, hotter chiles from Yunnan, Hunan, and Guizhou provinces are often preferred.

4.   Remove all the oil from the wok except for 1 tablespoon. Reheat the oil over high heat, then add the Sichuan peppercorns and chile bean paste and stir-fry 30 seconds, stirring constantly. Add the reserved pork, reserved sauce, chile flakes, chile oil, and ground sesame seeds and stir-fry until the sauce thickens, about 1 minute. Pour the meat and sauce over the tofu and bok choy and serve immediately.

MAKES 2 SERVINGS

Fish-Fragrant Pork Threads

This famous Sichuan preparation is an example of the complex combination of flavors—in this case salty, sweet, sour, and pungent—that typifies Sichuanese cooking. There are a number of theories about the name of this dish, which contains no fish. One is that it makes the pork taste like fish (which it doesn't). Another dubious theory is that the sauce was used to flavor fish first and pork later. One interesting theory related by Fuchsia Dunlop in *The Land of Plenty* (W. W. Norton, 2003), was proposed by Chef Xiao Jianming of the Piaoxiang Restaurant in Chengdu, who says that the dish actually tastes like a kind of tiny crucian carp called *ji yu*. It's often translated as "pork with hot garlic sauce" on restaurant menus. The black mushrooms called for are hard to find in their fresh state outside of Chinese markets, but dried black mushrooms are a fine substitute. Cutting the pork into the thin strips called for is made much easier if the pork is partially frozen first.

1/4 cup vegetable oil

1 pound pork loin, cut into 1 x 1/4-inch strips

1/2 pound fresh black mushrooms or 1 ounce dried black mushrooms soaked in tepid water for 15 minutes and drained, or 1/2 pound bamboo shoots or parboiled carrots cut into the same size as the pork pieces

8 scallions, 4 sliced into 1-inch pieces and 4 chopped

2 tablespoons Chile Oil (page 474)

2 tablespoons red pepper flakes

2 tablespoons finely chopped fresh ginger

12 large garlic cloves, finely chopped

4 teaspoons brown sugar

1/4 cup soy sauce

2 teaspoons Chinese black vinegar or white vinegar

2 teaspoons cornstarch (optional)

1.   In a wok, heat the vegetable oil over high heat, swirling the wok to coat the sides, then cook the pork until it turns color, about 1 minute, stirring. Remove the pork with a skimmer and set aside. Add the mushrooms and the 4 sliced scallions and cook for 1 minute, stirring constantly. Add the chile oil, red pepper flakes, ginger, and garlic, and stir-fry for another 30 seconds.

2.   Stir the brown sugar into the soy sauce to dissolve. Add this to the wok along with the vinegar, reserved pork, and chopped scallions. Toss well, reduce the heat to medium, cover, and simmer until the sauce is thicker, about 1 minute. If the sauce is not syrupy, mix the cornstarch with a tablespoon of water to make a paste, add it to the wok, and cook 1 minute. Serve immediately.

MAKES 4 SERVINGS

Pork and Peanuts in Hot and Spicy Sauce

This pork preparation from Sichuan will be moist and golden, punctuated by nearly blackened dry red chiles. It's a delicious and very hot preparation that should be savored slowly with some steamed rice on the side.

1/4 cup peanut oil

1/4 cup roasted unsalted peanuts

3/4 pound boneless pork shoulder, cut into 1/2-inch cubes

1 1/2 teaspoons salt, or more to your taste

4 large egg whites

2 1/2 tablespoons cornstarch

1/4 cup beef broth (homemade or canned)

2 teaspoons rice wine (*mirin*) or vermouth

2 teaspoons soy sauce

1 tablespoon very finely chopped scallions

1 teaspoon ground ginger

2 large garlic cloves, thinly sliced

1 teaspoon sugar

6 tablespoons vegetable oil

1/4 cup dried red de arbol chiles, cut in half and seeded

1 small green bell pepper, cut into 1/2-inch squares

2 teaspoons Chile Oil (page 474)

1. In a small skillet, heat the peanut oil over high heat, then fry the peanuts until golden brown, about 30 seconds or less, stirring. Remove and cool the peanuts.

2. In a medium-size bowl, toss the pork cubes with 1 teaspoon salt. In a large bowl, beat the egg whites until they form peaks, then mix with 2 tablespoons of the cornstarch. Add the pork cubes, mix well, and set aside.

3. In a small bowl, mix the beef broth with the remaining 1/2 tablespoon (1 1/2 teaspoons) cornstarch, remaining 1/2 teaspoon salt, rice wine, soy sauce, scallions, ginger, garlic, and sugar and set aside.

4. In a wok, heat 5 tablespoons of the vegetable oil over medium-high heat, then cook the pork and egg white mixture until the pork turns color and the egg whites solidify into smaller light golden pieces, 1 to 2 minutes. Remove with a skimmer and set aside. Add the chiles to the wok and cook until they begin to darken, about 30 seconds. Remove and set the chiles aside with the pork. Add the remaining 1 tablespoon of vegetable oil to the wok and heat over high heat. Add the green pepper and stir-fry for 30 seconds. Return the pork cubes and chiles to the wok and stir-fry for 1 minute. Stir the reserved sauce to blend it, then add to the wok and cook for 1 minute. Add the peanuts and chile oil and cook, stirring and tossing until thickened. Serve immediately.

MAKES 4 SERVINGS

sassy
seafood

One of the reasons most types of seafood do so well when married to chiles is that the taste of fish and shellfish actually falls within a narrow range. Remember that if you think fish is "fishy," that means you've gotten rotten fish. Fresh fish never smell "fishy"; they smell briny or oceany. The recipes in this chapter represent seafood cookery from most of our hot cuisines, even from landlocked Sichuan province. Many of these cuisines have access to the freshest fish, and seafood is an integral part of the diet. Although one would think that Americans, surrounded on three sides by great bodies of water, should have a great fish cooking tradition, most Americans don't cook fish at home, and therefore the quality of the seafood available to us is not the best. For this reason you will almost always have to buy your seafood at fish stores or ethnic markets. Should you buy fish at the supermarket? Well, here's the test: walk by the fish counter and if there is a smell, forget it. Once you've got your seafood, go make Spicy Fish with Black Bean Sauce (page 290), and you may wonder what the heck that stuff was they served you at the local Chinese restaurant.

Spicy Shrimp with Ají Sauce

his famous and fabulous Peruvian dish is called *picante de camarones*, which basically means "hot shrimp." It's an over-the-top dish that is rich and satisfying. The *ají* (pronounced ah-hee) sauce used in this dish is made with the fresh yellow chiles called *ají amarillo fresco* in Peru. As these are unlikely to be found in your supermarket, you can replace them with the yellow chile sauce. If you are using fresh shrimp and any of them have their eggs attached, remove the coral and add it to the skillet in step 2 at the same time you add the walnuts. Peruvians always serve this with boiled yellow potatoes (you can use Yukon gold), wedges of hard-boiled egg for garnish, and steamed rice to cut through the heat.

4 pounds fresh large shrimp with their heads or 2 pounds headless shrimp, heads and/or shells removed

3 tablespoons unsalted butter

1/4 cup extra-virgin olive oil

2 medium-size white onions, finely chopped

4 large garlic cloves, mashed in a mortar with 1 teaspoon salt

2 medium-size tomatoes, peeled, seeded, and chopped

1 tablespoon finely chopped fresh tarragon leaves

1 teaspoon dried thyme

1/4 cup Yellow Chile Sauce (page 406)

1/2 cup dry white wine

1 teaspoon salt, or more to your taste

1 teaspoon freshly ground white pepper

4 slices of white bread, crusts removed and soaked in half and half or milk

1/4 cup water

1/2 pound walnuts, coarsely chopped

2 3/4 cups heavy cream

1 tablespoon flour mixed with 1 tablespoon water (optional)

1. Bring a large pot of abundantly salted water to a boil over high heat, then plunge the shrimp in until they turn orange-red and are firm, about 3 minutes. Drain and set aside.

2. In a large skillet or casserole, melt the butter with 1 tablespoon of the olive oil over medium-high heat, then cook the onions, garlic, and tomatoes until the onions are soft, about 6 minutes, stirring. Add the remaining 3 tablespoons olive oil, tarragon, thyme, yellow chile sauce, and wine. Season with 1 teaspoon salt and 1/2 teaspoon white pepper and bring to a boil. Cook until most of the wine has evaporated, about 3 minutes, then reduce the heat to low and simmer until a little denser, about 3 minutes, stirring occasionally. Squeeze the liquid out of the bread and add the soaked bread to the skillet along with the water, walnuts, and cream and cook until creamy and saucy, about 30 minutes, stirring occasionally and making sure the sauce does not boil. If a thicker sauce is desired, add the flour and water mixture to the sauce, while stirring.

3. Add the reserved shrimp, add more salt if desired and the remaining white pepper, and heat the shrimp for about 5 minutes. Serve immediately.

MAKES 6 SERVINGS

Vatapá Stew

*V**atapá** stew is one of those distinctive Brazilian dishes, this one from Bahia in northern Brazil, which was born in the Amazon from the convergence of Portuguese colonial, native Amazonian Indian, and African slave cultures. This type of cooking is distinguished by the copious use of *dendê* oil, extracted from an African palm tree and the same red palm oil used in West African cooking. The Afro-Brazilians of today are descended from slaves mostly obtained from West Africa north of the equator before about 1550. They were originally from Lower Guinea and the Niger River delta, and later from Angola. Some cooks use fresh ginger or fresh coriander leaves too. *Vatapá* is traditionally accompanied by *pirão de arroz com leite de coco* (see page 386).

¹/₄ cup extra-virgin olive oil

2 pounds sea bass, grouper, or halibut fillets, cut into 2-inch pieces

2 pounds fresh large shrimp with their heads or 1 pound headless shrimp, heads and/or shells removed

1 small onion, finely chopped

1 large ripe tomato, peeled, seeded, and chopped

3 habanero chiles, finely chopped

1 coconut, shell cracked, flesh removed, peeled, and grated, or 2 cups dried shredded unsweetened coconut

2¹/₂ cups boiling water

¹/₂ cup roasted unsalted peanuts, coarsely ground

3 tablespoons dried ground shrimp

6 coriander seeds

2 teaspoons salt, or more to your taste

1 teaspoon freshly ground black pepper, or more to your taste

1 tablespoon rice flour *or* 1 tablespoon arrowroot powder mixed with 2 tablespoons water

¹/₄ cup red palm oil *or* ¹/₄ cup walnut oil mixed with 1 teaspoon paprika

1. In a large skillet, heat the olive oil over medium heat, then cook the fish and shrimp in two or three batches until light golden, about 4 minutes in all, turning once. Make sure the fish and shrimp don't touch one another in the skillet. Remove with a spatula and set aside.

2. Add the onion to the skillet and cook over medium heat until translucent, about 5 minutes, stirring. Add the tomato and habanero chiles, reduce the heat to low, cover, and cook for 10 minutes. Stir in the coconut, then add the boiling water, peanuts, dried shrimp, coriander seeds, salt, and pepper. Bring to a boil over medium heat, reduce the heat to low, and simmer, covered, for 15 minutes.

3. Pour the sauce through a sieve into a bowl, pushing with the back of the wooden spoon, pressing down hard to extract as much liquid as possible. Return the strained sauce to the skillet, stir in the rice flour mixture, and cook over medium heat until the mixture thickens slightly, about 5 minutes, stirring constantly. Add the red palm oil and blend it into the sauce, then add the reserved fish and shrimp and simmer until heated through, about 5 minutes. Transfer to a serving platter and serve immediately.

MAKES 6 SERVINGS

Mahimahi with Green Chile and Cilantro Cream Sauce

This Mexican preparation from the Pacific is called *pescado en salsa verde*, fish in green sauce. You could use just about any kind of firm-fleshed fish, but mahimahi (also called dolphinfish) is both perfect and authentic. The dish appears to be very hot, but the crème fraîche moderates the heat successfully. Serve with rice and tortillas.

6 mahimahi steaks (about 2 pounds)

Juice of 1 lime

Salt and freshly ground black pepper to taste

3 green bell peppers

4 fresh green finger-type chiles or 6 green serrano chiles

1 cup crème fraîche

3 tablespoons finely chopped fresh coriander (cilantro) leaves

1 tablespoon extra-virgin olive oil

1. Place the fish steaks in a glass or ceramic baking dish, add the lime juice, and salt and pepper and marinate for 2 hours in the refrigerator.

2. Preheat the oven to 425°F. Place the bell peppers and chiles in a baking dish and roast until the skin blisters black, 30 to 40 minutes. The chiles will probably be done first, so remove them first. When cool enough to handle, peel the peppers and chiles and remove their stems and the bell pepper seeds. Place the bell peppers and chiles in a blender with the crème fraîche and coriander and blend until smooth, about 2 minutes. Add salt and pepper if desired.

3. In a large skillet, heat the olive oil over high heat, then brown the fish steaks on both sides, turning with a spatula, about 3 minutes in all. Reduce the heat to low, add the sauce from the blender, pushing the fish steaks around a bit and spooning some sauce over them, cover, and simmer until cooked through, about 18 minutes. Serve immediately.

MAKES 6 SERVINGS

Shrimp in Pumpkinseed-Coriander Sauce

T he tiny oval chile known as *pequín*, *piquín*, or *chilipequín*, or *chiltepin* when in the wild state, gets its name from the Spanish word for "small" and is much used in Mexican cooking. These chiles are also known as bird's-eye chiles or *chile mosquito*. These chiles can be bought dried through the Internet, and the only place I've seen them fresh in this country is at farmers' markets and urban supermarkets. Serve with plain rice and flour tortillas.

3 pounds fresh shrimp with their heads or 1¹/₂ pounds headless shrimp, heads and/or shells removed and reserved

¹/₃ cup roasted salted pumpkinseeds

³/₄ pound medium-size tomatoes, peeled, seeded, and coarsely chopped

1 small onion, coarsely chopped

¹/₃ cup canned pimientos, drained and chopped

10 dried or fresh *piquín* chiles, crumbled or roasted and finely chopped, or 1 dried de arbol chile, crumbled

Leaves from 5 sprigs fresh coriander (cilantro), chopped

1 teaspoon ground coriander

1 large garlic clove, finely chopped

¹/₂ teaspoon sugar

Salt and freshly ground black pepper to taste

2¹/₂ tablespoons vegetable oil

1¹/₂ tablespoons freshly squeezed lime juice

1. Put the shrimp shells and heads, if any, in a saucepan and cover with cold water. Bring to a boil over high heat, reduce the heat to low, and simmer for 15 minutes. Drain the broth, setting aside ³/₄ cup and saving the remainder for another purpose. Discard the heads and shells.

2. Grind the pumpkinseeds in a spice mill until pulverized. Transfer to a blender and add the tomatoes, onion, pimientos, chiles, fresh coriander, ground coriander, garlic, sugar, and salt and pepper. Blend for 2 minutes until a smooth puree.

3. In a large skillet, heat 1¹/₂ tablespoons of the vegetable oil over medium heat, then cook the shrimp until most have turned pink-orange and are firm to the touch, about $2^1/_2$ minutes. Remove the shrimp from the skillet with a slotted spoon and set aside.

4.   Add the remaining 1 tablespoon vegetable oil to the skillet. Pour in the puree and cook, uncovered, over medium heat, stirring frequently, until it is thicker and bubbling vigorously, about 5 minutes. Stir the reserved $^3/_4$ cup of shrimp broth into the sauce and cook until half the liquid has evaporated, about 8 minutes. Add the reserved shrimp and cook over low heat for 2 to 3 minutes. Stir in the lime juice and serve immediately.

MAKES 4 SERVINGS

tacos

If there is any food that an American knows as Mexican, it's tacos. Thanks to Tex-Mex restaurants and chains like Taco Bell it is firmly in place as a Mexican food. There's only one problem: those crisp U-shaped hard corn tacos filled with ground beef, lettuce, and orange-colored cheese are not Mexican, but rather purely American. A real Mexican taco—two soft corn tortillas wrapped around well-seasoned roasted meat with a tomato-chile sauce, chopped onion, and coriander leaves, all slightly greasy from the griddle—is a heavenly and sublime experience. A taco can be stuffed with anything, and in Mexico it is. Often freshly made, corn tortillas are stuffed with thick stews, barbecued meats, boiled potatoes, eggs, or grilled pork, beef, or chicken. Cheese and chiles are also used. Tacos are always an informal food and are great for parties, lunches, or snacks.

Shredded Shrimp and Serrano Chile Tacos

T his dish is from the Mexican state of Sinaloa and is called *tacos de machaca de camarón*. It's a fun recipe because you finely chop the shrimp, spice it dramatically with chiles, and then roll it into tortillas. It's ideal for parties because everyone can make their own taco. It's very nice to sprinkle some of the garnish inside the taco before you wrap it up. Because the preparation is very hot, these mild garnishes both temper the heat and provide a delightful counter to the chiles. This recipe is adapted from one by Marilu Monem de Lopez.

3 tablespoons corn oil

3 tablespoons unsalted butter

1 very large white onion, finely chopped

6 fresh green serrano chiles, finely chopped

1 fresh green poblano chile, roasted, peeled, seeded, and finely chopped

1¾ pounds tomatoes, cut in half, seeds squeezed out, and grated against the largest holes of a grater

2 teaspoons dried oregano

2 pounds fresh medium-size shrimp with their heads or 1 pound headless shrimp, heads and/or shells removed, meat finely chopped or ground in a food processor until shredded

Salt and freshly ground black pepper to taste

4 large warmed flour tortillas

FOR GARNISH (CHOOSE 1 OR 2)
Shredded iceberg lettuce

Chopped ripe tomatoes

Chopped scallions

Chopped coriander

Shredded cabbage

In a large skillet, heat the corn oil and butter over medium heat, then cook the onion until golden, about 10 minutes, stirring occasionally. Add the serrano and poblano chiles, tomatoes, and oregano and simmer until the sauce is thick, about 25 minutes, stirring occasionally. Add the shrimp, reduce the heat to low, and simmer until very thick with no remaining liquid, about 25 minutes, stirring occasionally. Season with salt and pepper to taste. Transfer to a serving platter and serve with tortillas and garnishes.

MAKES 4 SERVINGS

sassy seafood

Squid with Chiles in the Style of Veracruz

Veracruz is the one area of Mexico where the old Spanish influence on cooking is still obvious. We know this whenever we see olives and capers (and almonds) in a dish. This recipe is very pleasant and a great way to introduce a neophyte to squid.

1/4 cup extra-virgin olive oil

2 pounds cleaned squid, bodies sliced into 3/4-inch rings, tentacles cut in half if large, washed and dried with paper towels

Salt and freshly ground black pepper to taste

1 medium-size onion, chopped

2 large garlic cloves, finely chopped

1 pound ripe tomatoes, cut in half, seeds squeezed out, and grated against the largest holes of a grater

4 fresh green finger-type chiles or 6 green jalapeño chiles, stemmed, seeded, and sliced

2 tablespoons finely chopped fresh parsley leaves

2 tablespoons finely chopped fresh coriander (cilantro) leaves

1 teaspoon dried oregano

1/2 teaspoon dried thyme

1 small bay leaf

16 pitted green olives

1 tablespoon capers, rinsed and chopped if large

1. In a large skillet, heat 2 tablespoons of the olive oil over high heat, then cook the squid rings and tentacles, seasoning with salt and pepper, until white, about 2 minutes. Remove with a slotted spoon and set aside, keeping warm. Discard the liquid in the skillet, wipe it clean with a paper towel, and add the remaining 2 tablespoons olive oil.

2. Heat the oil over high heat. Add the onion and garlic and cook until soft, about 4 minutes. Add the tomatoes, chiles, parsley, coriander, oregano, thyme, and bay leaf. Stir, season with salt and pepper, reduce the heat to low, cover, and cook until the liquid of the tomatoes has almost evaporated and the chiles are soft, about 12 minutes. Raise the heat to medium-high, uncover, and cook until the sauce is thick, about 2 minutes.

3. Add the reserved squid, olives, and capers, reduce the heat to medium, and cook until all the liquid is gone and it is saucy looking and the squid is tender but with a little bite to it, about 10 minutes, stirring occasionally. Serve immediately.

MAKES 4 TO 6 SERVINGS

Catfish Stew

When you're in Louisiana you hear about crawfish constantly. But the Cajuns do enjoy other seafood, including catfish. This rich stew is made with catfish in Bayou country, but you could use any firm-fleshed fish such as mahimahi, monkfish, opah, grouper, striped bass, or shark. Serve with rice, dumplings, or cornbread.

3/4 cup (1 1/2 sticks) unsalted butter

1 cup finely chopped red bell peppers

2/3 cup finely chopped green bell peppers

2 fresh green finger-type chiles or 3 green jalapeño chiles, seeded and finely chopped

1/2 cup finely chopped celery

5 scallions, trimmed of outer green portions and finely chopped

2 tablespoons finely chopped fresh coriander (cilantro) leaves

1/4 cup Cliff's Cajun Seasoning (page 412)

1/2 cup dry white wine

2 cups shrimp broth (homemade or canned)

2 cups heavy cream

Zest from 1/2 orange

1 bay leaf

1 1/2 pounds catfish fillets, cut into 1-inch cubes

6 slices Italian or French bread, lightly toasted

1. In a large casserole or stockpot, melt 1/2 cup (1 stick) of the butter over medium-high heat. When the bubbles subside, add the red bell peppers, green bell peppers, chiles, celery, scallions, and coriander. Add Cliff's Cajun Seasoning and cook for 8 minutes, stirring frequently.

2. Pour in the white wine and let it cook for 3 minutes, stirring frequently. Add 1 cup of the shrimp broth and 1 cup of the heavy cream. Add the orange zest and bay leaf. Reduce the heat to medium and cook for 20 minutes.

3. Pour in the remaining 1 cup shrimp broth and 1 cup heavy cream. Cook for 30 minutes. Add the catfish and cook until firm, 15 minutes. Remove and discard the bay leaf. Serve immediately in soup bowls with bread slices on the side for dipping into the stew.

MAKES 6 SERVINGS

sassy seafood

Shrimp Creole

Recipes of every kind abound for this well-known Louisiana dish. But there are certain ingredients that always appear in shrimp Creole, namely shrimp, tomatoes, onions, and chiles. Some cooks also add Tabasco or Worcestershire sauce. Creole cooking is a bit different from Cajun cooking. Creole cooking was born in New Orleans in the early eighteenth century as a mixture of three basic traditions, French, Spanish, and Afro-Caribbean. There were other influences, including Sicilian, Native American, and Mexican. As Paul Prudhomme pointed out, Creole cooking is a sophisticated city cooking that exists only in the home today, as restaurants have blended the distinction between Creole and Cajun. This recipe is adapted from an unattributed source in a New Orleans promotion on a travel Web site, but I feel that it must come from a very good cook because it evidences not only a good taste but a sophisticated balance of flavors. The original recipe called for olive oil, which I presume to be a modern introduction, since traditional Creole cooking is more likely to use butter or animal fat. The use of Scotch bonnet chiles in this recipe, rather than the more common use of jalapeño or serrano, points to an early introduction by Afro-Caribbean cooks who were familiar with the Scotch bonnet. This dish is traditionally eaten with rice.

3 pounds fresh jumbo shrimp with their heads or 1¹/₂ pounds headless jumbo shrimp, heads and/or shells removed and reserved

2 tablespoons freshly squeezed lime juice

2 teaspoons salt, or more to your taste

1 teaspoon freshly ground black pepper, or more to your taste

3 tablespoons unsalted butter

1 medium-size onion, finely chopped

12 scallions, white and light green parts only, finely chopped

4 shallots, finely chopped

6 large garlic cloves, finely chopped

2 Scotch bonnet chiles or habanero chiles, seeded and finely chopped

One ¹/₂-inch cube fresh ginger, finely chopped

1¹/₂ teaspoons curry powder

2¹/₄ pounds ripe tomatoes, peeled, seeded, and chopped

1 cup finely chopped fresh parsley leaves

¹/₄ cup finely chopped fresh coriander (cilantro) leaves

1 teaspoon fresh thyme leaves, finely chopped

1 bay leaf

¹/₃ cup dark rum

2 tablespoons tomato paste

1. Put the shrimp heads and/or shells in a saucepan and cover with water. Bring to a boil over high heat, reduce the heat to low, and simmer until needed.

2. Place the shrimp in a large bowl and pour the lime juice over them. Season with salt and pepper and set aside until needed.

3. In a large skillet, melt the butter over medium heat, then cook the onion, scallions, shallots, 5 of the garlic cloves, the chiles, ginger, and curry powder until the mixture is soft and yellow, about 5 minutes. Stir in the tomatoes, $1/2$ cup of the parsley, the coriander, thyme, and bay leaf. Increase the heat to high and cook, stirring, for 1 minute. Stir in the rum and bring to a boil.

4. Strain the shrimp broth, reserving 1 cup. Add the shrimp broth and tomato paste to the skillet. Reduce the heat to medium and simmer until thickened, about 20 minutes, stirring frequently.

5. Add the shrimp to the skillet, reduce the heat to low, and stir to coat the shrimp with the sauce. Simmer, turning occasionally, until the shrimp are curled and orange-pink, about 5 minutes. Stir in the remaining 1 clove garlic and cook 1 minute. Sprinkle with the remaining $1/2$ cup of parsley and cook 1 minute. Serve immediately.

MAKES 6 SERVINGS

fresh shrimp

Fresh shrimp as described in my recipes means never-having-been frozen shrimp. Just so you know that I don't have some secret supplier, fresh shrimp is nearly impossible to find and I can't find it often. Even when I do, it's only once a year. Nearly all commercial shrimp is flash-frozen, and what you are eating when you buy shrimp at the supermarket or fish store is defrosted shrimp. Is there really such a difference? Yes, there is. I know people brought up on fresh shrimp who refuse to eat frozen shrimp because you might as well eat imitation crabmeat. Fresh shrimp are always sold with heads on, and if you ever encounter them buy ten pounds and make a bunch of shrimp recipes.

the piquant cuisine of
the cajuns

In early seventeenth-century France, people from Provence immigrated to Nova Scotia, then called Acadia, establishing a colony. By the mid-eighteenth century, as the British position in Canada became stronger, many of these French people moved to the other important French colony in the Americas, Louisiana, where the French had arrived in the early 1700s. They settled in the bayou country to the west of New Orleans, and slowly the pronunciation of their name, Acadians, was shortened to Cadiens, and then transformed into Cajuns. Their cooking was based on local ingredients, rural French home cooking strained through their experience in maritime Canada. A style of cooking arose among the Cajuns that distinguished itself from the French aristocratic cooking existing in the city of New Orleans, which was Creole. Cajun cooking was also based on French cooking, but it was less sophisticated—rougher, bolder, and hotter.

Creole cooking arose in the urban homes of French families that could afford to employ a cook, often African slaves from Senegambia in West Africa, and later free black settlers from Haiti. The style of cooking became Creole, a mixture of homestyle spicy cooking of African slaves from the West Indies and Africa based on classic French technique and sensibilities with a potpourri of Sicilian, Mexican, Native American, and Spanish influences. In New Orleans, the Sicilians were responsible for today's "red gravy," a spicy tomato sauce, and muffaletta, a kind of large sandwich. The cooking of Louisiana was notable even at this time. The English novelist William Makepeace Thackeray said of New Orleans in the 1850s, "the old France-Spanish city on the banks of the Mississippi where of all cities of the world, you can eat the most and suffer the least, where the claret is as good as at Bordeaux, and where ragout and a bouillabaisse can be had the like of which was never eaten in Marseilles or Paris."

Cajun cooking resembles Creole cooking in that the same products are used, typically, crayfish, shrimp, oysters, pork, zucchini, chayote, okra, eggplant, and tomatoes, but also with a significantly greater use of chile, especially in dried and ground forms. The most famous chile of the Cajuns is the Tabasco chile, which is also the only South American chile cultivated commercially on a large scale in the United States. It's not clear when the first Tabasco chile came to Louisiana, but sometime before the U.S. Civil War some seeds or pods came into the hands of Edmund McIlhenny. McIlhenny married into the Avery family, which owned the Avery Island plantation. The Tabasco chiles were planted there, and eventually a commercial empire grew that continues to produce the famous Tabasco sauce.

Barbecued Shrimp

This is a Creole way of preparing shrimp in New Orleans that actually has nothing to do with barbecue pits or barbecuing. The dish consists of fresh shrimp baked in an ocean of seasoned melted butter. When you see this much butter you know the French have arrived on the scene. In fact, Creole cooking in Louisiana is a mixture of French, African, Spanish, Italian, Acadian (Cajun), and Choctaw Indian influences. This dish may have been invented at Pascal's Manale Restaurant on Napoleon Avenue in New Orleans, but it is popular everywhere in South Louisiana. My recipe is adapted from both the way the restaurant does it and Joyce Lafaye Crews's recipe published by the Ursuline Academy Cooperative Club in New Orleans in *Recipes and Reminiscences of New Orleans* (1971). You should always accompany Barbecued Shrimp with French bread and beer—and a bib, since it's a messy meal.

4¹⁄₂ cups (9 sticks) unsalted butter

1 medium-large onion, very finely chopped

12 large garlic cloves, very finely chopped

3 celery stalks, very finely chopped

¹⁄₄ cup finely chopped fresh parsley leaves

2 tablespoons chopped rosemary leaves

2 tablespoons cayenne pepper

1 teaspoon dried thyme

1 teaspoon dried oregano

1 tablespoon salt, or more to your taste

2 tablespoons freshly ground black pepper

1 cup lager beer, at room temperature

¹⁄₄ cup Worcestershire sauce

1 teaspoon Tabasco sauce

2 teaspoons fresh lemon juice

7 pounds fresh shrimp with their heads or 3¹⁄₂ pounds headless shrimp, rinsed well and drained

1. In a large casserole, melt half the butter over high heat, then cook the onion, garlic, celery, parsley, rosemary, cayenne, thyme, oregano, salt, and black pepper until the onion and celery are soft, 2 to 3 minutes, stirring. Add the remaining butter, and, once it melts, add the beer, Worcestershire sauce, Tabasco sauce, and lemon juice. Taste and add more salt and pepper seasoning if desired. Turn the heat off and keep warm until needed.

2. Preheat the oven to 350°F. Place the shrimp in a large baking casserole or 8 individual baking dishes and cover with the seasoned butter, making sure the shrimp are pushed down into the melted butter. Bake until the shrimp are orange-pink, about 30 minutes. Serve immediately.

MAKES 8 SERVINGS

sassy seafood

Crayfish Étouffée

The crayfish is a small lobster-like crustacean ubiquitous in Louisiana, from license plates to tourist brochures. The tail meat is used in this recipe, and Cajuns would save the heads to make what they call "crawfish water" or broth, for which crayfish heads are put in a stockpot with celery, onions, carrots, garlic, bay leaf, and thyme and simmered for more than an hour. Some cooks let their whole finished étouffée stand overnight in the refrigerator to let the seasonings "come home." You can use shrimp or lobster meat in place of the crayfish. It is important to make this in a cast-iron skillet, which retains the heat that is necessary to complete step 1. Serve over cooked rice with homemade biscuits or cornbread, celery seed coleslaw, and green beans.

FOR THE SPICE MIX

1 teaspoon salt

1 teaspoon cayenne pepper

1/2 teaspoon freshly ground black pepper

1/2 teaspoon freshly ground white pepper

1/2 teaspoon dried oregano

1/4 teaspoon thyme

FOR THE ROUX

1/3 cup vegetable oil

1/4 cup unbleached all-purpose flour

1 medium-size onion, chopped

2 garlic cloves, finely chopped

2 celery stalks, chopped

1 small green bell pepper, chopped

2 medium-size tomatoes, peeled and chopped

1 cup fish broth (homemade or canned), clam juice (fresh or bottled), or "crawfish water" (see headnote)

1 bay leaf

4 teaspoons hot sauce, such as Tabasco sauce, Crystal sauce, or Louisiana Red Sauce (page 413)

1 pound crayfish tail meat

1/2 cup (1 stick) unsalted butter

1/2 cup chopped scallions, white and green parts

1. In a small bowl, mix the spice ingredients. In a large cast-iron skillet, make the roux by heating the vegetable oil over high heat until it begins to smoke, then gradually whisk in the flour with a long-handled metal whisk, stirring constantly until it is smooth. Continue stirring constantly until the roux is rust brown, about 2 1/2 minutes. Be careful you don't burn the flour. Remove the skillet from the heat and stir in the onion, garlic, celery, and bell pepper. Stir in half the spice mix and continue stirring as the mixture and skillet cool down, about 5 minutes.

2. Add the tomatoes, fish broth, and bay leaf to the skillet and bring to a boil over high heat, stirring constantly. Reduce the heat to low and simmer until it thickens to a sauce, about 45 minutes. Add the hot sauce, crayfish, butter, scallions, and the remaining spice mix and simmer until the crayfish is cooked and the butter melted, about 10 minutes. Remove the bay leaf and serve immediately.

MAKES 4 SERVINGS

MAKING ROUX FOR CAJUN COOKING

When you set out to make gumbo or many other Cajun dishes you will start with a roux. All oral gumbo recipes start with the instruction, "First, make a roux." Derived from French cuisine, a roux is simply the blending of flour and a cooking fat—butter or vegetable oil in Creole and Cajun cooking—over heat to form a paste that serves as a thickener in the recipe. Making Cajun roux is tricky because you are doing a controlled burn, and if you burn it too much, you will have to discard it and start over. So the rule of thumb if you are a novice is to start it over medium heat, stir almost constantly, don't fiddle with the heat by raising it, and remember that patience is a virtue. Generally, the darker the meat, the lighter the roux, and the lighter the meat, the darker the roux. A chicken gumbo, therefore, would have a chocolate-colored roux, while the gumbo on page 266 would call for a caramel-colored roux. As one Cajun cook suggested about the length of time for making a good roux, it's "not a bad time to pop open a beer."

Andouille Sausage, Shrimp, and Oyster Gumbo

It's hard to say how gumbo was invented, although its connection to Africa is not in doubt. One legend is that it came about when okra was introduced to Mobile, Alabama, in 1704 by 25 French mademoiselles known as the "Cassette girls," who arrived in search of husbands. They came by way of the West Indies, where they had acquired okra from African slaves who called the plant gumbo and used it in stews also called gumbo. Today, a gumbo does not have to contain okra. The most popular ingredients in gumbo are andouille sausage, shrimp, oysters, crab, duck, chicken, and, among more rural cooks, alligator, squirrel, venison, and nutria. I'm wild about gumbos, especially when they mix meats with seafood, as in this recipe. Serve over rice.

2 tablespoons vegetable oil

1 pound smoked andouille sausage or Polish kielbasa, sliced

1/4 cup unbleached all-purpose flour

1 small red bell pepper, seeded and chopped

1 small green bell pepper, seeded and chopped

1 medium-size onion, thinly sliced

6 cups cold water

1 bay leaf

2 tablespoons salt

20 ounces fresh shrimp with their heads or 10 ounces headless shrimp

24 oysters, shucked, liquid reserved

One 14-ounce can Italian plum tomatoes with their liquid

1/2 teaspoon dried thyme

1/2 teaspoon dried oregano

2 teaspoons cayenne pepper

Freshly ground black pepper to taste

1/2 teaspoon Tabasco sauce

1/2 cup sliced shallots

2 tablespoons finely chopped fresh coriander (cilantro) leaves

1. In a large skillet, heat the vegetable oil over medium heat and brown the sausage, about 8 minutes. Transfer to a platter with a slotted spoon. Pour off all but 2 tablespoons of fat and make a roux by adding the flour and stirring almost constantly with a whisk or wooden spoon for about 45 minutes or until dark golden brown, adjusting the heat downward if it is cooking too fast.

2. Add the red and green bell peppers and onion. Reduce the heat to low and cook until the vegetables are soft, 6 to 10 minutes, stirring occasionally. Add a few tablespoons of water to scrape up any residue on the bottom of the pan.

3. In a saucepan, bring the water to a boil with the bay leaf and salt. Drop the shrimp into the boiling water and boil for 2 minutes. Remove the shrimp with a slotted ladle, reduce the heat to low, and let the water simmer for 15 minutes. As you peel the shrimp throw the heads and/or shells back into the simmering water.

4. Strain the shrimp broth, discarding the heads and/or shells and bay leaf. Pour the broth into a clean pot and bring to a boil over high heat. Stir in the roux mixture, the sausage, oyster liquid, tomatoes, thyme, oregano, cayenne pepper, black pepper, Tabasco sauce, and shallots and simmer for 2 hours over low heat, stirring occasionally.

5. Stir in the shrimp, oysters, and coriander leaves and cook until the shrimp are orange and the edges of the oysters have curled up, 2 to 3 minutes. Serve immediately.

MAKES 4 SERVINGS

Red-Hot
Red Snapper

find it amusing that Jamaicans name their culinary preparations either very colorfully, such as Stamp and Go (page 29) or Run Down, or in the simplest way possible. For example, I made up this name, because in Jamaica this dish is un-interestingly called "red snapper." Well, it is certainly much more than that—it is a fiery hot preparation best served with a bland food such as plain white rice. One of the reasons tourists never have any idea that real Jamaican food is so spicy-hot is that they are not served that food in tourist restaurants.

2 tablespoons extra-virgin olive oil

2 green bell peppers, chopped

3 large garlic cloves, finely chopped

1 medium-size onion, chopped

1 Scotch bonnet chile or habanero chile, seeded and finely chopped

1 pound red snapper fillets, cut into 1-inch pieces

Salt and freshly ground black pepper to taste

In a large skillet, heat the olive oil over medium-high heat with the green peppers, garlic, and onion and cook until soft, about 10 minutes, stirring frequently. Add the chile, stir, and add the fish, tossing so it is well covered with the vegetables. Season with salt and pepper, cover, reduce the heat to medium, and cook 5 minutes. Stir again, and cook until the fish is firm but not breaking apart, about another 5 minutes. Serve immediately.

MAKES 4 SERVINGS

Blaff

This famous dish from Martinique is said to get its name from the sound the fish make when they hit the boiling water. The preparation is known in Jamaica, too, where it is called escovitch. In the Caribbean, a cook would use local small mackerel or amberjack, but red snapper also works very well. One could also use fish steaks, although they won't provide as much flavor as the whole fish. In Jamaica, some cooks use the berries and leaves of the bay-rum tree, which they call malagueta pepper, in the marinade. In Martinique, cooks add baby scallions to the boiling liquid. Blaff cooks very quickly. Serve with white rice and boiled or Fried Plantains (page 389).

Juice of 8 limes

3 large garlic cloves, finely chopped

1 Scotch bonnet chile or habanero chile, finely chopped

6 allspice berries, crushed, or 1/2 teaspoon ground allspice

1 teaspoon salt

1 teaspoon freshly ground black pepper

4 whole cleaned red snapper (4 1/2 to 5 pounds in all), scored in 3 places on both sides

6 cups water

1 small onion, sliced

1 *bouquet garni*, tied in cheesecloth, consisting of 3 sprigs thyme and 3 sprigs parsley

1. In a large ceramic or glass dish, mix half the lime juice, the garlic, chile, half the allspice, the salt, and pepper. Swish the fish in this mixture and marinate for 1 hour in the refrigerator.

2. In a large casserole, skillet, or fish poacher that can hold all the fish, bring the water to a boil with the onion, the remaining allspice, and the *bouquet garni*. Place the fish and its marinade into the boiling water and return to a boil, about 4 minutes. Turn the fish, turn off the heat, and let sit 4 minutes. Immediately remove the fish and serve with the remaining lime juice drizzled over the top.

MAKES 4 SERVINGS

Fish Stew in Beer

The Jamaican name of this dish is Brown Fish Stew, and it's my guess that it is so named because of the beer. This is a pretty hot dish, as the traditional Scotch bonnet chiles are one of the two hottest chiles in the world. Other traditional fish to use are red snapper, kingfish, or Spanish mackerel.

4 tablespoons unsalted butter	2 cups amber beer
2 pounds mahimahi steaks, cut 1 inch thick	1 Scotch bonnet chile or habanero chile, seeded and finely chopped
2 medium-large onions, 1 cut into thick slices, 1 cut into thin slices	1 green bell pepper, finely chopped
1 tablespoon all-purpose flour	Salt and freshly ground black pepper to taste

1. In a large skillet, melt 2 tablespoons of the butter over medium-high heat, then cook the fish steaks on both sides until lightly brown, about 4 minutes, turning once. Remove and set aside.

2. Melt the remaining 2 tablespoons butter in the skillet and add the thick-cut and thin-cut onions. As they cook, sprinkle in the flour, and cook until the onions are golden, about 15 minutes, stirring and separating the rings. Add the beer, chile, bell pepper, and salt and pepper and let it cook and thicken, about 25 minutes. Reduce the heat to low, add the fish steaks, spooning some sauce over them, cover, and simmer until the fish is cooked through and firm and the sauce is gravy-like, about 15 minutes, turning once and adding a little water if the sauce gets too thick. Serve immediately.

MAKES 6 SERVINGS

Swordfish in the "Sauce That Dances"

*I*n Algeria, this preparation is called *kalb al-bahr shatitha*. The first part of this name, *kalb al-bahr*, is the Arabic name for dogfish, an unfortunate name for a delicious small shark also known as Cape shark on the eastern U.S. coast. Any firm-fleshed fish such as another kind of shark or swordfish works very well here. I use swordfish because it's easy, if expensive, to get. The second part of the Algerian name means literally the "sauce that dances," meaning that it is very piquant. The spicy-hot food "dances" in your mouth, and it also "dances" in the skillet, since it is cooked quickly. The word *shatitha* derives from *shatta*, a variety of chile. This is a spectacular dish with swordfish and wonderful served with fettuccine.

3 tablespoons extra-virgin olive oil

1 large garlic clove, finely chopped

1 fresh green finger-type chile or 2 green jalapeño chiles, seeded and finely chopped

1 bay leaf, finely crumbled

1/2 teaspoon dried thyme

1 teaspoon hot paprika

1 teaspoon salt, or more to your taste

1 teaspoon ground cumin

1 teaspoon ground coriander

1 teaspoon freshly ground black pepper

2 teaspoons cayenne pepper

1 teaspoon *Harisa* (page 414)

3 tablespoons water

4 to 6 swordfish steaks (about 1 3/4 pounds)

1 pound ripe tomatoes, peeled, seeded, and chopped

In a bowl, mix together the olive oil, garlic, chile, bay leaf, thyme, paprika, 1 teaspoon salt, cumin, coriander, black pepper, cayenne pepper, *harisa*, and water. Pour into a large skillet or stove-top earthenware tagine or casserole with a cover. Bring to just boiling over high heat, then reduce the heat to low, add the fish and tomatoes, salt lightly, cover, and cook until the fish is firm, about 25 minutes. Serve immediately.

MAKES 4 TO 6 SERVINGS

Octopus Stew

This preparation is octopus as you've never had it: hot, spicy, and luscious. It is a specialty of the island of Djerba off the coast of Tunisia. The octopus men of Djerba have a history of catching octopus that goes back to the time of the Carthaginians. This stew is traditionally cooked in an earthenware stew pot that sits atop an earthenware brazier filled with lump hardwood coals. This is how I first had it, and it sure was memorable.

1 small cleaned octopus (about 1¼ pounds)

6 tablespoons extra-virgin olive oil

1 medium-size onion, chopped

3 large garlic cloves, sliced

2 tablespoons tomato paste dissolved in 1 cup water

1 tablespoon *Harisa* (page 414)

½ teaspoon ground caraway

1 teaspoon cayenne pepper

1 teaspoon freshly ground black pepper

3 cups fresh or canned crushed tomatoes

2 cups diced pumpkin or winter squash flesh (about ½ pound)

6 cups water

Salt to taste

½ cup cooked chickpeas, drained

1. Put the octopus in a medium-size pot of water to cover, bring to a gentle boil, and cook 40 minutes. Drain, and, when cool enough to handle, rub off the skin and dice.

2. In a large stockpot, heat the olive oil over medium-high heat and cook the onion and garlic, stirring frequently so the garlic doesn't burn, until the onion is translucent, about 6 minutes. Add the tomato paste dissolved in water, the *harisa*, caraway, cayenne pepper, and black pepper. Stir and cook, covered, for 5 minutes, stirring or shaking the pot occasionally. Add the crushed tomatoes, pumpkin, octopus, the water, and salt, and boil for 20 minutes. Add the chickpeas and continue cooking until the stew is thick and everything is tender, 45 minutes to 1¼ hours. Serve immediately.

MAKES 4 SERVINGS

Sea Bream en Papillote

En papillote is the French term for wrapping foods in parchment paper for steaming. In the West African nation of the Ivory Coast, this method of cooking fish uses banana leaf for wrapping the fish, which may be cooked on an open fire. In West Africa a common fish is gilt-head bream, what the former colonial rulers, the French, call *daurade*. In North America, the fish closest in taste would be a porgy (scup), but redfish and red snapper work very well, too. This recipe comes from the southern portion of the Ivory Coast and is known as *bikosso*, while in the Congo it is known as *mamboke*. The whole fish is deeply scored through the backbone but kept attached so it does not separate into separate steaks. The distinctive red palm oil that makes African cooking so wonderful is worth ordering via the Internet. Serve with rice or yams.

4 whole cleaned *daurade* (gilt-head bream), porgies, redfish, or red snapper (about 1¼ pounds each)

2 medium-size onions, finely chopped

4 large garlic cloves, finely chopped

1 small bunch fresh parsley, leaves only, finely chopped

2 habanero chiles, seeded and finely chopped

Zest from 1 green (unripe) lemon or ripe lemon

¼ teaspoon ground nutmeg

3 tablespoons red palm oil *or* 3 tablespoons walnut oil mixed with ⅛ teaspoon hot paprika

4 sheets aluminum foil, almost twice as long as the fish

Juice from 2 lemons

Salt and freshly ground black pepper to taste

1. Cut the fish into 1-inch-thick steaks, making sure that you don't go all the way through the backbone, and turn them into separate steaks. In a bowl, toss the onions, garlic, parsley, chiles, lemon zest, nutmeg, and red palm oil together.

2. Place a fish on each piece of aluminum foil. Divide the onion-garlic mixture among the fish, pushing the mixture into the cuts. Squeeze the lemon juice over the fish. Season with salt and pepper. Wrap the fish up and crimp the aluminum foil tightly, making sure the foil is not punctured.

3. Preheat the oven to 350°F. Place the fish packets in one or two baking dishes and bake until the fish flakes, 45 minutes. Serve immediately.

MAKES 4 SERVINGS

Shrimp and Eggplant in Spicy Sauce

The cooking of Ghana in West Africa consists mostly of stewing, and nearly everything is eaten with fufu, made from pounded plantains, cassava, or African yams. This wickedly hot shrimp stew could also be accompanied by *banku*, a fermented corn dough that, when boiled, becomes *kenkey*, a kind of West African tamale. This spicy sauce is called *sesew-froi* in Ghana. It can be served with rice or *Fufu* (page 393).

1 large eggplant (about 1¹/₂ pounds), peeled and cut into 1-inch cubes

1¹/₂ teaspoons salt

1 pound ripe tomatoes, peeled and coarsely chopped

10 scallions, coarsely chopped

2 habanero chiles

2 fresh green serrano chiles

2 tablespoons peanut oil

1 cup fish or shrimp broth (homemade or canned) or clam juice (fresh or bottled)

¹/₂ teaspoon ground ginger

2 tablespoons tomato paste

¹/₄ cup finely chopped fresh parsley leaves

2 pounds fresh shrimp with their heads *or* 1 pound headless shrimp, heads and/or shells removed

1. Place the eggplant in a medium-size saucepan, add water to cover, and add 1 teaspoon of the salt. Bring to a boil over high heat and cook until the eggplant is tender, about 10 minutes. Drain and set aside.

2. In a blender, puree the tomatoes, scallions, and habanero and serrano chiles until completely smooth.

3. In a large, heavy casserole, heat the peanut oil over medium heat, then add the vegetable puree and cook until dense, about 10 minutes, stirring frequently. Add the fish broth, bring to a boil, then reduce the heat to low and simmer, covered, for 10 minutes, stirring occasionally. Add the remaining ¹/₂ teaspoon salt, the ginger, tomato paste, parsley, shrimp, and reserved eggplant. Stir and continue simmering until the shrimp are firm and orange-red, 10 minutes. Serve immediately.

MAKES 4 SERVINGS

sassy seafood

Grilled Shrimp with Piri-Piri Sauce

This fantastically hot shrimp dish from Mozambique is made with *piri-piri*, a word that comes from Portuguese Africa and refers to a very hot red chile sauce. This preparation of grilled shrimp is still known there by its Portuguese name, *camarão grelhado piripiri*. Some people think that the Ethiopian spice mix known as *Berbere* (page 417) is a corruption of *piri-piri*. *Piri-piri*'s home is truly Mozambique where they eat it in what some would call excess. Some Mozambiquan versions use only lemon juice. Versions from West Africa use tomatoes and sometimes red wine. This preparation can also be poached in water and lemon juice, but I think grilled is too spectacular to pass up. Grilled shrimp with fiery sauces are popular in coastal Africa. For instance, a dish from Cameroon is made by grilling skewered prawns over a hardwood fire made with aromatic woods and dipping them in a peanut sauce seasoned with wild herbs, chopped onions, and lots of ground red chile. The very name of the nation of Cameroon derives from "shrimp," which are so abundant in its coastal waters, coming from the Spanish and Portuguese words for shrimp, *camaron* and *camarão*, respectively. The colossal shrimp called for in this recipe have about 12 headless shrimp to a pound. Buy the largest shrimp available.

2 habanero chiles

5 red long finger-type chiles or 7 red jalapeño chiles or 4 red cherry or cascabel chiles

2 tablespoons ground red chile or cayenne pepper

1 tablespoon hot paprika

4 large garlic cloves

³/₄ cup peanut oil

3 tablespoons fresh lemon juice

2 teaspoons salt

4 pounds fresh colossal shrimp with their heads, heads left on and shells removed, or 2 pounds headless shrimp, shells removed and saved for making broth

6 tablespoons unsalted butter, melted

3 tablespoons fresh lemon juice

Six 10-inch-long wooden skewers

1.   Place the habanero chiles, other red chiles, paprika, garlic, peanut oil, lemon juice, and salt in a blender and blend until smooth. Transfer to a bowl, mix the shrimp into the sauce, and leave to marinate in the refrigerator for 4 to 6 hours.

2. Prepare a hot charcoal fire or preheat a gas grill on high for 15 minutes. In a small bowl, stir the butter and lemon juice together. Skewer the shrimp in two places lengthwise, 4 shrimp per skewer, making sure they don't touch each other. Grill 3 inches from the fire until slightly blackened, firm, and orange-pink, 4 to 8 minutes in all, turning once. Remove from the grill, arrange on a serving platter, and pour the lemon butter over the shrimp. Serve hot.

MAKES 4 SERVINGS

 # Bengali Fish Stew

West Bengal is part of India and East Bengal is Bangladesh. In both Bengals fish is extremely popular and in both Bengals the most famous dishes are fish dishes. Although there are a variety of styles of cooking fish in Bengal, the two main ones are cooking fish in spices and cooking fish in yogurt. In West Bengal mustard oil is used prominently as a cooking fat, while in Bangladesh coconut oil is more common. Two of the most popular fish used in this preparation, called *machher jhol*, are *rohu* and pomfret. Many cooks also add two vegetables to the stew, such as potatoes and eggplants in small dice. Serve with rice.

Salt to taste

1/2 teaspoon ground turmeric

1 teaspoon hot paprika

1 1/4 pounds sea bass, cod, or halibut steaks, cut into 2-inch cubes

3 tablespoons mustard oil or vegetable oil

3 large onions, finely chopped

4 large garlic cloves, crushed

4 fresh green finger-type chiles or 6 green jalapeño chiles, seeded and finely chopped

1/4 teaspoon ground cumin

1/4 teaspoon mustard seeds

1/8 teaspoon ground cinnamon

1/8 teaspoon ground cloves

1/8 teaspoon ground cardamom

1 1/2 pounds ripe tomatoes, cut in half, seeds squeezed out, and grated against the largest holes of a grater

1 tablespoon fresh coriander (cilantro) leaves, chopped

1/4 cup water

1/2 cup whole plain yogurt or Stabilized Yogurt (page 278)

the cuisine of bengal

The *Dakarnava* (a tantric Buddhist work), the *Daker-Vachana*, and the *Khanar Vachana* are all works of the earliest Bengali literature of the tenth and eleventh centuries and are full of aphorisms indicating the abundance of produce derived from good agriculture. Though rice is a staple food throughout Bengal, there are two distinct styles of cooking. Both styles of Bengali cuisine differ in the choice of spices used and the way in which dishes are prepared. East Bengali food is exemplified by the cuisines of Chittagong and Dhaka, where there is a greater emphasis on fish and a smaller one on dal than elsewhere in India. The food of West Bengal, as in Calcutta or the Pargagas, is distinguished by the liberal use of poppy seeds. Mustard is used in three ways: oil is used to fry foods, seeds are crushed to yield a piquant spice, and greens are used as a cooked vegetable. Fish and prawns are common in both cuisines, although East Bengalis prefer fish from big rivers and West Bengalis prefer farm-raised fish, estuary fish, or the river fish called *hilsa*, which is a favorite. This fish is oily like mackerel or salmon and even releases a lot of oil when fried.

1.　Mix the salt, $^1/_4$ teaspoon of the turmeric, and the paprika on a plate. Dredge the fish steaks on both sides in the mixture. In a large skillet, heat the mustard oil over medium-high heat and brown the fish on both sides, about 3 minutes in all, turning once. Remove and set aside.

2.　Add the onions and garlic to the skillet and cook until soft and yellow, about 15 minutes, stirring frequently. Add the chiles, cumin, mustard seeds, cinnamon, cloves, cardamom, and the remaining $^1/_4$ teaspoon turmeric. Cook for 2 minutes, stirring, then add the tomatoes, coriander leaves, and water. Reduce the heat to low and cook until the sauce is dense, about 15 minutes. Add the yogurt and salt to taste and stir to blend. Return the fish to the skillet, cover, and simmer until the fish flakes, about 10 minutes. Make sure that the broth never becomes too hot or the yogurt might separate, unless you are using Stabilized Yogurt. Serve immediately.

MAKES 4 SERVINGS

Fiery Fish and Yogurt Stew

This Bengali dish is called *dohi machh*, which means "yogurt stew." It is much hotter than the previous recipe, and you will find it delightful accompanied by basmati rice. Bengali cooks like to use a prized freshwater carp called *rui* or *rohu* for this dish. Remember too that the yogurt should not come to a boil, only be heated through; otherwise it will separate. Serve with Rice Pilaf (page 396).

2 medium-size red onions, 1 coarsely chopped, 1 thinly sliced

6 large garlic cloves, coarsely chopped

One 1½-inch cube fresh ginger, peeled and coarsely chopped

1½ cups water

1½ teaspoons salt, or more to your taste

½ teaspoon ground turmeric

1½ pounds halibut, cod, or carp steaks, cut into 6 portions

2 cups whole plain yogurt or Stabilized Yogurt (page 278)

5 tablespoons mustard oil or vegetable oil

Seeds from 5 cardamom pods

5 whole cloves

½ cinnamon stick

3 bay leaves

1 teaspoon cayenne pepper

4 dried red de arbol chiles

6 fresh green finger-type chiles or 8 green jalapeño chiles, seeded and chopped

1. Place the chopped onion, garlic, and ginger in a blender with ½ cup of the water and blend until smooth and frothy. Set aside. Mix ½ teaspoon of the salt and the turmeric on a plate. Rub the fish pieces on all sides with the spices and set aside. In a small bowl, beat the remaining 1 cup water into the yogurt.

2. In a large wok or casserole, heat 4 tablespoons of the mustard oil over high heat. Cook the fish on both sides until lightly browned, about 3 minutes, turning once with a spatula. Remove and set aside.

3. Add the remaining 1 tablespoon mustard oil to the wok and heat over medium heat. Add the cardamom seeds, cloves, cinnamon, and bay leaves and cook for 30 seconds, stirring. Add the sliced onion and cook until lightly browned, 3 to 4 minutes, stirring. Add the reserved onion and garlic paste, the cayenne pepper, and the remaining 1 teaspoon salt. Cook until the sauce turns a reddish brown color, 4 to 7 minutes, stirring. Remove from the heat and cool for 10 minutes.

4. Add the yogurt to the wok and set over low heat, stirring a bit so it blends. Add the fish and the green and red chiles, and stir very gently to mix. Simmer gently until the fish is cooked through, 10 to 15 minutes, spooning the sauce over the fish as it cooks. Do not let the yogurt come to a boil or it will separate, unless you are using stabilized yogurt. Serve immediately.

MAKES 6 SERVINGS

strained yogurt and stabilized yogurt

Strained yogurt is just that. It's yogurt that is placed in a cheesecloth-lined strainer and drained of its liquid over a 24-hour period until it is a thick cheeselike spread. It is used in cooking and makes a delicious snack. Strained yogurt is very popular in the Arab world, where it is known as *labna*, *lubny*, or *lubany*.

Stabilized yogurt is yogurt that is cooked for several minutes. Sometimes this is necessary before using cow's milk yogurt in cooking, because otherwise it will separate if heated beyond a certain point.

1 quart whole plain yogurt

1 large egg white, beaten

1 tablespoon cornstarch

1 teaspoon salt

In a saucepan, beat the yogurt with a fork until smooth, then beat in the egg white, cornstarch, and salt. Put the saucepan over high heat and start stirring in one direction with a wooden spoon. As soon as it starts to bubble, after about 6 minutes, reduce the heat to medium and boil gently until it is thick, about 5 minutes. Set aside until needed. Stabilized yogurt will keep in the refrigerator for up to 3 weeks.

MAKES 1 QUART

Goan Fish Curry

There are many dishes described as "fish curry" from Goa, from Bengal, and elsewhere and they can always be different. This preparation from Goa is unique because you make the coconut milk by spicing the coconut, then putting the spiced coconut shavings in a blender. Although Goan food is considered simple, it shows influences of the Portuguese, who made it a colony from 1511 until India reclaimed it in 1961. Goan food is also very, very hot, of that there is no doubt. Halibut has a rather heavy bone and therefore 2 pounds will serve four people. This dish can also be made with shrimp.

4 halibut or cod steaks (about 2 pounds)

1 medium-size onion, thinly sliced

4 fresh green finger-type chiles or 5 green jalapeño chiles, seeded and julienned lengthwise

Salt to taste

2 cups tightly packed fresh or dried shredded unsweetened coconut

6 large garlic cloves

One $1/2$-inch cube fresh ginger, peeled

8 dried red de arbol chiles, seeded

1 tablespoon coriander seeds

$1^1/_2$ teaspoons cumin seeds

4 black peppercorns

$1/2$ teaspoon ground turmeric

$3^1/_2$ cups warm water

2 tablespoons tamarind paste (see page 329)

1. Wash the fish, then pat dry with paper towels and place in a bowl. Toss with the onion, green chiles, and salt. Set aside in the refrigerator.

2. In a large bowl, combine the coconut, garlic, ginger, red chiles, coriander seeds, cumin seeds, peppercorns, turmeric, and 3 cups of the water. Blend this mixture in a blender, in batches if necessary, until smooth.

3. Pour the liquid through a strainer into a bowl, squeezing as much liquid as you can out of the coconut mixture with the back of a wooden spoon. Put the mixture back into the blender with the remaining $1/2$ cup water and blend again for 1 minute. Strain the liquid again, pressing as much liquid out as you can.

4. Pour the coconut milk into a deep pan or casserole. Cook over medium heat, stirring occasionally until thicker, 30 minutes. Add the tamarind paste and cook for 1 or 2 minutes while it softens. Add the fish and cook until it begins to flake, about 12 minutes, turning once or twice. If the sauce is evaporating before the fish is fully cooked, cover and add a little water. Serve immediately.

MAKES 4 SERVINGS

sassy seafood

Blistering Hot Shrimp with Tomatoes

Sometime between A.D. 750 and 850, a group of Persians who practiced Zoroastrianism fled from Muslim persecution to Hormuz on the Persian Gulf, and then to the island of Diu off Gujarat in western India. They became known as Parsis and formed a thriving mercantile community mostly around Mumbai, formerly Bombay, and a little north. The cooking of the Parsis is a blend of Persian and Gujarati. This Parsi dish is called *jhinga patia*, which means something like "shrimp preparation" in Gujarati, the language spoken by Parsis. The one thing you should remember about Parsi cooking is that the Parsis like very, very hot food. This recipe calls for extra-colossal shrimp that are about 8 to the pound of headless shrimp. If you can't find them, then use the largest shrimp available at the market. This dish is delicious with plain Rice Pilaf (page 396).

¹/₄ cup fresh lemon juice

¹/₃ cup apple cider vinegar

1 teaspoon ground cumin

1 teaspoon ground turmeric

¹/₂ teaspoon ground red chile or cayenne pepper

¹/₂ teaspoon freshly ground black pepper

4 teaspoons salt

2 pounds fresh extra-colossal shrimp, heads and shells removed, or 1 pound headless extra-colossal shrimp, shells removed

¹/₄ cup vegetable oil

1 teaspoon black mustard seeds

2 tablespoons finely chopped fresh ginger

1 tablespoon finely chopped garlic

1 cup finely chopped onions

1³/₄ pounds tomatoes, peeled, seeded, and coarsely chopped

2 tablespoons palm sugar or brown sugar

3 tablespoons finely chopped fresh coriander (cilantro) leaves

3 tablespoons finely chopped habanero chiles or fresh bird's-eye chiles

1. In a large bowl, combine the lemon juice, vinegar, cumin, turmeric, ground red chile, black pepper, and 3 teaspoons of the salt, stirring until blended. Marinate the shrimp in this mixture for 30 minutes at room temperature, turning the shrimp occasionally.

2. In a large skillet, heat the vegetable oil over medium heat until a light haze forms, then add the mustard seeds, shake the skillet, and immediately add the ginger, garlic, onions, and the remaining 1 teaspoon salt. Cook the onions until light golden and soft, 7 to 8 minutes, stirring occasionally.

3. Add the tomatoes and cook for 4 minutes. Add the palm sugar and coriander and cook for another 4 minutes, stirring. Add the chiles and cook for 1 minute. Remove the shrimp from the marinade and add to the skillet, turning in the sauce until coated on all sides. Continue to cook over medium heat until the shrimp are quite firm and pink-orange, 8 to 10 minutes. (Extra-colossal shrimp take longer to cook than you expect because they are so big. Adjust the cooking time downward if you are using smaller shrimp.) Serve immediately.

MAKES 4 SERVINGS

the soul of gujarati cuisine

There were two powerful influences behind the movement to vegetarianism in the Indian state of Gujarat. The first was the influence of Jainism, through the teachings of Mahavira before the sixth century A.D. Jainism arose as a religion as a protest against Hinduism. The central doctrine of Jainism is that everything in the universe, including matter, is eternal and that spirits retain consciousness of identity through incarnations. The second great influence was in the fifteenth century when Vaishnavaism, which promotes vegetarianism, became popular through the teachings of Vallabhacharya, who formed the Pusti-Marga sect. Today, Gujarat has the highest proportion of vegetarians in India, about 70 percent of the local population.

the piquant cuisine of thailand

The beginnings of Thai cuisine are to be found in the steep mountain valleys of Yunnan province in China. In Yunnan, about the time of the Han dynasty (first century A.D.), tribes known as the T'ai began to emigrate south into today's Thailand. Modern Thais date the beginning of the Thai nation to 1238, when the independent kingdom of Sukhothai Syam was established.

Thailand is a country entirely in the tropics and a country that was never ruled by any European power. These two geographical and historical attributes have determined to some extent the context of Thai cuisine. At the same time, Thailand has never been an insular country, so it adopts outside ideas and influences. Several historically important culinary influences were Hindu influences from India, especially the curries, and influences from China, Burma, and Vietnam. Later there were Muslim influences from India, especially the use of dried spices. As in so many culinary cultures, there developed a more formal palace cuisine that contrasted with peasant cooking.

There are four main regional cuisines in Thailand. Central Thailand, where Bangkok is the capital, is an extremely fertile area and considered to be the home of classic Thai cooking. Northern Thailand is mountainous with little agriculture. They like their rice sticky in the north, unlike the south. A variety of chile pastes are essential to northern Thai cuisine. The first is called *nam prik num*, or young chile paste, made by pounding together fresh green chiles with roasted eggplant. The second is called *nam prik awng* and is made by pounding dried red chiles, ground pork, tomatoes, lemongrass, and various other herbs into a paste. The third chile paste is *nam prik puu*, which is a curious chile paste made by pounding small field crabs into a paste and then cooking the paste in water until it becomes a slightly sticky black liquid and then mixing it with shallots, chiles, and garlic. The third regional cuisine, which has hot food, too, is Northeast Thailand or Issaan, which is also Thailand's poorest region. The fourth region is the South, where it is said one finds Thailand's hottest cuisine.

In both northern and southern Thai cooking, a central concept is the balance of flavors, a concept that characterizes Chinese cooking as well. Peasant cooking is characterized as being more piquant than palace cooking. It seems likely that the already piquant cuisines of Sichuan and Yunnan were a major reason why contemporary Thai cuisine tends to be hot and spicy. It's possible that a plant today called "jungle chile" was used as a pungent spice before the introduction of the chile. There is no doubt, though, that ginger and black pepper, especially in its green berry form, were two of the pungent spices used in Thai cooking before the chile.

It is not known exactly when the chile arrived in Thailand, but it seems likely that it was more or less the same time as its arrival in the Indo-Malaysian archipelago, by virtue of Portuguese traders from India. It is possible that the chile found its way to Thailand from the other direction, with Spanish galleons coming across the Pacific from Acapulco to Manila. The chiles of Thailand, *prik kee nu*, mouse-dropping chile, and *prik kee fa*, sky-pointing chile, being the two most important ones, are native to South America, while the third Thai chile, *prik yuak*, banana-stalk chile, seems to be originally from Mexico. But unlike Mexico, where there are perhaps 90 different cultivars, Thailand only grows about a dozen, of which only the three above truly predominate in the cuisine.

Although their food is very spicy-hot, Thais don't eat huge quantities of chile-flavored food. Small amounts of very spicy-hot food are eaten with huge amounts of rice.

Stir-Fried Catfish Dry Curry with Chiles and Ginger

Pad cha is a "dry" curry, which means that no broth is used. This preparation can be made with small cubes of fried catfish or it can be made with mixed fish, such as swordfish, yellowtail, and mahimahi. The fish is cooked quickly first and then the other ingredients are stir-fried before the fish returns to the wok to finish cooking. Garnished with either Thai basil or coriander, it is excellent with steamed rice.

3 tablespoons peanut oil or vegetable oil

1 pound catfish fillets or mixed firm-fleshed fish, cut into small cubes

1 tablespoon green peppercorns

15 fresh green Thai chiles, stemmed and halved lengthwise, or 6 fresh green serrano chiles, stemmed and quartered lengthwise

1^1/$_2$ tablespoons finely chopped fresh ginger

4 large garlic cloves, finely chopped

1 teaspoon freshly ground white pepper

2 shallots, thinly sliced

2 tablespoons coarsely chopped fresh basil or coriander (cilantro) leaves

1. In a large wok, heat the peanut oil over high heat and, once it is smoking, cook the fish (in 2 batches if your wok is small) until crispy, 3 to 4 minutes. Remove the fish from the oil with a slotted spoon and set aside, keeping warm.

2. Add the peppercorns, chiles, ginger, garlic, white pepper, and shallots to the wok and cook until softened and some liquid has evaporated, 4 to 5 minutes. Add the basil, cook 1 more minute, and pour over the reserved fish. Serve immediately.

MAKES 4 SERVINGS

the three basils of thailand

Thai cooks use three kinds of basil in their cooking. The three types are Thai sweet basil, called *bai horapha* in Thai, with small flat green leaves with pointy tips; lemon basil, called *bai mangluk*, with light green leaves and a distinct lemony flavor; and holy basil, called *bai kaprow*, with a distinctive violet shade to the leaves and stems and a zesty flavor. They can be found in Thai or Asian markets if there are any in your area; otherwise, use regular basil in the recipes.

Fish with
Red Curry Sauce

This delicious preparation from the central region of Thailand is adapted from Chat Mingkwan's *The Best of Regional Thai Cuisine* (Hippocrene, 2002) and is best made with a fish that can hold up to some vigorous cooking, ideally catfish, but monkfish or red snapper should work well. I like this preparation because it is quick to make and ideal for a cook who has had a harried day. This Thai curry is an example of a "wet" curry, contrasted with "dry" curries such as the previous recipe, Stir-Fried Catfish Dry Curry with Chiles and Ginger. Thai red curry paste can either be homemade or store bought. Kaffir lime leaves are sold in Thai markets or via the Internet. You can also try using lime zest or, if you have access to a lemon tree, lemon leaves. Serve with steamed rice.

2 cups coconut milk

20 dried red bird's-eye chiles or 5 dried red de arbol chiles

3 tablespoons Red Curry Paste (page 423)

1/4 cup Thai fish sauce

2 tablespoons palm sugar or granulated sugar

1 pound catfish, monkfish, or red snapper fillets, cut into bite-size pieces

2 tablespoons green peppercorns

1 cup shredded bamboo shoots, drained

FOR THE GARNISH

3 kaffir lime leaves, stacked, rolled into a cigarette shape, and very thinly sliced, or 2 teaspoons lime zest

2 tablespoons finely chopped fresh red Thai chiles or any fresh red chile

1/2 cup coarsely chopped fresh basil leaves

1. In a large wok, heat 1/2 cup of the coconut milk over medium heat, then stir in the dried red chiles and red curry paste and stir until it is blended and fragrant, about 3 minutes.

2. Add the remaining 1 1/2 cups coconut milk, the fish sauce, and sugar and bring to a boil over high heat. Add the fish, green peppercorns, and bamboo shoots and simmer until the fish is cooked through, about 8 minutes. The sauce should be somewhat thickened by now (but still soupy). If it isn't, remove the fish and bamboo shoots with a skimmer and set aside while you reduce the liquid a bit, then return the fish to the wok.

3. Arrange the fish on a shallow serving platter and ladle the sauce over it. Garnish with the lime leaves, fresh chile, and basil. Serve immediately.

MAKES 4 SERVINGS

The Drunkard's Deep-Fried Fish in Garlic Sauce

Although in Chinese cuisine "drunken" dishes refer to those that are marinated in alcohol, in Thai cuisine "drunken" dishes refers to the idea that they are eaten by drunks, those revelers who believe that the dish will "line the stomach" so you can drink more alcohol. This preparation is called *pla kapong kimao*, *kimao* meaning "drunk" in Thai. The recipe calls for whole fish, and a 1-pound fish such as a red snapper would be ideal. You can use whatever is available, but leave the head and tail on and have the fishmonger scale and clean it.

It may seem tricky to deep-fry a whole fish, and it is. Care must be paid to the whole process, especially the vessel you'll cook the fish in and the instructions for turning the fish so that you don't splash hot oil. A wok works wonderfully for frying a whole fish. A wide skillet can be used if you don't have a wok. Some Thai cooks use tapioca starch instead of flour to coat the fish, believing that it clings to the fish better.

8 large garlic cloves, finely chopped

25 fresh green Thai chiles or 10 fresh green serrano chiles or 7 fresh green jalapeño chiles, coarsely chopped

25 fresh red Thai chiles or 10 fresh red serrano chiles or 7 fresh red jalapeño chiles, coarsely chopped

3 scallions, thinly sliced

1/4 cup chopped fresh coriander (cilantro) leaves and/or stems and roots

1/3 cup Thai fish sauce

3 tablespoons palm sugar or granulated sugar

3 tablespoons fresh lime juice

1 teaspoon freshly ground black pepper

4 to 6 cups peanut oil or vegetable oil for frying

Four 1-pound whole cleaned fish such as red snapper

All-purpose flour, for dredging

3 tablespoons peanut oil

6 kaffir lime leaves, thinly sliced, or 1 tablespoon lime zest

1/4 cup chopped fresh basil leaves

1. In a bowl, toss together the garlic, green and red chiles, scallions, coriander, fish sauce, sugar, lime juice, and black pepper.

2. Preheat the frying oil to 325°F in a deep-fryer or wok. Preheat the oven to "warm." Score each fish in three places on both sides. Dredge well in the flour, including the body cavities, and pat off any excess. Cook the fish one at a time until crispy, 8 to 9 minutes. Remove from the oil and place on an ovenproof serving platter, keeping warm in the oven while you cook the remaining fish.

3. As you begin to cook the last fish, heat the 3 tablespoons peanut oil over medium heat in a wok or skillet, then add the chile mixture and cook, stirring continuously, for 3 minutes. Add the lime leaves and basil and continue to cook for 2 minutes. Remove from the heat. Pour the sauce over the fish and serve immediately.

MAKES 4 SERVINGS

 # Redfish with Green Chile and Coriander-Tamarind Sauce

Most travelers report on the extraordinary heights that Thai fish cookery reaches. But there is no mystery because it all rests upon very, very fresh seafood. This recipe, called *pla tort sahm rot*, is adapted from David Thompson's *Classic Thai Cuisine* (Ten Speed Press, 1993). He first encountered it at Hua Hin, a resort town about three hours south of Bangkok that is highly regarded for its cooking and for the seafood that comes to shore within sight of the restaurant where he first ate it. Ideally, you will want to use two 1- to 1½-pound fish, so you will be at the mercy of your local market. Best bets are red snapper, porgies, ocean perch (also known as redfish), and striped bass.

12 large garlic cloves, chopped

12 fresh green finger-type chiles or 14 green jalapeño chiles, chopped

½ cup chopped fresh coriander (cilantro) leaves

2 teaspoons salt

6 to 8 cups safflower or peanut oil, for frying

2 whole cleaned 1½-pound redfish, rockfish, or red snapper, washed and dried with paper towels

All-purpose flour, for dredging

6 tablespoons palm sugar or granulated sugar

¼ cup tamarind water (see page 329)

¼ cup Thai fish sauce

½ cup water

Leaves from 8 leafy sprigs fresh coriander (cilantro), for garnish

1. Place the garlic, chiles, coriander, and salt in a food processor and process until very finely chopped. Transfer to a mortar and pound until mushy.

2. Preheat the frying oil to 325°F in a deep-fryer or an 8-inch saucepan fitted with a basket insert. Dredge each fish in flour, patting off any excess, and fry one at a time until crispy on both sides, 12 to 15 minutes per fish. Set aside on a platter and keep warm.

3. In a medium-size skillet, heat 2 tablespoons of oil from the deep-fryer over medium-high heat, then cook the contents of the mortar until sizzling and fragrant, about 3 minutes, stirring. Add the sugar, tamarind water, fish sauce, and water, reduce the heat to medium, and cook until saucy, about 4 minutes, stirring. Pour the sauce over the fish and garnish with the coriander. Serve immediately.

MAKES 4 SERVINGS

Shrimp Hash in Coconut Cream

This intriguing recipe called *lon gung* is adapted from a recipe published in 1926 and ascribed to Mom Luang Yingdin Clamarakpitjan, which was discovered by David Thompson, author of several important books on Thai food. The final dish should be creamy, slightly sour, salty, a little sweet, and fiery hot. This is a rich dish that is best served as a main course with some rice.

1 1/2 cups coconut milk (see page 90)

1/4 teaspoon salt

6 ounces uncooked shrimp, very finely chopped

2 tablespoons palm sugar or granulated sugar

2 tablespoons tamarind water (see page 329)

1 tablespoon Thai fish sauce

1/2 small green mango, julienned

4 shallots, thinly sliced

8 fresh green finger-type chiles or 10 green jalapeño chiles, julienned lengthwise in 1/2-inch lengths

2 tablespoons coarsely chopped coriander (cilantro) leaves

In a saucepan, bring the coconut milk and salt to a boil, then add the shrimp and cook until firm and orange, about 3 minutes, stirring constantly to break up the clumped shrimp pieces. Add the sugar, tamarind water, fish sauce, mango, shallots, and chiles and cook until boiling again, about 3 minutes. Sprinkle with coriander leaves and serve.

MAKES 4 TO 6 SERVINGS

Bicol Express

Bicol, on the southern portion of the island of Luzon, is the only region in the Philippines whose culinary culture fits the definition of piquant as described in this book. Filipino cuisine is otherwise not spicy-hot at all. This unusually named dish is a mixture of chiles with bits of meat or fish and other spices simmered in coconut cream (*gata*). Naga City is one of the provinces in the Bicol region and home of Bicol Express. In Legazpi this dish is extremely spicy, and one glance at the finished dish with its huge amount of red and green chiles is quite alarming. This recipe is adapted from *Celebrity Recipes plus Home and Garden* magazine, published in the Philippines. It is best accompanied with plain white rice. All of the slivered chiles called for in the ingredients list should amount to 4 cups. Fresh bacon (pork belly) is usually available at Asian markets. If you are unable to find it you can use regular bacon, previously blanched in boiling water for 5 minutes.

22 red jalapeño chiles or 30 red serrano chiles, sliced into 1/4-inch slivers

22 green jalapeño chiles or 30 red serrano chiles, sliced into 1/4-inch slivers

1 tablespoon salt, or more to your taste

2 cups coconut milk (see page 90)

1/2 pound fresh pork belly or blanched bacon, diced or sliced

3 large garlic cloves, finely chopped

2 shallots, chopped

1/2 teaspoon ground turmeric

1 tablespoon finely chopped fresh ginger

1/4 teaspoon shrimp paste

Freshly ground black pepper to taste

1 cup coconut cream (see page 90)

2 pounds fresh shrimp with their heads or 1 pound headless shrimp, heads and/or shells removed

1.   Place the chiles in a large bowl of water with 1 tablespoon salt. Let stand for 30 minutes, then drain and rinse and drain again.

2. In a large wok or skillet, combine the coconut milk with the pork, garlic, shallots, turmeric, ginger, shrimp paste, salt to taste, and pepper and bring to a boil. Reduce the heat to low and simmer for 10 minutes. Add the chiles, increase the heat to medium, and cook until half of the liquid has evaporated, about 15 minutes. Pour in the coconut cream and continue cooking until oil begins to come out from the cream, about 5 minutes, then add the shrimp and cook until pink-orange and firm, about 3 minutes. Serve immediately.

MAKES 4 SERVINGS

Spicy Fish with Black Bean Sauce

There aren't many fish recipes from Sichuan because of its isolation from the coast. Most of the fish that is eaten is either lake or river fish. But this is one dish that uses fresh saltwater fish, namely the pomfret, a prized fish in the South China Sea. Pomfret can be found in fish stores on the West Coast of North America, while on the East Coast you could replace pomfret with butterfish or pompano. The caul fat used in this recipe is always available in Chinese markets, at good butchers, and, if you order it, in supermarkets. Many supermarkets that make their own sausages will also carry it. Serve with Stir-Fried Hot Bok Choy (page 382) or steamed rice.

---

4 whole cleaned pomfret (about 2¹/₂ pounds in all) or other small fish, scored in 3 places on both sides

1 tablespoon rice wine (*mirin*) or vermouth

1 to 2 teaspoons salt, to your taste

1 scallion, very finely chopped

3 tablespoons red chile flakes

3 tablespoons fermented black bean paste (see page 431)

2¹/₂ tablespoons finely chopped fresh ginger

2 tablespoons soy sauce

2 tablespoons finely chopped pork fat or pork caul fat

¹/₄ pound pork caul fat, unraveled carefully

---

1. Place the fish in a large skillet or fish poacher, just barely cover with water, and bring to a very gentle boil, then turn the heat off.

2. Remove the fish from the skillet and transfer to a large glass baking dish, sprinkle with the rice wine and salt, cover with plastic wrap, and marinate for 1 hour in the refrigerator. Reserve the liquid in the skillet.

3. In a small bowl, stir together the scallion, red chile flakes, fermented black bean paste, ginger, soy sauce, and pork fat. Spread the mixture over the surface of the fish. Carefully unravel the caul fat into 4 approximately 8-inch squares and arrange them on a work surface. Lay each seasoned fish over a piece of caul fat and fold the sides over to encase the seasoning.

4. Place the fish back in the skillet, stuffing side up, with the reserved liquid from the first poaching, making sure the liquid does not go more than halfway up the sides of the fish. Turn the heat to high and steam until the caul fat has melted and the fish is cooked through, about 8 minutes. Transfer the fish to individual plates or a serving platter and spoon the sauce over the fish. Serve immediately.

MAKES 4 SERVINGS

Fish with Chiles and Sichuan Peppercorns

The insane use of chiles and Sichuan peppercorns, as in this recipe, is a hallmark of the cooking of Chongqing, Sichuan's second city. Not much fish is eaten in this inland province, and those fish that are eaten are usually freshwater fish such as carp. When you eat this dish, you should pull the fish out of the fragrant oil it swims in with your chopsticks; don't eat the oil, or the chile and spices. The ingredients list calls for a quarter pound of dried chiles—that's a lot of chiles, so be prepared. You will soon see why a bland-tasting whitefish is perfect for this dish. Serve with steamed rice.

1¼ pounds carp, whitefish, or bass fillet, cut into ½-inch-thick slices

6 scallions, white and green parts, crushed with the side of a chef's knife or cleaver and cut into 2-inch pieces

Two 1-inch cubes fresh ginger, 1 peeled and crushed, 1 peeled and thinly sliced

2 teaspoons rice wine (*mirin*) or vermouth

½ teaspoon salt

1 cup peanut oil

2½ tablespoons Sichuan chile bean paste (see page 98)

3 large garlic cloves, thinly sliced

¼ pound dried red de arbol chiles, seeded and broken in half

2½ teaspoons Sichuan peppercorns, ½ teaspoon crushed, 2 teaspoons whole

¼ cup cornstarch mixed with 3 tablespoons cold water

1. Place the fish slices in a large glass or ceramic bowl and toss with 1 of the scallions, the crushed ginger, wine, and salt. Marinate in the refrigerator for 1 hour.

2. In a wok, heat ¼ cup of the peanut oil over high heat, swirling to coat the sides. As it begins to smoke, reduce the heat to medium-high, then add 1 tablespoon of the chile bean paste and stir-fry until it is red and fragrant, about 30 seconds. Add the sliced ginger, the remaining 5 scallions, the garlic, 6 dried chiles, and the ½ teaspoon crushed Sichuan peppercorns, and continue to fry until the scallions are soft, 3 to 4 minutes, tossing and stirring frequently. Remove to a deep serving bowl.

3. Bring a large pot of water to a boil. Discard the ginger and scallion from the fish marinade. Add the cornstarch-water mixture to the fish and toss well to coat. Drop the fish slices in the boiling water and do not stir. Let the water return to a boil. When the fish slices are just cooked, 1 to 2 minutes after the water has returned to a boil, remove them with a slotted spoon or skimmer and transfer them to the serving bowl.

4. Pour the remaining ¾ cup of peanut oil in the wok and heat over high heat until it is beginning to smoke, then add the remaining 1½ tablespoons of the chile bean paste and stir-fry until sizzling vigorously, about 30 seconds. Add the remaining chiles and the remaining Sichuan peppercorns and stir-fry until they are crisp and darker, reducing the heat if necessary to keep them from burning, about 2 minutes. The longer you cook them the more fragrant they will be. Pour the oil with the chiles over the fish and serve immediately, while the ingredients are still sizzling.

MAKES 4 SERVINGS

Batter-Fried Spicy Shrimp

Shrimp is not found often on the Sichuanese table, but this preparation called *laht sha* is unique to Sichuan. The shrimp is cooked twice: first it is batter-fried, then stir-fried in a spicy sauce. It's one of the most wonderful shrimp dishes you'll ever have, and it will be all the better if you make this at that time of year when fresh shrimp might be in your fish store—as rare as that is. Serve with steamed rice.

6 cups vegetable oil, for frying, plus 1 tablespoon for the wok

1¹/₂ pounds fresh shrimp with their heads or ³/₄ pound headless shrimp, dried with paper towels, heads and/or shells removed

¹/₂ teaspoon salt

4 teaspoons sugar

¹/₈ teaspoon freshly ground white pepper

1 large egg

2 tablespoons all-purpose flour

3¹/₂ teaspoons cornstarch

2 tablespoons soy sauce

1 tablespoon apple cider vinegar

1 tablespoon sesame oil

1 tablespoon red chile flakes

2 large garlic cloves, finely chopped

1. Preheat the frying oil to 360°F in a deep-fryer or an 8-inch saucepan fitted with a basket insert. In a large bowl, toss the shrimp with the salt, ¹/₂ teaspoon of the sugar, and the white pepper, mixing well. Set aside until needed.

2. Meanwhile, in a medium-size bowl, beat the egg and then add the flour and cornstarch, whisking until smooth. Dip the shrimp in the batter and deep-fry until golden, 2 to 3 minutes, cooking in two batches if necessary to prevent overcrowding. Remove and drain the shrimp on paper towels.

3. In a small bowl, combine the soy sauce, vinegar, sesame oil, the remaining 3¹/₂ teaspoons sugar, and the red chile flakes. In a wok, heat the 1 tablespoon vegetable oil over high heat, then add the garlic to the wok and stir-fry for 1 minute. Add the reserved sauce and, once it is bubbling, add the cooked shrimp and mix thoroughly. Serve immediately.

MAKES 4 SERVINGS

sassy seafood

Spicy Octopus

This dish is called *nak ji bok eum* in Korean. Octopus is usually sold frozen and will need to be defrosted first, but frozen octopus is also, thankfully, already cleaned, which will save you a lot of work. In preparing this dish, it is important that the octopus not be too tough and chewy, so after you boil it for 20 minutes, slice off a little bit of the tentacle and taste it. If it is still very chewy, boil the octopus for another 10 to 20 minutes. The Korean items mentioned in the ingredients list are available in Korean markets or through the Internet.

1 small cleaned octopus (about 1½ pounds), body quartered, tentacles cut into 3-inch lengths, rinsed and drained well

Salt to taste

¼ cup Korean red chile paste (*koch'ujang*)

2 tablespoons ground Korean red chile or 1 tablespoon cayenne pepper

1 tablespoon soy sauce

1 tablespoon sugar

2 tablespoons sesame oil

1 tablespoon sesame seeds

5 large garlic cloves, finely chopped

Vegetable oil for coating wok

½ medium-size onion, sliced ⅓ inch thick

2 fresh green jalapeño chiles, thinly sliced on the bias

2 scallions, white and green parts, sliced into ¼-inch-thick slices on the bias

1 small carrot, peeled and thinly sliced into sticks or rounds

4 shiitake mushrooms, quartered

1.   Place the octopus in a large pot with cold water to cover and bring to a boil with a little salt. Boil until the octopus is firm, 20 minutes. Drain and set aside.

2.   In a large bowl, toss the octopus with the chile paste, ground Korean red chile, soy sauce, sugar, sesame oil, sesame seeds, and garlic. Let marinate for 15 minutes.

3.   Rub the inside of a wok or deep nonstick skillet with vegetable oil, then heat the pan over medium-high heat. Cook the octopus, onion, chiles, scallions, carrot, and mushrooms until the octopus is tender but chewy, about 8 minutes, tossing frequently. Be careful that the heat is not too low or the octopus will be soggy, and not too high or it will burn. Serve hot or at room temperature.

MAKES 4 TO 6 SERVINGS

Stir-Fried Spicy Squid

This Korean dish, called *oh jing oe bul-go-ki*, is best made with large squid that are about a pound each. If the large squid can't be found, try the "calamari steaks" that are often sold frozen in supermarkets and fish stores, or otherwise use any squid that you find. The key to a successful preparation is cooking over very high heat so that the squid don't release too much of their moisture, which would make them braise more than stir-fry. Serve with steamed rice.

1/4 cup Korean red chile paste (*koch'ujang*)

2 tablespoons sugar

3 large garlic cloves, finely chopped

1 teaspoon sesame oil

1 teaspoon toasted sesame seeds

2 pounds whole cleaned squid, bodies cut into strips and tentacles left whole or cut in half if large

4 dried shiitake mushrooms, soaked in tepid water for 15 minutes, cut in half

1 small onion, diced

3 large fresh green jalapeño chiles, julienned

2 tablespoons vegetable oil

1.　In a large bowl, mix together the red chile paste, sugar, garlic, sesame oil, and sesame seeds. Add the squid, toss well, and marinate in the refrigerator for 30 minutes to 1 hour. Add the mushrooms, onion, and chiles to the marinade and toss again.

2.　Heat a large wok or cast-iron skillet over very high heat for at least 10 minutes. Add the vegetable oil and, once it is very hot, stir-fry the squid mixture until glistening and syrupy, about 8 minutes. Serve immediately.

MAKES 4 SERVINGS

Kimchi and Tofu Stew

This is a kind of stew made with kimchi called *kimchi chigae*. Kimchi is the spicy-hot flavorful Korean version of sauerkraut; its base is cabbage. Most young modern Korean cooks buy already prepared kimchi from the supermarket. This dish can be partially prepared a bit ahead of time. You can complete step 1, and then when you are ready to serve you can go on to step 2. Clams are always found in a traditional *kimchi chigae*, and Koreans prefer smaller clams, so buy Manila clams or the smallest littlenecks you can find. This recipe was prepared for me by my friend Unjoo Lee Byars, who buys fresh tofu from a local Korean market in Los Angeles.

1 tablespoon canola or vegetable oil

1/2 pound pork shoulder, cut into 1/2-inch cubes

2 cups vegetable broth (homemade or canned)

2 pounds kimchi, cut into 2-inch pieces

1 pound medium-firm tofu, cut into 1-inch cubes

7 fresh shiitake mushrooms, sliced 1/4 inch thick

2 teaspoons bonito flakes

18 small littleneck clams (about 1 inch in diameter) or 12 regular littleneck clams (about 2 inches in diameter), washed well

1.   In a large skillet, heat the canola oil over high heat, then brown the pork, about 4 minutes. Add the vegetable broth and kimchi, stir, and add water, about 1 cup, to cover. Cover and bring to a boil. Once it has been boiling for 1 or 2 minutes, add the tofu and mushrooms, pushing them down into the broth. Reduce the heat to medium-low, sprinkle with the bonito flakes, stir very gently, cover, and cook gently for 10 minutes. Turn the heat off and let sit for at least 15 minutes, or until you want to move on to step 2 to serve.

2.   Bring the *kimchi chigae* to a boil, add the clams, cover, and cook until they all open, 5 to 8 minutes. Discard any clams that remain firmly closed. Serve immediately.

MAKES 6 SERVINGS

volatile
vegetables

Nothing escapes the chile, so it seems. Vegetables are important components of our hot cuisines because so many of these cultures are or were quite poor. Not all of these vegetable recipes are vegetarian recipes because in traditional cultures, excepting some in India, vegetarianism is mostly unknown. But meat is sparse and used to flavor foods, almost like a condiment, as opposed to being the focus. The range of dishes made with vegetables is quite remarkable. Try the Shakhshukha (page 307) for an eye-opener or make your own Chiles Rellenos (page 300) and eat it all yourself (be careful because you just might). Pockmarked Old Woman's Bean Curd (page 316) from Sichuan is quite an amazing dish, and I'll bet you've never even had it before in a Chinese restaurant. It's easy to make, too.

Pumpkin Stew with Chiles and Cheese

T his pumpkin stew is so rewarding that I think serving it as a main course makes a lot of sense. It's colorfully orange and white and soul-warming from the chiles. This recipe is popular in Peru and Bolivia. Although I found it on the Internet, it is adapted from the original source, Felipe Rojas-Lombardi's *South American Cooking* (HarperCollins, 1991). Serve with a green salad on the side.

1 tablespoon vegetable or safflower oil

1 medium-size onion, finely chopped

2 large garlic cloves, finely chopped

6 fresh green serrano chiles, finely chopped

2 pounds pumpkin or other winter squash, peeled and cubed

2 medium-size white potatoes, peeled and cubed

1 cup water

2 teaspoons salt, or more to your taste

$1/2$ teaspoon freshly ground black pepper, or more to your taste

$1/4$ cup half-and-half

$1^1/4$ cups (about 6 ounces) diced Mexican *queso blanco* or farmer's cheese

In a casserole, heat the vegetable oil over medium-high heat, then cook the onion, garlic, and chiles until soft, about 5 minutes, stirring. Add the pumpkin, potatoes, water, salt, and black pepper. Stir, then cover, reduce the heat to low, and simmer until the pumpkin and potatoes are tender, 40 to 45 minutes. Add the half-and-half and 1 cup of the cheese and cook until the cheese has melted, about 5 minutes, stirring gently. Season with more salt and pepper if desired and garnish with the remaining cheese. Serve immediately.

MAKES 6 SERVINGS

volatile vegetables

Chiles Rellenos

This famous preparation, found not only everywhere in Mexico but also in every Mexican restaurant in the United States, is filled with either a *picadillo*, a ground pork stuffing, or with a cheese stuffing. In this recipe, I stuff poblano chiles with cheese, although you can also use New Mexico (Anaheim) chiles. In Mexico, the typical cheese used would be a *queso fresco*, a cheese like a crumbly farmer's cheese, or *queso Chihuahua*, a cheese like a mild cheddar. Many Mexican cheeses are sold in this country now, though they are all very similar since Mexico is not known for its cheeses except for *queso fresco*. In this recipe, I use a combination of Monterey Jack and mild white cheddar, since these are good melting cheeses and are readily available. One of the trickiest parts of making *chiles rellenos* is preparing the chiles for stuffing. They must be skinned by blistering them over a burner, which not only removes the skins but partially cooks them, too. Then the seeds must be removed without puncturing the chile and without damaging the stem. This process of cutting out the seeds renders the chile a *capón*, that is, like a capon (castrated chicken), since it is now "castrated." Some people like the chiles to be cooked until very soft and others like them a little firm. For the first option, keep them over the flame for an extra 4 minutes when blistering the skin, and fry for 1 minute longer than required for "golden."

1 pound ripe tomatoes, peeled and seeded

$1/2$ small onion, quartered

2 large garlic cloves, chopped

$1^1/2$ tablespoons pork lard

3 whole cloves

4 whole black peppercorns

1 bay leaf

1 cinnamon stick

$1/8$ teaspoon dried thyme

2 cups chicken broth (homemade or canned)

4 fresh large poblano chiles

$1^1/2$ cups shredded Monterey Jack and white cheddar cheese, combined

2 cups vegetable oil, for frying

3 large eggs, separated

Salt to taste

All-purpose flour, for dredging

1. Put the tomatoes, onion, and garlic in a blender and blend until very smooth. In a large skillet, melt the lard over high heat, then cook the tomato puree until bubbling vigorously, about 3 minutes, stirring. Add the cloves, peppercorns, bay leaf, cinnamon stick, thyme, and chicken broth, bring to a boil, and cook at a boil for 3 minutes. Reduce the heat to medium and cook until it is a slightly dense,

poblano, ancho, and pasilla chiles

American supermarkets regularly label poblano chiles as pasilla chiles. Here's what you need to know to buy the right item: a poblano chile, generally, is a dark green–colored heart-shaped chile about the size of a small fist. When a poblano chile is sold in its dried state, it is called an ancho chile. A pasilla chile is a darker green than a poblano and is longer and narrower.

smooth sauce, about 25 minutes. Keep hot over low heat while you continue the preparation.

2. Meanwhile, hold the chiles with tongs over a high flame, or under a broiler, until the skin starts to blister and blacken all over, turning the chiles so they blister evenly, 8 to 10 minutes. Place the chiles in a paper bag for 15 minutes to allow the skin to come off readily. Wash the skin off under running water. Make a slit running three-quarters down one side of each chile and carefully remove the seeds and any thick white veins with a sharp paring knife, making sure that you don't cut all the way through the flesh of the chiles when you are removing the sturdily attached seeds and also making sure that the stems remain intact and attached. Pat the chiles dry with paper towels and stuff with the cheese, evenly divided and molded with your hands into an oval shape to fit into the opening. Set aside on a paper towel–lined plate and cover with paper towels to absorb more water. If the chiles are wet, their batter will not adhere to them properly for frying.

3. Preheat the frying oil in a large skillet for 10 minutes over medium-high heat or to 375°F. Prepare the batter by beating the egg whites in a medium-size bowl until they form stiff peaks. Add the salt and the yolks, one at a time, beating each one in before adding the next one. Pat the chiles dry again, making sure the outside is completely dry, then dredge in the flour, tapping off any excess, and dip into the batter completely. Cook the chiles, in batches if necessary so that the skillet isn't crowded, until golden, about 4 minutes, turning once with tongs. Remove to an ovenproof dish to keep warm in a low oven as you continue cooking the chiles.

4. Transfer a few ladlefuls of sauce to a wide, shallow platter and place the fried chiles in the center so the broth comes up about halfway. Serve immediately.

MAKES 2 TO 4 SERVINGS

volatile vegetables

Callaloo

Callaloo, also spelled callalu, is the name of a Caribbean vegetable stew and also the name for a number of plants used in this and other dishes in Jamaica and Trinidad. The vegetable called callaloo used in this stew is the leaves from Indian kale (also called malanga or yautia) or Chinese spinach (also called Tahitian taro, tannier spinach, or belembe) or taro (also called dasheen, tannia, or cocoyam). To make matters a little more complicated, the roots of all these plants can have different names than the leaves. Another name for this callaloo preparation is "run down" or "pepperpot," and it can also be made with the addition of tomatoes, potatoes, chayote, scallions, and bell pepper. Apparently it is similar to the one made on Tobago, according to Jessica Harris, author of *Sky Juice and Flying Fish: Traditional Caribbean Cooking* (Simon & Schuster, 1991), who also tells us that cassareep, a condiment prepared from cassava juice, salt, and pepper, is used in the preparation of pepperpot in Guyana, Trinidad, and Grenada, an inheritance from the aboriginal Arawaks. Although it may be possible to find fresh callaloo in Caribbean markets, I find Swiss chard to be an excellent substitute.

2 pounds Swiss chard or spinach, heavy stems removed, rinsed well, and chopped

1 large onion, finely chopped

5 large garlic cloves, 3 finely chopped and 2 lightly crushed

2 ounces salt pork, chopped

1 1/2 cups coconut milk (see page 90)

5 cups water

1/2 pound fresh crabmeat, picked over

1/2 pound small okra, ends trimmed

1 Scotch bonnet chile or habanero chile, seeded and finely chopped

Salt and freshly ground black pepper to taste

Put the Swiss chard, onion, garlic, salt pork, coconut milk, and water in a large stockpot. Bring to a gentle boil over medium heat and when the salt pork is tender, about 20 minutes, add the crabmeat, okra, chile, salt, and pepper and cook until the vegetables are soft and bubbling gently, about 12 minutes. Serve hot.

MAKES 6 SERVINGS

how to grow and harvest chiles

Chiles do well in dry and warm weather. If you want to try growing your own chiles, sow the seeds indoors two to three months before the spring frost-free date, and transplant them outside when they are about five inches high or about three weeks after the average frost-free date. Place the plants two-and-a-half feet apart in rows three feet apart. Protect your transplanted chile plants with translucent plastic containers with the bottoms cut out. Harvest chiles as you need them and as they ripen. They are fully ripe when their skin turns red, yellow, orange, or some color other than green. Keep in mind that chiles get more piquant as they ripen.

Beans and Greens Stew

Traditionally, this Algerian stew called *al-buqul*, which means "greens," or specifically "legumes," would be cooked longer than I cook it here because the dried legumes would need lots of cooking. I save time by using canned chickpeas and fava beans. The dried white beans, though, do taste much better than the canned here, and they do have to be cooked until almost tender, about 1½ hours, before adding to the stew. The kind of canned fava beans you are looking for are the round ones called "bath fava" or "foul medammes," the transliterated name most likely to be found on the labels of those sold in Middle Eastern markets and in the international section of supermarkets. Mallow is an important part of this stew, but unfortunately it is sold only in farmers' markets, perhaps sold under its Japanese name, *fuyu aoi*, or Chinese name, *yuan ye jin kui*. So either you'll have to rely on the farmer or use something else. As we don't have any leafy vegetable remotely similar to mallow in our supermarkets, I suggest you substitute kale or Swiss chard.

volatile vegetables

1 cup small dried white beans

Leaves from 3 bunches mallow (about ³/₄ pound), well washed, all stems removed and chopped coarsely, or ³/₄ pound Swiss chard or kale, stems removed

¹/₂ cup extra-virgin olive oil

4 large garlic cloves, thinly sliced

1 tablespoon tomato paste dissolved in ¹/₄ cup water

1 dried red de arbol chile

1 tablespoon cayenne pepper

1¹/₂ teaspoons freshly ground black pepper

1¹/₂ teaspoons salt

2¹/₂ cups cold water

1¹/₂ cups cooked chickpeas, drained

1¹/₂ cups cooked fava beans, drained

1 cardoon stalk, diced and boiled for 1 hour in water with ¹/₄ cup vinegar, or 4 large fresh artichoke hearts, diced, or 3 celery stalks, cut into 1-inch lengths

2 medium-size potatoes (about 10 ounces), peeled and diced

1 cup fresh fava beans (from about 1¹/₄ pounds of pods), skinned

1 cup fresh or frozen peas

¹/₂ cup pitted green olives

Leaves from 1 bunch fresh coriander (cilantro), finely chopped

1. Bring a medium-size saucepan of water to a boil over high heat and cook the white beans until tender, about 1¹/₄ hours. Drain.

2. Bring a large pot of water to a boil over high heat and cook the mallow until wilted, but floating on top, 10 to 12 minutes. Drain and set aside.

3. In a large casserole, heat the olive oil over medium-high heat, then cook the garlic with the tomato paste–water mixture, the dried chile, cayenne pepper, black pepper, and salt until the water is nearly evaporated, 6 to 8 minutes, stirring frequently so the garlic doesn't burn. Add the water, chickpeas, white beans, and fava beans, reduce the heat to medium, and cook until almost tender, about 50 minutes. Add the cardoon, potatoes, fresh fava beans, peas, and olives. Stir and cook until the potatoes are almost tender, 40 to 45 minutes.

4. Add the coriander and mallow, reduce the heat to low, and simmer until the stew is thick and syrupy, about 15 minutes. Remove and discard the dried chile. Serve hot or cold.

MAKES 8 SERVINGS

Spinach Balls in Zesty Tomato Sauce

T his Tunisian stew, called *mubattan sabanikh*, is really quite extraordinary, both in taste and in its form. The name of the dish is interesting in this respect because *mubattan* derives from the verb "to hide," and in this dish the spinach is hidden by taking an unusual form (a ball). The balls of spinach are formed with rice and then floured and deep-fried and finished in a syrupy, chile-laced tomato sauce that hides them further. To keep the spinach balls from falling apart when they are in the sauce, the spinach should be well drained after wilting, and the balls should be fried until crisp. Leftover rice would come in handy for use in this recipe.

2 pounds spinach, trimmed of heavy stems, washed well several times

³/₄ cup cooked short-grain rice, such as Arborio rice

¹/₄ cup finely chopped onions

¹/₄ cup finely chopped fresh parsley leaves

2 teaspoons *Tabil* (page 415)

Salt and freshly ground black pepper to taste

6 to 8 cups olive oil or vegetable oil, for frying

2 large eggs, beaten

All-purpose flour, for dredging

¹/₄ cup extra-virgin olive oil

3 tablespoons tomato paste dissolved in 2 cups water

2 teaspoons *Harisa* (page 414)

2 teaspoons cayenne pepper

1. In a large saucepan or stockpot, place the spinach with only the water adhering to it from its last rinsing, cover, and wilt over high heat, about 4 minutes, turning once or twice. Remove and drain well, pressing excess water out in a strainer with the back of a wooden spoon. Chop the spinach very finely.

2. In a large bowl, mix together the spinach, cooked rice, onion, parsley, *tabil*, salt, and pepper. Form into 10 balls, each the size of a little egg.

3. Preheat the frying oil to 360°F in a deep-fryer or an 8-inch-diameter saucepan fitted with a basket insert. Dip the spinach and rice balls in the beaten eggs and then dredge in the flour, patting off any excess. Cook until crisp and light golden, 3¹/₂ to 4 minutes, cooking in 2 batches if necessary so the frying oil is never crowded. Drain on paper towels.

volatile vegetables

4. In an earthenware casserole (preferably) over medium-high heat, heat the olive oil and add the tomato paste–water mixture, using a heat diffuser if necessary. Stir in the *harisa* and cayenne pepper. Season with salt and pepper and bring to a boil. Reduce the heat to low, cover, and cook until the tomato and olive oil are separated, about 10 minutes. Add the spinach balls, raise the heat to high, and cook until the oil emulsifies and the sauce is slightly syrupy, 5 to 6 minutes. Serve immediately.

MAKES 2 TO 4 SERVINGS

the voyage of african food

No matter where one looks one will see the culture of Africa as it rides the slave ships with those poor souls transplanted to the New World. Food is a great example, as we can see by the migration of the Nigerian *akara*, the black-eyed pea fritters with hot chile sauce that made its way first to Brazil. In Nigeria, *akara* is made with the black-eyed peas mashed up with onion and chiles and deep-fried in red palm oil, and served as a "small chop," that is, an appetizer. The dish reappears in the New World as the identical black-eyed pea fritters called *acarajé* in the Bahia region of Brazil, where we find that among the deities of the Candomblé religion are those called Orishas, and each has a unique personality and favorite food. Yansan, the wind spirit, likes the black-eyed pea fritters called *acarajé*. In Bahia, they are made with the addition of dried shrimp and also served with a fiery sauce. The fritters are made by the *quituteiras*, experts at making tidbits, and no Bahian festival is complete without them. They are fried in the rich red palm oil until they puff up, then they are cooled and split down the middle, and the hot chile sauce goes inside the split. This dish is known in Martinique as *acras de zieu noi's* and is made with the same dried black-eyed peas, but uses Scotch bonnet chiles and garlic and is fried in corn oil.

Shakhshukha

I've written about *shakhshukha* before and so have many food writers, all describing this Algerian and Tunisian dish as a kind of spicy ratatouille finished with eggs. Yet, even given the popularity of Mediterranean cooking in this country I don't know if this dish is really known that well. The ratatouille analogy is fair enough, although I think this dish is more substantial and it is made in countless different ways. *Shakhshukha* is not an Arabic word, but a Turkish one, and the dish appears to derive from the nearly identical Turkish dish called *menemen*.

2 large green bell peppers

1 pound ripe plum tomatoes

1 fresh green finger-type chile or 2 green jalapeño chiles

2 small eggplant (14 to 16 ounces), peeled and sliced into ¹/₂-inch-thick rounds

Salt to taste

1 cup extra-virgin olive oil

2 medium-size zucchini (8 to 9 ounces), peeled and sliced into ¹/₂-inch-thick rounds

10 large garlic cloves, finely chopped

¹/₄ cup finely chopped fresh parsley leaves

4 large eggs, beaten

Freshly ground black pepper to taste

1 teaspoon cayenne pepper

1. Prepare a hot charcoal fire or preheat a gas grill on high or preheat the oven to 425°F. Place the bell peppers, tomatoes, and chile on the grilling grate or in a baking tray and grill or bake until the skin blisters black all over the peppers and chile and the skins are coming off the tomatoes, 30 to 40 minutes (less time for the chile). Once cool enough to handle, peel the peppers and tomatoes and remove their seeds. Cut the peppers into strips and the tomatoes into rounds.

2. Lay the eggplant pieces on some paper towels and sprinkle with salt. Leave them to drain of their bitter juices for 30 minutes, then pat dry with paper towels. Cut all the eggplant slices in half.

3. In a large casserole, heat the olive oil over medium-high heat, then add the eggplant and cook until light golden, about 4 minutes, turning only once. Remove the eggplant with a slotted ladle, set aside to drain, and let the oil cool significantly, about 20 minutes with the heat turned off.

4. Turn the heat to low, then add the zucchini, peppers, tomatoes, garlic, and parsley to the casserole. Season with salt, pepper, and cayenne pepper, cover, and simmer until most of the liquid is evaporated, about 30 minutes. Add the eggplant.

volatile vegetables

5. Season the eggs with a little salt and pepper and a few tablespoons of the broth from the casserole. Make a well in the center of the casserole, raise the heat to high for a minute, then stir the eggs into the well and let them set for a minute. Cook, scrambling the eggs until they are congealed, about 6 minutes, folding, not stirring. Serve hot.

MAKES 6 SERVINGS

Vegetable Kurma

This is a dish from Lucknow, in the Indian state of Uttar Pradesh, that I adapted from the recipe by Sanjay Kumar and Nivedita Srivastava, who posted theirs on the Internet. A *kurma* is a traditional Mogul preparation, a style of cooking derived from the great Muslim empire of India that was founded in 1526 by Baba, who claimed descent from the Mongol conqueror Genghis Khan. It is a thick, spicy, rich brown curry, filled with wonderful flavors from vegetables, nuts, and fruit. The gravy is creamy from the yogurt and spicy from the *masala*. This preparation goes great with Lamb Keema (page 213). The white cheese, or paneer, can be replaced with a Mexican *queso fresco* or a Syrian white cheese available in Middle Eastern markets, but you can also use farmer's cheese or drained cottage cheese in a pinch.

One $^1/_2$-inch cube fresh ginger, peeled

2 large garlic cloves

Leaves from 6 sprigs fresh coriander (cilantro)

4 fresh green finger-type chiles or 5 green jalapeño chiles

$^3/_4$ cup water

6 tablespoons vegetable oil

6 ounces white cheese (see headnote), cut into 12 cubes

$^1/_4$ cup whole milk

$^3/_4$ cup cauliflower florets, broken into small pieces

$^3/_4$ cup green beans, ends trimmed and cut into $^1/_2$-inch pieces

$^3/_4$ cup diced carrots

$^3/_4$ cup fresh or frozen peas

$^3/_4$ cup diced peeled potatoes

Salt to taste

$^1/_2$ teaspoon *garam masala* (see box at right)

$^1/_2$ teaspoon ground turmeric

$^1/_2$ teaspoon ground cumin

$^1/_2$ teaspoon ground red chile

$^1/_2$ cup fresh or canned tomato puree

$^1/_2$ cup whole plain yogurt

$^1/_2$ cup cubed pineapple

1 tablespoon whole unsalted cashews

1 tablespoon sliced or slivered almonds

1.   Place the ginger, garlic, coriander leaves, and green chiles in a blender with ¹/₄ cup of the water and blend until a smooth paste, scraping down the sides of the blender when necessary.

2.   In a large skillet, heat the vegetable oil over high heat until very hot, then cook the pieces of cheese until golden brown, about 30 seconds. Remove the cheese with a spatula and set aside, discarding any burnt bits. Remove 2 tablespoons of the oil from the skillet and mix it with the ginger-garlic paste. Let the skillet cool for 3 minutes, then add the ginger-garlic paste to the pan and cook over medium heat for 5 minutes, sprinkling it with the milk.

3.   Add the cauliflower, beans, carrots, peas, potatoes, salt, *garam masala*, turmeric, cumin, and ground red chile. Cook for 2 minutes, stirring, then add the tomato puree and the remaining ¹/₂ cup water. Reduce the heat to low and simmer, partially covered, until the vegetables are soft, about 1 hour.

4.   Stir in the yogurt, then add the fried cheese, pineapple, cashews, and almonds and cook for 3 minutes, stirring. Serve immediately.

MAKES 4 SERVINGS

indian spice blends

There are three spice blends used predominantly in Indian cooking. These are curry powder, which is sold everywhere, *garam masala*, and *panch phoron*. The most prominent spice in curry powder is coriander seed. It also contains turmeric, which is what makes the spice look golden, and lesser amounts of cumin, fenugreek, fennel, yellow mustard seeds, cloves, white pepper, and very little red chile pepper. *Garam masala* is used mostly in northern India, especially in Mogul cuisine, but can be found in South Africa used in Cape Malay cooking (page 420). Although it is found premade in jars in many Indian markets and large supermarkets, it can be made at home by blending together equal amounts of ground cumin, coriander, cardamom, and black pepper, and then adding a much lesser amount of cloves, nutmeg, cinnamon, and saffron. It's usually a rust color. *Panch phoron* (see page 366) is a spice mix typical in Bengali cuisine. It is a blend of equal amounts of ground cumin, fennel, and black mustard with a little lesser amount of nigella and fenugreek. This spice mix is usually sold premixed but unground in Indian markets.

Yam Curry in Chile Gravy

This dish, from the southernmost Indian state of Tamil Nadu, is called *sennaikkai kootu* in Tamil, which means something like "curry in gravy," and it is appropriately fiery, which is typical of most southern Indian cooking. Tamil Nadu is known for its spicy-hot vegetarian fare. The yams used in this old and traditional preparation are Old World yams. Some varieties of American sweet potatoes are called yams, but they are from an entirely different plant family.

1 cup pigeon peas or split green peas

1 pound yams, malanga, *ñame*, or sweet potatoes, peeled and cut into 1/2-inch cubes

1/2 teaspoon ground turmeric

1/2 cup tamarind pulp or 1 ounce tamarind paste

1/2 coconut, shelled, peeled, and flesh cut up into chunks, or 1 cup dried shredded unsweetened coconut

1 teaspoon chickpea flour, gram flour, or corn flour

10 fresh red finger-type chiles or 14 red jalapeño chiles, seeded and chopped

Pinch of asafoetida

1 tablespoon vegetable oil

1/2 teaspoon black mustard seeds

1/2 teaspoon black gram (*urad dal*) or black lentils

1 teaspoon dried shredded unsweetened coconut

6 small curry leaves (see page 372) (optional)

Salt to taste

1 cup coarsely chopped fresh coriander (cilantro) leaves

1. Place the pigeon peas in a saucepan with cold water to just barely cover and boil over high heat until tender, about 25 minutes. Drain and set aside. Place the yams in a saucepan with salted water to cover by 1 inch, add the turmeric and tamarind, and boil until tender over high heat, about 25 minutes.

2. While the yams are cooking, place the fresh coconut, chickpea flour, red chiles, and asafoetida in a food processor and grind completely, scraping down the sides when necessary. Add this mixture to the yams and cook at a boil for 1 minute.

3.   In a small skillet, heat the vegetable oil over medium heat, then cook the mustard seeds, black gram, and coconut until the mustard seeds start to jump, about 2 minutes. Add this mixture to the yams along with the cooked pigeon peas. Add the curry leaves, if using, season with salt, and cook on low heat, uncovered, until dense, completely tender, and not so liquidy, 1 to 1^1/$_4$ hours. Garnish with the coriander leaves and serve.

MAKES 6 SERVINGS

fresh coconut

Many supermarkets now sell coconuts with a pre-cut band around the fruit that only requires a hard tap with a hammer to split the coconut open. Before doing that, though, you will want to drain the water inside the coconut, which you can do by carefully pouring the water out after you crack the coconut open or by driving a few nail holes into the softer bottom of the coconut and letting the water drip out. After you have removed the shell, the coconut flesh can be pulled away from the shell. If the flesh does not come off easily, then slip a dinner knife in between the shell and flesh and pry the flesh out. Try to keep the flesh in large pieces because you will need to use a vegetable peeler to scrape off the brown peel from the white flesh. Once you've scraped off the peel, you have the white fresh coconut meat ready to use as the recipe suggests.

Vegetable Curry in Yogurt Gravy

This classic Hindu vegetarian stew called *avial* is from the Indian state of Kerala on the southwestern tip of the subcontinent, which is known for its spicy foods. In this recipe, there is a delightful contrast between blazing heat and sweetness. It is related to the previous recipe, as it too is a kind of *kootu*, a curry in gravy. It's a very appealing taste. Some cooks also use tamarind pulp for the stew. Typically, one would also serve some rice pilaf on the side. Do not add the yogurt to the stew until the end; otherwise it will separate if it cooks, unless you use stabilized yogurt.

1 small eggplant (about ½ pound), peeled and cut into 1-inch cubes

1 teaspoon salt, plus extra for sprinkling

1 tablespoon coconut oil or vegetable oil

1 small sweet potato (about ½ pound), peeled and cut into 1-inch cubes

½ cup shelled fresh or frozen green peas or 1 cup whole snap peas

1 cup green beans, ends trimmed and cut into 1-inch lengths

1 carrot, peeled and sliced

1 small onion, sliced

½ cup chopped green bell pepper

8 fresh green finger-type chiles or 10 fresh green jalapeño chiles, finely chopped

¾ teaspoon ground turmeric

¼ teaspoon ground cumin

1 cup water

1 medium-size tomato, peeled and diced

Pulp of ½ green mango, diced

⅓ cup dried shredded unsweetened coconut

1 cup whole plain yogurt or Stabilized Yogurt (page 278)

1 tablespoon unsalted butter, at room temperature

1. Lay the eggplant pieces on some paper towels and sprinkle with salt. Leave them to drain of their bitter juices for 30 minutes, then pat dry with paper towels.

2. In a large stockpot over high heat, combine the eggplant, coconut oil, sweet potato, green peas, green beans, carrot, onion, bell pepper, chiles, turmeric, and cumin. Add the water and teaspoon of salt and bring to a boil, then reduce the heat to low and simmer, uncovered, until the vegetables are soft and very little water remains, 1 to 1¼ hours. Add the tomato, mango, and coconut, stir, and simmer until they blend into the stew, about 15 minutes. Remove from the heat and stir in the yogurt and butter. Serve immediately.

MAKES 4 TO 6 SERVINGS

White Cheese in Tomatoes and Cream Sauce

This preparation is a Mogul dish from northern India that is made with paneer, a kind of soft curd cheese that is pressed together in lumps, like cottage cheese, which I recommend you use if you can't find paneer. The cubes of soft cheese are embedded in tomato sauce, which should be made from fresh tomatoes for an extraordinary dish. This can accompany rice or Indian breads.

2¹/₂ pounds ripe tomatoes, cut in half, seeds squeezed out, and grated against the largest holes of a grater

¹/₄ cup vegetable oil

One 1-inch cube fresh ginger, peeled and finely chopped

1 bay leaf

Seeds from 2 cardamom pods, crushed

2 teaspoons ground fenugreek

1 teaspoon ground red chile or cayenne pepper

Salt to taste

¹/₂ teaspoon *garam masala* (see page 309)

¹/₄ cup heavy cream

¹/₂ pound paneer, cubed, or cottage cheese, drained by squeezing out liquid and formed into lumps by squeezing in your hand, or farmer's cheese or Mexican *queso fresco* or *queso asadero*, cubed

1 tablespoon finely chopped fresh coriander (cilantro) leaves

1. Place the tomatoes in a food processor and blend until a smooth puree. In a large skillet, heat the vegetable oil over medium-high heat, then add the tomato puree, ginger, bay leaf, cardamom, fenugreek, and ground chile. Cover and cook until bubbling furiously for a few minutes, about 6 minutes in all. Reduce the heat to low, add the salt, *garam masala*, and cream, stir, and simmer until dense, about 45 minutes, stirring occasionally.

2. Add the cheese and cook until it is soft and hot, about 5 minutes. Transfer to a serving platter or bowl and garnish with coriander leaves. Serve immediately.

MAKES 4 SERVINGS

volatile vegetables

Eggplant Curry

This was the first Indian dish that I successfully cooked. It's a recipe from Tamil Nadu in south India and I've liked it all these years. It is not terribly hard to do. The tastes are very spicy-hot and luscious and it goes well with Rice Pilaf (page 396).

3 small eggplant (about 3 pounds), peeled, sliced lengthwise into ¹/₂-inch-thick slices, then sliced into ¹/₂-inch-thick pieces

1 teaspoon salt, plus extra for sprinkling

10 tablespoons vegetable oil

3 large onions, thinly sliced

4 large garlic cloves, finely chopped

1 tablespoon ground coriander

1 teaspoon ground red chile or cayenne pepper

¹/₄ teaspoon ground turmeric

6 fresh green or red finger-type chiles or 8 green or red jalapeño chiles, seeded and finely chopped

¹/₂ cup dried shredded unsweetened coconut

Juice and pulp of 1 small lemon

1 bay leaf

1 teaspoon toasted sesame seeds, crushed

1 cup water

1 teaspoon palm sugar or brown sugar

1 teaspoon black mustard seeds, toasted or pan-fried without oil until they begin to pop

2 tablespoons finely chopped fresh coriander (cilantro) leaves

1. Lay the eggplant pieces on some paper towels and sprinkle with salt. Leave them to drain of their bitter juices for 30 minutes, then pat dry with paper towels.

2. In a large skillet, heat 4 tablespoons of the vegetable oil over medium-high heat, then brown half of the eggplant pieces on both sides, about 6 minutes in all. Remove and set aside. Add another 4 tablespoons vegetable oil to the skillet, and, once it is heated, cook the remaining eggplant and set aside.

3. In a large casserole or stockpot, heat the remaining 2 tablespoons vegetable oil over medium-high heat, then cook the onions, garlic, ground coriander, ground red chile, turmeric, and fresh chiles until soft, about 5 minutes, stirring occasionally. Add the coconut and cook another 2 to 3 minutes, stirring. Add the lemon juice and pulp, teaspoon of salt, bay leaf, sesame seeds, and water. Stir, add the reserved eggplant, cover, reduce the heat to low, and simmer until the eggplant is very tender and the sauce is thick, about 1¹/₂ hours. Add the sugar and mustard seeds, stir, and cook for 5 minutes. Stir in the coriander leaves and remove and discard the bay leaf. Serve immediately.

MAKES 6 SERVINGS

some like it hot

Spicy Cabbage in Coconut Milk

This spicy Indonesian cabbage dish is called *sayur kol*. It is thought that the Indonesian word for cabbage comes from the Dutch word *kool*. This preparation can easily be served as a main course. I call for a range of shrimp paste because it has a strong flavor that one needs to adjust to, so if you have never used it start with the smaller amount.

1/2 to 1 teaspoon shrimp paste

2 tablespoons peanut oil

3 curry leaves (see page 372)

2 medium-size onions, grated

2 large garlic cloves, very finely chopped

4 fresh red finger-type chiles or 5 red jalapeño chiles, very finely chopped

Two 2-inch-long strips lemon rind, white pith removed

1 1/2 cups coconut cream (see page 90)

1 teaspoon salt

1 pound savoy or green cabbage, cored and shredded

3 tablespoons tamarind water (see page 329)

1. Wrap the shrimp paste in aluminum foil and roast in a hot toaster oven at 400°F for 5 minutes, turning once.

2. In a large wok or saucepan, heat the peanut oil over high heat, then cook the curry leaves for 10 seconds. Add the onions, garlic, chiles, and shrimp paste and cook until the mixture turns a darker color, about 6 minutes, stirring so that it doesn't stick. Add the lemon rind, coconut cream, and salt, stir well, and bring the liquid to a near boil. Add the cabbage, reduce the heat to low, and simmer, uncovered, until the cabbage is cooked but still crisp, about 5 minutes. Stir in the tamarind water and serve.

MAKES 4 SERVINGS AS A MAIN COURSE OR 6 SERVINGS AS A SIDE DISH

volatile vegetables

Pockmarked Old Woman's Bean Curd

There are a few stories about the origin of the name of this Sichuan dish. One says that it is named after the smallpox-scarred wife of a late nineteenth century Qing dynasty restaurateur. Another story is that an old woman with a bad complexion sold this tofu dish from a street stand in Chengdu during World War II, and that it was a fabulous and well-loved preparation whose reputation spread far and wide. The pockmarked old lady's stand became famous and today the same stand exists as a modernized, state-owned, full-size restaurant. In any case, this dish is one of the most famous of Sichuan preparations and typifies fiery peasant cooking. The meat used—here it's pork—could also be ground beef, though that is a bit unusual in Sichuan, as there is not a lot of beef eaten. Chinese yellow bean paste can be found in Chinese markets, in the international aisle of some supermarkets, and on the Internet at www.thecmccompany.com.

4 tablespoons vegetable oil

1 pound extra-firm tofu, cut into $1/2$-inch cubes, drained on paper towels

$1/4$ pound ground pork or beef

1 scallion, chopped

3 large garlic cloves, finely chopped

2 tablespoons yellow bean paste

1 tablespoon finely chopped fresh ginger

1 tablespoon red chile flakes

1 tablespoon ground Sichuan peppercorns

$1/2$ cup water

1 tablespoon rice wine (*mirin*) or vermouth

2 tablespoons soy sauce

1 teaspoon cornstarch

1 teaspoon sesame oil

1. In a wok, heat 3 tablespoons of the vegetable oil over high heat, then cook the tofu until golden, about 2 minutes. Remove with a slotted spoon and set aside. Add the pork to the wok and brown, tossing constantly and breaking up the meat, 1 to 2 minutes. Remove with a slotted spoon and set aside.

2. Add the remaining 1 tablespoon vegetable oil and heat over high heat. Add the scallion, garlic, yellow bean paste, ginger, chile flakes, Sichuan peppercorns, reserved tofu, and reserved pork, stirring and tossing gently but constantly to coat the tofu with the liquid. Add the water, rice wine, soy sauce, and cornstarch, and bring to a boil. Cover, reduce the heat to medium, and simmer until the water is evaporated and absorbed, 3 to 5 minutes. Drizzle on the sesame oil and serve.

MAKES 2 TO 4 SERVINGS

pizzazz pasta, napalm noodles, and fiery rice

What's the difference between pasta and noodles, you may ask? Well, for the purposes of this book "pasta" is made with hard wheat or blended wheat flours and "noodles" refers to those products made with other flours, such as rice, mung bean, or sweet potato starch. Whatever you call them, pasta and noodles are some of the favorite foods in all our hot cuisines. If you want to see what they're cooking in the Florida Keys that will send you into orbit, try Cayobo's "Devil's Nightmare" Pasta (page 324). In Tunisia, they're making a Vermicelli with Chicken and Chickpeas (page 325) that will give you insight into how versatile pasta can be. If you try some of the Asian noodle dishes, you may never eat anything else again—they're that good.

Rice is the staple food in many parts of the world, especially southeast Asia. Many dinners in hot zones around the world are built on rice. This chapter is filled with spicy-hot rice recipes that people eat as main courses. Remember, though, that so many of the other recipes in the beef, chicken, pork, and lamb chapters can be or are always eaten with rice. This chapter takes rice to another level—these aren't plain rice dishes (for those, go to "Cool Accompaniments," page 385). A Shrimp and Chile Fried Rice (page 347) or a satisfying Mango Rice (page 343) will convince you of that in an instant.

Wicked Spaghetti with Chipotle Chiles in Adobo and Pine Nut Sauce

I invented this preparation long ago, long before I began writing cookbooks. I went through a period in the mid-1980s when I just loved super-hot food and dreamed up all kinds of spicy stuff. I call this wicked spaghetti because it has an extremely hot sauce. You will need very little to flavor a lot of pasta. To fully enjoy the heat it is best to cut it with something such as a salad afterward, or with cheese or bread.

One 7-ounce can chipotle chiles in adobo sauce, chiles chopped and sauce reserved

$1/2$ cup dry red wine

1 tablespoon tomato paste

$1^1/_2$ tablespoons pine nuts

Salt to taste

$1^1/_4$ pounds spaghetti

1 to 2 cups freshly grated Pecorino cheese

1. In a saucepan, heat the chipotle chiles and their sauce with the red wine, tomato paste, and pine nuts over medium heat until heated through, about 10 minutes.

2. Meanwhile, bring a large pot of abundantly salted water to a rolling boil, then cook the pasta until *al dente*. Drain without rinsing. Toss with the sauce and serve with lots of Pecorino cheese.

MAKES 6 SERVINGS

pizzazz pasta, napalm noodles, and fiery rice

Red Pepper Linguine with Scallions and Shrimp

This Creole preparation that one would find in the home cooking of the Italian community of New Orleans would be best with fresh scallops and fresh shrimp, but you may not be able to find fresh. The flavors, though, will bring everything through, as this is a hot and rich dish that is quite filling.

FOR THE SHRIMP SEASONING

1 teaspoon salt

2 teaspoons Cliff's Cajun Seasoning (page 412)

1/2 teaspoon cayenne pepper

1/4 pound small shrimp, shelled and cut into thirds

FOR THE LINGUINE AND SAUCE

9 ounces fresh red pepper linguine or any fresh pasta

1 teaspoon vegetable oil

3 tablespoons unsalted butter

1/2 cup chopped scallions

3 tablespoons finely chopped celery

3 tablespoons finely chopped red bell pepper

1 tablespoon finely chopped fresh mint leaves

2 tablespoons dry white wine

1/2 cup heavy cream

1/3 cup freshly grated Parmesan cheese

1. In a bowl, mix the seasoning ingredients together, then toss with the shrimp. Set aside.

2. To make the linguine and sauce, bring a large pot of abundantly salted water to a vigorous boil, then cook the pasta until *al dente*. Drain without rinsing. Transfer to a bowl and toss with the vegetable oil.

3. In a skillet, melt the butter over medium heat, then cook the scallions, celery, red bell pepper, and mint until soft, 4 minutes, stirring or shaking often. Add the shrimp and stir for 1 minute. Pour in the wine and continue cooking until it is nearly evaporated, about 90 seconds. Add the cream, stir, and cook for another 90 seconds, shaking the pan. Add the Parmesan cheese, stir, and turn off the heat. Add the linguine and toss to mix. Serve immediately.

MAKES 2 SERVINGS

Darlene's Special Pasta

I made up this dish in the early 1980s when I was going through my newly found Cajun phase, which I later discovered was actually a Paul Prudhomme phase. This dish is named after a long-lost friend of mine. I cooked a dinner for the two of us that was to be purposely spicy and hot, and I told her that if it was any good I would name this special dish after her. Well, it was delicious, so here you go.

2 pounds fresh large shrimp with their heads or 1 pound headless shrimp, heads and/or shells removed and reserved

2 cups water

FOR THE SEASONING
1 tablespoon salt

1 1/2 teaspoons freshly ground black pepper

1/2 teaspoon freshly ground white pepper

1 1/2 teaspoons cayenne pepper

1/4 teaspoon dried oregano

1/4 teaspoon garlic powder

1/4 teaspoon finely chopped fresh basil

FOR THE SAUCE AND SPAGHETTI
1/2 cup (1 stick) unsalted butter

1/2 celery stalk, finely chopped

1/4 cup finely chopped green bell pepper

1/4 cup finely chopped red bell pepper

3 scallions, finely chopped

1 fresh or canned artichoke bottom, finely chopped

3 fresh green serrano chiles, finely chopped

3 tablespoons cognac

1/2 cup heavy cream

12 shucked raw oysters

1 pound spaghetti

1. Place the heads and/or shells of the shrimp in a saucepan and cover with the water. Bring to a boil over high heat, then reduce the heat to low and simmer while you continue the preparation.

2. Make the seasoning mix by tossing all the ingredients together in a small bowl. In a large bowl, sprinkle the shrimp with 3 tablespoons of the seasoning mix and set aside.

3. To make the sauce, in a large skillet, melt 1/4 cup of the butter over medium-high heat, then cook the celery, green bell pepper, red bell pepper, scallions, artichoke, and serrano chiles until softened, about 5 minutes, stirring almost constantly. Strain the simmering shrimp broth, pour 1 cup into the skillet, and cook until it is almost evaporated, stirring. Add the cognac and cook for

2 minutes. Add the cream, the reserved shrimp, the oysters, and remaining ¹/₄ cup butter. Cook until the oysters begin to shrivel on the edges, which should be at about the same time the butter finishes melting, about 5 minutes, stirring often.

4. Meanwhile, bring a large pot of abundantly salted water to a rolling boil, then cook the pasta until just *al dente*. Drain without rinsing. Once the sauce is nice and velvety, add the pasta. Cook the spaghetti, tossing well, for 1 to 2 minutes over high heat. Serve immediately.

MAKES 6 SERVINGS

Spaghetti with Veal, Oysters, and Artichokes

Although Cajun cooking has old and traditional recipes in its repertoire, many of its famous dishes known to Americans are actually the invention of chef Paul Prudhomme, who was responsible for popularizing Cajun food in the 1980s to a wider public, dishes such as blackened redfish or blackened anything for that matter. His first book, *Chef Paul Prudhomme's Louisiana Kitchen* (Morrow, 1984), is a treasure trove of traditional and innovative dishes, and this recipe is adapted from one in that book. I've tweaked a few things, but otherwise this is Chef Paul's magnificent creation.

12 oysters, shucked, liquid reserved

1¹/₂ cups cold water

Juice of 2 lemons

2 medium-size fresh artichokes

¹/₂ cup chopped scallions, light green and white parts

¹/₂ cup (1 stick) unsalted butter

³/₄ pound spaghetti

2 tablespoons vegetable oil

6 tablespoons unbleached all-purpose flour

2 teaspoons salt

2 teaspoons freshly ground white pepper

1¹/₂ teaspoons onion powder

1 tablespoon cayenne pepper

1 teaspoon hot paprika

³/₄ pound veal scallopine, cut into 1¹/₂ x ¹/₄ x ¹/₄-inch strips

1 cup heavy cream

1. Place the shucked oysters and their juices in a bowl with the water and refrigerate for 1 hour. Strain and reserve the oysters and the water separately.

2. In a large pot, bring salted water and the lemon juice to a boil over high heat, then cook the artichokes until the bracts come off easily and the heart is tender, about 40 minutes. Drain, and, once the artichokes are cool enough to handle, remove the bracts and scrape off any tender flesh from the bottoms of their insides. Scoop out the choke and discard. Thinly slice the artichoke bottom and the inside flesh of its stem after removing the stringy outside. You should have about $2/3$ cup of artichoke flesh. Place in a small bowl along with the chopped scallions and 2 tablespoons of the butter and set aside.

3. Meanwhile, bring a large pot of abundantly salted water to a rolling boil, then cook the pasta until *al dente*. Drain without rinsing, toss with the vegetable oil, and set aside.

4. In a medium-size bowl, combine the flour, salt, white pepper, onion powder, cayenne pepper, and paprika. Toss the veal in the spice mix. Remove the veal from the spiced flour, shaking off any excess flour.

5. In a large nonstick skillet, melt $1/4$ cup ($1/2$ stick) of the butter over high heat, then cook the veal until golden brown and crispy on all sides, about 4 minutes, stirring and turning. Add the artichoke mixture. Cook for 2 minutes, shaking the pan vigorously back and forth. Pour in $1/4$ cup of the oyster water and cook for 1 minute, shaking the pan. Add the remaining 2 tablespoons butter, the remaining $1^1/4$ cups oyster water, and the cream and continue cooking until the sauce is bubbling, about 2 minutes. Add the oysters and cook for 2 minutes. Add the reserved pasta and toss until the pasta is just coated and heated through, about 2 minutes. Serve immediately.

MAKES 4 SERVINGS

Cayobo's "Devil's Nightmare" Pasta

T his recipe is from Cayobo's Reggae Lounge in Key West, Florida, created by a guy nicknamed Cayobo who renovates old conch houses. It's not a traditional recipe but a new invention, Cayobo says, which came about when he was experimenting with pasta and chiles. The bananas and orange cut the heat, but it's still one hell of a hot meal. Having spent much time in the Florida Keys, I can tell you that this dish is typical of wacky Keys cooking by those very distinctive Keys personalities— and really good, too.

2 tablespoons extra-virgin olive oil

1 medium-size onion, finely diced

1 red bell pepper, finely diced

4 Scotch bonnet chiles or habanero chiles, finely chopped

2 bananas, peeled and sliced 1/2 inch thick

1/4 cup fresh pineapple juice

Juice of 3 oranges

1/4 cup fresh lime juice

1/4 cup chopped fresh coriander (cilantro) leaves

1/4 cup freshly grated Parmesan cheese

1 pound fettuccine

2 tablespoons unsalted butter

Salt and pepper to taste

1. In a large skillet, heat the olive oil over medium heat, then cook the onion and bell pepper until soft and orange-tinged, about 10 minutes, stirring. Add the chiles, bananas, pineapple juice, and orange juice. Cook until the bananas are soft, about 5 minutes, stirring gently. Remove from the heat and stir in the lime juice, coriander, and Parmesan cheese.

2. Meanwhile, bring a large pot of abundantly salted water to a rolling boil, then cook the pasta until *al dente*. Drain without rinsing, and toss with the butter. Toss again with the sauce and salt and pepper to taste, mixing well. Serve immediately.

MAKES 6 SERVINGS

Vermicelli with Chicken and Chickpeas

This Tunisian preparation is traditionally served on the ninth day of Ashura, the holiday during the Muslim month of Muharram, sacred to the Shi'ites because Husayn, the son of Ali who was married to the Prophet Muhammad's daughter, was martyred on this day at Karbala in Iraq in A.D. 680. This was the event that created the Sunni-Shi'ite schism. Broken vermicelli is an old type of pasta in North Africa. Make sure you use chicken thighs and not breast meat, which will dry out in this recipe.

½ cup extra-virgin olive oil

1 pound boneless chicken thighs, trimmed of fat and cut into small cubes

1 small onion, chopped

1 cup cooked chickpeas, drained

2 tablespoons tomato paste dissolved in ½ cup water

1 tablespoon *Harisa* (page 414)

2 teaspoons cayenne pepper

Salt to taste

5½ cups water

¾ pound vermicelli, broken into 1-inch lengths

1 tablespoon clarified butter

Freshly ground black pepper to taste

1. In a large casserole, heat the olive oil over high heat, then cook the chicken cubes and onion until golden, about 3 minutes, stirring a few times. Add the chickpeas, tomato paste–water mixture, *harisa*, cayenne pepper, and salt. Stir, reduce the heat to medium-high, and cook for 5 minutes. Add 1½ cups of the water to barely cover the pieces of meat. Bring to just below a boil, then reduce the heat to low, cover, and simmer for 1 hour.

2. When the chicken is almost cooked, add the remaining 4 cups of water, bring to a boil, and add the vermicelli. Cook until the pasta is soft, about 15 minutes. Add the clarified butter, season with black pepper, and stir to blend. Serve immediately.

MAKES 4 SERVINGS

pizzazz pasta, napalm noodles, and fiery rice

Pasta Balls with Merguez Sausages

Muhammas is the Tunisian Arabic name for what Middle Eastern groceries sell as *moghrabiye*, the name for dried and toasted pasta balls that are the size of coriander seeds. They are also sold as "toasted pasta balls" and as "Israeli couscous." This richly flavored and hot springtime dish uses merguez sausages (*mirqaz* in Tunisian Arabic), which are absolutely delicious, highly spiced Tunisian lamb or beef sausages that I used to order everywhere when I was in Tunisia but which were all but unavailable in this country years ago. Today a number of excellent merguez sausages are available, and the ones I use are made by Fabrique Délice or d'Artagnan, both available through the Internet. I call for mutton or lamb fat in this recipe and that's easily enough found—just ask the butcher or, if they make you buy something, get the fattiest cut of lamb, such as shoulder chop, and cut off the fat and reserve the meat for another purpose.

6 tablespoons extra-virgin olive oil

1 ounce mutton or lamb fat, chopped

1 medium-size onion, finely chopped

1 flat piece plain beef or lamb jerky (about 2 ounces), chopped

3/4 pound merguez sausages (see page 453), casings removed and crumbled

2 large ripe tomatoes (about 1 pound), peeled, seeded, and chopped

2 tablespoons tomato paste diluted with 1/4 cup water

2 tablespoons *Harisa* (page 414)

1 teaspoon *Tabil* (page 415)

1 tablespoon freshly ground black pepper

1 tablespoon cayenne pepper

4 cups (1 pound) skinned fresh fava beans

2 cups fresh or frozen peas

2 cups water

Salt to taste

1 pound toasted pasta balls

3 fresh red finger-type chiles or 4 red jalapeño chiles, seeded and finely chopped

5 dried rosebuds, crumbled (optional)

1. In a large casserole, heat the olive oil with the mutton fat over medium-high heat until the fat has been sizzling for 1 minute, then cook the onion until it is soft, 4 to 5 minutes, stirring. Add the beef jerky, merguez sausages, tomatoes, diluted tomato paste, *harisa*, *tabil*, black pepper, and cayenne pepper. Stir, and cook for 1 minute. Add the fava beans and peas, add the water, and bring to a boil. Reduce the heat to low and simmer, uncovered, for 30 minutes. Cover and simmer until the vegetables are tender, another 15 minutes, stirring occasionally.

2. Meanwhile, bring 2 quarts of lightly salted water to a rolling boil, then cook the pasta, uncovered, until soft and the water nearly evaporated, about 15 minutes. Taste the sauce and add salt if desired, then add the sauce to the pasta, stir to mix well, and cook over low heat for about 5 minutes. Transfer to a serving bowl and sprinkle the chopped fresh chiles and rosebuds on top. Serve immediately.

MAKES 8 SERVINGS

Pasta Balls with Dried Octopus

This recipe comes from Sofia Azouz, the wife of Taoufik Ben Azouz, a San Diegoan who has a small company making some amazing Mediterranean products, including Turkish-style *pide* bread, stuffed grape leaves, *spanakopita*, *muhammara*, and baklava that they sell at local farmers' markets in southern California. As the Tunisian-American community is small, Sofia said that years ago she used to ask friends heading for Tunisia to bring back the little round couscous or pasta balls called *muhammas*, but that today she finds them without a problem in this country, usually called *moghrabiye*. Dried octopus was also unavailable here for years, but today you might find it in Japanese or Asian markets. Dried foods are common in Tunisia, where the extreme desert aridity helps in preserving foods. This dried little octopus will swell up in the broth and be delicious and intensely flavored. If you can't find dried octopus, use a 1-pound fresh or frozen cleaned octopus.

1/2 cup extra-virgin olive oil

2 tablespoons tomato paste dissolved in 1 cup water

2 tablespoons *Harisa* (page 414)

10 large garlic cloves, pounded in a mortar until mushy with 2 teaspoons salt

1 tablespoon *Tabil* (page 415)

2 teaspoons hot paprika

2 teaspoons freshly ground black pepper

1 tablespoon ground caraway

3 quarts water

Two 15-ounce cans cooked chickpeas, drained

1 dried octopus or one 1-pound fresh octopus

Salt to taste

6 ounces toasted pasta balls

1. In a stew pot, preferably earthenware, heat the olive oil over medium heat, then add the tomato paste dissolved in water, the *harisa*, garlic, *tabil*, paprika, black pepper, and caraway. Cook for 10 minutes, stirring occasionally, and then add the 3 quarts water and bring to a boil over high heat. Add the chickpeas and dried or fresh octopus and cook until softer, about 30 minutes.

2.   Remove the octopus and cut up into bite-size portions. Return the octopus to the pot and continue to cook until tender, about 30 more minutes. Add salt if desired. Add the pasta balls and cook until soft, 10 to 12 minutes. Serve immediately.

MAKES 8 SERVINGS

Seashells with Monkfish

I n Tunisia, the word "macaroni," as in Italy, is a generic term referring to any kind of pasta. The Tunisians are fond of pasta dishes such as this one and, unlike in Italy, pasta is eaten not as a first course but as the main course. The pasta is also not cooked *al dente*, but rather until tender. This hot dish is made with monkfish, a very firm-fleshed fish that is ideal for rough cooking. If you replace it with something else, make sure it is also a very firm-fleshed fish, such as shark, swordfish, or catfish.

7 tablespoons extra-virgin olive oil

1 small onion, finely chopped

6 large garlic cloves, finely chopped

One 15-ounce can cooked chickpeas, drained

3 tablespoons tomato paste

1 1/2 cups water

2 tablespoons *Harisa* (page 414)

2 teaspoons *Tabil* (page 415)

2 teaspoons ground red chile or cayenne pepper

Salt and freshly ground black pepper to taste

1 3/4 pounds monkfish, cut into small fist-size portions

3/4 pound ridged seashell-shaped pasta, such as *conchiglie*

Freshly grated Gruyère cheese (optional)

1.   In a large casserole, heat the olive oil over medium-high heat, then cook the onion and garlic until translucent, 4 to 5 minutes, stirring. Add the chickpeas, tomato paste, water, *harisa*, *tabil*, and 1 teaspoon of the ground chile. Bring to a boil, then reduce the heat to very low and simmer until somewhat thicker, 20 to 30 minutes. Season with salt and pepper.

2. Rub the monkfish pieces with salt, pepper, and the remaining 1 teaspoon ground chile. Add the monkfish to the casserole, turn the heat to medium-high, and cook until firm and cooked through, about 12 minutes.

3. Meanwhile, bring a large pot of abundantly salted water to a boil, then cook the pasta until *al dente* or tender. Drain without rinsing. Add the pasta to the casserole and cook for 2 minutes, tossing the pasta with the sauce. Serve immediately with the cheese, if desired.

MAKES 4 SERVINGS

Drunkard's Fried Noodles with Seafood

This Thai preparation is called drunkard's fried noodles because the blast of chile is thought to be sobering. A favorite lunch or late-night snack, this spicy stir-fry consists of wide rice noodles like fettuccine, fresh basil leaves, chicken or pork or mixed seafood, seasonings, and a healthy dose of fresh sliced chiles. For the tamarind water, take a half-inch cube of tamarind paste, which can be bought in Indian or Chinese markets or the Internet, and let it soak in several tablespoons of hot water for 15 minutes.

35 fresh green Thai chiles or 15 fresh green serrano chiles, stemmed and quartered lengthwise

4 lemongrass stalks, tough outer portions removed and finely chopped

8 large garlic cloves, finely chopped

1 1/2 teaspoons salt, or more to your taste

Juice from 3 limes

1/4 cup Thai fish sauce

1/4 cup tamarind water (see headnote)

3/4 pound wide rice noodles (*pad Thai*)

1/4 cup peanut oil

1 pound mixed shrimp, scallops, and squid

4 shallots, thinly sliced

2 teaspoons freshly ground white pepper, or more to your taste

1. In a mortar, pound the chiles, lemongrass, garlic, and salt until mushy. Set aside. In a small bowl, mix the lime juice, fish sauce, and tamarind water together and set aside.

where's the pad thai?
where's the larb?

I think *pad Thai* and *larb* are the two most familiar Thai dishes, especially to Americans who regularly eat at Thai restaurants. The noodle dish *pad Thai* is probably the best known Thai dish outside of Thailand. And *larb* or *larp*, a salad of minced meat, shallots, and dressing, is probably a close second as one of the best known Thai salads found outside Thailand, served in virtually every Thai restaurant in North America. But the reason there are no recipes for these two dishes in this book is that neither is notably or traditionally hot with chiles.

2.   Bring a large saucepan of lightly salted water to a boil and cook the rice noodles until supple, about 3 minutes. Drain and set aside.

3.   In a wok, heat the peanut oil over high heat until nearly smoking, then cook the seafood until it turns opaque, about 1 minute. Add the shallots and the chile-garlic mixture and cook for 1 minute. Add the lime juice mixture and cook for 2 minutes. Add the noodles, white pepper, and more salt if desired, and cook until little liquid is left, about 3 minutes. Serve immediately.

MAKES 4 SERVINGS

Rice Noodles with Corn and Ginger

I made up this recipe when I became confident enough with my Thai cooking. I learned a lot from friends like Su-Mei Yu, author of *Cracking the Coconut* (Morrow, 2000), by going to Thai Town in Los Angeles, by talking to the street vendors at the Wat Thai temple's weekend food festival in the San Fernando Valley, and then by cooking Thai dishes nonstop for months. I was quite proud of myself since this was the first dish I created all by myself and my girlfriend and I loved it.

1/2 pound thin rice noodles	6 cherry tomatoes, cut in half
3 tablespoons peanut oil	15 fresh green Thai chiles or 6 fresh green serrano chiles, chopped
Kernels from 1 cooked ear of corn	
1 large shallot, chopped	1 tablespoon Thai fish sauce
One 1-inch cube fresh ginger, peeled and finely chopped	2 tablespoons fresh lime juice
	2 tablespoons coarsely chopped fresh mint leaves
4 large garlic cloves, finely chopped	
1/2 small green mango, peeled and julienned	1/4 cup coarsely chopped fresh coriander (cilantro) leaves

1. Bring a large saucepan of lightly salted water to a boil and cook the rice noodles until supple, about 3 minutes. Drain and set aside.

2. In a wok, heat the peanut oil over medium-high heat, then cook the corn, shallot, ginger, garlic, mango, tomatoes, chiles, fish sauce, and lime juice until sizzling vigorously and the chiles are soft, about 5 minutes. Add the noodles and toss until well coated, 2 to 3 minutes. Add the mint and coriander, toss again, and cook for 1 minute. Serve immediately.

MAKES 4 SERVINGS

pizzazz pasta, napalm noodles, and fiery rice

Rice Noodles with Pork and Mint

I became enamored of this dish when I was at the very beginning of researching this project and a good friend recommended a Thai restaurant with an unlikely name in the Westwood section of Los Angeles, an area better known for UCLA students than Thai food, called Mr. Noodle. I ordered this dish, *kwaytiow pad kee mau*, which was a stir-fry of big flat noodles with pork, tomato, and mint and I thought it very good, plenty hot, and a fine dish to include here. The noodles box is sometimes labeled "extra wide." Everything cooks quickly, so make sure your ingredients are prepared and ready to go.

1/2 pound 1/2-inch-wide rice noodles

3 tablespoons Thai fish sauce

1/4 cup vegetable, canola, or peanut oil

2 teaspoons soy sauce

1 tablespoon palm sugar or light brown sugar

1/2 teaspoon salt

1/2 teaspoon freshly ground black pepper to taste

4 large garlic cloves, finely chopped

35 fresh red Thai chiles or 10 fresh red finger-type chiles or 15 fresh red serrano chiles, finely chopped

1/4 pound ground pork

3/4 cup loosely packed, coarsely chopped fresh basil leaves

6 cherry tomatoes, quartered

1 tablespoon finely chopped fresh mint leaves

---

1. Bring a large pot of salted water to a rolling boil, then cook the noodles according to the package instructions. Drain, rinse in a colander, and set aside in cold water. In a small bowl, mix together the fish sauce, 1 tablespoon of the vegetable oil, the soy sauce, sugar, salt, and pepper and set aside.

2. In a large wok, heat the remaining 3 tablespoons vegetable oil over high heat, swirling the wok to coat the sides. Add the garlic and cook, stirring constantly, until golden, about 15 seconds. Add the chiles and cook for another 15 to 30 seconds, stirring. (Remember to keep the vent hood on full blast to avoid irritation to your eyes, nose, and throat.) Add the pork and stir-fry until browned, about 2 minutes, breaking up any lumps. Add the fish sauce mixture and cook until the sauce is bubbling, about 1 minute. Drain the noodles and add to the wok. Cook, tossing constantly, until they have absorbed the sauce, about 1 minute. Add the basil and tomatoes and continue cooking and tossing until the basil leaves wilt, about 1 minute. Transfer to a serving platter and garnish with the mint. Serve immediately.

MAKES 4 SERVINGS

Ants Climbing a Tree

C hinese writers and cooks will tell you that the name of this dish comes from the fact that when you hold up the thin noodles with your chopsticks, the bits of meat clinging to them appear like ants climbing a tree. Some other names for this authentic Sichuan dish are ants climbing a hill, ants climbing a log, ants creeping up a tree, and ants on the tree. Interestingly, this dish is thought by the Sichuanese to be bland. I include it because, first, it's a wonderful taste, and second, it has enough chiles in it to be considered quite hot by many North Americans. The noodles used in this preparation are made from mung or soy beans and are called bean thread noodles as well as Oriental vermicelli, cellophane noodles, or glass noodles. They are usually found in the international/Asian section of the supermarket. If you're not inclined to use chopsticks, think about it for this dish—it's more fun to eat that way and you can better understand its name.

1 tablespoon soy sauce

2 teaspoons sesame oil

2 teaspoons Chile Oil (page 424)

1 tablespoon sugar

1/2 pound ground pork

1/4 pound bean thread noodles (2 bunches)

1/4 cup peanut oil

8 dried red de arbol chiles, seeded and cut in half

2 teaspoons finely chopped fresh ginger

1 teaspoon red chile flakes

4 scallions, white and light green parts, chopped

1/4 cup water

1. In a medium-size bowl, stir together the soy sauce, 1 teaspoon of the sesame oil, the chile oil, and sugar. Add the ground pork and marinate for 15 to 30 minutes. Soak the noodles in hot water until they are pliable, about 5 minutes. Drain well, then cut them with kitchen scissors into shorter lengths.

2.   In a wok, heat the peanut oil over high heat, then cook the chiles and ginger for 15 seconds. Add the pork and stir-fry constantly, breaking it up, until it has lost its pinkness, about 1 minute. Add the chile flakes and scallions and stir, and then add the noodles, stirring all the time. Add the water and cook until the liquid has been absorbed and evaporated, about 3 minutes. Sprinkle the remaining 1 teaspoon sesame oil on top and toss. Serve immediately.

MAKES 4 SERVINGS

the piquant cuisine of korea

Korea is the one case that shoots down the tropical/perspiration hypothesis (page xii). Korea is not tropical, it is not near the Equator, and is, in fact, cold and temperate. Korea does not even lie within the so-called hot zone of the Tropics of Cancer and Capricorn, and it never was on any major spice route. Yet the Koreans are said to have the highest per capita consumption of chile in the world. The chile probably met its first Korean in China rather than Korea. Likely it was a Portuguese Jesuit in Beijing who interacted with the Koreans and a dried chile containing seeds may have exchanged hands. Alternatively, it's possible that the Dutch brought the chile to Korea much later, in the mid-seventeenth century.

Before the chile's arrival, pungency in Korean food came from radishes and mustard. The chiles most popular in Korea are a finger-type variety known as *koch'u*, about three inches long with smooth skin that tapers at the end. They resemble Anaheim or New Mexico Red chiles. This chile is the basis for the hot red chile powder known as *koch'u karu* that is sold in three grades: coarse for making kimchi, flakes or threads known as *sil koch'u* that are used as a zesty garnish, and fine for making the hot red chile paste known as *koch'ujang*, which is used in nearly all Korean prepared dishes. It is a complex paste, traditionally made in the home but today often bought in the market in tubs of different sizes, made with barley malt powder, water, sweet rice flour, hot red chile powder, fermented soybean paste, salt, and soy sauce.

Oriental Noodles
with Beef and Chicken

This extravagant dish called *chapch'ae* is typically found on a Korean party table, as it can be made to feed a good number of people and it can be prepared beforehand and served at room temperature. To make and serve this properly, have a large wooden salad bowl ready. Mung bean and sweet potato starch noodles are firm vermicelli-like noodles that can be found in Asian markets and some better supermarkets. If you are absolutely unable to find them, use bean sprout noodles that are found in the international/Asian section of your supermarket. At a Korean market you might find some of the other traditional ingredients that could find their way into this dish, such as dried day lilies or bellflower roots. Some cooks might also add cucumbers or carrots. Whatever is added should be cut in thin julienne. Korean cooks will instruct you to cook each component separately, and that's how I learned it and how I instruct you. But if you are pressed for time, you can use the first marinade mentioned for all the ingredients and cook them all together using a large wok and I'm sure it would taste fine. This recipe is adapted from the one in Hi Soo Shin Hepinstall's *Growing Up in a Korean Kitchen* (Ten Speed Press, 2001).

2 tablespoons rice wine (*mirin*) or vermouth

4^1/$_2$ teaspoons sugar

10 scallions, white and light green parts only, finely chopped

4 large garlic cloves, finely chopped

1 tablespoon fresh lemon juice

2 tablespoons finely chopped walnuts

1 tablespoon toasted sesame seeds

^{1}/$_4$ teaspoon salt, or more to your taste

^{1}/$_4$ teaspoon freshly ground black pepper, or more to your taste

^{1}/$_4$ pound boneless, skinless chicken breast, sliced into ^{1}/$_8$-inch-thick strips

^{1}/$_4$ pound beef tenderloin, sliced into ^{1}/$_8$-inch-thick strips

3 tablespoons vegetable oil

1 ounce dried shiitake mushrooms, soaked in tepid water for 10 minutes

2 tablespoons soy sauce

2^1/$_2$ tablespoons sesame oil

5 cups water

1 tablespoon distilled vinegar

^{1}/$_2$ pound napa cabbage, stem part only, cut into 3 x ^{1}/$_4$-inch strips

^{1}/$_2$ pound spinach, heavy stems removed, washed well, and sliced into 3-inch strips

2 large eggs, separated

^{1}/$_2$ pound mung bean and sweet potato starch noodles

2 fresh red jalapeño chiles, cut into ^{1}/$_8$-inch-thick slices

2 fresh green jalapeño chiles, cut into ^{1}/$_8$-inch-thick slices

1^1/$_2$ teaspoons coarsely chopped pine nuts

2 teaspoons ground Korean red chile or 1 teaspoon ground red chile

1. In a small bowl, stir together a marinade of 1 tablespoon of the rice wine, 1½ teaspoons of the sugar, 4 scallions, 1 garlic clove, the lemon juice, walnuts, sesame seeds, ¼ teaspoon of salt, and ¼ teaspoon of black pepper. Place the chicken and beef in their own small bowls, then divide the marinade between the two, mixing well so both meats are well coated.

2. In a wok or skillet, heat 1½ teaspoons of the vegetable oil over medium heat and, once it is very hot, cook the chicken until light golden, about 4 minutes, tossing. Transfer to a large bowl, such as a wooden salad bowl, where you will put all the ingredients side by side until their final tossing. Pour another 1½ teaspoons of the vegetable oil into the same skillet and cook the beef until brown, 1 to 2 minutes. Transfer to the bowl next to the chicken.

3. Drain the mushrooms and squeeze out as much liquid as possible. Slice into thin slivers and set aside. In a small bowl, combine 1 tablespoon of the rice wine, 1 tablespoon of the soy sauce, 1 tablespoon of the sesame oil, 4 scallions, 2 garlic cloves, and a pinch of salt and pepper. Divide in half to marinate the mushroom and cabbage separately. Place the mushrooms in a small bowl and toss with half the marinade. Reserve the other half of the marinade for the cabbage. Add 1 tablespoon of vegetable oil to the skillet you cooked the meat in and heat it over medium heat until hot, then add the mushrooms and cook until soft, 4 to 5 minutes, stirring. Transfer to the bowl next to the meat.

4. In a large saucepan, bring the 5 cups of water to a boil with the distilled vinegar and some salt. Plunge the cabbage into the boiling water for 3 minutes, then remove with a slotted spoon and squeeze as much liquid out as possible. Reserve the cooking water in the pot. Place the cabbage in a medium-size bowl and toss with the reserved half of the marinade. Transfer to the wooden bowl, next to the other cooked ingredients.

5. In the same pot you used to cook the cabbage, return the water to a boil if it isn't already boiling, then plunge the spinach in until it wilts, about 10 seconds. Drain immediately and run under cold water to stop its cooking. Then squeeze out as much liquid as you can. Transfer the spinach to the bowl you tossed the cabbage in and toss it with the remaining 2 scallions, 1 garlic clove, 1½ teaspoons of the sesame oil, and a bit of salt and pepper. Add the spinach to the wooden bowl, next to the other ingredients.

6. Put the egg whites and the egg yolks into separate small bowls and beat both seasoned with a little salt and pepper. In a large nonstick skillet, heat 1$\frac{1}{2}$ teaspoons of the vegetable oil over medium heat, then pour the egg whites in and tilt the pan so the whites cover the bottom of the pan. Reduce the heat to medium-low and cook until the eggs are set but not dry, about 2 minutes. Flip with a spatula and cook the other side for 1 minute. Transfer to a lightly oiled plate to cool. Heat another 1$\frac{1}{2}$ teaspoons of the vegetable oil in the same skillet, then pour in the egg yolks and repeat as with the egg whites. Remove and place on top of the egg whites and roll both into a cigar. Slice crosswise into $\frac{1}{8}$-inch slices, unravel, and separate and set aside next to the other food in the wooden bowl.

7. Meanwhile, bring a large pot of lightly salted water to a rolling boil, then cook the noodles according to the package directions. Drain in a colander and rinse with cold water to stop the cooking. Cut the noodles into 5-inch strands with kitchen scissors, transfer to a bowl, and toss with 1$\frac{1}{2}$ teaspoons of the sesame oil. Place next to the other foods in the wooden bowl. Add the red and green chiles to the bowl and toss everything together with your hands, then add the remaining 1 tablespoon soy sauce, remaining 1 tablespoon sugar, and remaining 1$\frac{1}{2}$ teaspoons sesame oil and toss again so everything is mixed very well.

8. Transfer the contents of the bowl to a large serving platter or to individual bowls. Sprinkle with the pine nuts and Korean red chile and serve.

MAKES 6 SERVINGS

Rice and Duck, Chiclayan Style

Called *arroz con pato a la Chiclayana*, this recipe is adapted from Maria Baez Kijac's informative (and delicious) *The South American Table* (The Harvard Common Press, 2003). She tells us that the dish is a specialty of the city of Chiclayo in northwestern Peru. Although it is traditionally made with *chicha de jora*, a fermented corn or quinoa drink, one can use dark beer with great satisfaction, as do many Peruvian cooks. This dish is ideal for dinner parties because it is a cook-ahead-of-time all-in-one dish, best accompanied by a simple salad. You need one 5-pound duck, cut into 8 pieces, breasts cut in half crosswise (to make 10 pieces altogether), wing tips cut off, as much skin removed as you can manage (and saved for rendering duck fat and making duck chitterlings out of the skin).

One 4- to 5-pound duck, cut into 10 pieces (see headnote)

Juice of 1 lemon

2 teaspoons salt, or more to your taste

$1/4$ teaspoon freshly ground black pepper, or more to your taste

$1/4$ cup extra-virgin olive oil

2 medium-size onions, finely chopped

8 large garlic cloves, finely chopped

2 tablespoons finely chopped fresh green serrano chiles

1 teaspoon ground cumin

$1/2$ teaspoon dried oregano

12 ounces dark beer (such as Guinness)

2 cups chicken broth (homemade or canned)

1 cup tightly packed fresh coriander (cilantro) leaves

2 tablespoons pisco or brandy

2 cups medium-grain rice, soaked in tepid water for 30 minutes or rinsed well in a strainer, drained

1 cup fresh or frozen peas

$1/2$ pound fresh green and red jalapeño chiles, seeded, deveined, and cut into thin strips, for garnish

1. Place the duck pieces in a ceramic or glass bowl or baking dish and toss with the lemon juice, $1/2$ teaspoon salt, and $1/4$ teaspoon black pepper. Cover with plastic wrap and marinate in the refrigerator for 4 hours.

2. In a large ovenproof casserole from which you can serve, heat the olive oil over medium-high heat, then cook the onions until soft, about 5 minutes, stirring. Add the garlic, chiles, cumin, oregano, and the remaining $1^1/2$ teaspoons salt, and cook for 1 minute, stirring. Add the duck pieces and toss with the onions until the duck is white on all sides, about 5 minutes. Add the beer and chicken broth, bring to a boil, then reduce the heat to low, cover, and simmer until the duck is cooked through, about 45 minutes. Season with more salt and pepper if desired.

3. Place the coriander and pisco in a blender or mini food processor and blend until very finely minced. There may not be enough liquid to make this work in a blender, in which case you are better off pounding the coriander in a mortar and then adding the liquid. Add this mixture and the rice to the casserole and stir. Cover, bring to a boil, then reduce the heat to medium-low and cook until the rice has absorbed most of the liquid, about 20 minutes. Add the peas, pushing them down into the rice, and cook for 5 minutes without stirring. Garnish the top with the sliced chiles and serve, or let sit in a very low oven until you are ready to serve.

MAKES 4 SERVINGS

Shrimp Rice

This Peruvian dish is not only rich in tastes and fiery hot but it also has an inviting orange-red color. The chile used in this preparation, called *ají amarillo*, is the most common chile used in Peruvian cuisine. The fruit grows up to five inches and matures from yellow to a deep orange. These Peruvian chiles can be purchased through the Internet, or you can use the substitutes I recommend.

8 teaspoons safflower oil or vegetable oil

8 large garlic cloves, mashed in a mortar

2 cups water

2 cups medium-grain rice

2 tablespoons salt

2¹/₂ pounds fresh shrimp with their heads or 1¹/₄ pounds headless shrimp, heads and/or shells removed

¹/₂ cup chopped onions

2 red bell peppers, finely chopped

2 tablespoons *Ají Panca en Pasta* (page 405)

3 fresh yellow chiles (*ají amarillo*) or 5 yellow *güero* chiles or 1 large habanero chile, finely chopped

1 tablespoon hot paprika

¹/₂ teaspoon freshly ground black pepper

¹/₄ cup lager beer

¹/₄ cup dry white wine

¹/₂ pound (1 cup) cooked fresh or frozen peas

1 tablespoon finely chopped fresh parsley leaves, for garnish

1. In a heavy saucepan with a heavy lid, heat 3 teaspoons of the safflower oil over medium-high heat, then cook 1¹/₂ mashed garlic cloves until sizzling and starting to turn color, about 1 minute. Add the 2 cups water and bring to a boil. Add the rice and 2 teaspoons of the salt, stir, reduce the heat to medium-low, cover, and cook without stirring until the rice is done, about 15 minutes. Remove the lid, drizzle with 2 teaspoons of the safflower oil, and rake the top of the rice with a fork. Turn the heat off and cover for 10 minutes, then uncover and let cool.

2. Bring a large saucepan of water to a boil. Add 1 tablespoon of the salt and cook the shrimp until they turn orange-pink, about 2 minutes. Drain and reserve the shrimp. If you are using fresh shrimp and there is any coral attached, separate the coral from the shrimp tail and reserve it.

3. In a large skillet or 12-inch paella pan, heat the remaining 3 teaspoons safflower oil over medium-high heat, then cook the remaining garlic, the onion, bell peppers, *ají panca en pasta*, fresh chiles, paprika, the remaining 1 teaspoon salt, and pepper until the liquid evaporates, about 5 minutes, stirring. Add the beer and shrimp coral, if any, and bring to a boil, stirring. Add the white wine and cooked rice. Stir gently until the rice takes on a uniform color from the other ingredients. Push the shrimp and cooked peas into the rice once it has been blended and colored, stirring ever so slightly, then simmer without stirring over medium-low heat until the rice dries and the shrimp are hot, about 5 minutes. Sprinkle the top with parsley and serve hot.

MAKES 4 TO 5 SERVINGS

Red Rice with Crispy-Fried Pork

This famous dish is called, simply enough, *arroz a la Mexicana*, Mexican rice, because it is made everywhere in Mexico. Depending on the region you're in, it will have variations, perhaps with meat or fish. This particular version comes from Oaxaca and is made with pork. It can be eaten either as a side dish or as a main course.

3 tablespoons pork lard

1 cup medium-grain rice, soaked in tepid water for 30 minutes or rinsed well in a strainer, drained

1 small onion, finely chopped

1 garlic clove, finely chopped

1/2 celery stalk, finely chopped

1 tablespoon finely chopped fresh parsley leaves

1 ripe juicy large tomato (about 10 ounces), cut in half, seeds squeezed out, and grated against the largest holes of a grater

1/2 cup fresh or frozen peas

1 large carrot, peeled and finely diced

2 fresh green jalapeño chiles, sliced

1 cup chicken broth (homemade or canned)

3 tablespoons fresh lemon juice

1 teaspoon salt

Freshly ground black pepper to taste

1 pound pork loin, cut into 3/4-inch cubes

4 sprigs coriander (cilantro), for garnish

1. In a heavy saucepan, melt 2 tablespoons of the lard over medium heat, then cook the rice and onion until lightly browned and sticking, about 7 minutes, stirring frequently. Add the garlic and cook for 1 minute, stirring.

2. Add the celery, parsley, tomato, peas, carrot, chiles, chicken broth, lemon juice, salt, and pepper. Bring to a boil, stir, reduce the heat to low, cover, and cook until the liquid is absorbed, about 15 minutes. Remove the rice from the heat, insert paper towels between the pot and the lid, and let sit for 10 minutes.

3. Meanwhile, in a medium-size skillet, heat the remaining 1 tablespoon lard over medium-high heat and cook the pork until crispy brown, 3 to 4 minutes. Turn and cook the other side until browned, another 3 to 4 minutes. Transfer the rice to a serving platter and fluff it with a fork. Add the fried pork and serve hot, garnished with coriander sprigs.

MAKES 4 SERVINGS

pizzazz pasta, napalm noodles, and fiery rice

Tomato Rice

The cooking of the Indian state of Andhra Pradesh is a melting pot of Hindu and Muslim cultures. Muslim emperors ruled from the fifteenth to the eighteenth century and they influenced the cuisine as much as the native Telegu-speaking Andhras. A result of the fusion of these cultures is a quite fiery food as we see in this rice preparation with tomatoes. The preparation is very simple and it can stand alone as a vegetarian meal.

3 tablespoons vegetable oil or clarified butter (*ghee*)

4 whole cloves

1/2 cinnamon stick

Seeds from 3 cardamom pods, crushed, or 1/4 teaspoon ground cardamom

One 1/2-inch cube fresh ginger, peeled and finely chopped

4 large garlic cloves, finely chopped

8 fresh green finger-type chiles or 10 fresh green jalapeño chiles, slit down the middle

2 medium-size onions, sliced

1 1/2 pounds tomatoes, peeled, seeded, and chopped

1 teaspoon ground red chile or cayenne pepper

1/2 teaspoon ground turmeric

3 teaspoons salt

2 cups long-grain basmati rice, soaked in tepid water for 30 minutes or rinsed well in a strainer, drained

3 cups water

1. In a large casserole, heat the vegetable oil over medium heat and cook the cloves, cinnamon, and cardamom for 1 minute, stirring. Add the ginger and garlic and cook for 1 minute, then add the chiles and onions and cook until the onions are golden, 10 to 12 minutes, stirring.

2. Add the tomatoes, ground chile, turmeric, and salt and cook for 4 minutes. Add the rice, stir, and pour in the water. Bring to a boil, reduce the heat to low, cover, and cook without stirring or uncovering until the liquid is absorbed and the rice is tender, 15 to 18 minutes. Serve hot.

MAKES 6 SERVINGS

Mango Rice

This vegetarian rice preparation is popular in the southern Indian states of Karnataka, Andhra Pradesh, and Tamil Nadu. Some cooks also add cashews or peanuts to the dish, and all versions include curry leaves (see page 372), which can be bought at Indian markets, some farmers' markets, and via the Internet, as can the black gram (which can be replaced with black lentils).

2 tablespoons unsalted butter or clarified butter (*ghee*)

2 cups long-grain basmati rice, soaked in tepid water for 30 minutes or rinsed well in a strainer, drained

2 teaspoons salt

4³/₄ cups water

¹/₄ teaspoon black mustard seeds

¹/₂ cup cooked chickpeas

¹/₂ ounce (2 tablespoons) black gram (*urad dal*)

Small bunch of curry leaves (about 2 dozen leaves)

¹/₂ teaspoon ground turmeric

3 fresh green finger-type chiles or 4 fresh green jalapeño chiles, seeded and chopped

2 dried red de arbol chiles, broken in half and seeded

1 mango, peeled and grated

Finely chopped fresh coriander (cilantro) leaves, for garnish

1. In a heavy saucepan, melt 1 tablespoon of the butter over medium-high heat. Add the rice and salt and cook for 2 minutes, stirring. Add 3¹/₂ cups of the water, bring to a boil, and stir. Reduce the heat to low, cover, and cook without stirring or uncovering until the liquid is absorbed and the rice is tender, 15 to 18 minutes.

2. Meanwhile, in a medium-size skillet, melt the remaining 1 tablespoon butter over medium-high heat and cook the mustard seeds, chickpeas, black gram, curry leaves, turmeric, and green and red chiles until they are soft, 4 to 5 minutes, stirring frequently. Add the mango and remaining 1¹/₄ cups water, season with salt, and cook for another 10 minutes, stirring. Cover, turn the heat off, and let sit for 10 minutes. Fold this mixture into the cooked rice and mix well. Sprinkle the top with coriander leaves and serve immediately.

MAKES 8 SERVINGS

pizzazz pasta, napalm noodles, and fiery rice

 # Spicy Eggplant Rice

T his type of rice preparation is popular in southern India, where heat from chiles is the norm. This rice dish is nice served with the traditional Goan Fish Curry (page 279). The green gram used in this recipe can be found in Indian markets as *moong dal*, or you can order it on the Internet.

¹/₂ pound eggplant, peeled and diced

1¹/₂ teaspoons salt, plus more for sprinkling

1¹/₂ tablespoons clarified butter (*ghee*)

1¹/₂ cups long-grain basmati rice, soaked in tepid water for 30 minutes or rinsed well in a strainer, drained

2¹/₄ cups water

3 tablespoons vegetable oil or mustard oil

1 teaspoon poppy seeds

¹/₂ teaspoon anise seeds

4 whole cloves

Seeds from 4 cardamom pods

One 2-inch cinnamon stick

1¹/₂ teaspoons mustard seeds

6 fresh red finger-type chiles, halved lengthwise, or 8 red jalapeño chiles, quartered lengthwise

6 fresh green finger-type chiles, split lengthwise, or 8 green jalapeño chiles, quartered lengthwise

1 tablespoon green gram (*moong dal*) or split green peas, soaked in water to cover until needed, then drained

1 large onion, finely chopped

Juice of 2 lemons

15 curry leaves

¹/₄ teaspoon ground turmeric

1. Lay the eggplant pieces on paper towels and sprinkle with salt. Leave them to drain of their bitter juices for 30 minutes, then pat dry with paper towels.

2. In a large, heavy casserole or saucepan with a tight-fitting lid, melt the clarified butter over medium-high heat and cook the rice for 2 or 3 minutes, stirring frequently. Add the water and 1¹/₂ teaspoons salt, increase the heat to high, and, once it begins to boil slightly, reduce the heat to low, cover, and cook without stirring or uncovering until the liquid is absorbed and the rice is tender, 15 to 18 minutes. Transfer the rice to a large platter, sprinkle 1 teaspoon of the vegetable oil over it, and toss with a fork.

3. In a small skillet, heat 2 teaspoons of the vegetable oil over medium heat and cook the poppy seeds, anise seeds, cloves, cardamom, and the cinnamon stick for 3 minutes. Remove and cool, then grind into a fine powder in a spice mill and set aside.

4. In a large skillet, heat the remaining 2 tablespoons of vegetable oil over medium heat and cook the mustard seeds and red chiles. Once the mustard seeds start to crackle and pop, add the green chiles and green gram and cook until the water content in the chiles evaporates, about 2 minutes. Add the chopped onion, chopped eggplants, and a little salt, and cook until the onion turns translucent and soft, 20 to 25 minutes. Add the lemon juice, curry leaves, and turmeric, mix well, and cook for 5 more minutes, stirring. Turn this mixture and the reserved spice mix into the rice and toss well. Serve hot.

MAKES 6 SERVINGS

Yogurt Rice

This preparation from Tamil Nadu is called *thair sadam* and is served with lemon pickle, *elumichai urukkai*, which you might be able to find at Indian markets. The dish should be hot temperature wise, so make sure the yogurt and cream are at room temperature before adding them.

1 tablespoon clarified butter (*ghee*)

1 cup long-grain basmati rice, soaked in tepid water for 30 minutes or rinsed well in a strainer, drained

1³/₄ cups water

1¹/₂ teaspoons salt

1 tablespoon vegetable oil

¹/₄ teaspoon black mustard seeds

¹/₂ dried red de arbol chile, crumbled, or ¹/₄ teaspoon red pepper flakes

2 fresh green finger-type chiles or 3 green jalapeño chiles, seeded and finely chopped

One ¹/₂-inch cube fresh ginger, peeled and finely chopped

4 curry leaves

1¹/₂ cups whole plain yogurt, at room temperature

3 tablespoons heavy cream, at room temperature

1. In a large, heavy casserole or saucepan with a tight-fitting lid, melt the clarified butter over medium-high heat and cook the rice for 2 to 3 minutes, stirring frequently. Add the water and 1 teaspoon of the salt, raise the heat to high, and, once it begins to boil slightly, reduce the heat to low, cover, and cook without stirring or uncovering until the liquid is absorbed and the rice is tender, 15 to 18 minutes. Transfer to a large bowl.

2.   Meanwhile, in a small skillet, heat the vegetable oil over medium-high heat, then cook the mustard seeds, red chile, green chiles, ginger, and curry leaves until the mustard seeds start to crackle and pop, about 1 minute. Pour this mixture over the rice and toss well. In a small bowl, beat the yogurt with the remaining $1/2$ teaspoon salt. Mix the yogurt with the rice, tossing well. Pour the cream over the rice and mix well. Serve hot.

MAKES 4 SERVINGS

Coconut Chile Rice with Pigeon Peas and Tamarind Juice

*I*n the city of Mysore in the Indian state of Karnataka, this is a favorite dish. It is fragrant, hot, and filling. The ingredients list appears exotic and it is—the pigeon peas, unsweetened coconut, black gram, fenugreek, asafoetida, *ghee*, tamarind, black mustard seeds, and curry leaves can only be found in Indian markets or on the Internet. I assure you it's worth the effort.

$1/2$ cup (about $1/4$ pound) dried pigeon peas or split green peas

6 fresh red finger-type chiles or 8 fresh red jalapeño chiles

$1^1/4$ cups fresh or dried or shredded unsweetened coconut

1 teaspoon yellow split peas

1 teaspoon black gram (*urad dal*)

$1/4$ teaspoon ground fenugreek

$1/2$ teaspoon ground turmeric

Pinch of asafoetida

2 tablespoons clarified butter (*ghee*)

1 cup long-grain basmati rice, soaked in tepid water for 30 minutes or rinsed well in a strainer, drained

$1^3/4$ cups water

1 teaspoon salt

$1/4$ teaspoon *garam masala* (see page 309)

$1/4$ cup tamarind water (see page 329)

1 tablespoon vegetable oil

$1/2$ teaspoon black mustard seeds

4 curry leaves (see page 372)

$1/4$ cup (1 ounce) unsalted cashews

1.   Bring a large saucepan of water to a boil, salt lightly, and cook the pigeon peas until soft, about 20 minutes.

2. Preheat the oven to 450°F. Place the chiles in one baking dish or tray and the coconut, yellow split peas, and black gram in another. Roast until the chiles are slightly blackened and the coconut is browning on the edges, about 25 minutes for the chiles and 10 to 12 minutes for the coconut. Remove the stems and seeds from the chiles. Transfer the contents of both trays to a food processor, add the fenugreek, turmeric, and asafoetida, and grind until a paste, scraping down the sides if necessary.

3. In a large, heavy casserole or saucepan with a tight-fitting lid, melt 1 tablespoon of the clarified butter over medium-high heat and cook the rice for 2 to 3 minutes, stirring frequently. Add the $1^3/_4$ cups water, salt, pigeon peas, coconut-chile mixture, *garam masala*, and tamarind water. Increase the heat to high, stir, and, once it begins to boil slightly, reduce the heat to low, cover, and cook without stirring or uncovering until the liquid is absorbed and the rice is tender, 15 to 18 minutes.

4. Meanwhile, in a small skillet, heat the vegetable oil over medium-high heat, then cook the mustard seeds, curry leaves, and cashews until the mustard seeds start to crackle and pop, 1 to 2 minutes. Transfer the rice to a serving platter, fluff the rice, and pour the mustard seed mixture over the top. Drizzle the remaining 1 tablespoon of melted clarified butter over the top, Serve immediately.

MAKES 6 SERVINGS

Shrimp and Chile Fried Rice

Fried rice is tricky to make. You start with steamed rice and make sure it is cool or cold and not warm. Fried rice requires a good bit of oil in order for the grains to remain separate and to make sure the final dish doesn't end up looking like risotto. Another thing you want to remember is that the eggs should begin to congeal before you start stirring them. So it's best to leave the eggs undisturbed for a bit until the white starts turning opaque. Then you can scramble them a bit, but not too much. You want the rice to be yellow from the yolk but you want to avoid making the rice creamy. Wait for the egg to cook before you add the next ingredient. Most Thai rice dishes are mild, one reason why they are popular with tourists, but this dish is quite hot.

3/4 cup peanut oil

3 large shallots, finely chopped

20 fresh green Thai chiles or 8 fresh green serrano chiles, finely chopped

1 tablespoon Red Curry Paste (page 423)

2/3 cup diced uncooked pork tenderloin or ham

1/3 cup diced or sliced raw pork belly or blanched bacon

4 cups cooked cold jasmine rice

3 large eggs, beaten lightly

1 cup cooked small shrimp

3 tablespoons Thai fish sauce

4 scallions, finely chopped, for garnish

2 tablespoons finely chopped fresh coriander (cilantro) leaves, for garnish

4 fresh red serrano chiles, split into quarters with a paring knife but keeping the chile whole and attached to the stem end, for garnish

1. In a wok, heat the peanut oil over medium-high heat and cook the shallots and chiles until the shallots are soft, about 5 minutes. Add the red curry paste and cook until blended into the shallots and the oil starts to separate, 3 to 4 minutes, stirring.

2. Add the pork tenderloin and pork belly and cook for 2 minutes, stirring. Add the cold rice and stir and toss thoroughly with a spoon or paddle until the rice is colored with the curry paste and heated through, 5 to 6 minutes. Raise the heat to high and push the rice to the sides, to make a well in the center of the wok. Pour the eggs into the well, let them set slightly, and then start to scramble the eggs in a small circular stirring movement. Once they are fully cooked, about 2 minutes, stir in the shrimp. Stir in the fish sauce, cook for 1 minute, then remove from the heat and transfer to a platter. Sprinkle with the scallions and coriander and decorate the borders with the red chiles. Serve immediately.

MAKES 4 TO 6 SERVINGS

Chicken Fried Rice

This Thai fried rice is called *kao pad gai* and it is delightful way to use up leftover rice. It's worth repeating here the tips for cooking fried rice that I have given elsewhere, because they are important. First, the rice must have been cooked properly in the first place. Second, the rice must be cold or cool and dry. When you come to fry the rice, make sure there's plenty of oil and that the oil is very hot before you start cooking. The cooked and cooled rice will be very sticky, so there is a limit to how unclumped you'll get the grains of rice. Rest assured that once the cold rice hits the very hot oil in the wok and you start stir-frying quickly, the grains will separate. Remember to have all your ingredients already prepared and lined up next to the stove because the cooking process happens quite rapidly.

¹/₄ cup peanut oil	4 cups cooked cold jasmine rice
6 large garlic cloves, finely chopped	1 large egg, beaten
3 shallots, thinly sliced	1 tablespoon Thai fish sauce
1 pound boneless chicken thighs, cut into 1 x ¹/₄-inch-thick strips	1 tablespoon soy sauce
	1 tablespoon green peppercorns
25 fresh red Thai chiles or 10 red serrano chiles or red finger-type chiles, chopped and pounded in a mortar until mushy	1 cup coarsely chopped loosely packed fresh basil leaves
2 small kaffir lime leaves, very thinly sliced, or 1 teaspoon lime zest	

1. In a wok, heat the peanut oil over high heat until smoking, swirling the oil to coat the surface. Add the garlic and cook for 5 to 10 seconds, then add the shallots and cook for another 15 seconds. Add the chicken and cook until it changes color, about 2 minutes. Add the chiles and lime leaves and cook until a bit dry, about 2 minutes, stirring constantly. Add the rice and cook, stirring constantly and quickly until the rice grains are separate, dry, and glistening, about 4 minutes.

2. Push the rice to the sides of the wok, making a well in the middle. Pour the egg into the center and let it set for a minute, then start to scramble the egg in small circular stirring movements. Once it has set, stir-fry the egg into the rice and cook for 1 minute. Stir in the fish sauce, soy sauce, green peppercorns, and basil and cook for another 30 seconds, stirring. Serve immediately.

MAKES 4 TO 6 SERVINGS

pizzazz pasta, napalm noodles, and fiery rice

Pork Fried Rice

Although pork fried rice is ubiquitous on Chinese take-out menus, this fried rice dish, called *kao pad moo*, is Thai, and it is one of my favorite fried rice dishes. As I've said in the two previous recipes, there are some key things to remember when making fried rice so that it doesn't turn into an unappetizing gloppy mess that looks like a pathetic risotto. Cook the rice properly, make sure it is cool or cold and dry, and use plenty of oil.

3 tablespoons vegetable oil

5 large garlic cloves, finely chopped

3 shallots, thinly sliced

2 tablespoons chopped fresh coriander (cilantro) roots and/or stems

1/4 pound pork tenderloin, very thinly sliced in strips

4 cups cooked cold jasmine rice

3 tablespoons Thai fish sauce

1 tablespoon palm sugar or granulated sugar

1 large egg, beaten

1/2 cup thinly sliced fresh red chiles, such as Thai chiles, finger-type chiles, or serrano chiles

2 small Persian cucumbers, julienned, or 1/2 regular cucumber, peeled, seeded, and julienned

2 scallions, thinly sliced on the bias

1/4 cup coarsely chopped fresh coriander (cilantro) leaves

1.   In a wok, heat the vegetable oil over high heat, swirling the wok to coat the sides with the oil, and cook the garlic until turning brown, 15 to 30 seconds, stirring constantly. Add the shallots and coriander root until sizzling furiously, about 1 minute. Add the pork and stir-fry until it loses color, about 2 minutes.

2.   Add the rice, stirring and tossing until the grains are broken up and it is mixed with the other ingredients, then add the fish sauce and sugar. Stir and toss until mixed well. Push the rice to the sides of the wok, making a well in the middle. Pour the egg into the center and let it set for a minute, then start to scramble the egg in small circular stirring movements. Once it has set, stir-fry the egg into the rice and cook for 1 minute. Add three-quarters of the chiles to the wok and toss with the scrambled egg and rice until well mixed. Transfer to a serving platter and sprinkle the top with the cucumbers, scallions, remaining chiles, and coriander leaves. Serve immediately.

MAKES 4 TO 6 SERVINGS

COUSCOUS

Couscous is a food product invented in North Africa and found also in West Africa, which in fact might be the place where the technique of steaming grains over broth was invented. Here's a brief primer on how to prepare it.

Couscous is made from scratch by rubbing and rolling together large grains of hard wheat semolina with finer grains of semolina sprayed with salted water to raise the humidity of the semolina so that the two sizes affix to each other to form couscous, the large grain serving as a kind of nucleus for the smaller grains. Couscous can be made from grains other than wheat, too. Today, in both its home in North Africa as well as the United States, couscous can be bought already made and even in an "instant" (that is, precooked) variety. Raw couscous made of wheat is sold in bulk in whole food stores, and I prefer buying it that way. In supermarkets, precooked and preflavored wheat couscous is sold in boxes along with boxed plain uncooked couscous. Although you can use the plain instant couscous in these recipes, they are written for use with uncooked couscous. And remember: couscous is *always* steamed and *never* boiled.

To cook couscous, start by spreading it on a platter and moistening it slightly with salted water, about 1 cup water for 3 cups couscous. Then rake, rub, pick up, and break up the couscous with your fingers to form separate pellets that are moist. Work the grains with your fingers in a circular rotating motion to separate and moisten them evenly. If the mixture becomes too wet, add a little dry couscous. The couscous should be evenly wet, not soggy, and uniform in size, about 3 millimeters in diameter. Continue this rubbing process until the final size of each pellet or couscous is about 1 millimeter in diameter and the pellets are separate from one another. Arrange the couscous on white kitchen towels and leave to dry for 1 to 2 hours, depending on the humidity that day, then rub a little olive oil in with your fingers. Now you are ready to steam the couscous, which is done one, two, or three times over boiling broth.

Couscous is cooked in a special kind of cooking vessel called a *kiskis*, known by the French word *couscoussière* in the West. This cooking ensemble consists of two parts, a potbellied stew pot and a colander-like top part that fits snugly over the bottom part and has holes in its bottom for the steam to rise through. Fine kitchenware stores sell *couscoussières*. A makeshift *couscoussière* can be made by placing a colander over a like-size pot.

The couscous goes in the top part and the broth goes in the bottom part. Cook the couscous as long as the recipe instructs and then remove it and dry it a bit before re-cooking as the recipe instructs. The way I tell whether the couscous is done is by tasting it. The couscous should taste tender (not *al dente* and not mushy), and the grains should be separate and taste moist (not wet and not dry).

Fiery Fennel Couscous

The Tunisians are big eaters of couscous and they like their broth very hot with chiles. This recipe, called *kisskiss bi'l-bisbas*, is a couscous typically served as a family lunch. The couscous is eaten in special bowls that look like cereal bowls, with each diner adding as much broth as desired. This couscous is also typically a winter dish, and that's when I would make it, too. Whole wheat couscous, which is more popular with older generations of Algerians and Tunisians, is harder to find than regular couscous, but should you see it in the market I suggest you use it because it makes the whole preparation so earthy to go along well with the fiery.

3 cups uncooked whole wheat or fine wheat couscous (about 1¹/₂ pounds)

4 teaspoons salt

6¹/₂ cups tepid water

1¹/₄ cups extra-virgin olive oil

1 medium-size onion, chopped

2 tablespoons tomato paste dissolved in ¹/₂ cup water

6 large garlic cloves, finely chopped

2 tablespoons hot paprika

1¹/₂ teaspoons ground coriander

1¹/₂ teaspoons ground caraway

4 whole cloves

2 tablespoons *Harisa* (page 414)

2 pounds fennel, leaves and some bulb, finely chopped

Leaves from ¹/₂ pound fresh coriander (cilantro), finely chopped

¹/₂ pound scallions, white and green parts, finely chopped

4 red potatoes (1¹/₂ pounds), peeled and diced

4 fresh Anaheim chiles or light green long peppers (*peperoncini*)

4 fresh large green jalapeño chiles

1. Place half the couscous on a large platter or baking pan with shallow sides. Dissolve 1 teaspoon of the salt in 1 cup of the water. Spread the couscous around and begin moistening it with the salted water a little at a time until all of the water is used—do not pour all the water in at once. Every time you add water, rub it into the grains, breaking up any lumps. Continue raking and rubbing in a circular motion until all the couscous pellets are moistened. If the mixture becomes too wet, incorporate a little dry couscous. Brush the little pellets of semolina with up to ¹/₄ cup of the olive oil so they are all coated. Cut a piece of cheesecloth and use it to cover the holes on the bottom of the top part of the *couscoussière* and up the sides. The cheesecloth is not used to keep the couscous from falling through—it won't—but to facilitate transferring it during the several drying processes. Transfer the couscous to the top portion of the *couscoussière* and set aside until needed.

2. In the bottom portion of a *couscoussière* or stockpot, heat the remaining 1 cup olive oil and cook the onion until yellow and soft over medium heat, about 6 minutes, stirring occasionally. Add the dissolved tomato paste, garlic, paprika, coriander, caraway, cloves, the remaining 3 teaspoons salt, and the *harisa*. Reduce the heat to low and simmer, adding up to $1^1/_2$ cups water from time to time during the next 10 minutes.

3. Increase the heat to medium, add 2 cups water to the bottom portion, place the top portion or strainer/colander on top, and add the chopped fennel, coriander leaves, and scallions to the couscous and steam them for 20 minutes, covered, fluffing the couscous once in a while with a fork. If you don't have a tight fit between the two sections you can wrap a kitchen towel around where they join.

4. Remove the top of the *couscoussière* or the strainer/colander and transfer the couscous to a cooling platter by picking up the ends of the cheesecloth and lifting it out. Break the couscous and vegetables up with your fingers, rubbing and aerating and tossing well. Add 2 cups water to the broth and return the couscous and vegetables to the top portion of the *couscoussière* or strainer/colander, and then place on top of the bottom portion. Steam over medium heat for 20 minutes, covered, fluffing occasionally with a fork. Transfer the couscous and vegetables to the platter again and leave to cool and dry for 1 hour.

5. Return the couscous to the top portion again and again place the top portion on top of the bottom portion. Add the potatoes, green long peppers, and chiles to the couscous. Steam over medium heat until the potatoes and peppers are tender, 45 minutes to 1 hour. Transfer the couscous to a large serving platter and pour one to two ladlefuls of sauce over the couscous. Stir and let the grains absorb the broth. Serve with the remaining broth on the side.

MAKES 6 TO 8 SERVINGS

USING PRECOOKED OR INSTANT COUSCOUS

It is more convenient to use precooked couscous in these recipes, though the flavor will not be as good. If you wish to use precooked packaged couscous, cook the meat and/or vegetables before adding the couscous to the top portion of the *couscoussière* or the colander. Then cook the couscous according to the package directions. However, if the package instructions call for boiling the couscous, don't do it. Instead, steam the couscous for twice the amount of time specified for boiling.

Fish Couscous

This Tunisian fish couscous is so different, far more delicate than the Tunisian lamb couscous. The fishing off Tunisian coasts has been good since the days of the Carthaginians, and a recipe like this, from the island of Djerba, makes me dream of Jason and the Argonauts. Even today Sfax has what many Tunisians consider the best fish cookery in the country. All along the coast down to Djerba and swinging around to Libya people make fish couscous with a wide variety of local fish, including gilt-head bream. Cooks throw all kinds of things into the aromatic steaming broth, such as chickpeas, quince, tons of chiles, black pepper, cinnamon, and even rose petal powder. Along the coast of western Libya, the ancient Tripolitania, cooks make fish couscous by deep-frying the fish first.

4 cups uncooked fine wheat couscous (about 2 pounds)

1¹/₂ to 2 cups lightly salted warm water

³/₄ cup extra-virgin olive oil

1 large onion, coarsely chopped

¹/₂ pound green bell peppers, chopped

One 6-ounce can tomato paste dissolved in 1 cup water

10 ounces Swiss chard, trimmed of heavy stems and julienned

Leaves from 1 bunch parsley (about 6 ounces), chopped

20 large garlic cloves (about 1¹/₂ heads garlic), peeled and lightly crushed

1 tablespoon *Harisa* (page 414)

2 teaspoons cayenne pepper

1 teaspoon ground cumin

Salt and freshly ground black pepper to taste

2 quarts fish broth (homemade or canned)

1 large boiling potato, peeled, and quartered

¹/₄ pound baby carrots

¹/₂ pound turnips, trimmed, peeled and quartered

2 medium-size zucchini, peeled and cut into thirds

2³/₄ pounds mixed fish fillets (at least 3 of the following or similar fish: grouper, gray mullet, porgy, monkfish, shark, ocean catfish, hake, cod, halibut), cut into large pieces

1. Place half the couscous in a large platter or baking pan with shallow sides. Spread the couscous around and begin moistening it with the salted water, a little at a time, until all of the water is used. Do not pour all the water in at once. Every time you add water, rub it into the grains, breaking up any lumps. Continue raking and rubbing in a circular motion until all the couscous pellets are moistened. If the mixture becomes too wet, add a little dry couscous and start again. Brush the little pellets of semolina with up to ¹/₄ cup of the olive oil so that they are all coated. Cut a piece of cheesecloth and use it to cover the holes on the bottom of the top portion of the *couscoussière* and up the sides. The cheesecloth is not used to keep the couscous from falling through—it won't—but to facilitate transferring it during the several drying processes. Transfer the couscous to the top portion and set aside until needed.

2. In the bottom of a *couscoussière* or a stockpot, heat the remaining olive oil over high heat and cook the onion and green peppers until the onion is soft, about 6 minutes, stirring frequently. Add the dissolved tomato paste, Swiss chard, parsley, garlic cloves, *harisa*, cayenne, cumin, salt, and black pepper. Reduce the heat to medium, stir, and cook for 10 minutes. Add the fish broth and bring to a boil.

3. Place the top portion of the *couscoussière* or the strainer/colander with the couscous on top of the bottom portion or stockpot. As soon as steam begins to rise through the couscous grains, about 4 minutes, reduce the heat to medium, cover, and cook for 18 to 20 minutes, stirring and breaking up any lumps of couscous with a fork. If steam is escaping where the two parts join, seal them with a kitchen towel. Remove the top portion and transfer the couscous to a cooling platter by picking up the ends of the cheesecloth and lifting it out. Break the grains up with your fingers, rubbing and aerating. Turn the heat off under the broth. Dry the couscous for 30 minutes to 1 hour.

4. Taste the broth and add some salt, if necessary. Add more fish broth or water, if necessary. Return the couscous to the top portion of the *couscoussière* or strainer/colander and place over the broth. Bring the broth to a boil and, as soon as the steam rises from the couscous, reduce the heat to medium and steam for 18 to 20 minutes. Remove the couscous to the cooling platter again and break up the grains with your fingers, rubbing and aerating. Turn the heat off under the broth. Dry the couscous for 30 minutes to 1 hour.

5. Replace the couscous on top of the *couscoussière* or strainer/colander a third time. Add the potato, carrots, turnips, and zucchini to the broth. Arrange the fish on top of the couscous. Cover, bring the broth to a boil, and cook for 25 minutes over medium-high heat.

what to drink with spicy food

There is something of a debate about what one should drink with chile-based piquant food. First, recognize that wine is completely lost and hopelessly wrecked by chile-hot foods, except perhaps those recipes rated with a 🌶. Water has no effect, although it is still fine to drink and cold water is always refreshing no matter what you eat. Beer is, of course, very refreshing, although it will not counteract the chile. Milk and yogurt drinks, such as the Indian *lassi*, are not only said to have some mild effect in countering the heat but are also delicious on their own. I imagine a milk shake might be nice to drink with very hot food, although it sounds too heavy to me. Jamaicans say you should drink ginger beer. West Africans are said not to drink anything. Perhaps the best drinks to have are slightly sweet ones, since sweetness seems to be a delightful complement to the chile-heat. Try apricot juice, mango juice, lemonade, and other fruit-based drinks, as well as Coke, root beer, and cream soda, all of which are wonderful with hot foods (although the carbonation of sodas might not help). After all these suggestions, I find that the two beverages I drink the most with hot food are beer and water.

6. Check the fish and, if it is perfectly steamed, flaking easily but still maintaining its shape, remove to a plate. Pour the couscous onto a large serving platter, fluffing with a fork. Stir in a ladle or two of broth and add black pepper. Stir and fluff so that it is well blended. Mold the couscous attractively on the platter and scatter the fish and vegetables around on top. Cover with sheets of aluminum foil and let rest for 10 minutes. Remove the foil and serve with the remaining broth on the side.

MAKES 8 TO 10 SERVINGS

hot
accompaniments

This chapter is filled with great side dishes to serve along with your main courses. They are spicy-hot, too, and can be used with plainer main courses if you like. If I were to use them that way, I would make a simple main course, such as a grilled steak or a roast chicken or poached fish. As many of the recipes in this chapter are all-vegetable recipes, you could increase the portions and serve them as full-fledged vegetarian main courses. Some of these recipes have very simple names that disguise their complex tastes, such as the Rice and Peas (page 362). Other recipes draw you to them simply because of their names, such as Baby Carrots in the "Sauce That Dances" (page 363).

Zucchini with Tomatoes, Corn, and Chiles

T his Mexican dish is excellent with *manchamantel* (see page 126). This delightful preparation can be made hotter if you like by using more chiles. It will also be a little nicer with fresh corn kernels rather than frozen. You could also cut up some other leftover vegetables (pumpkin is especially nice) and heat them with this dish in the same saucepan.

2 tablespoons extra-virgin olive oil

1 pound small zucchini, sliced ¼ inch thick

1 medium-size onion, thinly sliced

2 large garlic cloves, finely chopped

1 roasted green bell pepper, peeled and cut into strips

2 fresh green finger-type chiles or 3 fresh green jalapeño chiles, seeded and cut into strips

Salt and freshly ground black pepper to taste

1 pound tomatoes, cut in half, seeds squeezed out, and grated against the largest holes of a grater

1 cup fresh corn kernels

3 tablespoons finely chopped fresh coriander (cilantro) leaves

1. In a large skillet, heat the olive oil over high heat and, when it is almost smoking, cook the zucchini, preferably in one layer, until light brown on both sides, about 6 minutes. Remove the zucchini with a slotted spoon or spatula and set aside.

2. Add the onion and garlic to the skillet and cook, stirring constantly, until soft and light brown, about 3 minutes. Reduce the heat to low, add the bell pepper and chiles, season with salt and pepper, cover, and simmer until soft, about 10 minutes. Stir in the tomatoes, corn, and coriander and continue cooking, covered, until the corn is almost tender, 20 to 25 minutes. Add the zucchini and cook until the vegetables are soft, about 10 minutes. Serve immediately.

MAKES 4 SERVINGS

hot accompaniments

Skillet-Fried Potatoes with Green Chiles

This Mexican preparation is called *papas con rajas*, potatoes with strips, "strips" being slices of chiles. This is a particularly nice accompaniment to Mahimahi with Green Chile and Cilantro Cream Sauce (page 254).

1¹/₂ pounds small waxy potatoes, such as Red Bliss

2 tablespoons pork lard

1 medium-size onion, finely chopped

2 fresh green finger-type chiles or 3 fresh green jalapeño chiles, seeded and cut into strips

1. Place the potatoes in a saucepan and cover with cold water, then turn the heat to high and cook for 20 minutes. Turn the heat off, let the potatoes rest in the water for 5 minutes, then drain and, when cool enough to handle, peel and cut into ¹/₄-inch-thick slices.

2. In a large skillet, melt the lard over medium heat, then cook the onion and chiles until soft, about 5 minutes, stirring. Raise the heat to high, add the potatoes and salt, and cook until golden, tossing and turning almost constantly, about 10 minutes. Serve hot.

MAKES 4 SERVINGS

Black Beans with Chiles

One will find black beans accompanying many dishes in Mexico. This simple combination is wonderful because the leftovers are so versatile. Add nearly anything to it and you have tomorrow's lunch, or crumble some cheese on top and spoon it into a tortilla and you've got a snack. I particularly like these beans with Carnitas (page 227) as a side dish.

1 cup dried black beans

1 small onion, quartered

1 large garlic clove, finely chopped

5 cups water

2 tablespoons pork lard

2 large fresh green serrano chiles, seeded and finely chopped

5 sprigs epazote (optional)

Salt to taste

1 cup crumbled Mexican *queso fresco* or shredded Mexican 4-cheese mix

3 tablespoons finely chopped fresh coriander (cilantro) leaves, for garnish

1. Place the beans in a saucepan with the onion and garlic, cover with the water, and bring to a boil. Reduce the heat to medium-low and cook until the beans are very tender, about $1^1/2$ hours. If the water has evaporated, add about $^1/2$ cup boiling water to keep the beans moist.

2. Meanwhile, in a medium-size skillet, melt the lard over high heat with the chiles. Once the chiles are sizzling and soft and the beans are tender, add 2 ladlefuls of the beans to the skillet and cook them until softer, about 5 minutes, stirring. Mash the beans in the skillet with a potato masher and return the contents of the skillet to the saucepan with the remaining beans, along with the epazote, if using, and salt. Cook the beans over low heat for 30 minutes, stirring occasionally. Transfer the beans to a serving plate or platter and sprinkle the cheese on top. Serve with a sprinkling of coriander leaves.

MAKES 4 SERVINGS

EPAZOTE

This musty herb, reminiscent of a combination of sage and parsley, is used in Mexican cuisine and can be found in farmers' markets in the western United States. The leaves of epazote were originally used as condiments in soups and stews made by Chinatects and Mezatects and other tribes in Mexico. Rather than concoct a substitute I recommend that you just consider it optional, as it can be hard to find.

hot accompaniments

Rice and Peas

It has been claimed that every household in Jamaica, no matter what class, makes "rice and peas," a nutritionally complete preparation. One writer called it the backbone of the island's cuisine, and, in fact, it is also known as "Jamaica's coat of arms." The Jamaican "rice and peas" is a great example of a peasant-based pan-Caribbean type of preparation. The combination of rice and beans—and in Jamaica the "peas" are actually red kidney beans or pigeon peas—appears in the Spanish islands as *moros y cristianos* (Moors and Christians), a dish that originated in Spain, and on French islands as *pois et riz* (peas and rice). Rice and peas is a typical dish on Sundays in Jamaica and is often served with meats. While there are regional variations around the Caribbean, Jamaica's is a notably fiery dish. Some cooks don't use the Scotch bonnet chiles in order to make the dish balance with spicier main courses. Another name used for this dish in Jamaica is "watchman," but I don't know what the reference or derivation of that name is.

1 cup (1/2 pound) dry red kidney beans, soaked overnight in water to cover and drained

1/2 small coconut, shelled, peeled, and grated, or 1 1/4 cups dried shredded unsweetened coconut

1 tablespoon salt

1 large garlic clove, finely chopped

1 teaspoon freshly ground black pepper

1 small onion, finely chopped

2 scallions, finely chopped

1 tablespoon unsalted butter

2 sprigs fresh thyme

1/2 teaspoon ground allspice

1 Scotch bonnet chile or habanero chile, finely chopped

2 1/2 cups medium-grain rice, soaked in tepid water for 30 minutes or rinsed well in a strainer, drained

1. Place the beans in a large pot with the coconut and cover by 2 inches with cold water. Bring to a boil and cook at a boil until tender, about 1 1/2 hours.

2. Add all the other ingredients except the rice, reduce the heat to medium-low, and simmer for 15 minutes. Reduce the heat to low, add the rice, and cook until it is tender, about 15 minutes. If the rice is still a little hard, add another cup of boiling water, cover again, and cook until tender. Serve immediately.

MAKES 8 SERVINGS

Baby Carrots in the "Sauce That Dances"

*I*n Algeria, this preparation not only can be served as a meze but the Algerian Arabic name also implies that the cook would probably use wild carrots to make this dish. In fact, this is a good recipe to use to experiment with varieties of carrots such as purple carrots or white carrots that you might encounter at the farmers' market. Remember when buying supermarket carrots that those so-called "baby" carrots in a bag are not young carrots at all; they are mature carrots that have been pared down to that shape. The recipe title implies that dishes with this sauce are highly seasoned and piquant and dance in your mouth from the chile burn.

2 pounds young carrots, trimmed and peeled	2 dried red de arbol chiles
1/4 cup extra-virgin olive oil	1 teaspoon ground caraway
2 tablespoons tomato paste	1 teaspoon ground red chile or cayenne pepper
1 cup water	Salt and freshly ground black pepper to taste
1 head garlic, peeled as much as possible without breaking the cloves off	1 tablespoon white wine vinegar

1. Bring a saucepan filled with lightly salted water to a boil and cook the carrots until almost tender, about 5 minutes. Drain and set aside.

2. In a large casserole or skillet over medium-high heat, add the olive oil, tomato paste, water, head of garlic, dried chiles, caraway, ground chile, salt, and pepper. Once the mixture begins to boil, reduce the heat to low, cover, and simmer for 10 minutes. Add the carrots and cook until completely tender, about 15 minutes. Add the vinegar, increase the heat to high, and cook for 2 minutes. Serve hot.

MAKES 6 SERVINGS

hot accompaniments

Cassava Ball Fritters

This Nigerian side dish is usually made with African yams, which are starchy and not sweet like American yams. As they are not readily found in this country, you can make it with cassava, a root vegetable also known as manioc and yucca that has a brown shiny skin and is yam-shaped but larger. Cassava can be found in most supermarkets. This dish is called *ojojo*, and it can be eaten along with any West African stew. Because there are so few ingredients, you may wonder how it will hold together to fry properly. It does so by using the natural water and starch in the vegetable itself. To release it you must first grate the cassava and then run it through a food processor so that it gets crumbly. Although it's much more work, you can also do this using a box grater.

1 pound cassava, peeled, cut in half lengthwise and then into thirds

2 to 3 teaspoons salt, to your taste

3 large green or red jalapeño chiles, seeded and finely chopped

6 to 8 cups peanut oil, for frying

1. Push the cassava through the feed tube of a food processor fixed with the fine grating attachment. Transfer to the regular blade and run the processor in pulses until the cassava is crumbly.

2. In a large bowl, combine the cassava, salt, and chiles. Form into 24 balls, each about the size of a golf ball. Preheat the frying oil to 350°F in a deep-fryer or an 8-inch saucepan fitted with a basket insert. Drop the balls into the hot oil, cooking in batches if necessary in order not to crowd them, and cook until golden brown, 4 to 5 minutes. Remove and drain on a paper towel–lined platter. Serve immediately.

MAKES 24 BALLS (6 SERVINGS)

Fried Plantains in Chile and Red Palm Oil Sauce

I n small roadside restaurants in the Ivory Coast this dish, *aloco*, is very popular. The plantains are fried in a pan of hot palm oil and seasoned with tomatoes, onions, and chiles, and usually served with grilled fish. Try to find red palm oil, but if that proves impossible you can use walnut or peanut oil, although they lack the authentic flavor and color of the palm oil. Red palm oil is available through the Internet and it is the ingredient that will make West African recipes taste West African. The plantains required for this preparation must be ripe, meaning that their skins will nearly be black. This means you will have to buy the unripe plantains from the supermarket at least a week before you want to make this dish.

1 cup red palm oil *or* 1 cup walnut oil mixed with 2 teaspoons hot paprika

3 ripe plantains, peeled and sliced ¹/₂ inch thick

Salt to taste

1 medium-size onion, chopped

2 large ripe tomatoes (about 1 pound), peeled, seeded, and chopped

3 fresh cherry chiles or 8 red finger-type chiles or 2 habanero chiles, chopped

1 tablespoon white vinegar (optional)

1. In a large skillet, heat the red palm oil over medium-high heat until nearly smoking. Salt the plantains and fry in 2 or 3 batches until golden brown on both sides, 4 to 5 minutes in all. Remove from the oil and drain on paper towels.

2. Add the onion, tomatoes, and chiles to the skillet with the oil that you cooked the plantains in and bring to a gentle boil, then reduce the heat to low and simmer until the sauce is thick and chunky, about 45 minutes, stirring frequently. Stir in the vinegar if using. Arrange the plantains on a serving platter and pour the sauce over them. Serve immediately.

MAKES 4 TO 6 SERVINGS

hot accompaniments

Red Lentil Dal

This Bengali-style dal called *masoor dal* is always made with red lentils because they disintegrate well, which is what you want to have happen to have a soft dal.

3 cups water

1 cup red lentils

1 tablespoon vegetable oil

1/2 teaspoon cumin seeds

1/2 teaspoon *panch phoron* (see box)

1 medium-size onion, sliced

1/2 teaspoon ground turmeric

1 1/4 teaspoons salt

1 fresh green finger-type chile or 2 fresh green jalapeño chiles, seeded and finely chopped

1. Bring a large saucepan filled with the 3 cups water and the red lentils to a boil and cook until most of the liquid has evaporated and the lentils are soft, about 12 minutes. Drain through a strainer and mash the lentils.

2. In a large skillet, heat the vegetable oil over medium-high heat and cook the cumin seeds and *panch phoron* for 1 minute. Add the onion and cook until golden brown, 6 to 8 minutes, stirring. Add the mashed lentils, turmeric, salt, and chile, reduce the heat to low, and simmer until dense and about the consistency of a bowl of oatmeal, about 15 minutes. Serve hot.

MAKES 4 SERVINGS

PANCH PHORON

Panch phoron is a spice mixture unique to Bengal. It consists of equal parts whole onion seed, celery seed, anise seed, fenugreek, cumin, nigella, and *radhuni*; mustard seeds can replace *radhuni*. *Panch phoron* is sold as a premixed spice in Indian markets. If you like, you can add 1/2 teaspoon to every Bengal dish that you make. *Panch phoron* is also available via the Internet.

the dals

The variety of dried legumes used in Indian cooking can become quite mind-boggling, and when you are in an Indian market you may find yourself walking back and forth in the aisle trying to figure out what's what. A dal is a dried legume. Sometimes the word specifically refers to split dried legumes. Adding to the confusion is the fact that Indian writers sometimes use the same word for two different legumes. Here's a little guide to help (or confuse) you more.

Arhal dal or *tur dal* (*toor dal*) are either split red gram or pigeon peas. But *tur dal*, and also *thuvar dal*, is used by some authors to mean yellow split peas. The English word "gram" derives from the Portuguese word for grain, which is what the early Portuguese voyagers to India called these little dried legumes in India. Gram generally means chickpea, specifically Bengal gram, but can also mean any dried legume. *Channa dal* is the whole or split chickpea, although some writers use it to refer to yellow split peas. Black gram (also *urd*) is *urad dal*. Horse bean, sword bean, and jackbean (*bada-sem*) are also identified as *urad dal* but they are a different species. *Urad dhuli dal* is the white version or split white gram. Sometimes *chowli* or *chowla dal* or *lobia* is the cowpea, also known as black-eyed pea. Green gram is more familiarly known as mung beans and in India is known as *moong dal*. *Kesari dal*, if eaten in quantity, causes a crippling disease called lythyrism. *Kulthi dal* is horse gram (different from the horse bean) or Madras gram. *Masoor dal* is split red or yellow lentils. To round out the dals, *matki* is moth or mat bean, *sem* (also *valpapdi*, *avarai*) is hyacinth bean, and *sutari* is rice bean. Whew.

Five-Legume Dal

The word "dal" refers to a variety of different legumes, of which lentils are one. In the Indian state of Rajasthan, known for its rich and colorful tradition of chivalry, romance, and hospitality, this dal is made with five different legumes. It's called *pachrangi dal* and the name comes from the Pachrangi tribe, which also gives its name to a kind of cloth, notable in the turbans worn by men because of its five-color stripes. Rajasthani cuisine is derived from both the harshness of the desert and from the Mogul and Persian influences that were so much a part of its history. Desert dwellers had little access to fresh vegetables, so a cuisine evolved around grains and legumes combined with meat and milk products. The cooking fat is *ghee*, and the chiles introduced by the Portuguese are used with abandon in this very hot cuisine. The mixture of onion, garlic, chiles, and other spices that is turned into the dal is known as *tarka*, a kind of tempering that is also found in the medieval cooking of Europe. These five dried legumes are sold in Indian markets almost exclusively, but are available from the Internet too. If you want to make this dish but are simply unable to get these particular legumes, then replace them with supermarket choices, such as green split peas, red lentils, brown lentils, black lentils, and dried chickpeas.

1/4 cup (2 ounces) dried yellow split peas, picked over

1/4 cup (2 ounces) dried black lentils, picked over

1/4 cup (2 ounces) dried green gram or mung beans

1/4 cup (2 ounces) dried red gram or pigeon peas

1/4 cup (2 ounces) dried split black gram or brown lentils

6 cups water

2 tablespoons clarified butter (*ghee*)

1 small onion, thinly sliced

One 1-inch cube fresh ginger, peeled and thinly sliced

5 large garlic cloves, finely chopped

Pinch of asafoetida

2 bay leaves

4 fresh green finger-type chiles or 5 fresh green jalapeño chiles, finely chopped

4 teaspoons salt

1/2 teaspoon ground turmeric

2 tablespoons ground coriander

2 dried red de arbol chiles, crumbled

4 ripe plum tomatoes (about 14 ounces), peeled, seeded, and chopped

1 teaspoon *garam masala* (see page 309)

1. Place the first five ingredients in a bowl, cover with water, and soak for 1 hour. Drain, place in a saucepan, and pour in the 6 cups water. Bring to a boil over high heat, then reduce the heat to medium-high and boil until the liquid is almost half evaporated and the dals are nearly tender, about 25 minutes. Reduce the heat to low until needed.

2. Meanwhile, melt the clarified butter in a skillet over medium-high heat and cook the onion and ginger until golden, 3 to 4 minutes, stirring frequently. Add the garlic, asafoetida, bay leaves, and green chiles. Cook for 1 minute, stirring, then add to the dal. Add the salt, turmeric, coriander, and red chiles, stir, reduce the heat to low, and cook for 15 minutes, stirring occasionally. Add the chopped tomatoes and cook for 10 minutes. Add the *garam masala* and cook for 2 minutes. Serve hot.

MAKES 8 SERVINGS

the cuisine of karnataka

Karnataka is an Indian state on the coast in the southwest portion of India, north of Kerala and Tamil Nadu and touching Goa to the north. The capital is Bangalore. The three distinct regions of Karnataka are a narrow coastal strip along the Arabian Sea, the hills of the Western Ghats, and expansive plains to the east that lead to the next-door-neighbor state of Andhra Pradesh. Karnataka is also known as a spice region that produces the "queen of spices" and "black gold," cardamom and black pepper, respectively. The cuisine of Karnataka varies in each region of the state, but generally in the northern part the food resembles that of Maharashtra and the coastal cuisine resembles that of Kerala. The Kannada housewife (a person from Karnataka) uses more lentils and coconuts than her neighbors. A typical Mysore meal is pure vegetarian and is cooked in sesame and ground nut oil. In the simple cuisine of the coastal areas, fish and seafood cooked in coconut oil play a role. People in northern Karnataka use millet as a staple food. Rice, another staple food, is served in a number of ways, including *chitranna* rice, which is flavored with lemon juice, green chiles, and ground turmeric and is sprinkled with fried peanuts and coriander leaves. The traditional Karnataka meal is served on a banana leaf.

Bengal Gram and Chile Dal

This dal is a recipe from the Indian state of Karnataka called *bele potoli*. The food of Karnataka is thought of as less hot than that of neighboring Andhra Pradesh, a relative comparison, as this dal is very hot, I think. "Bengal gram" is the Anglo-Indian phrase for yellow split peas, although it also is the word for chickpeas. If you can't find yellow split peas in the supermarket, use green split peas.

1 cup (about ¹/₂ pound) dried yellow split peas (Bengal gram), soaked overnight in water to cover and drained

8 fresh green finger-type chiles or 10 fresh green jalapeño chiles, seeded

1 teaspoon cumin seeds

Salt to taste

3 tablespoons vegetable oil

1 teaspoon mustard seeds

Pinch of asafoetida

¹/₂ teaspoon ground turmeric

1 teaspoon ground red chile or cayenne pepper

2 cups water

3 tablespoons chopped fresh coriander (cilantro) leaves

1. Place the yellow split peas in a food processor with the chile, cumin seeds, and salt and grind coarsely. Set this dal mixture aside.

2. In a large nonstick skillet, heat the vegetable oil over medium-high heat, then cook the mustard seeds, asafoetida, turmeric, and ground chile until the mustard seeds start to crackle, 1 to 2 minutes. Add the ground dal to the skillet and stir well. Add the water, reduce the heat to low, cover, and cook, stirring frequently, until the split peas are soft and most of the water has been absorbed, about 40 minutes. Add the coriander leaves and stir. Serve hot.

MAKES 6 SERVINGS

Spinach and Lentil Dal

T his hot side dish is called *dal palak*, which simply means "lentil spinach." Serve it with any kind of Indian lamb dish and rice or Naan (page 398). If you can't get fenugreek leaves, sometimes available at farmers' markets, just leave them out. Dried mango powder, called *amchur*, is readily available in Indian markets, but can also be bought on the Internet.

1 teaspoon chopped garlic

1¹⁄₂ teaspoons ground cumin

1 cup red lentils

1³⁄₄ pounds spinach, heavy stems removed and chopped

¹⁄₂ pound fenugreek leaves, chopped (optional)

2 tablespoons vegetable oil

2 fresh green finger-type chiles or 3 large fresh green jalapeño chiles, seeded and finely chopped

2 dried red de arbol chiles, crumbled

1 large onion, finely chopped

1 teaspoon ground fenugreek

¹⁄₂ teaspoon mango powder (*amchur*)

¹⁄₂ teaspoon ground turmeric

¹⁄₂ cup water

2 teaspoons salt

1. Place the garlic and cumin in a mortar and mash them until mushy. Put the lentils, spinach, and fenugreek leaves into a large saucepan and pour in enough water to barely cover them. Bring to a boil, covered, over high heat. Reduce the heat to low and cook until the lentils are almost falling apart, about 5 minutes, partially covered. Remove from the heat and set aside.

2. In a large skillet, heat the vegetable oil over high heat, then cook the cumin and garlic paste for 10 seconds, stirring. Add the fresh chiles and the dried chiles and cook for 1 minute. Add the onion and cook until soft and yellowed, 4 to 5 minutes, stirring. Add the ground fenugreek, mango powder, and turmeric. Add the 1/2 cup water and simmer until the liquid evaporates, about 3 minutes. Add the reserved spinach mixture, strained with a skimmer, and the salt, and cook on high heat until thick, about 7 minutes. Serve hot.

MAKES 8 SERVINGS

Spinach and Pigeon Pea Curry

This preparation from the southern Indian state of Karnataka is called *soppu palya*. It is a typical side dish preparation from North Karnataka, where it is usually eaten with a variety of rotis (griddled unleavened breads) made from wheat or millet. The final dish should look mushy and creamy.

1 cup pigeon peas or split green peas, picked over for stones and rinsed	6 fresh red finger-type chiles or 8 fresh red jalapeño chiles, seeded and split lengthwise
1 cup water	2 cups shredded unsweetened dried or fresh coconut
1 1/2 pounds spinach, heavy stems removed and chopped	One 1-inch cube tamarind paste
5 tablespoons vegetable oil	1 teaspoon ground turmeric
1 tablespoon coriander seeds	Salt to taste
	2 medium-size onions, chopped

1. Put the pigeon peas in a medium-size saucepan, cover with cold water by 3 inches, and bring to a boil over high heat. Salt lightly and cook until the peas are *al dente*, 10 to 12 minutes, stirring once or twice. Be careful that you don't cook too long or the pigeon peas will disintegrate and become mush. Drain, reserving 1 cup of the cooking water, and return the peas to the saucepan.

2.   In another medium-size saucepan, bring the 1 cup water (not the reserved water) to a boil over high heat, then cook the spinach until soft, about 5 minutes. Transfer the spinach and the liquid it cooked in to the saucepan with the pigeon peas and stir it in.

3.   In a medium-size skillet, heat 1 tablespoon of the vegetable oil over medium-high heat, then cook the coriander seeds and chiles until the seeds are slightly browned and the skin of the peppers is crinkly, about 4 minutes, stirring. Place this mixture in a food processor with the coconut and tamarind pulp and grind until a paste. Add this paste to the pigeon pea mixture along with the turmeric. Season with salt and mix well.

4.   In the skillet you used to cook the chiles, add the remaining 4 tablespoons of vegetable oil and heat over high heat, then cook the onions until golden and starting to get crispy, about 6 minutes, stirring occasionally.

5.   Add the cooked onions to the pigeon pea mixture with the reserved 1 cup of cooking liquid and cook over medium heat until it comes to a boil. If the mixture looks too dry and it is difficult to stir, add up to 1 more cup of water. Serve hot.

MAKES 6 SERVINGS

curry leaves

Curry leaves have nothing to do with curry. They are the slightly pungent and aromatic leaves of a small tree native to the Himalaya region and are used in Indian cooking. They are usually found in Indian markets, sometimes fresh as well as frozen, and they are sold at some farmers' markets, especially in southern California.

Spinach with Coconut

his dish from Kerala is known as a *thoren*, a kind of stir-fry dish that can be made with any number of shredded vegetables. It is made with shredded coconut cooked in oil seasoned with mustard seeds, dried red chiles, and fresh curry leaves. The Dundicutt chiles that are typically used in Indo-Pakistani cooking can be ordered from www.penzeys.com (see page 429). The de arbol chiles are the name of the regular whole dried red chile found in the supermarket.

---

²/₃ cup shredded unsweetened dried or fresh coconut

¹/₂ teaspoon ground cumin

¹/₂ teaspoon cayenne pepper

¹/₂ teaspoon ground turmeric

1 teaspoon salt

8 fresh green Thai chiles or 2 large green jalapeño chiles

2 tablespoons vegetable oil

1 teaspoon black mustard seeds

1 small onion, finely chopped

6 dried Dundicutt chiles or 2 dried de arbol chiles, crumbled

10 curry leaves (optional; see box at left)

2¹/₂ pounds spinach, heavy stems removed

1. In a blender, combine the coconut, cumin, cayenne, turmeric, salt, and green chiles with enough water to make the blades spin, about ¹/₂ cup. Run until smooth.

2. In a wok or large skillet, heat the vegetable oil over medium-high heat, then cook the mustard seeds until they start to crackle and pop, about 1 minute. Add the onion, dried chile, and curry leaves, if using, and cook until they start to soften, about 2 minutes. Add the spinach and cook until it starts to wilt, stirring constantly, about 5 minutes. Stir in the coconut mixture and continue cooking until the spinach is tender, about 5 minutes. Serve hot.

MAKES 4 SERVINGS

hot accompaniments

the piquant cuisine of india

The earliest writings of ancient India, the Vedas, set down about 1800 B.C. to 1200 B.C., indicate spices used in Indian cooking. The earliest spices on record are mustard, asafoetida, sour citrus, turmeric, black pepper, and long peppers. By the Buddhist era (sixth century B.C.), we know that ginger, cloves, cumin, and vinegar are prominently used in cooking. Spicy relishes are used during and after meals. By this time, Indians are trading with the Greeks, and a little later with the Romans, and they note that their traders are interested in black pepper. In ancient Tamil culture, black pepper was a prized spice where it grew in its home of Kerala. *Kari*, a pepper-spiced dish derived from the Tamil word, became the modern-day curry, and fits into a thriving trade in black pepper.

Although the home of black pepper is on the Malabar Coast in the state of Kerala, we know it had diffused to Malaysia before the fifth century A.D. Even with this evidence in trade, it's difficult to determine how people actually cooked and how pungent they liked their food. The evidence that they liked hot food is more than circumstantial, though. In a poem called the *Naishadha Charita*, written around A.D. 1000, a mustard-flavored yogurt served at a marriage feast was so piquant that diners had to "scratch their heads," which must be a reference to sweating caused by the pungency of the mustard.

The chile arrived with the Portuguese, who landed on the Malabar Coast in 1498 and moved to Cochin to the south because it had a better harbor. They captured Goa in 1510. Jean Andrews, the author of several books on chiles, speculates that Jesuits carried the seeds of the chile to grow in their mission gardens.

The first clearer evidence of the chile in India comes from the testimony of the south Indian composer Purandaradasa (1480–1564) who seemed aware of its attributes when he wrote: "I saw you green, then turning redder as you ripened, nice to look at and tasty in a dish, but too hot if an excess is used. Savior of the poor, enhancer of good food, fiery when bitten, even to think of [the deity] Panduranga Vittala is difficult." Once the chile entered India, it changed forever how Indians spiced their food. Duarte Barbosa, the sixteenth-century geographer, tells us that the "flesh or fish or vegetable" eaten in Calicut by locals is flavored with so much pepper that "no man from our countries would be able to eat it."

Today the use of chiles is prominent in India from Kashmir in the north to Tamil Nadu in the south. Generally, it can be said that southern Indian food is hotter than northern Indian food. In the south, coconuts, coconut milk, and tamarind are used with spices such as fenugreek, coriander seeds, mustard seeds, and curry leaves to give a flavor quite different from northern Indian, which features *garam masala* and cumin. Another big difference between north and south in India is the southern technique of frying spices in hot oil first to draw out a distinctive aroma and flavor, while northern cooks grind their spices to a powder first and use them in combination with onions, tomatoes, and yogurt.

Eggplant Bharta

A *bharta* is a class of dishes usually made by boiling or roasting a vegetable over fire, then mashing it together with a variety of seasonings, but usually some combination of onions, garlic, tomatoes, mustard oil, ginger, and fresh green chiles or dried red chiles. This is a Bengali dish, very nice to eat with some Naan (page 398).

2 medium-size eggplant (about 2 1/2 pounds)

Salt to taste

3 tablespoons vegetable oil or mustard oil

1 medium-size onion, finely chopped

2 large garlic cloves, crushed until mushy

2 fresh green finger-type chiles or 3 green jalapeño chiles, seeded and finely chopped

1 teaspoon ground cumin

1/4 teaspoon ground turmeric

1/4 cup finely chopped fresh coriander (cilantro) leaves

1/2 cup whole plain yogurt

1. Preheat the oven to 425°F. Cut the eggplants in half, place in a baking dish, and roast until the skin is crispy, about 35 minutes. Remove the eggplant from the oven and, once it has cooled, remove the flesh and mash it in a colander. Season with salt and let it drain for 30 minutes.

2. In a large skillet, heat the vegetable oil over medium heat, then cook the onion until golden, 8 to 10 minutes, stirring. Add the garlic, chiles, cumin, turmeric, coriander, and salt to taste and cook for a few minutes. Add the eggplant and continue cooking until the eggplant mixture is rather dense and dry, 15 to 20 minutes. Stir in the yogurt and remove from the heat. Serve hot.

MAKES 4 TO 6 SERVINGS

punjabi cuisine

Punjab is one of India's smallest states, north of Delhi. The Punjabis are hard-working people and because the land they live on is irrigated by five major rivers, it is green and abundant. When you eat in an Indian restaurant in America, what you are eating is basically Punjabi cuisine. When you order tandoor chicken, or chicken tikka, or stuffed parathas, you are ordering Punjabi food, especially when you order lassi with it. Much of Punjabi cuisine has been influenced by the Moguls.

Mustard Greens and Chiles

T his dish, called *sarson ki saag*, is from the Punjab. Serve with roti and Lamb Keema (page 213) or Lamb in Spicy Cardamom and Rose Water–Flavored Yogurt Sauce (page 210). The gram flour is found in Indian markets, but you can also use chickpea flour or fine corn flour.

2 cups water

2 pounds mustard greens, heavy stem ends trimmed and finely chopped

1/2 pound spinach, heavy stems removed and finely chopped

1/4 cup clarified butter (*ghee*)

One 1-inch cube fresh ginger, peeled and very finely chopped

4 large garlic cloves, very finely chopped

2 fresh green finger-type chiles or 3 fresh green jalapeño chiles, seeded and very finely chopped

2 dried red de arbol chiles, seeded and crumbled

Salt to taste

2 tablespoons gram flour, chickpea flour, or fine corn flour, sifted

1 tablespoon unsalted butter

1. Bring a large saucepan filled with the water to a boil over high heat. Add the mustard greens and spinach and cook until soft, about 5 minutes. Drain well through a strainer, pressing out excess liquid with the back of a wooden spoon, or let it sit to drain for 45 minutes.

2. In a large skillet, melt the clarified butter over medium heat, then add the ginger, garlic, green chiles, and red chiles and cook until light brown, 3 to 4 minutes, stirring. Add the reserved greens and salt. In a small bowl, mix the gram flour with a little water, 2 to 3 tablespoons, and add to the greens. Reduce the heat to low and simmer until the liquid is mostly evaporated and the greens look mushy, about 30 minutes. Serve hot with the butter on top.

MAKES 4 TO 6 SERVINGS

hot accompaniments

Cabbage Curry

This dish from the Indian state of Kerala is very simple to make, but you want to be sure you don't cook the cabbage too much. It should not be as soft as the onion, but almost. I like to serve this with Kashmiri Kebab (page 214).

¹/₄ cup vegetable oil or mustard oil

1 teaspoon black mustard seeds

3 medium-size onions, thinly sliced

4 fresh green finger-type chiles or 8 fresh green serrano chiles, chopped

5 curry leaves

1 pound green cabbage, cored, outer leaves removed, and shredded

2 to 3 teaspoons salt, or more to your taste

2 tablespoons dried shredded unsweetened coconut

1. In a large skillet, heat the vegetable oil over medium heat, then cook the mustard seeds until they start to crackle and pop, 1 to 2 minutes. Add the onions, chiles, and curry leaves and cook until golden and soft, about 20 minutes, stirring.

2. Add the cabbage and salt, toss well to mix, cover, reduce the heat to low, and cook until the cabbage is soft and wilted with only the tiniest of bite to it, stirring occasionally, about 12 minutes. Add the coconut and cook until fragrant, about 3 minutes. Serve hot.

MAKES 4 SERVINGS

Chiles and Onions with Boiled Cheese

This recipe, called *ema datshi*, comes from a Bhutanese native, Kunzang Namgyel, who says that if you've been to Bhutan and not eaten this, you have not been to Bhutan. The Bhutanese like their food hot, and chiles are widespread. How chiles got to Bhutan is a good question, and no one has ever written about it. I believe they arrived in Bhutan from Goa. The only other alternative is that chiles came from Sichuan over the Himalayas. You can also eat raw chiles dipped in salt to accompany this dish if you like to be authentic. The cheese used in this preparation cannot be found outside Bhutan. It is a local cheese made by farmers that doesn't dissolve when put in boiling water. The best substitute is Syrian white cheese, available in Middle Eastern markets, or a Mexican *queso fresco*, available in Latin American markets and many supermarkets. Serve with steamed rice and a main course.

1/2 pound fresh green jalapeño chiles, seeded and quartered lengthwise

1 medium-size onion, chopped

1 tablespoon vegetable oil

1 3/4 cups water

1 pound tomatoes, peeled, seeded, and chopped

5 large garlic cloves, smashed

1/2 pound firm Syrian white cheese or Mexican *queso fresco*

1 tablespoon finely chopped fresh coriander (cilantro) leaves

Put the chiles, onion, and vegetable oil in a medium-size saucepan and pour in the water. Bring to a boil, then reduce the heat to medium and cook for 8 minutes. Add the tomatoes and garlic and boil for another 2 minutes. Add the cheese and cook for 3 minutes. Add the coriander, turn off the heat, stir, cover, and let sit for 2 minutes. Serve hot.

MAKES 4 SERVINGS

hot accompaniments

Stir-Fried Spinach with Chiles

This simple dish from Sichuan can accompany just about any other dish. The secret here, besides fresh spinach, is making sure most of the water is dried off the spinach from its washing. This entire dish will cook in 4 minutes.

3 tablespoons peanut oil

2 pounds spinach, heavy stems removed

6 dried red de arbol chiles, broken into thirds

One 2-inch cube fresh ginger, peeled and cut into matchsticks

$^1/_2$ teaspoon salt, or more to your taste

$1^1/_2$ teaspoons cornstarch mixed with 1 tablespoon water

1. In a wok, heat the peanut oil over high heat until it is nearly smoking. Add the spinach, chiles, and ginger and stir-fry until wilted and dark green, about 2 minutes. Season with salt.

2. Stir the cornstarch and water to make it smooth, then pour it into the wok and cook until the sauce is thick, tossing constantly, about 2 minutes. Serve immediately.

MAKES 4 SERVINGS

the hot spices: ginger

Ginger is the rhizome of a plant native to southeast Asia or southern China, and perhaps India, which grows to three feet tall on partly shaded slopes. It has long, slender leaves and yellow flowers with a purple edge and has been cultivated in Asia for more than 3,000 years. Ginger is propagated by splitting the root and rarely by seed, indicating that it has been under human cultivation for so long that it has lost one of its natural attributes in the wild. Its pungency is caused by a viscid oil, gingerol.

Before the discovery of the chile, ginger and black pepper were the two most piquant spices. India today is a major producer of ginger. The English name "ginger" derives from the Latin, which in turn borrowed the word from the Greeks, who themselves seem to have adopted a form of the Sanskrit word in antiquity.

In China, ginger was first mentioned by Confucius. Ginger was one of the first spices to reach the Mediterranean through trade. Dioscorides, the Greek physician of the first century A.D., writes about ginger growing in Eritrea and Arabia and describes this small rhizome and its use fresh in soups and stews. The Arabs took ginger to East Africa in the thirteenth century. Although the word for ginger appears in the Koran in connection with the ginger-flavored water of Paradise, the Meccans of the Arabian Peninsula did not trade in this spice. The Portuguese took it to West Africa and the Spaniards to the Indies in the early sixteenth century with Francisco de Mendoza, son of the viceroy of New Spain, who cultivated it there.

In medieval times, when ginger was a very important spice, there were three or four grades on the market in Europe. The first was *beledi*, ginger native to the west coast of India, derived from the Arabic word for "country style" or "common." The second was *micchino*, ginger that had passed through the Mecca spice market—also known as *mequin* and *colombino*—from the name of the port of Kulam in the princely state of Travancore on India's southwestern coast along the Arabian Sea, in today's Kerala state. There was also *sorratin*, a ginger from Surat, considered the best.

Stir-Fried Hot
Bok Choy

This Sichuanese dish called *la baicai* is very simple. Bok choy is a rather bland type of cabbage, which is to its advantage in this preparation. This can accompany nearly any of the other Sichuanese preparations; it is very versatile.

1/4 cup peanut oil	1 tablespoon salt
1 tablespoon Sichuan chile paste (see page 98)	1/2 cup water
2 pounds bok choy, sliced 1 inch wide	1 tablespoon cornstarch mixed with 1/4 cup water

In a wok, heat the peanut oil over high heat, then cook the chile paste and bok choy together, stir-frying so the bok choy is coated well with oil and paste, until it wilts, about 4 minutes. Add the salt and the water and let boil until the leaves are very soft and the stems are separating, 10 to 12 minutes. Pour the cornstarch and water mixture over the bok choy and stir-fry until a little denser, about 30 seconds. Serve immediately.

MAKES 4 SERVINGS

on woks

The standard cooking vessel of the cuisines of China and southeast Asia is the wok, which is the Cantonese pronunciation of *guo*, or pan, in Chinese. Traditionally, woks were made of cast iron, but today they are made of a variety of materials. Woks are very easy to find and I recommend that you buy one for general-purpose cooking as well. The best woks are those made of heavy-gauge steel with a flat bottom and sloping sides and not the ones made of cast aluminum or stainless steel, which don't hold the heat well enough. The sloping sides are necessary for stir-frying, the most important cooking technique in China. A steel, also called carbon steel, wok will rust, so it needs to be seasoned first. Season the wok by rubbing the inside entirely with a little vegetable oil and heat over medium heat for 1 hour. Turn the heat off, cool, and repeat the process. The wok is now seasoned. Sometimes woks lose their seasoning and you have to re-season them, which simply means you repeat this process.

Buy a large wok, one that is 12 to 14 inches in diameter, as you will never regret that size. Woks are often sold with a circular ring stand that is meant to adapt them to American stoves and hold the wok in place. But do not use these ring stands. They keep the wok too far away from the heat source and you will not be able to attain the high temperatures needed for stir-frying. Only use a soft sponge and warm water to wash your wok, and never any abrasives, or elbow grease, otherwise you will have to re-season the wok. Fill the wok with warm water as soon as you finish cooking, then go and eat and enjoy yourself. In the meantime, the wok is soaking and the water is lifting up all the little bits of food. Wash with the sponge until clean, then dry thoroughly inside and out, rub with a thin film of oil, and store for the next time.

The most important thing to remember when cooking with a wok is not to overload it with food. The ideal wok for serving four to six people is one with a widest diameter of 14 inches. For larger ones you will need to visit a restaurant-supply store, as home kitchen stores generally don't carry them. The three most essential cooking implements for using with a wok are a Chinese spatula (also called a paddle), a skimmer, and a shallow ladle. All of these will be available at the same store at which you buy the wok.

Spinach with Ground Red Chile and Sesame Seeds

This Korean preparation can be served as an appetizer or as a side dish, which is the way I like to make it. I first bought this from the "salad" bar at the California Korean Market in Koreatown in Los Angeles, which is like no salad bar you've ever seen. Displayed were more than 25 different preparations ranging from recognizable dishes like this spinach one to completely mysterious dishes, one of which I was wild about: minuscule crabs, about 1/2 inch in diameter, cooked with spicy Korean red chile flakes or red chile threads (called *sil koch'u* and sold in Korean markets). Young Korean-American yuppies, like their urban American counterparts, are more likely to stop by this salad bar to shop for dinner than they are to make it. But freshly made is, well, fresher.

1 tablespoon white vinegar	2 tablespoons soy sauce
2 1/2 pounds spinach, heavy stems removed	1 tablespoon sesame oil
1 large garlic clove, finely chopped	2 teaspoons ground Korean red chile or 1 teaspoon cayenne pepper
1 scallion, white and light green parts only, finely chopped	1/4 teaspoon salt
2 1/2 teaspoons toasted sesame seeds	1/2 teaspoon freshly ground black pepper

1. Bring a large saucepan of water to a boil with the vinegar, and then plunge the spinach in for 10 seconds and drain in a colander. Immediately spray cold water over the spinach to stop its cooking. Squeeze the water out of the spinach by pressing it against the holes of the colander with the back of a wooden spoon, then dry further by damping with paper towels. Chop very coarsely.

2. In a large bowl, mix together the garlic, scallion, sesame seeds, soy sauce, sesame oil, 1/2 teaspoon of the ground red chile, salt, and pepper. Add the spinach and mix well. Transfer to a serving platter and garnish with the remaining ground red chile. Serve at room temperature.

MAKES 4 SERVINGS

cool accompaniments

T here should be a proverb that goes something like this: "Every hot needs a cool." When it comes to spicy-hot food, a cool accompaniment is a cool thing. Physiologically, it doesn't do a thing to moderate the burn, but psychologically it is very pleasant. The recipes in this chapter are traditional ones from piquant cuisines, but they have no chiles (or very few) in them. Of course, you can also make a variety of other foods, such as mashed potatoes, if you want a bland side dish to accompany fiery dishes.

Rice and Coconut Pudding

This Brazilian rice dish from Bahia is called *pirão de arroz com leite de coco* and is the traditional accompaniment to *Vatapá* Stew (page 252), one of the most magnificent shrimp dishes you'll ever taste. It can be served straight from the molds or you can remove it first. Remember that this pudding is not a dessert—it's meant to be a bland accompaniment to fantastically hot food. I suspect that it was invented in Bahia by African slaves who remembered their *Fufu* (page 393).

4 cups coconut milk (see page 90)	1 teaspoon salt
¾ cup rice flour	

1. In a heavy saucepan, heat 3 cups of the coconut milk over medium heat until tiny bubbles form around the edge. Combine the remaining 1 cup coconut milk with the rice flour and salt in a small bowl, and, stirring constantly, pour it into the heated coconut milk. Reduce the heat to low and cook, stirring, until thick and smooth, about 2 minutes.

2. Pour the pudding into 6 individual custard molds and cool to room temperature. Cover with plastic wrap and refrigerate for 4 hours. Remove from the refrigerator and serve cool (not cold) or at room temperature.

MAKES 6 SERVINGS

Green Rice

Arroz verde is a famous Mexican rice preparation that is excellent with steaks. This recipe is adapted from *The Art of Mexican Cooking* (Bantam, 1989) by Diane Kennedy.

1¹/₂ cups medium-grain rice

2¹/₂ cups chicken broth (homemade or canned)

2 large garlic cloves, coarsely chopped

1 cup firmly packed coarsely chopped fresh parsley leaves

¹/₂ cup firmly packed coarsely chopped fresh coriander (cilantro) leaves or epazote leaves

3 tablespoons pork lard

2 tablespoons safflower oil

¹/₄ cup finely chopped white onions

2 roasted poblano chiles, peeled, seeded, and cut into strips

1¹/₂ teaspoons salt

1. Put the rice in a strainer and let the strainer rest in a bowl of very hot water for 10 minutes. Drain and rinse under running water. In a blender, puree 1 cup of the chicken broth with the garlic, parsley, and coriander until smooth, about 2 minutes. Set aside.

2. In a large, heavy skillet or casserole, melt the lard with the safflower oil over medium-high heat, then cook the rice until it sticks to the bottom of the skillet, 4 to 5 minutes, stirring occasionally. Add the onion and chiles and continue cooking until the onion is soft, about 3 minutes.

3. Add the green puree to the rice and continue cooking over high heat, stirring and scraping the bottom of the pan until the rice has absorbed all of the liquid, about 3 minutes. Pour in the remaining 1¹/₂ cups of the broth, add the salt, and cook uncovered over high heat without stirring until the liquid has been absorbed and there are air holes in the rice, 8 to 10 minutes. Remove from the heat, cover with a paper towel, and place the lid on top. Set aside in a warm place for the rice to swell up, about 10 minutes. Transfer to a serving platter by scraping up the crust from the bottom of the skillet or casserole. Serve hot.

MAKES 4 SERVINGS

cool accompaniments

Jicama and Cucumber Salad

This is a nice accompaniment to spicy-hot Jamaican dishes. This recipe was invented by Sarah Pillsbury (she likes jicama) and me. The Georgia Peach and Vidalia Onion Hot Sauce is a commercial product that either you have or you don't. If you don't, just leave it out or make it by combining the following in a blender: 2 tablespoons red chile flakes, $1/3$ ripe peeled and pitted peach, 2 teaspoons sugar, 1 teaspoon white wine vinegar, $1/3$ cup chopped Vidalia onion, $1/2$ teaspoon salt, and a pinch each of nutmeg, cloves, and allspice.

2 medium-size cucumbers, peeled, split lengthwise, and seeded

1 small jicama, peeled, quartered, and thinly sliced

$1/2$ green bell pepper, finely diced

1 large garlic clove, finely chopped

1 tablespoon finely chopped fresh mint leaves

2 tablespoons finely chopped fresh coriander (cilantro) leaves

2 tablespoons extra-virgin olive oil

2 teaspoons apple cider vinegar

2 teaspoons tangerine juice

$1/2$ teaspoon Georgia Peach and Vidalia Onion Hot Sauce (optional)

In a medium-size bowl, toss all the ingredients together. Serve at room temperature.

MAKES 4 SMALL SERVINGS

Shredded Cabbage Salad

This crisp salad is a very nice accompaniment to Mexican or Jamaican dishes.

1 small head green cabbage (about $1^{1}/4$ pounds), cored, quartered, and thinly sliced

8 scallions, trimmed and chopped into $1/4$-inch pieces

Salt and freshly ground black pepper to taste

$1/4$ cup extra-virgin olive oil

1 tablespoon white wine vinegar

3 tablespoons mayonnaise

1 large garlic clove, finely chopped

In a large bowl, toss the cabbage and scallions together, then toss again with the salt and pepper. In a small bowl, whisk the olive oil, vinegar, mayonnaise, and garlic together. Toss with the cabbage and serve.

MAKES 6 SERVINGS

Fried Plantains

You will want to make this recipe as an accompaniment to any hot dishes from the Caribbean or Africa. This method of cooking the plantains is really the one that works the best. "Green" means the plantain is not ripe.

$1/2$ cup vegetable oil, plus more as needed

3 large green plantains, peeled and cut into 2-inch lengths

Salt to taste

1. In a small skillet, heat the vegetable oil over medium heat, then cook the plantain pieces, 4 at a time, until golden on all sides, turning with tongs, 5 to 6 minutes. Reduce the heat if they are cooking more quickly. Remove the plantains from the oil and carefully and gently pound them with a rolling pin or the side of a cleaver until flattened to $3/8$ inch thick. Set aside and continue cooking and pounding the remaining pieces, adding more oil to the skillet if necessary.

2. Remove to a paper towel–lined baking dish and season with salt. You can serve them immediately, keep them warm in an oven, or serve them at room temperature.

MAKES 4 TO 6 SERVINGS

Fried Cassava

*T*his preparation is one that I first had in a Salvadorean restaurant in Alexandria, Virginia, where there is a community of Salvadorean immigrants. Salvadorean food is not hot at all, but this preparation, which is also popular in the Caribbean and Africa, is a great foil for spicy foods. The secret here is not in the frying but in the boiling. The cassava, which is like a potato on steroids, must be boiled first to make it tender. As it becomes tender it splits up along its natural grain and looks as if it will fall apart. That's when you remove it from the water and let it dry before frying until it is crispy golden and crunchy. Don't worry about making too much, as leftovers reheated in the oven are just as crunchy and delicious.

2 pounds cassava, peeled

Salt to taste

6 to 8 cups peanut or vegetable oil, for frying

1. Cut the cassava into rectangles about 5 inches long and 1 inch thick. Bring a large saucepan of water to a boil, add salt, and boil the cassava until the pieces start to break apart, 30 to 35 minutes. Drain and cool on paper towels.

2. Preheat the frying oil to 360°F in a deep-fryer or an 8-inch saucepan with a basket insert. Fry the cassava pieces until golden and crispy. Remove and drain on paper towels, but salt them immediately. Serve hot.

MAKES 6 SERVINGS

Boiled Plantain and Cassava

*T*his dish, from the Ashanti region of Ghana, is called *ampesi*, and it is usually eaten as an accompaniment to fiery hot West African dishes. This dish hopped the Atlantic with the slave trade, as we know from the identical preparation found in Brazil. This combination of cassava and plantain, once it has been pounded thoroughly, can also be turned into *Fufu* (page 393). You could substitute malanga, yautia (cocoyam), bananas, or yams in any combination or all together. Some cooks boil the vegetables whole and others cut them up. Cassava is a large and long brown-skinned tuber that has white flesh. When fully cooked, split it open lengthwise; the flesh can be easily scooped out and the peel removes itself almost like a banana peel.

1 plantain

1 small cassava (about 1½ pounds)

1 tablespoon unsalted butter

1 tablespoon peanut oil

1 cup water

Wash the plantain and cassava very well, but do not peel or cut them, then place in a large pot of water and bring to a boil. Reduce the heat a little and cook until easily punctured with a fork, about 25 minutes for the plantain and 30 to 35 minutes for the cassava. Drain and peel them both. Place the flesh of both in a medium-size bowl and mash them well with the butter and peanut oil. Place in a saucepan with the 1 cup water and cook over medium heat, stirring frequently, until softer, about 10 minutes. Serve hot.

MAKES 4 SERVINGS

cool accompaniments

Sweet Puff-Puffs

Puff-puffs are very popular in Nigeria and Cameroon, where they are sold as street food. They are basically beignets and very appetizing when eaten with, rather than after, very hot food.

1 tablespoon active dry yeast

$^1/_4$ cup tepid water

$1^1/_2$ cups unbleached all-purpose flour

$^1/_2$ cup sugar

3 cups vegetable oil, for frying

Sugar, for garnish

1.   In a small bowl, dissolve the yeast with the tepid water. In a large bowl, mix the flour and sugar together. Add the dissolved yeast to the flour mixure and blend until a stiff dough forms. Cover with a kitchen towel and let sit in a warm place for 3 hours.

2.   In a deep skillet, heat the frying oil to about 350°F, then drop tablespoon-fuls of the dough into the oil and fry until golden brown, 5 to 6 minutes, cooking in batches so the skillet is never crowded. Drain the puff-puffs on paper towels, sprinkle with sugar, and serve warm.

MAKES 4 SERVINGS

Fufu

Fufu or foofoo is one of the most common starch dishes of West Africa. As a staple food, it is usually served with other foods. It is a kind of pudding, or mush, made from a variety of starchy root vegetables, including African yam, sweet potato, and plantains. The most common *fufu* is made from fermented cassava flour. The cassava flesh is soaked in water for three days and then grated and placed under weights so the liquid is driven out. Then when it is quite dry it is ground, covered with water, and left overnight to drain in a strainer. In West Africa, you will see women standing over a large wooden mortar dropping a thick long pestle repeatedly onto the cassava, pounding and pounding until it is completely mashed. Once the cassava flour is pounded enough, it is put in a pot and cooked with water like a polenta until white, almost translucent, and completely smooth. Small pieces the size of marbles are pinched off by the diner, rolled into a ball, and swallowed whole. Another kind of mush is called *gari* and is made with roasted grated cassava cooked with water. This recipe is based on cassava flour, which can be obtained through the Internet. I was told that this recipe feeds two, but Africans eat enormous amounts of *fufu*. *Fufu* can be made to accompany any of the West African recipes. If you can't find fermented cassava flour, make this with corn flour or rice flour instead.

2¹/₂ cups water		3 cups fermented cassava flour

Bring the water to a boil in a large saucepan, preferably cast iron, over high heat. Slowly add some cassava flour (about 1 cup), and stir with a wooden spoon until blended. Reduce the heat to low and stir to break up any lumps. Add the rest of the flour and stir until the pudding is stiff, soft, and smooth, and pulls away from the saucepan, less than 5 minutes. Mound on a plate and serve.

MAKES 4 TO 6 SERVINGS

Mango Chutney

This is a great accompaniment to any of the Caribbean curries, especially Curry Goat (page 218). For an Indian-style chutney on the hot side, replace the ginger with half a cup of freshly grated coconut, the onion with four finely chopped green chiles, the vinegar with lemon juice, and add five more garlic cloves, a handful of fresh mint leaves, and one-half teaspoon ground cumin.

2 ripe mangoes, peeled, pitted, and chopped

1½ tablespoons freshly grated ginger

1 small onion, chopped

1 small garlic clove, finely chopped

¼ cup raisins

3 tablespoons sugar

1 teaspoon salt

¼ cup white wine vinegar

3 tablespoons water

Bring all the ingredients to a boil in a nonreactive saucepan over high heat. Once it reaches a boil, reduce the heat to low and simmer until the liquid has evaporated, 1 to 1¼ hours. Remove from the heat and allow the chutney to cool completely. Store in jars in the refrigerator for up to 6 months.

MAKES 1½ CUPS

Dumplings

These dumplings can be used with any stew recipe from Southwest American, Cajun, or Caribbean cuisine. When cooking dumplings, you lay them on top of the stew, place the cover on, and leave it on until they're done without stirring, looking, or uncovering.

1 cup unbleached all-purpose flour

½ teaspoon baking powder

½ teaspoon salt

1 tablespoon unsalted butter

⅓ cup milk

In a medium-size bowl, mix together the flour, baking powder, and salt. Work the butter into the flour until it looks like coarse oatmeal. Add the milk and mix until it can be formed into a consistent dough. Dump the dough out onto a lightly floured surface and flatten until it is 1 inch high. Cut into 6 pieces and use as instructed in the main recipe.

MAKES 6 DUMPLINGS

Johnny Cakes

Whereas the johnny cakes of Rhode Island are a kind of pancake made with cornmeal, these Jamaican johnny cakes are fried dumplings that can be eaten with very spicy food.

2 cups unbleached all-purpose flour	1/4 cup (1/2 stick) unsalted butter
1 teaspoon baking powder	4 to 6 tablespoons water
1 teaspoon salt	1 cup vegetable oil, for frying

1. In a bowl, sift together the flour, baking powder, and salt. Cut in the butter with a knife or pastry cutter until the mixture looks like rolled oatmeal. Add the water, 1 teaspoon at a time, until the dough can be formed with a firm consistency. Knead the dough for about 5 minutes, until a smooth ball. Wrap in plastic wrap and refrigerate for 1 hour.

2. Remove the dough from the refrigerator. In a skillet, heat the frying oil over medium-low heat, then break off pieces of the dough, a little smaller than golf ball size, and flatten them until about 2 inches in diameter.

3. Cook the disks until light golden, 3 to 5 minutes, making sure you don't crowd them in the skillet. Remove to a paper towel–lined platter to drain. Serve hot.

MAKES 12 JOHNNY CAKES FOR 6 SERVINGS

cool accompaniments

Raita

A raita is an Indian yogurt relish served with other foods. It is usually made with cucumber, but can be made with carrots, onions, or other vegetables. Raita arrived in India with the Moguls, and it is a famous Muslim dish in the Arab world as well. In Greece it is known as tzatziki.

1 cup whole plain yogurt	Salt and freshly ground black pepper to taste
2 teaspoons water	Pinch of cayenne pepper
1/2 cup seeded and finely chopped cucumber	1 teaspoon very finely chopped fresh coriander (cilantro) leaves or mint leaves
1/8 teaspoon ground cumin	

In a bowl, whisk the yogurt and water together. Add the cucumber, cumin, salt, and pepper and mix again. Transfer to a serving bowl and sprinkle with cayenne pepper and coriander leaves. Serve cold or cool.

MAKES 4 SERVINGS

Rice Pilaf

T his is the basic rice pilaf recipe that you can use for any recipe calling for pilaf as an accompaniment to spicy food. The best rice to use for pilaf is basmati or patna long-grain rice, which are available in supermarkets as well as ethnic markets. An American long-grain rice is okay to use, too, but not converted rice. This recipe is self-explanatory, but if you hesitate about making pilaf, then read the box at right.

2 tablespoons clarified butter (*ghee*) or unsalted butter	3 1/4 cups water
	2 teaspoons salt
2 cups long-grain rice, soaked in tepid water for 30 minutes or rinsed well in a strainer, drained	1/2 cup boiling water, if needed
	Freshly ground black pepper (optional)

1.   In a large, heavy casserole or saucepan with a tight-fitting lid, melt the clarified butter over medium-high heat, then cook the drained rice for 2 to 3 minutes, stirring frequently. Add the water and salt, increase the heat to high, and, once it begins to boil, reduce the heat to very low and cover. Do not stir or uncover the rice for 12 minutes.

2. Remove the cover and check whether the rice is cooked and the liquid absorbed by pushing a fork to the bottom of the pot in the middle. If not, cook for another 3 minutes and check again.

3. If the water is absorbed but the rice is still hard, add the boiling water and continue cooking until done. The rice can be served immediately or you can cover the pot with a paper towel, replace the lid, and let sit for 10 minutes. When ready to serve, transfer to a serving platter, season with pepper if desired, fluff the rice, and serve.

MAKES 6 SERVINGS

how to cook rice pilaf

Rice pilaf is a method of cooking rice in the Arab world from North Africa to the Middle East, as well as in Turkey, Iran, Central Asia, and the Indian subcontinent. A proper rice pilaf, at its simplest, will consist of fluffy grains of long-grain rice that remain separate from one another after they are cooked. The best rices for pilaf are the long-grain basmati or patna rices, which are sold commonly in supermarkets, Middle Eastern markets, Greek markets, and Indo-Pakistani markets throughout this country. A long-grain American rice is also fine, but not converted rice. The distinguishing characteristic about rice pilaf is that, once cooked, the grains of rice are tender and each is completely separate from the other, without any stickiness. The rice should be fluffy and fragrant. To achieve this you first need to soak or rinse the rice to wash away the starch that will, if left unwashed, turn rice into sticky rice or risotto. The second step is to fry the rice briefly in some fat. The third step is to pour in the liquid in which the rice will cook, add some salt, and bring it to a boil. The rule of thumb for the ratio is 2 parts liquid to 1 part rice, and 1 teaspoon salt for each cup of raw rice. But that ratio depends on the age of the rice so I would say use a little less than 1$\frac{1}{2}$ parts liquid to 1 part rice to play it safe, because you can always add boiling water to the rice if it is not tender. After the liquid comes to a boil, reduce the heat to very low, cover the pot with a heavy lid, and let it cook until all the liquid is absorbed and the rice is tender. The most important thing during this time is to never take the lid off and never stir the rice. After about 12 minutes, take a look at the rice to test for doneness. It might require another few minutes.

Naan

This popular Indian bread is ideally cooked on the inside walls of a tandoor oven. It is originally a Middle Eastern bread and probably arrived in India millennia ago. You can make something close to naan in a home oven, although unless you have a tandoor oven it won't be quite the same. If you like you could also follow the directions for Griddled Arabic Flatbread (page 401) and cook the naan on a grill. This recipe is easily doubled. Naan bread is a wonderful accompaniment to spicy-hot Indian foods of all kinds, not just tandoori foods.

1/2 cup whole plain yogurt	1/4 cup unsalted butter, melted
3/4 cup warm water	1 large egg
1 teaspoon active dry yeast	3 cups bread flour (preferably) or unbleached all-purpose flour
2 teaspoons sugar	
1 teaspoon salt	Vegetable oil, for greasing the pan and hands

1. In a bowl, beat together the yogurt and water. Add the yeast, sugar, salt, butter, and egg and blend well. Add the flour and stir with a wooden spoon until blended. The dough will be very soft and sticky. Oil your hands and knead the dough for 10 minutes, or use an electric mixer, following the manufacturer's instructions, for 4 to 5 minutes. Leave the dough in the mixer bowl or transfer to a lightly greased bowl, cover with a kitchen towel, and let rest in a turned-off oven until it triples in size, 3 to 4 hours.

2. Preheat the oven to 500°F. On a well-floured work surface, punch down the dough and divide into 8 balls, flattening each out into 5-inch disks. Because the dough is so sticky you must have a good amount of flour to avoid sticking. Form the 8 disks into oblong loaves about 8 inches long and 1/4 inch thick. Arrange the loaves on a lightly buttered baking sheet and bake in the middle of the oven until they puff up and brown, 5 to 6 minutes. Remove and brush with butter to serve. If you have a grill going you can grill the naan for a few seconds to create a tandoor-oven effect.

MAKES 8 NAAN

Poori Bread

This bread is a little different from what you find in Indian restaurants. The dough is cut into triangles and deep-fried. It can be served with any Indian meal but is nice with Chile Chicken with Coconut and Cashews (page 144).

2 cups unbleached all-purpose flour

1¹/₂ teaspoons salt

2 tablespoons vegetable oil

³/₄ cup water

6 to 8 cups vegetable oil, for frying

1. In a bowl, mix the flour, salt, and vegetable oil. Add enough of the water to make a stiff dough, and knead the dough for 3 minutes. Form balls of dough the size of lemons and roll each one into 4-inch-diameter disks. Cut each disk into two triangles, re-forming the cut-off edges into a new ball of dough and cutting triangles until the dough is used up.

2. Preheat the frying oil to 360°F in a deep-fryer or an 8-inch saucepan fitted with a basket insert. Fry the triangles in batches in the oil until golden brown and puffy, 1 to 2 minutes. Serve immediately or keep warm in an oven.

MAKES 12 POORI

Injera

This is the most refined of Ethiopian breads, although it is actually closer to a pan-cake. It is made from finely ground teff, an annual grass grown almost exclusively in Ethiopia as a cereal crop, with a little grown in South Africa for hay. Teff is a very old grain that may have seen its use, in the form of straw, in the making of pyramid bricks in Egypt from 3359 B.C. For making *injera*, the grain is ground into flour that is then mixed with water in a clay container, where it ferments. At this point the batter is mixed with a small quantity of a thin yellowish fermented fluid saved from the previous fermentation of the making of *injera*, called *irsho*, and the resulting thin watery paste is left for about 72 hours to ferment. The product, now called *absit*, produces a clean looking, thin *injera*. The dough is baked for a few minutes in covered trays and is elastic and spongy with a slightly sour taste. Because teff is expensive, the bread is also made with millet or wheat flour. Once cooked, the *injera* is a spongy, pancake-like bread served at room temperature. The bread is used as a utensil to pick up the cooked foods, much of which are stews in Ethiopia. As teff is hard to find in the United States (though I have occasionally found teff flour at Whole Foods markets), Ethiopian restaurants often use wheat flour mixed with buckwheat flour or millet flour. A server brings trays covered by large disks of *injera* and then places the various foods (if there is more than one dish) onto different areas of the pancake. Diners rip off small pieces of the *injera* from the unused portions on the tray to pick up bite-size portions of the main courses, and consume the whole morsel in one swallow.

2 cups self-rising flour *or* 2 cups unbleached all-purpose flour mixed with 2 teaspoons baking powder

^{1}/$_2$ cup buckwheat flour

^{1}/$_2$ teaspoon baking soda

1 cup club soda

2 to 2^1/$_2$ cups water

About 6 tablespoons vegetable oil

1.   In a bowl, mix together the self-rising flour, buckwheat flour, and baking soda. Add the club soda and the water, and mix until a smooth, thin batter forms. The batter should look like waffle or pancake batter.

2.   In a 9-inch nonstick skillet, heat 1 tablespoon vegetable oil over medium heat, then pour ^{1}/$_2$ cup of batter into the skillet and spread it around with a spatula to cover the entire surface of the skillet, trying to make the entire pancake about ^{1}/$_4$ inch thick. As the *injera* cooks, little bubbles should appear all over it.

Make sure you do not brown the *injera*. When the entire surface is cooked and little bubbles appear everywhere, 2¹/₂ to 4 minutes, remove the *injera* from the skillet and cool. Add a little more oil to the pan, and repeat the process until all batter is used. If not serving the *injera* immediately, let it cool, then wrap well in plastic wrap or aluminum foil and freeze for up to 6 months.

MAKES ABOUT SIX 9-INCH "PANCAKES"

Griddled Arabic Flatbread

*T*his simple bread is found everywhere in the Arab world, with slight variations. It can be used with any of the North African or Indo-Pakistani dishes in the book and is especially good to spread with the Yemeni Jewish relish known as *Zhug* (page 421). I think the best way to cook it in order to resemble a real Middle Eastern bread is to turn your grill into a mock clay bread oven. To do this you need a grill, of course, and either a baking stone or quarry tiles. Some bakers make the bread using a "starter" dough saved from a previous batch. If you like using starter doughs, which I think make for more flavorful bread, then save one of the 16 balls of dough you will make in this recipe, well-wrapped in the freezer, for a future batch.

4 teaspoons active dry yeast	1 tablespoon salt
2¹/₂ cups tepid water	2 teaspoons sugar (optional)
6¹/₂ cups unbleached all-purpose flour	

1.   Dissolve the yeast in the water in a large bowl or the bowl of an electric mixer. Add the flour, salt, and sugar if using, and mix until an elastic ball of dough is formed. Knead for 10 minutes. If using an electric mixer, follow the instructions of the manufacturer.

2.   Divide the dough into 16 balls and arrange them on a lightly greased baking tray. Cover the baking tray with a clean kitchen towel and leave to rise until doubled in size in a warm, draftless place, such as a turned-off oven, for at least 2 hours and preferably longer.

3. Prepare a hot charcoal fire with more coals than you usually use, or preheat a gas grill on high for 15 minutes with a baking stone or quarry tiles. After the preheating, put the cover down and let heat for another 20 minutes. By this time the temperature will be 600°F to 650°F.

4. Roll the balls of dough out on a floured surface until about 8 inches in diameter. Place as many disks of dough as will fit on top of the baking stone and close the cover. Do this quickly so that not too much heat escapes. Flip the bread when the bottom has turned golden brown and blackened in spots, 1 to 2 minutes. Turn and cook for another 1 to 2 minutes and remove. Continue cooking the remaining disks of dough. If you are not going to serve the flatbread right away, freeze them for up to 6 months.

MAKES 16 FLATBREADS

basic sauces, pastes, and seasonings

In this chapter, you will find all those basic items that make cooking all the other recipes in the book easier. The various chile pastes, sauces, and seasonings used in cooking piquant foods from around the world can be made ahead of time, and many will keep for months if frozen or refrigerated. It is important that you make these condiments first, because you don't want to find out in the middle of a recipe that you need some *Ají Panca en Pasta*, essential to that fabulous-sounding Peruvian dish you're making. I keep all kinds of clean empty jam jars around to store this stuff, and I can whip up a lot of these recipes as easily as if I were making a grilled cheese sandwich. Most of the sauces, condiments, and mixes in this chapter are very hot, though a few are not hot at all, but for all of them you can choose how much you want to use to make a dish more or less piquant.

Ají Panca en Pasta

Ají panca is the name of a particular Peruvian chile that is considered to be of mild pungency; nevertheless, by any measure, it is still a hot chile. When it is ripe it is nearly purple in color, and at that time it is picked and sun-dried. This chile paste is a kind of South American *Harisa* (page 414) and is used as a condiment in the cooking of a variety of Peruvian dishes. It is made by soaking the dried chiles in water and then blending them into a paste. Some Peruvian cooks also boil the dried chiles. It can be refrigerated for a month. As this South American chile is available only on the Internet at this time, I make some suggestions for substitutes.

10 dried *ají panca* chiles or a combination of 3 dried pasilla chiles, 3 dried guajillo chiles, and 8 dried red de arbol chiles

2 fresh *ají panca* chiles or fresh red jalapeño chiles

1/2 teaspoon ground cumin

1/2 teaspoon salt

1 tablespoon safflower oil

In a bowl, soak the dried chiles in warm water to cover until very soft, 3 to 5 hours. Remove and place in a food processor with the fresh chiles, cumin, salt, and safflower oil. Puree until smooth, about 2 minutes. Transfer to a jar or container and refrigerate until needed.

MAKES ABOUT 1 1/4 CUPS

all about chiles

So much of this book is about chiles. There are so many different kinds of chiles and different names for them, but even with this knowledge you may go to the supermarket only to discover they carry two kinds, jalapeño and serrano. The reason I've gone into such depth is that the better armed you are with knowledge and the more you make demands for special chiles and other foods from your supermarket manager and staff, the more likely they are to go to the trouble to find these products and start selling them. Remember when the only types of lettuce you could find in the produce section were iceberg and romaine? Now, you can find a dozen different lettuces . . . and mushrooms . . . and herbs . . . and all other varieties of foods. The reason is that informed consumers asked for them—it's as simple as that.

dried red de arbol chiles and finger-type chiles

You will find these two names used throughout the book. The common supermarket-variety whole dried red chile that is two to three inches long and slender is a cultivar known as de arbol chile, and that's how I refer to it throughout the book. The supermarket jar of red chile flakes is made from de arbol chiles. As for fresh finger-type chiles, this is an expression that covers a number of different cultivars that are long and slender, such as cayenne chile or chile japones. Sometimes these are called long red chile and long green chile. Remember that, in the end, you use what you can find.

Yellow Chile Sauce (Ají)

A bowl of *ají* appears on every table in Bolivia and Peru as a condiment to soups, stews, seviches, and nearly everything else. It is made with fresh yellow chiles called *ají amarillo fresco*. In your supermarket, look for yellow chiles, banana chiles, Hungarian wax chiles, or yellow *güero* chiles. Other chiles one could use are mirasol chiles, also known as guajillo chiles, that are hot yellow chiles. Look for yellow chiles about three inches long and one inch wide at the stem. You could also make this with red or green chiles. The red finger-type chiles are about four inches long and a half inch wide at the stem and the green chiles are your typical large jalapeño chiles. In this recipe, I've adapted the chiles used to create something akin to South American chiles. You can put this sauce on the table whenever you are having a Peruvian or Bolivian dinner.

20 fresh yellow chiles or 18 fresh red finger-type chiles or 12 large fresh green jalapeño chiles, seeded and coarsely chopped

1 habanero chile, seeded and chopped

1 tablespoon extra-virgin olive oil

1/4 cup water

2 teaspoons salt

Place the chiles, olive oil, water, and salt in a blender and process until smooth, adding a little more water if necessary to make it puree and to scrape down the sides. Store in the refrigerator for 1 week or freeze indefinitely.

variation The salsa can be made with dried yellow chiles.

MAKES ABOUT 1¹/₄ CUPS

 # Rocoto Chile Sauce

This *salsa de rocoto* is served with a variety of foods such as the Shrimp Soup from Rinconada (page 76) and grilled chicken or rib eye. The *rocoto* chile is a potent chile that one rarely finds outside of South America. It is *the* chile of the Indians of the highlands of both the western and eastern sides of the Andes. The sixteenth-century chronicler Garcilaso de la Vega called this chile *rocot-uchu* and *locoto*, an alternative name even today. When ripe it ranges from orange-yellow to yellow to red. In this popular Peruvian sauce the color is pink and quite attractive.

4 fresh *rocoto* chiles or 5 large fresh red jalapeño chiles or 3 fresh red serrano chiles and 1 habanero chile

6 tablespoons vegetable oil

1 medium-size onion, coarsely chopped

¹/₄ pound farmer's cheese, *queso fresco*, *queso ranchero*, *queso cotija*, ricotta cheese, or domestic feta cheese

1 teaspoon salt

1. Place the chiles in a saucepan and add water to just cover them. Bring to a boil. As soon as it comes to a boil, turn the heat off and strain. Repeat.

2. Place the chiles in a blender and puree with the vegetable oil, onion, cheese, and salt until smooth, 2 or 3 minutes. Store in a jar in the refrigerator for up to 1 month.

variation Replace the cheese with ¹/₂ cup evaporated milk, replace the onion with the juice of 1 lime, and increase the oil by ¹/₄ cup.

MAKES ABOUT 1¹/₄ CUPS

basic sauces, pastes, and seasonings

Llajwa

This chile sauce is a Bolivian table sauce, also spelled *llajua*, made with *rocoto* chiles. Traditionally, it was made in a mortar called a *batan*, which is like a Mexican *metate*, a grinding stone that is large and heavy and not moved about. A food processor is quite convenient. The salsa should not be smooth; it should have some texture to it. I like to serve this salsa with grilled lamb heart or grilled steak. This recipe is adapted from one in Jean Andrews's *The Pepper Trail* (University of North Texas Press, 1999).

3 plum tomatoes (about 1/2 pound), peeled and seeded

1 small red onion, chopped

2 yellow *rocoto* chiles or 5 red serrano chiles, seeded and chopped

Juice of 1 lime

1/4 cup tightly packed fresh coriander (cilantro) or parsley leaves

Salt to taste

Place all the ingredients in a food processor. Pulse several times until well blended, but still chunky. This is best used right away, though you can refrigerate it for up to 1 week.

MAKES 1 CUP

how to buy, store, and prepare chiles for cooking

When buying fresh chiles, look for firm, fleshy, glossy-skinned chiles without blemishes. The skin should not be wrinkled and the stems should be firm. They should feel relatively heavy. Fresh chiles can be kept wrapped in paper towels in the refrigerator for up to three weeks. Pay attention when handling chiles, because the volatile chemical in chiles, capsaicin, is so potent that contact with the skin will cause the capsaicin to adhere to it. When transferred to a mucous membrane such as eyes, nose, or mouth, it can be very highly irritating. *Do not* touch your eyes, nose, or mouth when handling chiles. As soon as you have finished preparing them immediately wash your hands thoroughly with soap and water. You might want to consider using thin disposable plastic gloves when cutting chiles.

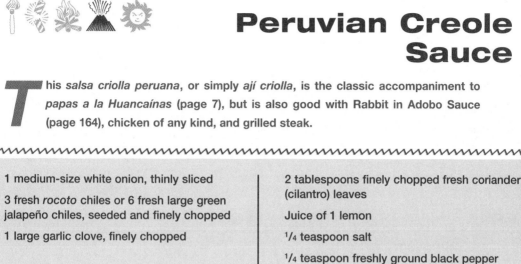

Peruvian Creole Sauce

This *salsa criolla peruana*, or simply *ají criolla*, is the classic accompaniment to *papas a la Huancaínas* (page 7), but is also good with Rabbit in Adobo Sauce (page 164), chicken of any kind, and grilled steak.

1 medium-size white onion, thinly sliced

3 fresh *rocoto* chiles or 6 fresh large green jalapeño chiles, seeded and finely chopped

1 large garlic clove, finely chopped

2 tablespoons finely chopped fresh coriander (cilantro) leaves

Juice of 1 lemon

¼ teaspoon salt

¼ teaspoon freshly ground black pepper

In a medium-size bowl, mix together all the ingredients. Cover with plastic wrap and refrigerate for 1 day before using.

MAKES ABOUT 2 CUPS

Xni Pec

This tomato and chile salsa from the Yucatán is also called *ixni-pec* (pronounced schnee-pek) and appears to have roots in Mayan times. The name *xni pec* is said to mean "dog's nose" in Mayan, perhaps because it's so hot it makes one's nose moist like a dog's. It is traditionally made with habanero chiles and the yellow chiles known as *chile xcatik* in the Yucatán, better known by their Mexican-Spanish name of *güero* chiles. These are the same small yellow chiles that southern Italians like to use in their *giardiniera* salads. Another traditional ingredient is the juice from bitter oranges (also called sour oranges or Seville oranges in English), a citrus that was part of the Old World foods that came to the New World after 1492. The diet of the ancient Maya was based on maize, beans, chiles, and squash, and they would not have known the orange. Bitter oranges, although available in the United States, are difficult to find, so a mixture of sweet orange and lime might work as a substitute. You'll want to use a navel orange, which tends to be less sweet than a Valencia or

basic sauces, pastes, and seasonings

juice orange. This recipe is adapted from one posted at the Center for Archaeological Research of the University of Texas at San Antonio. Serve with grilled foods, as a dip for tortilla chips, or with tamales.

2 pounds ripe tomatoes, cut in half, seeds squeezed out, and grated against the largest holes of a grater	1 habanero chile, chopped
	Juice from 1 bitter orange *or* 1/2 navel orange and 1 lime
1 medium-size onion, chopped	2 teaspoons salt, or more to your taste

In a medium-size bowl, mix together all the ingredients. Store in the refrigerator and use within 1 week.

MAKES 1 QUART

Red Sauce

This Mexican *salsa roja* is actually a fiery sauce from Baja California called *salsa de chile de arbol*. This typically is a sauce used over enchiladas, as a dip for tortilla chips, or spread on grilled steak. These simple red sauces are found all over Mexico and there are probably hundreds of variations. Some people make the salsa with some texture to it and others add coriander (cilantro) leaves.

15 large dried de arbol chiles, seeded	1 ripe large tomato (about 10 ounces), roasted until its skin blisters black, peeled, seeded, and chopped
2 large garlic cloves	
One 1/4-inch-thick sliced onion	1/2 teaspoon salt, or more to your taste

1. Place the chiles in a saucepan with the garlic and onion and water to barely cover. Bring to a boil over high heat and cook for 10 minutes. Drain and set aside, reserving 1/4 cup of the water.

2. Place the tomato in a blender with the reserved water and chiles and puree. Strain through a sieve. Season with salt to taste. Store in the refrigerator for up to 1 week.

MAKES ABOUT 1 1/2 CUPS

Ocean Park-Style Hot Sauce

I t's fun to start fooling around with making your own hot sauces. I call this Ocean Park style, since I live in the Ocean Park section of Santa Monica, California, and I bought all these ingredients at the Main Street Farmer's Market there. This sauce is great spread on grilled flap steak, a cheaper skirt steak–like cut that is traditionally used for *carne asada* in Santa Monica.

³/₄ pound jalapeño chiles	1 teaspoon ground cumin
2 teaspoons dried oregano	1 teaspoon ground coriander
¼ teaspoon Tabasco sauce	½ cup red wine vinegar
1 teaspoon ground red chile	1 tablespoon extra-virgin olive oil

1. Preheat the oven to 425°F. Place the jalapeño chiles on a rack in a baking dish and roast until the skin blisters, about 15 minutes. Remove the peppers and, when cool enough to handle, remove the seeds and peel off as much of the skin as you can.

2. Put the peppers and all the other ingredients in a blender and blend until very smooth, about 2 minutes. Transfer to a bottle or jar and refrigerate. This will keep for several months.

MAKES ABOUT 2 CUPS

Cliff's Orange Devil Sauce

N eedless to say, when you write a book like this you do get caught up in the world of chiles. I've tried tons of different hot sauces and I grow my own chiles, even saving the seeds for future crops. I have one habanero chile plant that produces so many fruit that I have to let them drop. One way to avoid that is to make your own hot sauce. This hot sauce is best for the plainest foods. Roasting the habanero chiles brings out a very sweet and fruity bouquet, but don't let that fool you. This is an extremely hot sauce, and serving yourself half a teaspoon will be plenty.

basic sauces, pastes, and seasonings

40 habanero chiles	1/2 teaspoon sugar
10 large garlic cloves, unpeeled	1/4 teaspoon salt
10 tablespooons apple cider vinegar	1/8 teaspoon freshly ground black pepper

1. Preheat the oven to 450°F. Place the chiles and garlic in a roasting pan and roast until black spots appear on the chiles, 15 to 17 minutes. Remove and cool.

2. Remove any stems from the chiles, remove the peels from the garlic, and place both in a blender. Add the vinegar, sugar, salt, and pepper and blend until smooth. Transfer to a small bottle, using a funnel, and store in the refrigerator for several months.

MAKES ABOUT 1 CUP

Cliff's Cajun Seasoning

There's a million of these so-called Cajun spice blends. Commercially, the two most famous are Tony Chachere's Creole Seasoning and Paul Prudhomme's Magic Seasoning blends. This recipe is similar to those.

1 tablespoon salt	1/2 teaspoon onion powder
1 teaspoon freshly ground black pepper	1/4 teaspoon ground coriander
1 teaspoon freshly ground white pepper	1/4 teaspoon ground cumin
1/2 teaspoon cayenne pepper	1/8 teaspoon dried basil
1/2 teaspoon paprika	1/8 teaspoon dried oregano
1 teaspoon garlic powder	1/8 teaspoon dried thyme

Place all the ingredients in a spice mill and run until ground. Alternatively, mix all the ingredients together in a bowl. Store in a jar and keep with your other spices.

MAKES 3 TABLESPOONS

Louisiana Red Sauce

When you taste your own freshly made hot sauce you'll wonder why you'd ever want to use something out of a bottle again. Some people call this Creole sauce, but that is a little different. You can use this sauce on anything, but I like to use it on chicken or pork. The chili powder called for in the ingredients list is not powdered red chile but rather the spice mix labeled "chili powder." This sauce is not an "insane" sauce using essence of capsaicin or anything like that, but it's damn hot.

1/4 cup (1/2 stick) unsalted butter

1 tablespoon chili powder

1 small onion, finely chopped

2 large garlic cloves, finely chopped

1/2 green bell pepper, finely chopped

1 celery stalk with a few leaves, finely chopped

2 fresh red jalapeño chiles, seeded and finely chopped

One 28-ounce can crushed tomatoes

3 bay leaves

1 1/2 teaspoons dried thyme

1 tablespoon Tabasco sauce

1 teaspoon salt, or more to your taste

1/2 teaspoon freshly ground black pepper

1. In a nonreactive saucepan, melt the butter over low heat, then add the chili powder and cook until it starts to foam, about 2 minutes, stirring. Add the onion, garlic, green pepper, celery, and chiles, increase the heat to medium, and cook until the vegetables are soft, about 5 minutes, stirring occasionally.

2. Add the tomatoes, bay leaves, thyme, Tabasco, salt, and black pepper. Bring to a boil, then reduce the heat to low and simmer until dense like a spaghetti sauce, about 30 minutes, stirring occasionally. Add more salt if desired and serve hot or at room temperature. Store in the refrigerator for up to 1 week or freeze for up to 6 months.

MAKES 3 CUPS

basic sauces, pastes, and seasonings

Harisa

*H*arisa is the most important prepared condiment used in Tunisian and Algerian cooking, and in fact, you really need to make this recipe and keep it in the refrigerator before attempting any other Tunisian or Algerian recipe. This famous hot chile paste is also found, to a much lesser extent, in the cooking of Morocco, Libya, and even western Sicily, where they use it in fish couscous. *Harisa* is sold in tubes by both Tunisian and French firms, and although the Tunisian one is better, neither can compare to your own freshly made version. To turn the *harisa* into a sauce for grilled meats, stir together 2 teaspoons *harisa*, 3 tablespoons olive oil, 2 tablespoons water, and 1 tablespoon finely chopped fresh parsley leaves.

¹/₄ pound dried guajillo chiles	¹/₂ teaspoon ground caraway seeds
1 ounce dried de arbol chiles	¹/₄ teaspoon ground coriander
5 large garlic cloves, peeled	1¹/₂ teaspoons salt
2 tablespoons water	Extra-virgin olive oil, for topping off
2 tablespoons extra-virgin olive oil	

1. Soak the chiles in tepid water to cover until soft, about 1 hour. Drain and remove the stems and seeds. Place in a food processor with the garlic, water, and olive oil. Process until a puree, stopping occasionally to scrape down the sides.

2. Transfer to a mixing bowl and stir in the caraway, coriander, and salt. Store in a jar and top off with olive oil, covering the surface of the paste. The *harisa* must always be covered with olive oil to prevent spoilage, so whenever you use some, always make sure to top off with a little olive oil. Properly stored in the refrigerator, it will keep for 6 months to 1 year.

MAKES 1 CUP

Tabil

Tabil, pronounced "table," means "seasoning" in Tunisian Arabic, although it also is the word for coriander. This is an important spice mix in all of Tunisian cooking and it varies from region to region, with some cooks adding dried powdered geranium or rose petals to the blend.

2 teaspoons garlic powder

1/4 cup coriander seeds

1 tablespoon caraway seeds

2 teaspoons cayenne pepper

Place all the ingredients in a spice mill and grind until powdery and homogeneous. Alternatively, place in a mortar and pound. Store in a jar and keep with your other spices.

MAKES ABOUT 1/4 CUP

Preserved Lemon

This is one of the most refreshing condiments used anywhere. Although it is typically used in Tunisian cooking, I find myself relying on preserved lemons when I make other kinds of foods and want a particular zestiness. It's easy to prepare, easy to store, and easy to use. I prefer using Meyer lemons for the lemons to be preserved, but the lemon juice in this recipe can come from any type of lemon.

2 thin-skinned Meyer lemons, washed well, dried, and cut into 8 wedges

1/3 cup salt

1/2 cup fresh lemon juice

Extra-virgin olive oil, as needed

In a small bowl, toss the lemon wedges with the salt and place in a 1/2-pint jar with a glass or plastic lid. Cover the lemons with the freshly squeezed lemon juice and screw on the lid. Leave the jar at room temperature for 7 days, shaking it occasionally. After 1 week, pour in olive oil to cover. Store in the refrigerator for up to 6 months.

MAKES 2 PRESERVED LEMONS

Ata Sauce

Ata is the generic term for chiles among the Yoruba people of Nigeria. *Ata funfun* resembles the jalapeño, while *ata wewe* is a Tabasco-like chile. *Ata rodo* is a relative of the habanero chile. Some West Africans actually eat this sauce with a boiled starch for breakfast. Some cooks make the sauce chunky. The pinches of spices called for means literally a pinch, about $1/16$ teaspoon. Typically, this sauce is served over fried or grilled meats or fish or with a bland *Fufu* (page 393).

---

3 red bell peppers, seeded and chopped

1 medium-size onion, coarsely chopped

$3/4$ pound ripe tomatoes, peeled and seeded

5 cherry chiles or 4 habanero chiles, stemmed and chopped

$1/2$ cup red palm oil *or* $1/2$ cup walnut oil mixed with 1 teaspoon paprika

1 teaspoon salt, or more to your taste

1 teaspoon ground dried shrimp

Pinch of ground ginger

Pinch of ground cardamom

Pinch of ground coriander

Pinch of ground nutmeg

Pinch of ground cloves

Pinch of ground cinnamon

1. Place the bell peppers, onion, tomatoes, and chiles in a blender and run until smooth.

2. In a saucepan or skillet, heat the red palm oil over medium heat, then cook the contents of the blender until bubbling, about 5 minutes. Add the salt, ground shrimp, and the spices and simmer for another 5 minutes. The sauce can be used like this, or you can add cooked meat or chicken to the sauce. Store in a container in the refrigerator for up to 4 weeks or freeze for up to one year.

MAKES ABOUT 1 QUART

Berbere

*I*n Amharic, the language of Ethiopia, the word *berbere* is the name of the fiery chile seasoning similar to *Harisa* (page 414). *Berbere*, though, refers to three things in Ethiopian cooking. It is the name of the dry spice mix that is the foundation for the paste, as well as the name of the paste itself. Also, the local chiles are known generically as *berbere*. One can make the analogy that the dry spice mix *berbere* is to the paste *berbere* as the Indian *masala* is to curry sauce. In his useful, but now dated book, *African Cooking* (Time-Life Books, 1970), Lauren van der Post already suggested the Ethiopian connection to India and speculates that the use of spices in Ethiopian cooking may have a lot to do with early spice traders from India and Java. This all-purpose spice mix is used in nearly every Ethiopian preparation, and there are many different recipes for the mix itself. One could also add ajwain seeds, turmeric, or cumin seeds, while Ethiopian cooks also use other spices such as rue and mint. The bulk of the spice used in this recipe is hot paprika, but one could easily use ground New Mexican chiles as well. The best way to store *berbere* is in a jar, topped with olive or vegetable oil. This way it will not go bad and you can keep it refrigerated for 6 months. Although it is quite easy to make this yourself, you could substitute the "chili powder" used in Southwestern U.S. cooking, though it will be different. In Ethiopian folklore it is thought that the excellence of a woman's *berbere* increased her chances of finding a good husband.

1 teaspoon ground ginger	2 tablespoons finely chopped onion
1 teaspoon ground cardamom	1 tablespoon finely chopped garlic
1/2 teaspoon ground coriander	2 tablespoons salt
1 teaspoon ground fenugreek	1 1/2 cups plus 3 tablespoons water
1 teaspoon ground ajwain seeds (optional)	2 cups hot paprika or ground New Mexican chile, *or* 1 cup hot paprika and 1 cup cayenne pepper
1/4 teaspoon ground nutmeg	
1/8 teaspoon ground cloves	2 tablespoons cayenne pepper
1/8 teaspoon ground cinnamon	1/2 teaspoon freshly ground black pepper
1/8 teaspoon ground allspice	

1. In a cast-iron skillet, dry roast the ginger, cardamom, coriander, fenugreek, ajwain (if using), nutmeg, cloves, cinnamon, and allspice by stirring the spices without any liquid or fat over low heat. Make sure you do not burn the spices, as this will only take about 2 minutes. Set aside to cool.

2. In a blender or mini food processor, blend the dry roasted spices, the onion, garlic, 1 tablespoon of the salt, and 3 tablespoons of the water until smooth.

3. Combine the paprika, cayenne pepper, black pepper, and the remaining 1 tablespoon salt in the cast-iron skillet and dry roast over low heat for about 1 minute. Transfer to a larger skillet or a saucepan and stir in the remaining 1$\frac{1}{2}$ cups water, $\frac{1}{4}$ cup at a time. Stir in the blender mixture and cook over very low heat, stirring vigorously, until thick, smooth, and dark, 10 to 12 minutes.

4. Transfer the *berbere* to a jar, packing it in tightly. Let the paste cool to room temperature, then cover with a thin layer of olive oil. Store in the refrigerator for up to 6 months.

MAKES ABOUT 2$\frac{1}{4}$ CUPS

Spiced Butter

Niter kebbeh is a spiced clarified butter used as a condiment in Ethiopian cooking. This recipe will provide you with enough to make all the Ethiopian recipes called for in this book. This butter is essential to use in the Ethiopian recipes, but you'll be tempted to use it in many other dreamed-up dishes because it is so colorful and aromatic.

1 cup (2 sticks) unsalted butter, cut into small pieces

1/2 small onion, coarsely chopped

2 large garlic cloves, finely chopped

1 teaspoon finely chopped fresh ginger

1/2 teaspoon ground turmeric

Pinch of ground cardamom

1/2-inch-long piece of cinnamon stick

1 whole clove

Pinch of ground nutmeg

1. In a large saucepan, melt the butter slowly over medium heat, making sure it does not brown. Increase the heat to high and, once the butter is bubbling, stir in the onion, garlic, ginger, turmeric, cardamom, cinnamon, clove, and nutmeg. Reduce the heat to very low and simmer uncovered for 45 minutes without stirring. Turn the heat off.

2. The milk solids should remain on the bottom of the saucepan and the butter on top will be clarified. Slowly pour the butter through a cheesecloth-lined strainer into a bowl, making sure no milk solids fall through. Transfer to a jar, cover tightly, and refrigerate until needed. The butter will keep for 1 month.

MAKES 1 1/2 CUPS

basic sauces, pastes, and seasonings

Cape Malay Garam Masala

The cooking of South Africa is not hot at all, but one community there, the Cape Malays, do have rather piquant food. This is not a native Zulu or other African influence but is an influence from the type of cooking the Cape Malays brought with them when they came from the Indo-Malaysian archipelago by way of India. This mixture can be used for all kinds of purposes on grilled foods or when making up your own stews and curries.

5 tablespoons ground coriander seed

2 tablespoons ground cumin

1 tablespoon freshly ground black pepper

1 teaspoon ground cinnamon

1/2 teaspoon ground cardamom

1/4 teaspoon ground nutmeg

In a small bowl, mix all the ingredients together. Store in a jar and keep with your other spices.

MAKES 3/4 CUP

South African Sambal

The Indo-Malaysian sambals hopped the Indian Ocean with the Cape Malays and are found as an integral part of every Cape Malay meal. The rule of thumb is cool sambals with hot dishes and hot sambals with cool dishes. You can use this sambal to accompany other Cape Malay dishes in the book or anything grilled.

1 medium-size cucumber, peeled, seeded, and finely chopped

1/4 cup finely chopped fresh coriander (cilantro) leaves

1/4 cup fresh orange juice

1 fresh green finger-type chile, seeded and finely chopped

Salt to taste

In a medium-size bowl, mix all the ingredients. Serve immediately or store in a jar in the refrigerator for up to 1 week.

MAKES 1 CUP

Zhug

This fiery green chile and coriander relish is usually served as a dip or spread with pieces of freshly baked or fried flatbread, such as *khubz tawwa*, a Yemeni home-cooked flatbread that is fried in an oiled pan. I suspect that *zhug* is a unique Yemeni Jewish preparation because several authors have mentioned that they never came across *zhug* in Yemen. Although the Yemeni population does enjoy a hot relish called *zahawigh*, I've never seen a recipe and I don't know if it's the same thing. In any case, I do believe that the Yemeni love of pungent food probably derives from either cultural contacts with Gujarati traders from the western coast of India or from interaction with Ethiopians. Some recipes call for parsley and others for tomatoes, but I like this version the best. If you like you can use the stems of the coriander, too, for a little different texture.

¹/₈ teaspoon ground cardamom	1 bunch fresh coriander (cilantro) leaves, leaves only
1 teaspoon freshly ground black pepper	
¹/₂ teaspoon ground cumin	6 large garlic cloves
¹/₂ teaspoon ground coriander	³/₄ teaspoon salt, or more to your taste
1 teaspoon caraway seeds	¹/₄ cup cold water
8 fresh green serrano chiles	3 tablespoons extra-virgin olive oil

1. In a small bowl, mix the cardamom, pepper, cumin, coriander, and caraway. Transfer to a food processor and add the chiles, coriander leaves, garlic, salt, water, and 2 tablespoons of the olive oil, and puree.

2. In a skillet, heat the remaining 1 tablespoon of olive oil over low heat, then cook the *zhug* until sputtering, 6 to 7 minutes. Turn the heat off, cool in the skillet, and store in a jar in the refrigerator for up to 1 week.

MAKES ABOUT ³/₄ CUP

basic sauces, pastes, and seasonings

Green Curry Paste

Thai green curry paste, which should be called thick green chile puree for Thai curry, is a staple of the Thai kitchen and is one of the first recipes you should make as it is the basis of many dishes. On the other hand, the convenience of store-bought jars of green curry paste is appealing, though the flavor does not compare to homemade. Jars are readily available in the international/Asian section of many supermarkets. Although we associate curry with India, the real meaning of the Tamil word *kari* or curry is "sauce." In Thailand, *kaeng*, or curry, really is a liquidy sauce, almost soupy. The word *kaeng* is a Mon (the original inhabitants of Siam) word that described the technique of making stewlike dishes. Su-Mei Yu, author of *Cracking the Coconut* (William Morrow, 2000), tells us that it is a curious word because it describes both the process of using clear liquid and the practice of using coconut cream for cooking. The word is also used for both non-spicy and spicy soups. Some food historians suggest that Thai curry may have come from the Ceylonese (Sri Lankans), who introduced the Mon to Buddhism in the seventh century.

1 teaspoon coriander seeds

1 teaspoon cumin seed

1/2 teaspoon salt

10 large garlic cloves

25 fresh green bird's-eye chiles or 6 jalapeño chiles

25 fresh green Thai chiles or 10 serrano chiles or finger-type chiles

One 1/2-inch cube fresh ginger or galangal, peeled

1 teaspoon shrimp paste

1/4 cup chopped fresh coriander (cilantro) root or stems

1/2 teaspoon chopped kaffir lime leaves or regular lime zest

1 lemongrass stalk, tough outer portions removed, tender portions chopped

4 shallots, chopped

1/2 teaspoon green peppercorns

1. Dry-roast the coriander and cumin in a cast-iron skillet over medium-high heat without any fat for 2 minutes, stirring and shaking the pan. Cool and transfer to a spice mill or mortar and finely grind.

2. Place all the ingredients in a food processor and puree until there are no bits of any ingredient visible, 5 to 8 minutes of continuously running the processor. Scrape the puree into a jar with a tight-fitting lid and store in the refrigerator for up to 1 month.

MAKES ABOUT 1 CUP

Red Curry Paste

Nam prik, or *nam prik kaeng ped daeng*, meaning spicy red curry paste, goes into every Thai curry, but it is also often served alone in Thailand. Placed in the center of the table, it is used as a dip for raw or parboiled vegetables, using only a tiny amount since the taste is powerful. This paste is used by all segments of Thai society. It is an ancient preparation, and records indicate that it was probably eaten in the twelfth and thirteenth centuries during the Sukhothai period. At that time it was likely that *prik* was made from peppercorns. The common flavoring ingredients of a *nam prik*, and there can be hundreds of versions, are saltiness from fish sauce, soy sauce, salt, or anchovies; sour from lime juice or tamarind; spicy from chiles; sweet from palm sugar; and aromatic from chile leaf, coconut cream, coriander root, garlic, shallots, or fresh turmeric, all bound with fermented fish or shrimp paste. Other ingredients can find their way in, such as raw eggplant, roasted mushrooms, or pineapple. Thai red curry paste is also found in jars in the international/Asian section of supermarkets.

2 teaspoons coriander seeds

2 teaspoons cumin seeds

Seeds from 3 cardamom pods

2 shallots, chopped

10 garlic cloves

15 dried red de arbol chiles, soaked in tepid water for 30 minutes and drained

10 fresh red Thai chiles or 6 fresh red serrano chiles, stemmed

One 1-inch cube fresh ginger or galangal, peeled

1 tablespoon shrimp paste

1 large lemongrass stalk, tough outer portions removed, tender portions chopped

1 tablespoon green peppercorns

1 tablespoon fresh kaffir lime zest or regular lime zest

1 tablespoon peanut oil

2 tablespoons water

$1/2$ cup chopped fresh coriander (cilantro) roots and/or stems

$1/4$ cup loosely packed fresh basil leaves

1 teaspoon salt

$1/2$ teaspoon ground nutmeg

$1/4$ teaspoon ground mace

1. Dry-roast the coriander, cumin, and cardamom in a small cast-iron skillet over medium-high heat without any fat for 2 minutes, shaking the pan. Cool and transfer to a spice mill or a mortar and finely grind.

2. Place the spice mixture in a food processor with the shallots, garlic, dried and fresh chiles, ginger, shrimp paste, lemongrass, green peppercorns, lime zest, peanut oil, water, coriander, basil, salt, nutmeg, and mace and run the processor until the mixture is completely smooth, 5 to 8 minutes of continuous processing. Scrape the puree into a jar with a tight-fitting lid and store in the refrigerator for up to 1 month.

MAKES ABOUT 1 CUP

Chile Oil

I t's certainly easy enough to buy chile oil in the supermarket, but it is also very easy to make it at home. The best way to make this is with a large bag of bright red dried de arbol chiles sold through a spice purveyor such as www.penzeys.com. There's one thing you need to be very careful about when doing this—and I learned the hard way through carelessness. When the chiles hit the oil at such a high temperature, they will release their pungent, irritating fumes, and if you are facing the oil it will hit you smack in the eyes and nose. This is not fun, so turn the exhaust fan to high and look and lean away from the oil as you do it. This oil is used in Sichuan and Thai cooking, but it's great for anything.

4 cups peanut oil | 1¹/₂ cups red pepper flakes

In a wok, heat the peanut oil over high heat. Once it starts to smoke, add the chile flakes and turn the heat off. Turn your head away, and do not lean over the wok or try to smell anything at this point. Let cool completely in the wok, and then cover and leave standing for 2 days. Strain the oil through a cheesecloth-lined sieve into a clean, dry storage bottle and discard the flakes. Store in a dark, cool place as you would other oils.

MAKES 1 QUART

Sambal Ulek

This is the simplest of the sambals used for Malaysian foods. You can make it by pounding it in a mortar or by putting it in a small blender. The mortar will work best. As it is very strongly flavored, use only about ¹/₂ to 1 teaspoon per person in a prepared dish. One does not eat this on its own.

12 dried red de arbol chiles, stems removed, soaked in water for 30 minutes, drained, and chopped

¹/₂ teaspoon shrimp paste

¹/₂ teaspoon salt

1 tablespoon tamarind juice or brown sugar

Place the chiles, shrimp paste, and salt in a mortar and pound until mushy. Add the tamarind juice and continue pounding until blended. Alternatively, grind in a mini food processor. Store in the refrigerator for several weeks.

MAKES ¹/₄ CUP

Indonesian Spice Paste for Seafood

This basic spice paste is called *base be pasih* and can be made in a food processor. There are many different spice pastes for different foods in Indonesia. This one is used with seafood.

12 large fresh red Thai chiles or 4 large fresh red jalapeño chiles, coarsely chopped

4 large garlic cloves, chopped

8 shallots, chopped

One 2-inch-long piece fresh ginger, peeled and chopped

1 small tomato, cut in half, seeds squeezed out, and grated against the largest holes of a grater

1¹/₂ teaspoons ground coriander

2 teaspoons ground turmeric

5 macadamia nuts

¹/₂ teaspoon shrimp paste

2 tablespoons vegetable oil

One 1-inch cube tamarind paste

1 lemongrass stalk, crushed slightly under a rolling pin

1. Place the chiles, garlic, shallots, ginger, tomato, coriander, turmeric, maca-damia nuts, and shrimp paste in a food processor and run until pasty.

2. In a skillet or saucepan, heat the vegetable oil over medium heat, then add the mixture from the processor and cook until sizzling nicely, about 5 minutes, stirring. Add the tamarind and lemongrass and stir until the tamarind melts and blends into the mixture, 3 to 5 minutes. Then turn the heat off and let cool. Remove and discard the lemongrass stalk. Store in the refrigerator for up to 1 month.

MAKES 1 CUP

Indonesian Spice Paste for Chicken

This Indonesian spice paste is called *base be siap*. Spice pastes based on chiles are used extensively in Indonesian cooking and different dishes require different kinds of spice pastes. This one can be used with chicken. Although this recipe is traditionally made with a root called zedoary, a plant related to turmeric and with properties similar to ginger, I do not include it as an ingredient here because zedoary for culinary purposes is nearly impossible to find in the United States.

3 large shallots, coarsely chopped

6 large garlic cloves

One ³/₄-inch cube galangal *or* one ¹/₂-inch cube fresh ginger, peeled

3 macadamia nuts

1¹/₄ teaspoons ground turmeric

2 tablespoons palm sugar or brown sugar

2 tablespoons vegetable oil

¹/₂ lemongrass stalk, tough outer parts removed, tender inner parts finely chopped

5 fresh green Thai chiles or 2 fresh green serrano chiles, thinly sliced

1. Put the shallots, garlic, galangal, macadamia nuts, turmeric, and palm sugar in a food processor and grind coarsely.

2. In a wok, heat the vegetable oil over medium-high heat, then cook the lemongrass and chiles for 1 minute. Add the mixture from the food processor and cook until the paste turns golden and mushy, about 3 minutes, stirring almost con-stantly. Let cool before using. Store in the refrigerator for up to 1 month.

MAKES ³/₄ CUP

Indonesian Chile Seasoning

Although this seasoning is used for many dishes in Malaysian and Indonesian cooking, it is only used in one recipe in this book (page 39). But once you make it, you will see why and why it can be used to season practically anything. Try experimenting by making something up, say, by tossing together a nice stir-fry of chopped chicken, shallots, and green beans!

³/₄ teaspoon shrimp paste

¹/₈ teaspoon salt

1 teaspoon vegetable oil

12 fresh green Thai chiles or 3 fresh green serrano chiles, quartered lengthwise

Crumble the shrimp paste with the salt in a small bowl. In a small skillet, heat the vegetable oil over high heat, then cook the chiles with the shrimp paste, stirring constantly for 1 minute. Turn the heat off and cool in the skillet. Once it is cool, store in the refrigerator for up to 2 weeks.

MAKES ABOUT 1¹/₂ TABLESPOONS

Korean Vinegar Chile Sauce

This is a vinegary hot sauce called *ch'o toenjang* that is used as a condiment for plainer Korean foods such as grilled meat or fish. The apple cider vinegar called for is an authentic ingredient, and you will find that sweet rice wine, also called *mirin*, is an important ingredient in Korean cooking. The consistency of this chile sauce is like a tomato puree. This recipe is from my friend Unjoo Lee Byars. I particularly like to dip strips of grilled pork tenderloin or swordfish into this sauce.

¼ cup Korean red chile paste (*koch'ujang*)

2 scallions, trimmed, white and light green parts only, finely chopped

1 tablespoon apple cider vinegar

½ teaspoon sugar

1 tablespoon sweet rice wine (*mirin*), cooking sake, or vermouth

In a small bowl, stir together all the ingredients. Store in the refrigerator for up to 1 month.

MAKES ½ CUP

Soy Dipping Sauce

This all-purpose Korean dipping sauce of soy and vinegar is called *ch'o kanjang* and can be used for everything from grilled beef to chive or scallion pancakes (see page 51).

2 tablespoons soy sauce

2 tablespoons rice wine (*mirin*) or vermouth

2 tablespoons rice vinegar or apple cider vinegar

1 tablespoon sesame oil

2 tablespoons fresh lemon juice

Salt to taste

1 tablespoon toasted sesame seeds

Freshly ground black pepper to taste

In a small bowl, stir together the soy sauce, rice wine, rice vinegar, sesame oil, lemon juice, and salt. Add the sesame seeds and black pepper. Store tightly covered in the refrigerator for up to 1 week.

MAKES ABOUT ½ CUP

internet
food shopping

As I began researching this Internet information, I realized that this book could not have been written and used 15 years ago. The Internet is amazing: with a Google search you can find practically anything. I've attempted to provide here as many reliable Internet sources as possible for the specialized foods used in this book. The best ones are listed here, but there are many more. Perhaps the best way to start is by going to http://phonebook.superpages.com/yellowpages/C-Grocery+Stores+%26+Supermarkets/ and clicking on your nearest city. Then click on "Ethnic Grocers" and start making phone calls. In the meantime, here are the best online resources I've found. The first part is a description of some of the Web sites and the second part is a list of where to find specific items used in the recipes.

All Web addresses have been active for more than two years and were checked for validity in the spring of 2005.

General Web Sites

www.adrianascaravan.com
One of the best sources for spices and other food items around the world—don't miss it
www.myspicer.com
An excellent source for spices of all kinds and especially hard-to-find South American chiles
www.penderys.com
A source for a large variety of dried chiles and hot sauces
www.thecmccompany.com
Probably one of the best sources for obtaining ingredients for preparing spicy-hot recipes from around the world. They sell everything from Cascabel chiles to Thai shrimp paste and kaffir lime leaves to Sichuan peppercorns and fermented black beans.
www.penzeys.com
An excellent source for dried chiles and spices

www.peruvianpeppers.com

A good source (maybe the only source) for the more unusual South American chiles used in Peruvian and Bolivian cooking

www.mexgrocer.com

For all your Mexican cooking needs, from chiles to tortillas

www.friedas.com

A great source for specialty fruits and vegetables

http://store.yahoo.com/chefshop

Asian ingredients

http://home.earthlink.net/~marutama/contactus.htm

Korean-style products made by Marutama, a Japanese-American company

http://safarimkt.com

Red palm oil for West African and Brazilian cooking

www.indianfoodsco.com

Offers a full line of Indian foods, including dried legumes

www.jbafricanmarket.com

A variety of African food products, including red palm oil

www.notinmylocalshop.com

African foods such as dried crayfish, African smoked fish, *egusi* seed, and red palm oil

www.afrikan-food.com

A good source for African food products such as bitterleaf, Maggi Seasoning Sauce, cassava leaf, and dried shrimp

www.hotpaste.com

A source for chile pastes used in Ethiopian cooking

www.quickspice.com

A very good source for all kinds of Asian food products

www.orientalpantry.com

A good selection of Asian spices and products, including bean sauces, soy sauces, oyster sauces, chile pastes, galangal, shrimp paste, etc.

www.ikoreaplaza.com

An excellent site for all Korean products, especially kimchi and the essential red chile paste *koch'ujang*

www.gourmetsleuth.com

Food products for Asian, Mexican, and Indian cuisines

www.malaysianfood.net

A good Web site with information on Malaysian food and food products used in Indo-Malaysian cuisine. You can order hard-to-find sambal ulek and dried shrimp paste.

http://importfood.com

Extensive online Thai market for food products, canned goods, and cooking equipment

www.templeofthai.com

Online Thai market for all items, including sambals for Indonesian cooking

www.asianfoodgrocer.com

Noodles, rice, and other Asian products

www.kgrocer.com
Korean food products of all kinds, as well as other Asian foods

www.koamart.com
All Korean food products

www.ethnicgrocer.com
Wide range of products from Asian and other cuisines

www.kingarthurflour.com
Excellent source for flours, unsweetened coconut, and potato starch

www.thaifoodandtravel.com
This excellent site provides a searchable database of Thai markets in the U.S. by ZIP code. Also excellent for Chinese and Indo-Malaysian shopping needs.

www.africanchop.com
An excellent site maintained by Elisabeth Jackson, author of *South of the Sahara*, with a thorough list of African food stores on the Web and local markets selling African foods, organized by state

www.ams.usda.gov/farmersmarkets/map
Maps of locations of farmers' markets in the U.S.

www.chinatownla.com
Information on, directions to, and a list of groceries and markets in Los Angeles's Chinatown

www.alibaba.com/catalogs
A good site to use for inquiries, with a huge database of worldwide suppliers

www.sweetfreedomfarm.com
For those with gardens, buy rare and unusual chile seeds from this company and grow your own chile plants

Where to Find Specific Items

African dried fish
www.jbafricanmarket.com
www.notinmylocalshop.com

African smoked fish
www.jbafricanmarket.com
www.notinmylocalshop.com

African yams (ñame)
www.friedas.com
www.notinmylocalshop.com

ajwain, dried ground
www.adrianascaravan.com

andouille sausage
www.cajungrocer.com

annatto (*achiote*) seed
www.adrianascaravan.com
www.myspicer.com

asafoetida
www.adrianascaravan.com
www.thecmccompany.com

baharat
www.adrianascaravan.com

banana leaves
www.adrianascaravan.com
www.friedas.com

berbere
www.adrianascaravan.com

black bean paste, fermented
www.koamart.com

black gram
www.adrianascaravan.com
www.indianfoodsco.com

bonito flakes
www.orientalpantry.com

cardoons
www.friedas.com

cassava flour
www.globalfoodcompany.com
www.notinmylocalshop.com

cassava leaves
www.jbafricanmarket.com

cassava root (yucca, manioc)
www.friedas.com

chiles
  African bird chile, ground
  www.adrianascaravan.com

aji amarillo chiles, whole or ground
www.adrianascaravan.com
www.myspicer.com
www.tjpmd.com
www.penderys.com

aji limo chiles, ground
www.adrianascaravan.com
www.tjpmd.com
www.penderys.com

aji mirasol chiles, whole or ground
www.tjpmd.com

aji panca chiles
www.tjpmd.com
www.penderys.com

ancho chiles
www.adrianascaravan.com
www.myspicer.com
www.thecmccompany.com
www.friedas.com

bird's-eye (bird) chiles, whole dried
www.adrianascaravan.com
www.friedas.com
www.thecmccompany.com

cascabel chiles
www.adrianascaravan.com
www.friedas.com
www.thecmccompany.com
www.penderys.com

cherry chiles, fresh
www.friedas.com

chipotle chiles
www.adrianascaravan.com
www.penderys.com

Dundicutt chiles
www.penzeys.com

finger-type chiles, fresh (cayenne, chilaca)
www.friedas.com

guajillo chiles, dried
www.adrianascaravan.com
www.myspicer.com
www.friedas.com
www.thecmccompany.com

habanero chiles
www.adrianascaravan.com
www.friedas.com

jalapeño chiles, fresh red and green
www.friedas.com

New Mexico (Anaheim) chiles
www.adrianascaravan.com
www.friedas.com

pasilla chiles, dried
www.adrianascaravan.com
www.myspicer.com

piquín chiles
www.penzeys.com
www.friedas.com
www.penderys.com

piri-piri chiles
www.adrianascaravan.com

poblano chiles
www.friedas.com

red de arbol chiles, dried
www.adrianascaravan.com
www.myspicer.com
www.friedas.com
www.penzeys.com

rocoto chiles
www.tjpmd.com
www.penderys.com

serrano chiles, fresh red and green
www.friedas.com

Tabasco chiles, dried
www.friedas.com

Thai chiles, fresh red and green
www.adrianascaravan.com
www.friedas.com

yellow banana chiles, fresh
www.friedas.com

yellow chiles (yellow Caribe), fresh
www.friedas.com

Chinese black vinegar
www.adrianascaravan.com
www.orientalpantry.com

chives, Korean/Chinese
www.friedas.com

chrysanthemum leaves
www.adrianascaravan.com
www.friedas.com

coconut cream
www.templeofthai.com

coriander root
www.importfood.com

cornhusks
www.adrianascaravan.com
www.friedas.com

couscous
www.thecmccompany.com

cubeb
www.adrianascaravan.com

curry leaves
www.adrianascaravan.com

dried anchovies
www.koamart.com

dried crayfish
www.globalfoodcompany.com

dried octopus
www.alibaba.com

dried rosebuds
www.adrianascaravan.com

dried unsweetened grated coconut
www.thecmccompany.com

egusi seed (melon seed), ground
www.globalfoodcompany.com
www.notinmylocalshop.com

epazote
www.adrianascaravan.com
www.friedas.com

fenugreek leaves
www.adrianascaravan.com

fermented black beans/bean paste
www.adrianascaravan.com
www.thecmccompany.com
www.koamart.com

fermented glutinous rice wine
www.koamart.com

fermented locust bean (*nététou, dawadawa,* or *soumbala*)
www.jbafricanmarket.com

fish pancakes (*tenpura* or *odang*), Korean or Japanese style
http://home.earthlink.net/~marutama/contactus

galangal
www.adrianascaravan.com
www.friedas.com

garam masala
www.adrianascaravan.com
www.thecmccompany.com
www.orientalpantry.com
www.ethnicgrocer.com

grains of paradise
www.adrianascaravan.com

gram flour
http://buy-ethnic-food.com
www.indianblend.com

green curry paste
www.adrianascaravan.com

green gram or mung beans
www.adrianascaravan.com
www.indianblend.com

green peppercorns
www.adrianascaravan.com
www.myspicer.com

hoisin sauce
www.adrianascaravan.com

kaffir lime leaves
www.adrianascaravan.com
www.orientalpantry.com

kimchi
www.friedas.com
www.kgrocer.com

Korean red chile, ground
www.kgrocer.com
www.ikoreaplaza.com

Korean red chile paste (*koch'ujang*)
www.kgrocer.com
www.ikoreaplaza.com

lemongrass
www.friedas.com
www.orientalpantry.com

long peppers
www.adrianascaravan.com

Maggi Seasoning
www.orientalpantry.com
www.globalfoodcompany.com

malanga
www.friedas.com

mango powder (*amchur*)
www.adrianascaravan.com
www.indianblend.com
www.thecmccompany.com

masa harina (Mexican corn flour)
www.thecmccompany.com

merguez sausages
Fabrique Délice, Sapar USA,
Hayward, CA 94544
(Tel: 510-441-9500)
www.ippi.com/dartagnan
www.themerguez.com

Mexican cheeses: *queso fresco, queso ranchero, queso chihuahua, queso cotija, queso panela,* and *queso asadero*
www.caciqueusa.com
www.cheese.com

millet flour
www.bobsredmill.com

miso (fermented soybean paste, *toenjang*)
www.asianfoodgrocer.com
www.ikoreaplaza.com

mung beans, dried
www.adrianascaravan.com
www.indianblend.com
www.orientalpantry.com

mustard oil
www.thecmccompany.com
www.indianblend.com

mustard seed, yellow, black, brown
www.adrianascaravan.com
www.myspicer.com

ñame (African yams)
www.friedas.com
www.notinmylocalshop.com

Noodles/Pasta

bean curd noodles
www.adrianascaravan.com
www.orientalpantry.com

bean thread noodles
www.orientalpantry.com

cellophane noodles
www.adrianascaravan.com

mung bean and sweet potato starch noodles
www.kgrocer.com
www.ethnicgrocer.com

Oriental-style starch noodles
www.quickspice.com
www.ethnicgrocer.com

Oriental-style vermicelli
www.quickspice.com
www.ethnicgrocer.com

pasta balls
www.adrianascaravan.com
www.easternlamejun.com

rice noodles
www.quickspice.com
www.kgrocer.com

rice vermicelli
www.adrianascaravan.com

wide rice noodles (*pad Thai*)
www.adrianascaravan.com

palm sugar
www.adrianascaravan.com

panch phoron
www.adrianascaravan.com

pea eggplants
(Thai eggplant)
www.friedas.com

pigeon peas
www.indianfoodsco.com

pink peppercorns
www.adrianascaravan.com
www.myspicer.com

prawn crackers
www.adrianascaravan.com

quinoa
www.adrianascaravan.com

red curry paste
www.adrianascaravan.com

red gram
www.indianfoodsco.com

red palm oil
www.globalfoodcompany.com
safarimkt.com
www.jbafricanmarket.com
www.notinmylocalshop.com

rice flour, nonglutinous
(*maep ssal karu*)
www.orientalpantry.com

rice vinegar
www.orientalpantry.com

rice wine (*mirin*)
www.orientalpantry.com

rose water
www.thecmccompany.com

seaweed
www.orientalpantry.com

shrimp, dried ground
www.adrianascaravan.com
www.orientalpantry.com

shrimp, whole dried
www.adrianascaravan.com

shrimp paste
www.adrianascaravan.com
www.orientalpantry.com

Sichuan peppercorns (see
also Tasmanian pepper)
www.thecmccompany.com

Sichuan chile bean paste
www.adrianascaravan.com
www.orientalpantry.com
www.thecmccompany.com

Sichuan chile paste
www.adrianascaravan.com
www.orientalpantry.com
www.thecmccompany.com

soybean paste (miso)
www.orientalpantry.com

star anise
www.adrianascaravan.com
www.orientalpantry.com
www.thecmccompany.com
www.caique.com

Syrian white cheese
www.easternlamejun.com

tamarind paste (water,
juice, etc.)
www.adrianascaravan.com
www.orientalpantry.com

tamarind pods
www.friedas.com
www.ethnicgrocer.com

Tasmanian pepper
www.adrianascaravan.com

Thai fish sauce
www.adrianascaravan.com
www.orientalpantry.com
www.thecmccompany.com

tomatillos
www.friedas.com

turmeric, fresh
www.friedas.com

white cardamom seeds
www.adrianascaravan.com
www.thecmccompany.com

yard-long beans
(asparagus beans)
www.friedas.com

yellow bean paste
www.thecmccompany.com

yellow split peas
www.ethnicgrocer.com

Measurement Equivalents

Please note that all conversions are approximate.

Liquid Conversions

U.S.	Metric
1 tsp	5 ml
1 tbs	15 ml
2 tbs	30 ml
3 tbs	45 ml
$1/4$ cup	60 ml
$1/3$ cup	75 ml
$1/3$ cup + 1 tbs	90 ml
$1/3$ cup + 2 tbs	100 ml
$1/2$ cup	120 ml
$2/3$ cup	150 ml
$3/4$ cup	180 ml
$3/4$ cup + 2 tbs	200 ml
1 cup	240 ml
1 cup + 2 tbs	275 ml
$1^1/4$ cups	300 ml
$1^1/3$ cups	325 ml
$1^1/2$ cups	350 ml
$1^2/3$ cups	375 ml
$1^3/4$ cups	400 ml
$1^3/4$ cups + 2 tbs	450 ml
2 cups (1 pint)	475 ml
$2^1/2$ cups	600 ml
3 cups	720 ml
4 cups (1 quart)	945 ml (1,000 ml is 1 liter)

Weight Conversions

U.S./U.K.	Metric
$1/2$ oz	14 g
1 oz	28 g
$1^1/2$ oz	43 g
2 oz	57 g
$2^1/2$ oz	71 g
3 oz	85 g
$3^1/2$ oz	100 g
4 oz	113 g
5 oz	142 g
6 oz	170 g
7 oz	200 g
8 oz	227 g
9 oz	255 g
10 oz	284 g
11 oz	312 g
12 oz	340 g
13 oz	368 g
14 oz	400 g
15 oz	425 g
1 lb	454 g

Oven Temperature Conversions

°F	Gas Mark	°C
250	$1/2$	120
275	1	140
300	2	150
325	3	165
350	4	180
375	5	190
400	6	200
425	7	220
450	8	230
475	9	240
500	10	260
550	Broil	290

index